STEPPE BY STEP

Mongolia's Christians —
from ancient roots
to vibrant young Church

HUGH P. KEMP

MONARCH
BOOKS

First published by Monarch Books 2000.

ISBN 1 85424 484 1

British Library Cataloguing Data
A catalogue record for this book is available
from the British Library.

Black and white photos taken by the author.
Cover photos: Paul Hattaway, Asian Minorities Outreach

Designed and produced for the publishers by
Gazelle Creative Productions Ltd,
Concorde House, Grenville Place, Mill Hill, London NW7 3SA.

'Hugh Kemp shines a bright and welcome light on Mongolia past and present. Who would have thought that Kublai Khan's mother was a Christian or that Mongolia had several Christian queens? Around the world Christians are seeing that God is doing a new work in Mongolia, where a burgeoning Church is making Jesus known to a new generation.'
– **Peter Lewis,** Cornerstone Evangelical Church, Nottingham

'Today's enthusiasts wrongly imagine that current missions are the first to burst into Mongolia. This personal odyssey shows the patient faithfulness of God in repeatedly sending messengers to the Mongols from many lands over two millennia... This book is a winner.'
– **Michael Griffiths**

'An important book for anyone interested in missions and mission history.'
– **James A. Tebbe,** International Director, Interserve

'A fascinating history of the Christian Church in one of the world's most fascinating countries. Kemp recounts the extraordinary exploits of missionaries over 1,500 years, concluding with the past decade when the Church was literally reborn.

This is an inspiring story, and an instructive and challenging account of how God has used his people to carry the gospel to the nations of Central Asia. I heartily recommend this book.'
– **Tom Hale,** author of Don't Let the Goats eat the Loquat Trees and On the Far Side of Liglig Mountain

'Hugh Kemp guides us through the exotic and intriguing history of the Mongols with a sure and entertaining hand. A "must read" for all who are interested in the remarkable birth of the Church among the ancient people.'
– **Marku Tsering,** author of Sharing Christ in the Tibetan Buddhist World

PUBLISHING

OMF International works in most East Asian countries, and among East Asian peoples around the world. It was founded by James Hudson Taylor in 1865 as the China Inland Mission. Our overall purpose is to glorify God through the urgent evangelisation of East Asia's billions, and this is reflected in our publishing.

Through our books, booklets, website and quarterly magazine, *East Asia's Billions*, OMF Publishing aims to motivate Christians for world mission, and to equip them for playing a part in it. Publications include:

- contemporary mission issues
- the biblical basis of mission
- the life of faith
- stories and biographies related to God's work in East Asia
- accounts of the growth and development of the Church in Asia
- studies of Asian culture and religion relating to the spiritual needs of her peoples

Visit our website at *www.omf.org*

Addresses for OMF English-speaking centres can be found at the back of this book.

Contents

To

Bilgée and Baisa

And on the steppe bleat the lambs,
A pure wind blows
Warm and caressing.
It reminds us of the past
And inspires many thoughts.
The young ones of the steppe
have given beauty to our encampment.
D. Natsagdorj

STEPPE BY STEP

Prester John, Ulaanbaatar, the Silk Road, Marco Polo, Kublai Khan. Nestorius, Pope Innocent IV, Ramon Lull, the Moravians, Mildred Cable. Conviction, bloodshed, ambition, courage, vision; warring tribes and careful scholarship; love of God and love of fellow men ...

Potent names and themes stud this account of the Christian Church among the Mongols. Master storyteller Hugh P. Kemp weaves his own travels and experiences into the narrative, showing how events of centuries past still resonate today. Marshalling his vast cast he describes how overzealous bishop Nestorius left his mark on East and West; how letters from Prester John, the mysterious Christian king, fired imaginations in the twelfth to fifteenth centuries; how Chinggis Khan unified the tribes and established his mighty rule; how Pope Innocent IV and Ramon Lull initiated Catholic missions, followed in turn by the Moravians and the London Missionary Society, the Swedish Mongol Mission and many others.

Despite opposition from kings, shamans and Communists, the seeds sown by tenacious missionaries, Christian traders, doctors, translators and priests are bearing fruit. The Church in Mongolia is being reborn, at the very point where the nation is seeking direction and finding its roots.

Steppe by Step completes the 'Asian Trilogy' of major volumes on the rebirth of Asian churches, from OMF Publishing and Monarch Books. The other two titles are *Killing Fields, Living Fields* and *China's Christian Millions: The Costly Revival.*

Hugh P. Kemp and his family first went to Mongolia in 1992, under sponsorship from Interserve, where they concentrated on church planting, Bible teaching and theological education by extension. Hugh is currently Dean of Studies for the Manawatu branch of the Bible College of New Zealand.

Preface

January 2000 and the turn of the millennium. All the celebrations have died down and the Y2K bug has come to nothing. With a new year and a new millennium, I sit and ponder an array of resolutions. Change is unsettling, yet if embraced, invigorating. What is God going to do in the next millennium? How will I fit in with his plans? Where will God take his reborn church of Mongolia in the decade, century, ahead?

I sit at my desk in a small New Zealand town, a long way away from the arena of this book, a long way away from my Mongolian friends and colleagues. Yet, in this electronic age, they are more accessible now than ever before. It has been eight years since I was asked to research and write this book by young Mongolian believers, eager to learn of their Christian heritage. The hardest part of the project has been reflecting on the last decade of the twentieth century where history became the present, and I became an active participant in it.

What God has done in Mongolia since 1990 has been nothing less than miraculous. God has come to Mongolia in power, and I have seen him at work with my own eyes. Thousands now give their allegiance to Jesus Christ, leaving behind their Shamanism, Buddhism, Communism, finding fulfillment and purpose in the good news of Emmanuel, God with us. But it is not the first time that the Mongol people have been awakened to the plans and purposes of God. Neither is it the first time that a Mongolian church has been established. Documenting the history of Christianity among the Mongol people is the aim of this book.

But with seeking to know the whats, wheres and whos of a people's story, one inevitably stumbles into the whys, the reflections, the predictions. Writing a history is by definition an interpretation, and this story is no exception. The reader will be frustrated that at points I have not included vital information (in their opinion) or that I have interpreted some incident from another angle. I trust the reader will be forgiving if my interpretations seem unreasonable or appear skewed. I am acutely aware that developments within the Christian community in Mongolia happen so rapidly that aspects of this book will be out of date before going to press.

A note is needed to clarify how I use some words. 'Catholic' is used as a term designating the Western European Church, as opposed to the Nestorian Eastern Church. I do not use it in the sense of the post-Reformation sixteenth-century church. Likewise, the word 'Nestorian' is used imprecisely at times. Catholic writers who use the word often mean 'non-Catholic' or 'heretic'. On other occasions the word is synonymous with 'Eastern Church', that is, the group of churches professing Eastern theology.

The adjectives 'Mongol' and 'Mongolian' are interchangeable according to the Oxford dictionary. I have chosen to use 'Mongol' as a generic adjective, and 'Mongolian' as someone or something relating to the modern state of Mongolia (formerly the Mongolian People's Republic or MPR) or to the Khalka dialect of the Mongol language.

The difference between 'Tatar' and 'Tartar' can be confusing. Of the Turkic pre-Mongol tribes in the twelfth century, the Tatars of eastern Mongolia were the most prominent at the rise of Temujin (that is, Chinggis Khan). Because they were his enemies, Temujin virtually exterminated the whole tribe, but the name 'Tartar' (with an 'r') has oddly remained, becoming a generic term for 'Mongol'. It became a convenient label used by Europeans to mean anyone Mongol — an expedient title, as it suggests that the Mongols had come from *tartarus*, that is hell. On the other hand the word may have come from Marco Polo's usage of the name Da-tu, which was the Mongolian word for the city that Kublai Khan built at the site of modern Beijing. A third possibility, suggested by Carpini, is that the word Tartar came from the name of the River Tartur in eastern Mongolia, that is, the Tartars are people from the area of the Tartur River. Note that 'Tatar' refers to the pre-Mongol eastern Asian Turkic tribe, and 'Tartar' (with an 'r') is a generic word for 'Mongol' that was used in Medieval Europe.

A note on the words 'Buddhism' and 'Lamaism' is needed. The type of Buddhism that the Mongols embraced was Lamaism from Tibet, otherwise called Tibetan Buddhism. Where 'Buddhism' alone is used, the sense is the Buddhist religion as a whole.

Several Mongolian words appear in the text and I have tried to keep their meaning clear throughout. There are many variant spellings of anglicised Mongol names, and I have chosen to use the spelling most generally accepted or closest to the Mongolian spelling in the current Cyrillic script. Likewise, I have not attempted to present a consistent form of Chinese place names; whatever seemed expedient from the sources I was referring to has been used. Please see the 'Where's Where' appendix for clarity.

Some of the anecdotal material has appeared as articles in Interserve's *Go* magazine and Bible College of New Zealand's *Reality* magazine. All the stories are true, although some names have been changed to respect anonymity.

I would like to acknowledge the help of so many who have brought this book to life. Marku Tsering, Michael Müller, Bryan Kernaghan, Magnus Kôpman and Takashi Shimamura have volunteered time and resources in the pursuit of elusive books and periodical articles on my behalf. Anne Windsor, PhD candidate at the University of Auckland, has translated journal articles from French into English. Denise James of the Deane Memorial Library has been very patient and helpful with my never-ending demands on her time. Librarians at the OMF centres in both Hong Kong and Singapore have given me time and space for research and for this I am very grateful. Thanks also to the Rev. Dr John Roxborogh of the Bible College of New Zealand, who graciously suffered my idiosyncrasies and propensity to get side-tracked, trying to keep me focused on the core research for the book, initially done for an MTh thesis. John has always been able to see the big picture in terms of this story benefiting the life of the modern Mongolian church.

I'd like to acknowledge and thank the host of checkers, proofreaders, critics, translators, advisers and imparters of information and wisdom: Katy Barnwell, Professor Charles Bawden, Professor Igor de Rachewiltz, P Bayarmagnai, Diane Benge, Dr Paul Ellingworth, Dr Lesley Francis, Margaret Jones, Chris Grantham, Margaret Gunzel, Monica Ruderstum, Martin Hickey, Elisabeth Lindgren, Graham Ogden, Tom Hale, Elizabeth Ostenson, Elon Svanell, Ewen Kitto, and friends and colleagues still resident in Mongolia. Thanks too to John and Agnes Sturt for their reflections on Reginald Sturt, and also to my parents, Ian and Elizabeth Kemp for the story of their trip to Ladakh, and Karen, my wife, for her personal reflections accompanying the chapter on the Cable and French trio.

Many Mongolian friends, colleagues and teachers have assisted in the evolution of the book: Tserenchuunt, Tserenchimeg, Uranchimeg, Janchivdorj, Dorjderem and Saruul all had the mammoth task of teaching me the subtleties and nuances of Mongolian language and culture. I thank specifically Professor Unurbayan of the Mongolian State Pedagogical Institute for his ability to walk me patiently through the wealth of relevant Mongol history.

Bayarmagnai, Mojik, Munkhoo, Buyanhisheg and Badamdorj along with the members of Everlasting Dawn Church in Ulaanbaatar have continued to remind me of the priority of this project, and consistently encouraged me to keep going. I am amazed at the work that God has done so quickly and deeply in the lives of so many in Mongolia in such a short time, and count it an immense privilege to have been a part of that. I hope it is only the end of the beginning.

Last of all I would like to acknowledge the untiring support of my wife Karen and our two girls, Anjali and Mikhaela who have given me the space, time and encouragement to keep on track. Without their patience, understanding, fortitude and humour,

Foreword

Back in the seventies when I was living in Beijing I had the chance to visit Ulaanbaatar, the capital of Mongolia, for a few days. However, the trip by rail took place in mid-January when I knew temperatures in the Mongolian capital could plummet to –40° celsius. So I chickened out — a decision which I have since much regretted. My only contact with Mongolians was to invite a junior diplomat then stationed at the Mongolian embassy in Beijing to come to the small foreigners' Christian fellowship which I helped start there back in 1976. He did come a couple of times before being transferred to Moscow. I often wondered how much of the gospel he had been able to understand.

This visit which 'might have been' but never in fact took place leads me to reflect on some far more serious 'might have beens' in the history of the Mongols. In the thirteenth century the Mongols carved out the greatest land empire in history. Their invincible warriors conquered Russia and penetrated Hungary and Poland to the borders of Germany. Medieval Europe quailed before them. There was nothing to stop the Mongol *blitzkrieg* from storming Paris and Rome and annihilating the cities of Christendom as they had already razed innumerable cities in central Asia. Then in 1241 the Khan Ogedei died and the Mongol armies voluntarily withdrew to elect a new Khan. Europe and Christian civilisation were saved. It was one of the great turning points of history. If Ogedei had survived a few more years the Mongol Empire might have stretched all the way across the Eurasian landmass from the Pacific to the Atlantic and the history of Christianity in Europe would have been entirely different from what we know today.

The Mongols also devastated the Islamic world. In 1258 Hulegu stormed Baghdad, the brilliant centre of the Abbasid Caliphate. It seemed that they would sweep across all the

Islamic countries. Only Egypt stood in their path. In 1260 a decisive battle was fought near Nazareth at Ain Jalut between the outnumbered Mongol army and the Muslim Mamelukes. The Mongols were defeated and driven back to Iran. Islam, too, was saved as an independent religious and political force.

For Christians, the most momentous and most tragic 'might have been' of Mongol history concerns Kublai Khan's request to the Pope in 1265 or 1266. Like most of the early Mongol Khans, Kublai was eclectic in his religious tastes and employed Buddhists, Muslims and Nestorian Christians at his court. According to Marco Polo, the Khan gave him a letter for the Pope requesting one hundred Christian missionaries — 'wise men of learning in the Christian religion and doctrine' — to come to Mongolia and China to preach their doctrine. In fact the Pope sent only two Dominican friars, who turned back half way. By the time the first handful of Catholic missionaries reached Beijing in 1294, Kublai had died, the Mongols had largely turned to Tibetan Buddhism and the opportunity had passed.

These are the great 'what ifs' of history. However, the book before you is more concerned to recount the history of what actually has taken place in the great saga of bringing the gospel to the Mongolian people. It is this which, for most of us, will be an eye-opener. Incontrovertible evidence is given showing that the Christian faith was brought to the Mongolian steppes as early as the seventh century by the Nestorians. Today it is largely forgotten that until the rise of the Jesuit Catholic missions in the sixteenth century and the Protestant missions in the nineteenth century the most far-reaching missionary movement by a long way was that conducted by the Nestorians. In the case of the Mongols their efforts lasted at least seven centuries, during which time they brought many Mongols to faith in Christ, including even queens and statesmen.

We are then given stirring, and sometimes heartbreaking, details of more recent missions over the last two centuries by the Moravians, the London Missionary Society, the Swedish Mongol Mission and the formidable Mildred Cable and her companions, leading up to the present and the planting of a young, vigorous church in many parts of Mongolia.

Hugh Kemp has unearthed many significant facts which are not easily obtained elsewhere. First-class research is presented in an enjoyable form. I hope this book will be widely read by all concerned for the cause of Christ among the Mongol peoples in Mongolia, Inner Mongolia and Siberia. For Mongol believers it gives an authoritative account of their precious Christian history and shows that the gospel first came to their ancestors over a millennium ago, not in Western dress, but brought peacefully by Asian monks and traders. This book also has a sobering message for Western missionaries. Far from bringing Christ to Mongolia for the first time as some think, they are building on the work and prayers of many previous generations. That should be both a humbling and an encouraging lesson.

Tony Lambert

Section **1**

Christianity During the Rise of the Mongols

Part **1**

Pre-Mongol Asia

Nestorius
the Overzealous Bishop

'My dearest wish is that God should be blessed in the heavens and upon earth.'

Nestorius

'How do you eat these?'

The first thing I had to learn in Mongolia was how to eat *buudz*. These are steamed dumplings. A small amount of minced mutton (the fattier the better) is placed on a circle of rolled dough. This is then folded over like an envelope, pinched and sealed. The final size could be anything between a walnut and a small fist. Several trays are then steamed together and they are presented to you stacked like a small mountain. A Mongolian hostess will accept no fewer than ten per person consumed at any meal.

'Just do it like I do.' My Mongolian friend had gone to great lengths to show me how to eat them. 'Take one at a time in your right hand, and as you bite, suck vigorously.'

The sucking, I was told, was to prevent the hot juicy fat from spurting across at my neighbour. Loud slurping noises accompanied the procedure. My classroom, I'm glad to say, was the privacy of my own home.

But now I was at church camp, and I had to eat them publicly. We were sitting around a trestle table, the noise of camp chatter from 150 young people filling the hall. This was our first camp together as a church. It was the week between Christmas and New Year and about –25°c outside. The snow was half a metre thick, and we had just come in from an hour of singing outside. I hoped the plate of *buudz* would dispel the incipient cold which could sneak into every small neglected gap in my clothing.

I desperately wanted to do things right. I managed my first *buudz* without incident, and feeling more confident, decided to engage my neighbour in conversation, more to convince myself that I was 'enculturating' than to learn anything that may come my way. My language ability at the time was at the level of *uuchlarai*, one of those all-purpose words in a language that can be used in a hundred different situations. It simply means 'I'm terribly sorry'.

Being distracted by my conversation, I forgot about the finer points of *buudz* eating. As I bit, I forgot to suck. A short, hot, greasy squirt of liquid fat erupted and plastered itself down my front. Thank goodness it didn't blind my neighbour. I fretted over my stupidity and said *uuchlarai* a dozen times to everyone at the table over my social ineptness. They forgave me.

I was guest speaker at this camp, and I hadn't made a very good start. The tables were soon cleared and I was on. The topic was 'An introduction to Christianity among the Mongols'. I had three sessions to deliver and the first was on the Nestorians. I wiped the greasy *buudz* fat from the front of my jacket and launched into my talk. I spoke passionately for over an hour via a translator.

I thought I did quite a good job, really, then during the question time one young man burst my bubble.

'*Bagsh-aa.*' He addressed me with the formal title of teacher. 'I understand that the Nestorians were heretics.'

Arguments about theology

In the centuries immediately following the life of Christ, debates raged among Christians in the Roman Empire on the nature of Jesus: how could the person Jesus be both God and human at the same time? Various theories were put forward, and most were hotly disputed and firmly put down by the bishops. However, as the decades passed, a core of orthodox belief emerged and a number of schools of Christian learning appeared. By the fifth century, Antioch, in the Roman province of Cilicia (modern south-east Turkey), and Alexandria, in northern Egypt, had become two centres with unique and different emphases in their understanding of who Jesus was. Simply put, the school of Antioch emphasised the humanity of Jesus, while the school of Alexandria emphasised his divinity.

Into this theologically-volatile environment, Nestorius was born in Cilicia, about the year 381. As a young man, he trained at Antioch, then entered the nearby monastery of St Euprepius. Here he gained a reputation as an excellent preacher. His presence was awe-inspiring; he was not only an eloquent speaker, but had 'fine eyes and red hair'. One contemporary described him as completely lacking in tact, with an inability to stop talking. The Byzantine Emperor, Theodosius II (408–450) came to consider him as another 'golden mouth', like John Chrysostom (c.347–407) who had also been a graduate of the school of Antioch.

In 428, Constantinople was embroiled in christological debate. Its bishopric had fallen vacant, and there were at least two contenders for the job. The Emperor wanted an outsider to help bring some stability, and invited Nestorius to accept the role. He obliged. At his induction on 10 April, he preached, 'Give me, O Emperor, the earth purged from heretics, and I will repay you with heaven.' He then embarked on a zealous campaign to rid Constantinople of heretics.

History is full of ironies. Within a very short time as bishop, Nestorius himself became embroiled in controversy and was accused of heresy. And this bears on a key issue for Christianity in modern Mongolia, 1600 years later. The label 'Nestorian' became attached to a distinct theology, which until recently was considered heretical. When the Mongols first encountered Christianity, it was this so-called heretical sect of 'Nestorianism' which they met. Would the modern church in Mongolia be proud of being associated with a so-called ancient heresy, if indeed it was a heresy? This then is the first major consideration: was Nestorius a heretic?

The start of the controversy

It was Anastasius, one of Nestorius' assistants, who inadvertently started the controversy. Anastasius criticised the use of the word *theotokos* in a sermon. *Theotokos* means 'God-bearer' in Greek, and was widely used in the church to describe Mary. In other words, Mary, the mother of Jesus, was the 'bearer of God'. The term had gained some respectability as a term which rightly described Mary's human role in bringing Jesus into the world, who was, to some degree divine (but to what degree was hotly debated). Nestorius defended Anastasius' use of the word, but personally preferred to use the word *christotokos*, or 'Christ-bearer'. *Theotokos* had become a word used by the bishops of the emerging mainstream of orthodox theology, and therefore, as soon as Anastasius and Nestorius criticised it, it opened them up to charges of heresy, specifically the heresy of compromising the divine nature of Jesus.

Not surprisingly, Bishop Cyril of the rival theological school of Alexandria was the main antagonist in humbling Nestorius. The Alexandrine school emphasised Jesus' divinity, and it seemed to Cyril that Nestorius was denying Jesus' divinity. (It is important to note that what we know of the argument is mainly written by Cyril.) Both sides appealed to the Emperor who called an ecumenical council to sort out the impasse.

This was the Council of Ephesus in 431. Much ecclesiastical swaggering and theological politicking went on behind the scenes, and Nestorius was unjustly condemned as a heretic without being present. Cyril, strong-minded and hot-tempered, conducted himself in a 'violent and un-Christian' manner and bribed conspirators to condemn Nestorius. The Papal legates were absent (still en route) and the Emperor himself pronounced the Council illegal. Cyril held it anyway.

Nestorius lasted only three short years as Bishop of Constantinople. The Council of Ephesus ordered him to be confined, initially at Ephesus, but then in his former monastery of St Euprepius near Antioch where he was under house arrest from 431 to 435. Here he started writing a defence of his teaching, which has survived in fragments. That Nestorius was able still to have some influence, even in banishment, caused some embarrassment, and he was therefore exiled by imperial order to Petra in Arabia (modern south-west Jordan), and then to an oasis in the Libyan desert, in about 436. However, even this was not to be his final home, as marauders carried him off to Panopolis (Akhmim), then to Elephantine (on the Nile), then back to Panopolis, where he died about 452.

Church history has been tough on Nestorius, considering what he was supposed to believe was written mainly by his opponents. He was condemned a heretic on the basis of misunderstanding. The differences between Cyril and Nestorius (and the Alexandrian and Antiochean schools) was merely one of emphasis. Neither bishop separated the divine and the human natures of Jesus. Their emphases were derived from the way they understood Scripture. The school of Alexandria liked to study Scripture allegorically, trying to find mystical allusions in the text. Alexandria had a 'high christology', emphasising the unity of the person of Christ. On the other hand, Antioch handled Scripture using strict logic and historical realism. Students did not speculate outside the biblical sources — in some ways it was pre-evangelical. Theodore of Mopsuestia, the tutor under whom Nestorius probably studied, was called 'The Interpreter' because of his exegetical rigour. Rational argument and common sense gave the Antiocheans an earthy, feet-on-the-ground style of doing theology — it had a 'low christology'. A clash with Alexandria was inevitable at some stage.

Nestorius' alleged teaching

What Nestorius supposedly taught was a 'prosopic union', a self-manifestation of an individual in other objects or forms. For example, a painter may consider that the brush he holds is an extension of himself as it puts upon the canvas what his inner soul wants to express. In one sense it is distinct (he could drop the brush), but in another sense it is a legitimate extension of not only his arm, but also his mind. The brush is in a sense part of himself. Likewise, I may consider this computer I'm writing on as a part of myself. It is at the same time separate from me (I can leave it and go and make myself a cup of coffee), but also in some sense it is a part of me as I can reveal my inner self through it to the reader. In a similar way, the Son of God used manhood as a self-manifestation.

Even this understanding of what Nestorius may have believed is highly debatable, remembering that what we know of his teaching was written by his enemies. In other words, we know what his enemies thought he taught. To make sense of Nestorius, we have to consider where his theology led historically, and that takes us east to Persia and so into Asia. Modern scholars are a lot less harsh on Nestorius than those of a century ago. This is mainly due to the fact that more of his documents have been discovered. Samuel Moffett, a professor from Princeton Theological Seminary in the USA summarises: 'Judged by his own works, which have come to light only in the last century, Nestorius seems scarcely as heretical as the West had always thought him.'[1]

Nestorius landed himself in hot water due more to his indiscretion and zeal than his theological conviction. His extrovert character and his high-profile anti-heresy preaching in Constantinople drew uncalled-for attention. He wrongly picked the forum of public debate to argue an issue that was best left in the classrooms of Antioch among sympathetic peers. It is more likely that the Antiochean theology (if it was indeed unorthodox) probably should be attributed more to Theodore than Nestorius. Nestorius found himself the victim of intrigue, and the hidden agendas of those who were vying for church power.

Nestorius' views were partially vindicated in the Council of Chalcedon in 451. He wrote a personal defence of his theology called *The Bazaar of Heraclides* under a pseudonym, and it seems that he was able to retain some dignity. He was thankful that truth prevailed:

'God didn't bring these things [the favourable rulings of Chalcedon] on my account, for who is Nestorius, or what is his life... or his death in this world? [God brought these things] because of the truth that God has given to the world.... My dearest wish is that God should be blessed.... As for Nestorius, let him remain anathema.'[2]

One can't help wondering whether differences between Cyril and Nestorius could all have been amicably ironed out had they got together over a capuccino in a Mediterranean cafe.

I must have looked odd standing up at the front, mouth gaping in indecision at the question, and a huge greasy streak down the front of my jacket.

The student repeated himself. 'Were the Nestorians heretics?'

I stammered my way through a feeble reply. I have no idea what I said or even if the translator had the foggiest idea of what I was talking about. What I did start to realise, however, was that Nestorius (and the Nestorians that were to follow) would prove to be the key to understanding Christianity among the Mongols. If we could clear up this accusation of heresy, then there was a whole lot of history that the Mongols could feel good about. I delivered my other two talks, in between doing battle with *buudz*.

One of my friends later took me aside.

'*Bagsh-aa*,' he said in a rather didactic but compassionate way. 'At *Tsagaan Sar*, our New Year festival, our Mongol women make about 5000 *buudz* for all the guests that visit. You'll be expected to eat several hundred.'

NOTES

1. Samuel Hugh Moffet, 'Mission in an East Asian Context: the Historical Context', *Princeton Seminary Bulletin*, 3 (1982): 249.

2. Nestorius in *The Bazaar of Heraclides*. English translation by B.R.Driver and L.Hodgson, Oxford, 1925. p 514. Quoted in WHC Frend, *Saints and Sinners in the Early Church; Differing and Conflicting Traditions in the First Six Centuries* (London: Darton, Longman and Todd, 1985) p 156. Language is modernised slightly.

Chapter 2

Alopen
and the 'Luminous Religion' in China

'Behold there was a highly virtuous man named Alopen [who carried] the true sutras with him.'
The Nestorian Stone

A Toyota Corolla is not the best vehicle in the world to travel in when the road looks as if it has been strafed by helicopter gun-ship fire. Potholes and *deweys* (small irrigation channels about ten centimetres deep) bedevilled this road. You could lose the car in a pothole, and break an axle in a *dewey*. Rural roads in Afghanistan lacked a certain aesthetic finish to them.

We were heading for Bamiyan, a broad valley in central western Afghanistan and, because we had an adventure gene in our family — inherited from a Spanish sea captain wrecked on the shore of the Shetland Islands while fleeing the British — we had chosen to go the long, adventurous, dangerous and challenging way to Bamiyan instead of the route that tourists use.

The Afghan countryside had an austere, unbroken, midsummer mustard-brown tone to it. Harsh and jagged landscapes burst up out of this; serrated blackness of rock buttresses bit into the azure blue sky. In the distance a mountain peak was cooled with snow. Broken mud forts guarded the entries to valleys like old witnesses to skirmishes that Old Man Time had eventually won. The valleys themselves were the only reprieve from the harsh landscape. A vivid deep green at the bottom of each revealed irrigation which brought life; the life that allowed children to play and goats to roam.

A cluster of houses and a network of stone walls gave away the presence of humanity. The burble of *deweys* and the distant song of a shepherd boy refreshed the ear from the immense silence of the road between. The children greeted us shyly with *salaam*, as they pondered the mystery of four strangers in a little car emerging from a mighty swirl of orange dust. After *naan* bread and sweet tea, we wound our way down the road back out into the wilds of central Asia — four adults and a heap of luggage in a navy blue Corolla, dodging potholes and *deweys*, bouncing through the shimmer of a desert mirage. If my memory serves me correctly, I think we had only nine punctures.

When we arrived in Bamiyan, we found a huge Buddha carved into the side of a mountain. Surrounding the Buddha were hundreds of caves which pockmarked the cliff-face. This apparently had been an ancient Buddhist monastery. We climbed up the pathway to the viewing platform above the head of Lord Buddha and looked out across the Bamiyan valley. It was broad, luscious and I could smell the fresh melons on the breeze. (I looked forward to what the bazaar would turn up. I'd already noticed three different types of melons, cashews, pistachios and dried apricots.) We explored the caves and examined the frescoes. The government evidently put some value on all this as there was scaffolding holding up Lord Buddha, and fences blocked some entrances to the caves. An Indian archaeological team was in charge of the restorations.

I struck up a conversation with one of the archaeologists who was delicately caressing a fresco with what looked like a small putty knife: 'If Afghanistan is a Muslim country, how did all this Buddhist stuff get here?'

The answer was simple. 'A branch of the old Silk Road came through here. Traders and armies travelled this road. Like Alexander the Great. He passed through and went east down the Kabul gorge over the Khyber Pass and into northern India.'

The historical significance of that appalling road we'd just travelled hit me. 'Do you mean to tell me that we have just followed in the footsteps of Alexander the Great in our Toyota Corolla?'

'Yes. Precisely. Melon?' My new archaeologist friend had been carving up a very large melon while he'd been talking. He handed me a piece. 'I don't know if it was the exact road, but you've got the idea.'

The Silk Road

In 635, Alopen, a Nestorian monk from Syria, arrived at Chang-an, the capital of the T'ang dynasty of China (618–907). His journey was long and arduous, sometimes on donkey, sometimes on foot. Danger from bandits, warfare and weather threatened him daily.

From as early as the first century before Christ, a standard route was being used for trade and exploration between China and the Middle East. This was the Silk Road — the only means of communication between Imperial Rome and Imperial China. In the west, it started in Antioch and Tyre, then went eastward through Persia. Alopen picked up the road from Baghdad, then followed a route joining the Central Asian oases: Merv, Bokhara, Samarkand, through the Tien Shan mountains to Kashgar. Alopen then had a choice: to take the northern or southern route around the Taklamakan desert. They converged at Tunhuang, from where the road led eastwards through the Gansu corridor and south-east on to Chang-an.

There were several subsidiary routes (like the one we had travelled in Afghanistan), including one that branched off southwards from Yarkand, through Leh, then Srinagar and south into India. Other branches wended north of the Gobi desert into Mongol heartland, via Uliastay, Urga then south again into China.

The Silk Road carried more than just Chinese silk. Initially the route was used by the Chinese to try to acquire horses from Arabia as early as 115 BC. It also carried armies. The more it was used, the more it had to be serviced with troops and forts to protect the movement of commerce. Caravans going to China carried gold, valuable metals, wool and linen textiles, ivory, coral, amber, precious stones, asbestos and glass. Westward-bound caravans carried furs, ceramics, iron, lacquer, cinnamon, rhubarb, bronze, jade, weapons, mirrors and silk. In addition to merchandise, the Silk Road carried ideas. The Greek influence in Chinese art arrived via the Silk Road. Buddhism came to

China from India in the same manner. Silkworms were smuggled back to Constantinople along the Silk Road.

Much in the way that Buddhism had travelled westward from India to Afghanistan, so Nestorian Christianity travelled eastwards, borne by Syrian traders initially, then by Syrian Nestorian monks.

Nestorians travel eastwards

There is some evidence to suggest that Alopen was not the first Christian in China, although he is often given that credit. Christians may have come to China as early as 300. The apostle Thomas probably made it to India, and legend has it that he may have reached China, probably by boat rather than via the Silk Road. However, the evidence for the establishment of a strong Christian presence isn't convincing, and the Nestorians are generally given the credit as the first Christians in Asia.

After the Council of Ephesus, Nestorius' followers moved east and joined the Eastern Church in Persia to avoid persecution in the wake of Nestorius' condemnation. The Eastern Church had grown from Jewish Christian roots, first in a Syrian environment, then with the Sassanid revolution about 226, in a Persian milieu, establishing monasteries along the Tigris and Euphrates rivers. Because Palestine, the home of Christianity, was on the eastern frontier of the Roman Empire, movement east took Christians out of the influence of Rome. Hence the Eastern Church was both politically distinct from Rome and theologically distinct from what became known as Western (ie Roman) Christianity.

The followers of Nestorius, and the movement that became known as 'Nestorianism' became closely linked with the economic success of Mesopotamia in general, and with Baghdad in particular. Initially Seleucia / Ctesiphon (near Baghdad) was the Nestorian centre but Baghdad itself became the Nestorian capital after the eighth century. Due to its strategic location on the Silk Road, Nestorian Syrian traders used Baghdad as a base from which to trade with China, founding Nestorian centres in many of the oases towns along the road.

These Nestorian centres became places of learning and spiritual life. Nestorian monks were disciplined by the austerity of the monastic life. There was a strict regime of prayer and Bible study. With so much commercial movement along the Silk Road, and with the constant threat of persecution, there was always stimulus to push the Nestorian frontiers further east. This meant that the Nestorian monasteries became what we would call missionary training schools.

And so Alopen arrived in Chang-an.

Alopen and the Nestorian Stone

We know about Alopen because around 1623, Chinese workers digging near the modern city of Xi'an, in China's Shaanxi province, made a remarkable discovery. This was on the site of Chang-an, the T'ang Dynasty capital. Workmen dug up a huge black granite stone engraved with both Chinese characters and Syriac words. It is, in essence, the 'calling card' of the Nestorians.

This stone is three metres high, one metre wide and about 30 cms thick. It has a title of nine characters: *Ta Ch'in Ching Chiao Lau Hang Chung-Kuo Pi* meaning 'The Monument of the Syrian Illustrious Religion's Coming to China'. *Ching chiao*, here translated as Illustrious Religion can also be translated as 'luminous' or 'light-bringing'. The stone itself declares that it was set up in 781, that it was written by a certain Ching-ching (also known as Adam), and that the Syrian Luminous Religion arrived in Chang-an in 635, brought by a monk called Alopen. It claims to be 'an orderly account… of the diffusion through the Middle Kingdom of the Luminous Teaching' and it contains three sections: a summary of Christian doctrine, a description of the arrival of various Syrian monks, and an account of the fortunes of the Luminous Religion between 635 and 781.

The discovery of the Nestorian Stone (also known variously

as the Nestorian Tablet, or the Hsian-fu Stone/Tablet/Stele) rocked the Christian world of the seventeenth century. Until then, it was assumed that Christianity had had no history in Asia at all, and that the Jesuits, who arrived in the seventeenth century, were the first Christians (notably Catholics) in Central Asia. The testimony of the Nestorian Stone changed all that.

The French philosopher Voltaire believed the Stone to be a 'pious fraud' set up by the Jesuits during the Ming dynasty (1368–1644) to show the Chinese that Christianity had been in China for a long time. 'The Jesuits have made us acquainted with it, therefore it is false.' Voltaire betrays his loathing of Jesuits here more than a rational assessment of the Stone's antiquity. Today its genuineness is beyond dispute. When it was discovered, China contained Franciscans, Dominicans and Jesuits from Portugal, Italy, Spain, France and Germany. For all of them to agree, and then to send rubbings to Europe, is testimony enough that it wasn't a fraud, contrary to Voltaire's speculation. All these foreigners in China were there by the grace of the Emperor. If any had lied about Chinese artefacts, it could have cost them their lives. One Father Alvares Semedo writes: 'I have seen, read, and considered this Stone at my leisure; and have been astonished that it was so complete, and the letters so entire and well formed, after the lapse of so many years'.[1]

The Chinese also knew of the Stone. It is mentioned in several Chinese manuscripts that pre-date the Jesuits and are as old as the Song dynasty (960–1280). The Nestorians were certainly astute enough to erect it. Tsien-che, on examination of the Luminous Doctrine in the late eleventh century, noted: 'As to the Luminous Doctrine, which has spread like a river, its professors are the most intelligent of all the barbarians [that is, non-Chinese]... they understand the [Chinese] characters.'[2]

Alopen then is the first documented Christian missionary in China proper. Ching-ching, the likely author of the Stone and who is himself named on it, revered Alopen as the first courier of Christianity to China. His arrival caused a magnificent flurry in the imperial court. The Stone records:

When the accomplished Emperor T'ai-tsung began his magnificent career in glory and splendour... behold there was a highly virtuous man named Alopen in the kingdom of Ta-ch'in. Auguring from the azure sky, he decided to carry the true *sutras* with him, and observing the course of the winds, he made his way through difficulties and perils.... The Emperor despatched his Minister, Duke Fang Hsuan-ling... to the western suburb to meet the visitor and conduct him to the Palace.[3]

Alopen's arrival at the imperial court at Chang-an opened the way for more Nestorian missionaries. The Stone contains a long list of Persians and Syrians who took up residence in Chang-an. Indeed, their arrival could be called the First Christian Mission to China, dating from 635 until 649 when the Emperor T'ai-tsung died, and the Mission lost its first patron. The Luminous Religion was Eastern Christianity, which, since the Council of Seleucia in 498, had become Nestorian. (It was this Council which made the formal split from Rome.) Its arrival in T'ang China was the result of continual persecution in its Persian homeland, and its new presence in China was to be the start of seven centuries of sporadic, yet significant influence throughout all of central Asia, including the Mongol homelands north of the Gobi desert.

'Thanks,' I said, taking the piece of melon from my new archaeologist friend.

I sank my teeth into the most juicy, exquisite melon I had ever tasted in my life. 'Buddhism must have come the opposite way then, brought here by Buddhist missionaries?' I slurped, wiping the juice from my chin.

'And why not? The Silk Road not only allowed for commerce (and armies) but more importantly, it was the channel of ideas from West to East, or in the case of Buddhism, like you say, from East to West. The main road was north of here but smaller branches networked around it. That's how Buddhism got here.'

That explained the anomaly of a Buddhist monastery in a Muslim country. It was all about ideas. The interchange of thought, culture, religion, worldviews, ways of doing things, ways of thinking. It's hard to imagine today, with our near-instant Internet communication, how significant a secure east-west route must have been. If you could control the Silk Road, then you could control central Asia. More immediately, if you could control the oases that were dotted along the Silk Road, you could influence whole towns and villages which grew up around each of them.

'I guess the monks liked this valley,' I said, trying to imagine what life would be like with a thousand monks living in the side of this mountain. 'If the melons were as good then as they are now, then perhaps it wouldn't have been too bad.'

NOTES
1. Huc, Regis Evariste *Christianity in China, Tartary, and Thibet* (London: Longman, Brown, Green, Longmans, and Roberts, 1857) 81, footnote.
2. Huc, Regis Evariste *Christianity in China, Tartary, and Thibet* (London: Longman, Brown, Green, Longmans, and Roberts, 1857) 79.
3. The Nestorian Stone, translated by Saeki, quoted in Samuel Hugh Moffet, *A History of Christianity in Asia*, VOL 1: Beginnings to 1500 (NY: Harper Collins, 1992) 291.

Chapter 3

Emperor T'ai-tsung,
Chinese Patron of Religions

'[His majesty] investigated "the Way" in his own forbidden apartments, and being deeply convinced of its correctness and truth, he gave special orders for its propagation.'

The Nestorian Stone

'Let's go do the British Museum.'

The suggestion caught me by surprise. It was immediately appealing though. I'd been sitting in a conference for four days, and was keen to get out and look around London. It was Saturday, and we had only two hours to spare.

'How on earth are we going to get around the British Museum in two hours?' I asked.

No problem. Armed with underground map, running shoes and an every-station tube pass, I launched myself with my two American conference delegate-friends into the bowels of London and emerged within a block of the museum. We had an hour and a half to go.

It seemed half of London was there too. Well not London so much, but Europe. The only English I saw or heard was the notice for the £2 compulsory donation and the little labels on the exhibits. Around me was the general chatter of any number of European languages with the odd bit of Middle Eastern and Asian as well. As a global nomad, born in India, married in Chile, and having lived in New Zealand and worked in Mongolia, I felt right at home.

'So that's where the rest of the Parthenon is,' I commented to my friends. I was standing in awe in the middle of a long hallway, surrounded by huge bits of Parthenon fresco. Decapitated statues of men, women and gods towered over me. I'd passed through Athens at the end of 1979 on a seven-week overland trip with my family from India to England. We'd broken down at Marathon Bay and had made a day trip into

Athens while we awaited parts from Europe for our dilapidated Ford Transit. I remembered how much the Parthenon dominates Athens, and I was intrigued to find that bits of it were in the British Museum.

Time was running out. I quickly looked at my guide book.

'Let's split up,' I suggested. 'I want to do the Chinese section.' My friends disappeared elsewhere.

I skimmed over the Ming section with its copious blue pottery and jogged back in time to the T'ang dynasty. Here I stopped. There was nothing too remarkable about the displays — some pottery (with brown and red patterns, not blue), some domestic utensils and a few portraits and images. And yet here was a moment in history that fascinated me. Captured in the glass cases was time standing still, a brief portrait of when China was at its greatest. And a time when Christianity arrived there to stay.

Who used this pottery and these utensils? I tried to imagine the Emperor T'ai-tsung eating from this plate or pouring from that jug. Perhaps it was a Christian sister who combed her hair with that comb? Maybe a Christian brother who wrote with that brush? I recalled that there was a full replica tourist village of the T'ang capital of Chang-an in Singapore and regretted not having visited it the last time I was there. For a few short minutes I was quite lost in my imaginings.

The golden age of Chinese culture

The T'ang Dynasty (618–907) is often regarded as the golden age of Chinese culture. People look back to an era like that with nostalgia, searching for the roots of modern life and the inspiration to 'be like that' again. It is the period in Chinese history that sets the standard by which all subsequent dynasties are judged. The replica Chang-an theme village in Singapore celebrates its stability, glory and cultural depth.

Chang-an was the centre of a unified China after two centuries of division between north and south. The opening of the Grand Canal, dug between 605 and 609, physically united the country, promoting a boom in economic growth. Political centralisation in Chang-an laid the foundation for three hundred years of relative stability. It was an era of strengthening and of standardising the political process, and codifying the legal system. Chang-an grew to be the biggest city in the world, with about a million residents, and became a cosmopolitan melting pot of traders, students, artists, pilgrims and diplomats. It was Tokyo, London and New York all rolled into one.

Emperor T'ai-tsung (r. 626–649) was the second T'ang emperor, reigning after his father, Li Yuan (r. 618–626). Together, they are considered the founders of the T'ang dynasty, although rather ignominious founders. Li Yuan emerged as the victor after the rebellions which overthrew the previous northern Sui dynasty (581–618). T'ai-tsung ruled three times longer than his father, but to establish himself, he killed his two brothers and ten nephews, and demanded Li Yuan abdicate in his favour. Once established, however, he proved to be wise and conscientious. He selected advisors to whom he was willing to listen, and from whom he would take criticism.

Emperor T'ai-tsung tolerates Nestorian Christianity

T'ai-tsung was emperor when Alopen arrived at Chang-an, and he gave Alopen a warm welcome. He sent his duke Fang Hsuanling to meet Alopen with a full imperial guard of honour, inviting him to the imperial palace. Here he took an interest in Alopen's literature. The Nestorian Stone records what followed: 'the *sutras* were translated in the imperial Library. [His majesty] investigated "the Way" in his own forbidden apartments, and being deeply convinced of its correctness and truth, he gave special orders for its propagation.'[1]

It would be unwise to think that T'ai-tsung exclusively favoured the Luminous Religion as the testimony of the Nestorian Stone may imply. Alopen had the good fortune to arrive at a time when the emperor was actively promoting a policy of religious toleration, mainly as a pendulum swing against the suppression of Buddhism by his father. T'ai-tsung had the challenging task of balancing the competing claims of three main religions: Taoism, Confucianism and the emerging Buddhism. He did not want to appear intolerant.

In spite of T'ai-tsung's welcome to Alopen, religious toleration never became a consistent political policy of the T'ang emperors. The fortunes of the Luminous Religion in T'ang China oscillated between persecution and tolerance, albeit begrudged tolerance due to the growing influence of the Buddhists. The stone itself must have been carved during a time of religious toleration. Its existence reflects both religious toleration and the importance of historical record keeping.

The stone says that T'ai-tsung built a monastery for the Luminous Religion in the Yi-ning ward of the city and twenty-one priests were ordained for it. Presumably the government must have given a grant of land and revenue for its upkeep. If this was so, then the Luminous Religion was not only tolerated but officially endorsed. However, the government required all foreign religions to be investigated, probably to check the potential spread of politically subversive ideas. Before any new religion could be established, a licence had to be issued. No propagation, study or worship was allowed without one, which is why Alopen had to proceed immediately to the emperor's palace so the emperor himself could verify the worth of this newly-arrived religion.

Through T'ai-tsung's patronage, Nestorianism gained respectability, and the various Nestorian monasteries dotted along the Silk Road (at least those under T'ang administration) grew with more arrivals from Syria. It was T'ai-tsung who allowed Nestorian Christianity to take root in central Asia.

But the accusation of 'heresy' still haunts us. Is the Nestorianism that arrived at T'ai-tsung's court one with which the modern Mongolian church would be proud to be associated? To answer this, and to establish how 'Christian' the

Luminous Religion was, we need to look in more detail at the Nestorian Stone.

What does the Nestorian Stone actually say?

At least nine formal translations have been made of the Nestorian Stone. The Stone has a difficult style and lots of classical quotations. It also has technical Buddhist and Taoist phrases and nuances, which makes translation difficult. The Stone's theology is orthodox and trinitarian: '...is this not the mysterious Person of our Three in One, the true Lord without beginning.' This Three-in-One 'holds the mysterious source of life and creates'. The Three-in-One created Man good and gave him dominion 'over the ocean of creatures'. The fall is caused by Satan: 'So-tan [Satan], propagating falsehood, borrowed the adornment of the pure spirit. He insinuated [the idea of] equal greatness [with God]... he introduced... evil.' The universal waywardness of humankind is illustrated: 'for all their activity they attained nothing, being consumed by their own feverish zeal. They deepened darkness on the road of perdition, and wandered long from the [way of the] return to happiness.'

The stone also affirms the incarnation and makes no reference to the worship of Mary as 'Mother of God' or 'God-bearer': 'The... Mi-shih-he [Messiah] veiling and hiding his true majesty, came to earth in the likeness of man. An angel proclaimed the good news; a virgin gave birth to the sage in Ta-ch'in [Syria, that is the Middle East].' This had been a major sticking point at the Council of Ephesus — Nestorius had insisted that the term *theotokos* (the God-bearer) should not be used of Jesus' mother Mary. The nativity star and the visitation of Persian wise men to Mi-shih-he's birth is mentioned on the Stone. The birth itself is portrayed as a fulfilment of Old Testament prophecy. The teaching of the Beatitudes is alluded to. 'The three which abide' — presumably faith, hope and love — are mentioned as part of the '[disclosure] of life'. The crucifixion is alluded to, and Mi-shih-he 'abolished death'.

The stone goes on to include various religious practices. It denounces the use of images and promotes the signing of the cross: 'the figure of ten [that is the cross; the Chinese pictogram '+' is the number 10] which is held as a seal lightens the four quarters to unite all without exception.' When the Nestorian monks arrived in China, they brought their *sutras* (that is, their Scriptures) and images. The canon of Scripture is 'twenty seven books which explain the great reformation to unlock the barriers of the understanding'. The doctrine of purgatory is opposed, but the stone does mention prayer of the 'protection of the living and for the dead'. It opposes the theory of transubstantiation, but holds to a real presence of Christ in the Eucharist. Church organisation and hierarchy is Eastern Orthodox. The stone also notes the Christian feasts, mentions vegetarianism and commends the use of Christian literature in Syriac (but doesn't prohibit the use of the vernacular). Piety is attained through baptism, regular worship (facing east), growing a beard and shaving the crown, reckoning lowly and noble people alike, community support without amassing personal wealth, seclusion, meditation, self-restraint and silence.[2]

Some have criticised the theology of the stone on grounds of syncretism with Buddhism and Taoism. Certainly there are Buddhist and Taoist terms in the inscription. The word used for God is *A-lo-he*, which was a Chinese adaptation of the Syriac term *Alaha*. The Buddhists had been using it (although in a different sense), and the stone in effect borrows it back from the Buddhists. The nature of humankind is described as 'the mysterious identity [of being and not-being]' using Buddhist terminology. The Stone uses the term 'divided body' when talking of members of the God-head. It is a phrase which is regularly used in Chinese literature when a spiritual being appears in two or more places at once. 'Hanging up a brilliant sun' is an allusion to the crucifixion, but is a term known to Buddhists as 'to hang up the Buddha sun'. The text uses the Taoist term 'the way' to signify the Luminous Religion. The symbol at the top of the Stone certainly invites the accusation of syncretism. A

Christian cross sits on a Buddhist lotus blossom surrounded by a Taoist cloud.

Perhaps the use of these Buddhist and Taoist terms and imagery could reinforce the notion that the Nestorians were the syncretistic heretics that the Western church has generally portrayed them to be. There must certainly have been contact with Buddhist monasteries in Chang-an, along with other religions that were engaged in contemplative spiritual disciplines, due to the proximity of their temples in the city. The wisdom and compassion mentioned on the stone might reflect the dialogue Nestorians had with Buddhists. But this is a simplistic answer.

The Nestorians: attempting to contextualise the gospel

The Nestorians were constrained by the language available to them to explain the gospel. They were the first generation of Christians ever to come to China, so they had no Christian terminology to draw on. They simply used the religious terms available, and injected them with new meaning. In modern jargon, they had to indigenise and contextualise the gospel. The fact that both Buddhist and Taoist terms are used betrays a search for 'the best fit' terminology to explain Christian doctrine. Were not the first Christians called 'followers of The Way'? (Acts 9:2; 24:14) So why not also in China? Considering how many other Buddhist and Taoist terms could have been used, it is surprising how clear the core Christian doctrine is on the stone. One of the original investigators of the stone in 1625, a Chinese scholar by the name of Chang Keng-Yu, believed its theology to be the same as that of Matteo Ricci (1552–1611), the Jesuit priest in China famous for his efforts to contextualise the gospel.

We must remember that the accusation of 'heresy' comes from Western (Roman) Christianity. Nestorians were formally independent from Rome by the end of the fifth century. This of itself does not mean that they were heretics. 'Heresy' as then used by the Roman church really meant politically 'non-Roman', rather than doctrinally unorthodox. During the thirteenth century, the Roman Pope (who was head of the Western church) sent Franciscan embassies to the Mongol Khans. These ambassadors (especially William of Rubruck) used the word 'heretic' quite freely to describe the non-Western / non-Roman Christians they discovered within the Mongol Empire. One modern Catholic critic of the Nestorians insists on the old terms of reference — the Nestorians were 'not in union with Rome, and in fact [were] enemies of Western Christianity'.[3]

We should not relegate the Nestorians to the category of heretics on the testimony of the Nestorian Stone. In fact, all credit is due to Alopen and his team of priests for making the genuine effort to contextualise the gospel into the language and thought forms of their Chinese hearers. The success of the Nestorians may have been precisely because of their assimilation into the culture around them, rather than because of their allegedly faulty theology. Later, when Western Christianity (ie Roman Catholicism) had gained a bridgehead in Asia, the Asians couldn't figure out why the Catholics always wanted to debate theology. Within the Confucian cultural environment, where propriety, conformity and community allegiance form a strong underlying ethic, it made sense for Nestorianism to assimilate to Chinese thought patterns.

The Christianity that arrived at T'ai-tsung's court was already partly Asian. Jesus was Asian, born in Asia. The Nestorians were Asian. Asians brought the gospel further into Asia to fellow Asians. The Nestorian Stone reveals the challenge to enculturate this gospel into Chinese thought forms. How the church relates to a new culture is a challenge that missionaries have wrestled with ever since the time of Christ. With the religious toleration afforded in the first instance by T'ai-tsung, coupled with the effort to contextualise the gospel quickly, it is not surprising that Nestorianism became well established throughout the T'ang Empire.

'Ten minutes please.' The custodian's warning jolted me out of my daydreams and I slowly made my way back to the foyer where I was joined by the crushing mass of humanity all converging at the main exit, trying to leave the museum at the same time. Thoughts of T'ai-tsung and Alopen stayed with me as I navigated my way back on the underground to my conference. Alopen was trying to contextualise the gospel, and T'ai-tsung gave him the space to do it. Wasn't that what we were supposed to be doing today in missions? I was still mulling over the similarities as I glanced at the programme for the evening's session.

'What's the topic tonight?' I asked the conference facilitator.

'Contextualising the gospel in a Buddhist culture,' he replied.

NOTES
1. The Nestorian Stone, translated by Saeki, quoted in Samuel Hugh Moffet, *A History of Christianity in Asia, VOL 1: Beginnings to 1500* (NY: Harper Collins, 1992) 291
2. P.Y. Saeki, *The Nestorian Monument in China*, (London: SPCK, 1916) 112ff.
3. H. Serruys, 'Early Mongols and the Catholic Church', *Neue Zetschrift für Missionswissenschaft* 19 (1963) 161.

Prester John,
Mysterious King of the East

*'... and having got into the snow and lost the way,
[the King of the Kerait] suddenly saw a saint, who
thus addressed him, "If you will believe in Christ, I
will show you a way on which you shall not perish."
Then did the king promise to become a sheep in
Christ's fold. Having been shown the way, the king
on reaching home summoned the Christian
merchants who were at his court and adopted their
faith.'*

Ebed Jesu, Metropolitan of Merv

I browsed the glass shop-counters at the State Department store
in Ulaanbaatar. A notice that read 'Do not lean on the glass'
had been used to seal over a large crack. Then I found what I
was looking for: Chinggis Khan lapel badges. I'd seen the
young guys around town (and in church) wearing them, and I
decided I'd like one too. I'd almost convinced myself I wanted
one just to show to friends at home in New Zealand, but deep
down I thought that if I wore one, I might be able to get in with
the crowd. It might be a small step towards enculturating.

Pictures of Chinggis Khan were everywhere in Ulaanbaatar
in 1992. Since the overthrow of the Communist party in 1990
and a turn to democracy with an elected parliament, the resulting sudden freedom meant Mongols could openly identify with
their pre-Communist history again. Pictures of Lenin came
down, and Chinggis went up. The textbooks were rewritten —
Chinggis was no longer the marauding barbarian that Russian
(and Western) historians had portrayed him to be. He was now
the skilful military strategist, the world conqueror, the astute
governor, and founder of the Mongol nation.

But I got a little confused. If Chinggis was ordained into the
Khanate in 1206, who was in central Asia before him? I put this

question to my language teacher, a professor at the State Pedagogical Institute.

'Who are the Mongols?' I asked him one day.

My professor replied by quoting *The Secret History of the Mongols*, the epic biographical poem of the life of Chinggis Khan.

'*The Secret History* records that Temujin (Chinggis Khan) "unified the people of the felt-walled tents". These were the Tatar, Taichuud, Merkit, Naiman, Kerait, Oriyat, Ongut, Mankut, Mongol and Uriangad tribes. He integrated them into his own growing empire.'

I practised for several minutes to get my tongue around the new names. I'd asked the same question of forty Mongolian students in a class the previous week and received a barrage of names of every sub-tribe that had ever existed on the Asian steppe. At least my teacher's list was shorter.

'In the thirteenth century, there were five main pre-Mongol tribes living on the Mongolian steppe: Naiman, Merged, Kerait, Taichuud and Tatar. In the modern era, it is easier to think of four main groupings: the Khalka, Oirod, Buriat and Inner Mongolians. The Khalka are the predominant tribal grouping of modern Mongolia.'

I'd read this in the Lonely Planet Guide to Mongolia. Modern Mongolia is eighty percent Khalka, I think it said.

My teacher's nationalistic passions were now aroused. He carried on enthusiastically.

'The Oirod Mongols are located in the western regions of Mongolia, also in Xinjiang province of China, and Khukh-nor region of Qinghai province of China. This group includes the "Russian" Mongols who live between the Don and Volga rivers in Russia, who are better known as Kalmuck Mongols.'.

'What is a Mongol tribe doing over in Russia?' I asked with some incredulity. I imagined they must have been left over after the Mongol conquests in the thirteenth century, and suggested this.

'Well not exactly. The Kalmuck Mongols were a part of the

larger tribal grouping of the Torguts. They didn't like being under the thumb of Chinese-Manchurian overlords. In the seventeenth century they simply up and left China and migrated to better pastures in Russia.'

'Is that the only tribe of Mongols living outside the original steppe?' I asked.

'No. The Oirod Mongols are also scattered throughout France, America, Taiwan, Hong Kong and Germany. The Buriat Mongols are located to the north of modern Mongolia in the Buriat Republic of Russia. Their provincial capital is Ulaan Ude. Buriat Mongols also live in modern Mongolia and China. The Mongols of the Inner Mongolian Autonomous Region of China are comprised of numerous sub-tribal groupings (called 'banners'), but we refer to them simply as "the Inner ones".'

'Why the "Inner" and "Outer" distinction?' This was a question that I'd wanted to ask for some time.

My teacher's answer was short. 'The Inner Mongolians sold out to the Manchus, but the Outer Mongolians didn't.' I suspected a tinge of bitterness in his voice.

It was nearly 5pm and my linguistic skills had been pushed to the limits. I tried to sum up. 'It sounds like you're saying that the tribes Chinggis conquered and absorbed can all be called "Mongols"?'

'Yes. He is the father of our nation.'

I fingered my new Chinggis Khan badge. It was still in my coat pocket as I hadn't been brave enough to put it on yet. 'That would explain why many of the young people wear the little round lapel badges,' I ventured.

He agreed. We put on our winter coats, and headed out onto the busy street to wait for a bus. He had one last comment.

'If you ask any of these people here the same question you asked me, they would tell you that Chinggis is the father of the nation and that the modern Khalka, Buriat, Oirad and Inner Mongolians are his descendants.'

Rumours in Europe

A rumour appeared in Europe in the early twelfth century that a great Christian king lived in the East. This rumour appeared in several versions but collectively they identified this king as 'Prester John' or 'Father John'. Letters from Prester John to European princes and popes started to circulate around the courts of Europe about the time when the Christian-Crusader kingdom of Edessa fell to the Muslim Turks in 1144.[1] One version reads:

> We have planned to visit the sepulchre of our Lord at the head of a great army, to combat and humble the enemies of the cross of Christ.... Our territory stretches from India... across the deserts to the place where the sun is born, and back by the ruins of Babylon... on one side the of a four months' journey, on the other side no one can know how great it is.[2]

Naturally, Europe was delighted. If the European Crusaders could attack the Muslims from the west, while Prester John did the same from the east, then the growing menace of Islam could be contained.

However, finding the exact identity of Prester John was a problem. Letters kept arriving from him well into the fifteenth century, addressed personally to a number of successive popes and kings. Prester John stories, in a number of European languages, circulated around Europe for a full three hundred years, during which time he evolved into an immortal priestly king, exceedingly powerful and rich. Although nobody had met him or knew of his precise name or location, Popes and kings replied to Prester John's letters. Pope Alexander III (r.1159–1181) wrote to Prester John in 1177, affirming the supremacy of Peter, and the authority of the Pope to regulate church affairs and doctrine, and exhorting him to 'repent from his [doctrinal] errors'.

Several theories have been put forward as to Prester John's identity, including Ethiopian kings descended from the Queen of Sheba. However, Prester John's name quickly became associated with central Asian Nestorianism. In 1143, the Bishop of Gabala, legate of the Church of Armenia, had written to Pope Eugene 3 (r: 1145–1153): 'Some years ago a prince named John, who dwelt... at the extremity of the east, professing along with his people Nestorianism, and uniting in himself the characters of sovereign and priest, came and waged war against Media and Persia.'

Prester John's alleged realm became focused on central Asia. One medieval European, Jacques de Vitry, declared: 'The Nestorians have mortally infected the greater part of the east with their doctrine, and especially the empire of the... Prince... called Priest or Prester John.' In 1237, Matthew of Paris reports a letter from a Brother Philip, which declares Nestorianism to be predominant in India, the Kingdom of Prester John, and the most distant states of the East.[3]

The Prester John letters have been shown to be fakes, products of wishful thinking in the light of the impotency of the Crusades to contain the rise of Islam. However, there was some truth in them, and the subject on whom the letters were based was probably a real king ruling a real kingdom, and he was probably a Nestorian Christian.

Who was Prester John?

Our trail to identify Prester John leads us to consider a letter from one Mar Philoxenus, an Eastern Church bishop who lived in the early sixth century. He writes to Abu Afr, a military governor, and mentions 'Christian Turks' resident in central Asia whose 'beliefs [are] orthodox... they are true believers and God-fearing folk'. The letter also reports that 'any time their bishop dies they come to the Nestorians and take another to replace him from Ctesiphon'. The letter then tells of four powerful kings of these Turks, apparently all contemporaries, well spread out across central Asia. Their names are Gawirk, Girk, Tasahz and Langu and all are called 'Tartars from Sericon'. Sericon is the name that Ptolemy gave to China.[4]

So far, the letter implies that east of Ctesiphon, the ancient Nestorian centre near Baghdad, there were Christians, in what we now know as China, at least by the sixth century. Each of these kings, so the letter says, ruled over 400,000 families. Assuming there are five people in a family, this would mean that there would be two million people under each king, or eight million in total. The supreme king was Idi Kut, 'Lord of the Kingdom', whose capital was five days from Karakorum (called a 'border town' in the letter). The site of Karakorum is where the later capital of the Great Khans was built, south-west of modern day Ulaanbaatar. The four kings could well have been the Khans of the four powerful Turkic tribes of the Kerait, Uighur, Naiman and Merkit of central Asia. And the letter calls them 'Christian Turks'. Because of the expansive Nestorian presence along the Silk Road, these tribes could easily have come into contact with Nestorian missionaries and traders.

This is in fact what must have happened. Bar Hebraeus (1225–1286), a Syrian-Jewish chronicler, records a letter sent from Ebed Jesu, Nestorian Metropolitan of Merv[5] to his superior, the Catholicos of Baghdad, which records the conversion of the Kerait tribe to Christianity: 'In the year 398 of the Hegira, a tribe called Keryt [that is, Kerait], living in the inner land of the Turks, was converted to Christianity, and their king was baptised.' At that time Ebedjesus, Metropolitan of Merv, wrote to the Nestorian Catholicos saying:

The king of the Keryt people... while he was hunting... and having got into the snow and lost his way, suddenly saw a saint, who thus addressed him, 'If you will believe in Christ, I will show you a way on which you shall not perish.' Then did the king promise to become a sheep in Christ's fold. Having been shown the way, the king on reaching home summoned the Christian merchants who were at his court and adopted their faith. Having received a copy of the gospels, which he worshipped daily, he sent me a messenger with the request that I should go to him or send him a priest who should baptise him.... Finally, he mentioned that the number of his people who had been converted was 200,000.[6]

The story is clear and reliable and there is little reason to doubt the sincerity of this letter or the genuine conversion of the Kerait Khan. The vision in the snow-storm must have been so real to the Kerait Khan that it led to his conversion. He subsequently made contact with Ebedjesus, who then wrote to the Nestorian Catholicos, possibly John, who reigned in Baghdad between 1001 and 1012. In response the Catholicos sent 'two priests and deacons' with altar furniture to baptise and continue the conversion of the Kerait.[7]

The date of the Kerait tribe's conversion is recorded as Hegira 398. This is an Islamic date which is equivalent to 1020.[8] It was unrealistic that the priests and deacons who were sent could adequately have taught and baptised a tribe of 200,000. It is impossible to verify the size of the tribe, but even for a tribe a tenth of this size, the response was hopelessly inadequate. Nonetheless, there was a significant presence of lay Nestorian merchants living and trading among the Kerait. A mass movement of sorts must have occurred, as the Kerait tribe through history has since been known as a Christian tribe.

Whatever the exact date, and whatever the extent of conversion, it is reasonable to conclude that the Keraits were nestorianised by the second decade of the eleventh century. It was this tribe which, over the next two hundred years, grew to become 'the most powerful and dominating tribe in the Mongolian steppes at the accession of Chinggis Khan'.[9]

Unc Khan of the Keraits

So the most likely contender for the title of 'Prester John' is the Khan of the Keraits. Bar Hebraeus makes the connection explicit, and names him as Unc Khan.[10] Unc Khan, who is mentioned in *The Secret History*, had initially been an ally and patron of Temujin, the young Mongol prince who later became Chinggis Khan. The given name of Unc Khan in *The Secret History* is Toghrul.

The alliance between Toghrul and Temujin grew as a result of an allied attack against the Tatar tribe of the eastern Gobi steppe. The Tatar had betrayed two Mongol princes into the hands of the Chinese Kin in 1161 and killed Temujin's father, Yesugei, in about 1167 by poisoning him at a 'friendly banquet'. The Mongols under the command of Temujin, together with the Keraits under the command of Toghrul, seeking to avenge these insults, exterminated the Tatars as they were being chased by the Kin prince Hsiang. In gratitude, Prince Hsiang gave the title 'Wang', which means 'king' in Chinese, to Toghrul who has been known since as 'Wang-Khan'. If the word 'Wang' is mongolised, it becomes 'Unc', hence the title 'Unc-Khan'.

However the alliance between Temujin and Toghrul did not last and with the confidence of the local religious priests, Temujin's armies defeated Toghrul, who had turned against Temujin due to contrived stories by bad counsellors. The whole Kerait tribe was then defeated by the rising Temujin and absorbed into his emerging pan-Mongol confederacy.

How 'Khan' becomes 'John'

Some dating problems emerge at this point. The defeat of Unc Khan and the Keraits was in 1204, and the conversion of the Kerait Khan was two hundred or so years before that. Unc Khan could not be the Kerait Khan that the original Prester John letters in the eleventh century were from or about. How then can this discrepancy be accounted for?

All central Asian Turkic tribal kings bore the title 'Khan'. Because of the guttural fricative sound of this word in Mongolian, Nestorian traders brought back stories to Europe, naming the kings as 'Chan', 'Caan', 'Ghan', 'Gehan' and then finally 'John'. John was a convenient name to give to a so-called Christian king. All the succeeding Kerait chiefs carried the title 'Khan', which accounts for the supposed longevity of Prester John. The holder of the title Unc Khan inherited this Prester John mythology — he was a 'type' of king that had evolved in the minds of the Europeans. Travellers in central Asia identified Prester John with the Khan of the Keraits, including William of Rubruck (Franciscan envoy to the Mongols between 1253 and 1255), Marco Polo (travelling to and from Asia between 1271 and 1295) and Odoric of Porderone (travelling to and from Asia between 1318 and 1330). The possibility that Prester John had some sort of priestly function was pure speculation on the part of Europeans.

But perhaps the fact that the Prester John letters were forgeries means that *a priori* no one should really be identified with the name. The letters were certainly a vain attempt to restore some hope at the losses incurred by the Crusaders at the hands of the Turks. They tended to be pompous and exaggerated, and had a dismissive tone against Eastern Orthodox Byzantines, betraying a sympathy with the Western Catholic church. Nevertheless, the forger must have heard of something happening somewhere in the east to spark his imagination. And that something was probably the presence of the Nestorians throughout central Asia.

———————

'What are you wearing a Chinggis Khan badge for?' His tone of voice was critical. Obviously my colleague had a problem with it.

'I'd like to identify in some way with my Mongolian friends in their current search for their own national identity. Seventy years of Communism is rather a large ball and chain to throw off.' I repeated what I'd learned the previous day: 'Chinggis Khan is the father of the nation, you know.'

He wasn't satisfied with my answer.

'But do we want these young Christians in these new churches emulating the brawn of Chinggis Khan? Do we want this new Mongolian nation to build itself on Chinggis Khan? As Christians, we must teach them to build the church and the nation on Jesus Christ, not Chinggis Khan.'

He had raised his voice and was waving his arms about. He felt quite passionate about this, obviously. He didn't wait for me to defend myself. 'Everything's up for grabs right now. The nation, the church, the institutions, the University, the parliament.... We have to be uncompromising in our proclamation of Jesus. Your Chinggis Khan badge is sending mixed messages.'

He had a point. The Jesus we were teaching about had to be a Mongolian Jesus, or at least we had to encourage the young Mongolian Christians to embrace Jesus without all of our own Western culture that so often got tangled up in the message. The priority must be to mongolise Jesus, not modernise Chinggis.

NOTES

1. This is modern day Orfa in SE Turkey.
2. J. Foster, *Setback and Recovery: AD 500–1500* (London:TEF/SPCK, 1974), 77.
3. R.E. Huc, *Christianity in China, Tartary, and Thibet* (London: Longman, Brown, Green, Longmans, and Roberts, 1857), 1:109.
4. A. Mingana in John Stewart, *Nestorian Missionary Enterprise; The Story of a Church on Fire* (Edinburgh: T and T Clark, 1928) 142 .
5. Modern day Mary in Turkestan.
6. H.H.Howorth, *History of the Mongols: From the 9th to the 19th Century* (London: Burt Franklin, 1876), 1:543.
7. H.H.Howorth, *History of the Mongols: From the 9th to the 19th Century* (London: Burt Franklin, 1876), 1:543. It can not be established if this was two priests, and a number of deacons, or alternatively two people, one of which was a priest and the other a deacon.
8. Other estimates of the date vary from 1001 to 1007 or 1009. Kenneth Scott Latourette, *A History of Christian Missions in China* (New York: Macmillan, 1929), 63.
9. H.H. Howorth, 'The Northern Frontagers of China. Part VIII. Article IV: The Kirais and Prester John', *Journal of the Royal Asiatic Society* (1889): 431.
10. Bar Hebraeus, *The Chronography of Gregory Abu'l-faraj, 1225–1286; the Son of Aaron, the Hebrew Physician commonly known as Bar Hebraeus, being the First Part of his Political History of the World.* Trans. E.A.W.Budge (Amsterdam: APA/Philo Press, 1932) 352.

Part **2**

Imperial Mongol Asia

Juvaini, Rashid and Bar Hebraeus,
Key Eyewitnesses of Christianity in the Mongol Empire

'Certainly no other Syrian writer possessed to such a wonderful degree the knowledge of the history, traditions and spirit of the Christian religion.'

E.A.W. Budge on Bar Hebraeus

'Why has no one ever told us this before?'

I'd just outlined in great detail the conversion of the Keraits to Nestorian Christianity and explained the evidence for a widespread presence of Nestorian Christianity across the central Asian steppe just prior to the ascendency of Chinggis Khan. I could see the question came from somewhere deep within her being. There were tears in her eyes. The room was silent as the hundred or so Mongolian young people contemplated the implication of what I'd just taught them.

'Are you saying that we have Christian roots from before the days of Chinggis Khan?' You could see the lights go on behind her eyes.

'Yes, that's exactly what I'm saying,' I replied.

'Why haven't we been able to learn about all this then?' This time from a young man I recognised. His name was Altangerel, or 'golden light', and his father was a professor of history at the university.

With many disillusioned Communists still hanging on to power, I wasn't sure how much to say in public. I didn't want to be too explicit. They'd have to fill in the gaps themselves.

'Maybe it's because the Communist government over the last seventy years hasn't taught you a balanced picture of your own history in your classes in school?' I suggested.

This drew approving nods and grunts. I'd noticed over the last year that the young people of Mongolia were becoming braver and more outspoken about the shortcomings of their previous government.

'It's also because you haven't been able to access the information here in Ulaanbaatar,' I continued. 'It's all quite readily available. You can go into any university library and pick the books off the shelf.'

This wasn't quite true. It's only in the libraries in the West that you can do this. I doubted very much if any of this information would be in the Ulaanbaatar State Central Library.

But then, life is full of surprises. I did spend some time during the following week at the Central Library and was incredulous at the Christian material I found. About ten items, some to do with Mongol imperial times, and also books on Protestant mission to Mongolia in the nineteenth century. None of it was important, nor was it in Mongolian, but it was there! The Communist leaders must have forgotten to burn it all during the religious purges of the 1930s.

I took the news of my grand discovery back to my students the following week. 'However, there are three key books missing in the library which are really important: *Juvaini*, *Rashid* and *Bar Hebraeus*. I don't imagine they'll be in modern editions, so I'm going to have to spend a lot of time looking for them.'

That was in 1993. I found *Juvaini* in 1995, but it wasn't until 1998 that I eventually found *Bar Hebraeus*. I located it via the World Wide Web in an obscure back-street second-hand bookshop in Amsterdam. I stroked the two volumes lovingly when they arrived in the mail and quietly hummed the praises of globalisation.

Although academics love to quote *Rashid*, I still haven't found a copy.

The rise and fall of Juvaini (1226–1283)

'Ala-ad-Din 'Ata-Malik Juvaini came from a noble Persian family who served for a long time in the governments of the

Persian-Khorazim Shahs. They were from the district of Juvain, near Nishapur in Khorasan, a province in modern north-east Iran. Khorasan was totally devastated by the Mongol invasion of 1220. Sporadic Persian resistance to the Mongols persisted through the following years, and in hunting down dissenters in 1232 and 1233 the Mongols captured Baha-ad-Din, Juvaini's father. Instead of executing him, the Mongol Governor of Khorasan honoured him with the title *sahib-divan* or Minister of Finance.

At age twenty-seven, Juvaini was in Karakorum, accompanying his father who had official duties to perform during Munkh Khan's reign (r. 1251–1259). During this sojourn, he undertook to write a formal history of the Mongols. The Juvain clan excelled in administration, record-keeping and bureaucratic duties, along with their loyalty to the Mongols, and Juvaini, like his father, was recognised by Hulegu, Munkh Khan's younger brother, who became the first of the Il-Khans (or 'subordinate' Khans) of Persia.

Hulegu esteemed Juvaini highly and enrolled him in his service. Juvaini's future was henceforth tied to Hulegu's and Juvaini accompanied him on his western campaigns. He witnessed the destruction by Hulegu of the Assassin stronghold of Alamut in 1256 and then Baghdad in February 1258. In 1259, Hulegu appointed him Governor over all the previous territories that the Caliph of Baghdad had governed: Arab Iraq, Lower Mesopotamia, Khuzistan and the city of Baghdad itself. After Hulegu's death in 1265, his son Abaqa retained Juvaini as Governor. In all, Juvaini served twenty years in administration in the Persian Il-Khanate, effecting much good for the peasantry, building a canal, and establishing many villages.

But he was not without his enemies, and his eventual fall came from accusations that he was in league with the Egyptian Mamalukes and squandering money from Baghdad's treasury (as much as 2.5 million dinars!). Juvaini was vindicated, but his accusers were persistent. Majd-al-Mulk, his chief accuser, was lynched by Muslims and Mongols after being condemned by

Tuguder Il-Khan (r. 1282–1284). The seed of doubt had been sown and the accusation of theft of money was renewed, although the alleged sum was never found. The authorities tortured Juvaini's servants and exhumed and insulted the corpses of his family and previous servants. On hearing this, Juvaini suffered a violent headache and died, though some records say he fell from a horse. The date was 5 March 1283, and he is buried in Tabriz.

Juvaini's *History of the World Conqueror*

Juvaini was in a unique and privileged position to observe first-hand the inner workings of the Mongol court. He knew many of the Mongols personally. In Karakorum he would have observed not only daily political life, but also the cosmopolitan nature of the town itself. During the reign of Ogedei, Karakorum became a settled encampment, with walls and buildings; it was the centre of patronage to kings and princes of conquered peoples. It was Mongol policy to send useful prisoners of war back to Karakorum to enhance technological and cultural life. So artisans, priests, ambassadors, engineers, administrators and linguists formed the core of its multi-ethnic diversity.

Juvaini started writing his *History of the World Conqueror* in Karakorum during his stay there in 1252–1253, and was still working on it in 1260 when he was appointed Governor of Baghdad. His *History* drew on his father's accounts of service to the Mongols, and eventually, he became a participant in the events themselves. It is a systematic, chronological account of the rise of the Mongols and their conquests. It was immediately recognised as authoritative and was freely quoted and referred to by historians of the day, both Arab and Persian. His style is in Persian prose literature, and although a Muslim, his point of view is remarkably conciliatory towards his Mongol overlords, justifying their invasions as being the will of God. He records events objectively and abstains from personal opinion, even though he witnessed many horrendous atrocities done by the Mongols.

With regard to Christians, Juvaini's testimony is accommodating and enlightening. On one occasion, he credits a report of an alleged miracle to Jesus and on another equates the justice of Munkh Khan to the breath of Jesus: 'Now the justice of the Emperor is like a compassionate physician who dispels the diseases of tyranny and oppression from the constitution of the world with one draught of awesome severity; nay, it is the breath of Jesus which in a moment raises the victims of injustice to life.'[1] In a similar vein, Juvaini praises at length the virtues of Queen Soyo, mother of Munkh, Hulegu and Kublai, whom he calls 'a follower and devotee of the religion of Jesus'.[2]

It is specific references like these which make Juvaini's *History* so valuable in establishing the extent and influence of Christianity among the Mongols of his time. Other sources refer to Nestorians in the Mongol court, and Juvaini confirms these. He is meticulous in his record of the genealogical connections among the Mongols, so is invaluable in tracing the influence of the Nestorians.

The bloody end of Rashid (c.1247–1318): prime minister and state physician

Fazl-ullah Rashid, better known as Rashid ad-Din served as a physician for seven Mongol Il-Khans in Persia from Abaqa Il-Khan to Oljeitu Il-Khan. He was born of a Jewish family, but not himself a practising Jew. He rose to great influence during the reign of Ghazan Il-Khan during which time he was appointed prime minister of the Il-Khanate.

However, court intrigue brought his final demise, some of it probably perpetrated by himself. He was accused of causing the death of Oljeitu Il-Khan due to a medical error of judgement. As a result, his son Ibrahim was executed before his eyes, and he himself was torn in two, labelled as a blaspheming Jew, and his head paraded through the streets of Tabriz. Abu Said (r:

1316–1335), last of the Il-Khans and successor to Oljeitu admitted that state affairs had not gone well after Rashid's fall, and with some regrets — and possibly to appease his conscience — he appointed Rashid's eldest son Ghaiassuddin to his father's former office.

Rashid's *Compendium*

Like Juvaini, Rashid was another outstanding Persian administrator who had great influence in the Mongol Il-Khanate. During his appointment to the Il-Khanate, he wrote his *magnum opus* the *Jami-ut-Tawarikh* or *Compendium of Histories*. This is a fuller and more detailed account of the affairs of the Mongols than Juvaini's, and in some places Rashid quotes Juvaini word for word. Not all of Rashid's *Compendium* has been translated into English. It has however been in other European languages for a longer time than Juvaini, and so has tended to overshadow Juvaini's record.

Rashid was a classical Persian scholar who was well read, not only in his own profession of medicine, but also in agriculture, architecture, metaphysics and Islamic theology. He was 'acquainted with' the Persian, Arabic, Mongol, Turkish and Hebrew languages. He was also wealthy and somewhat pretentious about the court, but nonetheless able and hard working. What we know of Rashid's way of operating 'reads like a bit of French romance'.

Like Juvaini, Rashid records the conventional history of his day, until the time when he too becomes eye-witness to contemporary events. Rashid records the outworking of the Mongol *yasa* or legal tradition that Chinggis Khan instigated, in which religious toleration was enshrined. His account of the oscillations of the Il-Khans' religious sympathies, Islam on one hand, and Nestorianism on the other, makes his writing indispensable for our purpose.

Bar Hebraeus (1225–1286): linguist and scholar

Gregory Abu'l Faraj was born in Malatiya, the main town of the eastern province of the Byzantine empire (modern day Malatia in Cappadocia, eastern Turkey). He was the son of a successful physician of Jewish descent, therefore known as 'son of the Hebrew' that is, Bar Hebraeus. His birth name, given to him by his father, was John, but he was also known as Gregory: his grave at the monastery of Mattai reads, 'This is the grave of Mar Gregory John... '. Bar Hebraeus also had an Arabic name, Abu'l Faraj, possibly received from his mother as a family nickname. She was likely to have been an Arab Christian.

Malatiya, during Bar Hebraeus' life, was a very prosperous town, being the convergence point of several caravan routes. In Roman times it had had a permanent garrison stationed there to guard the bridge over the Euphrates tributary on which it was built. The hinterland contained rich soil for both agriculture and horticulture, and this, combined with an ideal climate, meant it was a prize over the centuries for Greek, then Arab, and finally Mongol armies.

Bar Hebraeus grew up with Hebrew as his mother tongue, but he was also proficient in Arabic, probably due to his mother's influence. Living in a Syrian cultural environment meant that Syriac was part of his repertoire, being the trade language of the area. His linguistic ability was phenomenal. Aside from his three 'working languages', he acquired at least a nodding acquaintance with Greek, Uighur, Chinese, Armenian and Mongol over the course of his life.

On leaving Malatiya, he went to the Great Library at Maragha, a monastery settlement about a hundred kilometres south of Tabriz (modern north-western Iran). Here he intended writing a history, mainly of the previous eighty years, basing his work on the *Chronicle* of Michael the Great, which stops in 1196. He wanted to build on this and document the rise of the Mongols and their arrival in Persia. The Library at Maragha was the best place for this research, as it contained ancient Syriac,

Arabic and Persian manuscripts and some contemporary manuscripts about the Mongols. His history grew to include a full world history from creation, and we have it today known as *The Chronography*.

Bar Hebraeus as Christian

In writing his *Chronography*, Bar Hebraeus was producing a history textbook for his own people, the Syrian Jacobites. The Jacobites were a Christian sect within the bigger umbrella now known as Orthodox Christianity. He wanted to stimulate his fellow Syrians to a love of history, language and literature. In his opinion, if they wanted to become an enlightened nation (rather than merely a Christian sect) they had to raise their level of learning, and build a knowledge of the literature of the cultures around them.

Bar Hebraeus had converted to Christianity and had been educated in medicine at Antioch and Tripoli. He went on to be ordained Jacobite Bishop of Gubos in 1246, then in 1264 was elected as Maphrian of the East, that is Archbishop of the Jacobite Syrian Orthodox Church. This was done with the full endorsement of the ruling Mongols, namely Dokuz-hatan, Hulegu's Queen (a Nestorian whom we meet again later), and Abagh Il-Khan, Hulegu's son and successor to the Il-Khanate. Such was the rapport that Bar Hebraeus had with the Mongols that he received a *yarlag* (imperial decree), allowing him to levy taxes for monastery and church upkeep.

Bar Hebraeus was in a unique position to be a cultural, theological, and linguistic mediator in the Mongol Il-Khanate. Not only did he have a good working knowledge of the languages of the Il-Khanate, but an immense intellect; he assimilated new facts quickly, and could astutely grasp their significance. He also had a remarkable memory, and tireless aptitude for study and writing. During his lifetime, he wrote at least thirty major tomes covering such diverse topics as physics, theology, logic, dialectics, astronomy, grammar, ethics, economics, politics, philosophy, church polity, interpretation of dreams, humour, spiritual disciplines, medicine, music and poetry, biblical commentary and various translations and abridgements of other Syriac, Arabic and Persian works. He had the uncanny ability to take a complex problem, interpret it, and rewrite it, or teach it at the level of the common person. He could write a whole book on philosophy within a month, as well as conduct his church duties!

These duties took him around the Il-Khanate, where he visited Baghdad, Nineveh and Tabriz, but finally settled back in Maragha. He was buried at the monastery of Mar Mattai in Mosul (modern day Al Mawsil, north Iraq). There is some reference in his writings to both Rashid (a contemporary) and also Yabhallah III, the Nestorian Patriarch, who was a Mongol from Kublai's kingdom (we meet him again later), with whom apparently he got on well.

When the Mongols attacked Persia and then eastern Syria, Bar Hebraeus could interview the refugees who moved to Maragha (near Tabriz, the Mongol Il-Khanate capital) especially after Baghdad fell to Hulegu in 1258. This gave a distinctive strength to his reporting. His style suggests he was an eyewitness to the Mongol arrival in Persia. He writes with directness and clarity, with a hint of intimacy towards the Mongols.

Bar Hebraeus' *Chronography* is of great worth to us as a source that records Christian sympathy and activity among the Mongols. It is Bar Hebraeus who tells of the infant baptism into the Nestorian church of the Mongol Il-Khans in Persia. He also records that Hulegu's wife Dokuz-hatan was a Nestorian Christian, and that Hulegu was sympathetic to Christianity. It is Bar Hebraeus who tells us that the Great Khan Guyuk was a Christian, and that Guyuk's officials and physicians were Christians (although he must have heard of this only second hand).

One may argue that as a Christian himself, Bar Hebraeus would have been predisposed to find Christian sympathies among the Mongols. On the other hand, precisely because he was a Christian, he could assess the nature of the Christianity he observed. He proved himself an original thinker and judged facts independently of others' opinions, being tolerant of all religions. He remained on good terms with the Nestorians, using the generic word 'Christian' in his writings, rather than specifying the sect he was writing about. He goes one step further than Juvaini and Rashid by telling us of the fate of Christians in the Il-Khanate, and records the various oscillations of the welfare of the Christian communities in the Il-Khanate due to the variable sympathies of the subsequent Il-Khans. Ernest Wallis Budge, his translator and commentator, declares that 'certainly no other Syrian writer possessed to such a wonderful degree the knowledge of the history, traditions and spirit of the Christian... religion'.[3] The Syrian Orthodox Church to this day venerates the name of Bar Hebraeus, and holds his writing in high esteem.

'Why has no one ever told us this before?' That question changed my life. During our first trip home to New Zealand in 1994, I was determined that I would start doing what I'd said was possible — 'picking books off library shelves' to research the Mongols' Christian history. I had access to that information and my Mongolian students didn't. I felt a gut compulsion to do something.

And the tears in their eyes told me that this was no passing academic interest in their own history. I'd touched on something deep within the corporate psyche of my students. I sensed it was all about identity. National identity. Personal identity.

'Bagsh-aa,' Altangerel cornered me. I could hardly hear him above the scraping of chairs as the students began leaving the hall. 'The lamas at the temple keep telling me that Christianity is a new religion from America. I can walk taller now as you've shown us plenty of evidence that we have some Christian roots as a nation. I think that if I do my numbers right, there must have been Mongol Christians in the thirteenth century before there were Mongol Buddhists!'

NOTES

1. 'Ala-ad-Din 'Ata-Malik Juvaini, *The History of the World Conqueror*, trans. John Andrew Boyle (Manchester: Manchester University Press, 1958), 110, 517.
2. This is an abbreviation of her full name, Soyorgachtani-bekh.
3. E.A.W. Budge in his preface to Bar Hebraeus', *Chronography*, (London: Oxford University Press, 1932) xvi.

Chinggis Khan,
World Conqueror and Astute Politician

'I am the punishment of God. If you had not committed great sins, he would not have sent a punishment like me.'
Chinggis Khan, berating the citizens of Bukhura

The office was abuzz. Three Mongols and five foreigners were huddled over a newspaper discussing its contents in rather agitated terms.

'The parliament has just passed a law discriminating against Christians,' one of my colleagues told me as I came in. It was Thursday 2 December 1993. I checked the clock on the wall to see how much time I had: it was 9.15am. I wanted to nip into the office to get the mail before heading off to class. I had only ten minutes.

'Discrimination?' I queried.

'Yes, the law is called The Law on the Relationship between the State and Religion. It says that Buddhism is to be the predominant religion of Mongolia.'

This didn't surprise me. The Tibetan form of Buddhism was plainly the major religion in Mongolia already. Merely describing this didn't mean that Christians would get discriminated against *per se.*

'It'll be interesting to read an English translation of it.' I wanted to get the facts right before jumping to conclusions.

One of the Mongolian office staff chipped in. 'The Law names Mongolia's official religions as Shamanism, Buddhism and Islam, with Buddhism as predominant. It also gives the state control over the locations of church buildings and prohibits teaching of religions outside those buildings.'

'What do you mean by "church buildings"?' I asked. I still wasn't too alarmed as no church in Mongolia had a building anyway.

The Great Khans and their Nestorian Queens

Key:
1. *Italics* denotes Nestorian queens
2. +: Maintaining Christian sympathies (or publicly Christian)
3. (k): Kerait
4. (m): Merkit
5. (o): Ongut
6. (#): Sequence of the Great Khans
7. [#]: Sequence of the Golden Horde Khans
8. {#}: Sequence of the Il-Khans

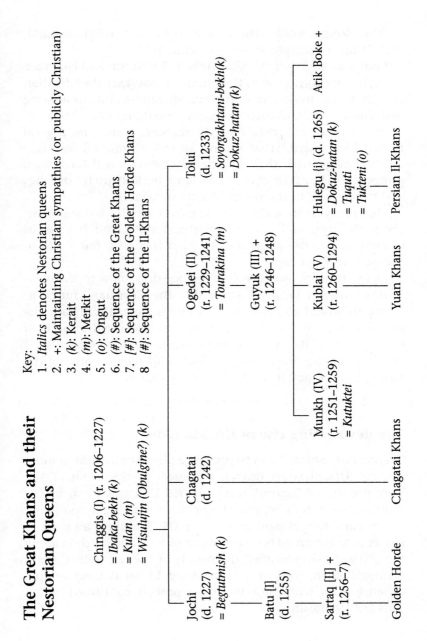

Chinggis (I) (r. 1206–1227)
= *Ibaka-bekh (k)*
= *Kulan (m)*
= *Wisulujin (Obulgine?) (k)*

Jochi (d. 1227)
= *Begtutmish (k)*

Chagatai (d. 1242)

Ogedei (II) (r. 1229–1241)
= *Tourakina (m)*

Tolui (d. 1233)
= *Soyorgakhtani-bekh(k)*
= *Dokuz-hatan (k)*

Batu [II] (d. 1255)

Munkh (IV) (r. 1251–1259)
= *Kutuktei*

Guyuk (III) + (r. 1246–1248)

Kublai (V) (r. 1260–1294)

Hulegu {i} (d. 1265)
= *Dokuz-hatan (k)*
= *Tuguti*
= *Tukteni (o)*

Arik Boke +

Sartaq [II] + (r. 1256–7)

Golden Horde

Chagatai Khans

Yuan Khans

Persian Il-Khans

'The Mongol word is the generic word for "a religious building". It means temple, mosque or church.'

I put it all together. 'So Shamanism, Buddhism and Islam are going to have to register as well, right?' I didn't see the Christian churches' registration as a problem. Singapore and Hong Kong had similar laws and their churches were doing fine.

'If Christian churches have to register, it may be a good thing,' I suggested. 'That means we will acquire all the legal rights that go with that. Registered churches will have legal protection. They'll be able to buy land, build church buildings and have access to the normal legal procedures.'

That really let the cat out of the bag. A very heated argument about the pros and cons of registered state churches versus unregistered house churches in China followed, but I had to excuse myself for class.

As I scuffed my way through the powdery snow to the polytechnic where I taught, I knew that the Christian church in Mongolia would go through some choppy months ahead. The new law was obviously in response to the rapid growth of Christianity in the previous three years. I mulled over what I knew about the relationship of state and religion among the Mongols. It all had its roots in Chinggis Khan.

The devastating rise of the Mongols

On the vast central Asian steppe, on a plain south-west of modern-day Ulaanbaatar, near the source of the Onan River, Temujin, son of Toghrul, was ordained Chinggis Khan by the shaman priest Bout-Tengri. The occasion was the grand *hural-tai*, or pan-Mongol parliament, of 1206. Temujin had risen to power through an *ad hoc* assortment of localised battles among the tribes. Having 'unified the people of the felt-walled tents', Chinggis Khan, lord of all the Mongols, set out on a rapid expansion for world dominance, a process continued by his sons and grandsons.

The testimonies of those that bore this storm are stupefying. Toung-Kien-Kan Mou in the *Annals of China* declares: 'they [the Mongols] annihilate empires as one tears up grass.' In the twelve years between 1211 and 1223, it is estimated that over eighteen million people died in northern China at the hands of the Mongols. In the west, Chinggis' successors continued the devastation. Gregor of Akanc, an Armenian, records the sacking of Baghdad in 1258: 'When they (the Mongols) arrived... they took at once the great and famous city of Baghdad, filled with many people and rare treasures, and countless gold and silver and pearls.' Rashid gives the number 800,000 as those killed in Baghdad under Chinggis' grandson Hulegu. In Russia, the *Chronicle of Novgorod* records the arrival of the Mongols:

The same year (1224), for our sins, unknown tribes came; no one exactly knows who they are, nor whence they came out, nor what their language is, nor of what race they are, nor what their faith is; but they call them Tartars.... God alone knows who they are... We have heard that they have captured many countries, slaughtered a quantity of the godless... and scattered others, who all died, killed thus by the wrath of God.[1]

Mongol expansion is constrained by the *yasa*

To Western critics, this annihilation of peoples and kingdoms seems random, but that was not the case. Mongol military strategy and social structure were exactly governed. It is probable that Chinggis instigated a *yasa* or some sort of legal code that demanded strict adherence by his troops and administrators. The existence of the *yasa* is described in full by Juvaini:

[Chinggis] established a rule for every occasion and a regulation for every circumstance; while for every crime he fixed a penalty. And since the Tartar peoples had no script of their own, he gave orders that Mongol children should learn writing from the Uighur; and that these yasas and ordinances should be written down on rolls. These rolls are called the *Great Book of Yasas* and are kept in the treasury of the chief princes. Whenever a khan ascends the throne, or a great army is mobilised, or the princes assemble and begin [to consult together] concerning affairs of state... they produce these rolls and model their actions thereon.[2]

The existence of the *yasa* is generally assumed among historians. The traditional view (based on Juvaini's account), is that at the 1206 parliament, Chinggis appointed Qadaq as judge, ordering him to write a corpus of law which was deposited with the princes and was permanently binding on all. *The Secret History of the Mongols* records this:

> Chinggis Khan made Shigi Khutukhu [that is Qadaq] the judge of all the people, saying: 'Let him write everything in a blue book, recording how he has divided the people, recording how he has judged the people, and for all generations let no one change anything. [Qadaq], after taking counsel with me, has written on the white paper of his blue book. Let no man who comes after us alter it.[3]

Another translation relates this slightly differently: '... writing in a blue book, make a register [that is, a permanent record]... of the judgements you have made'.[4]

What form did this 'Blue Book' take? Perhaps instead of drawing up a legal code as such, Qadaq was making a record of the legal judgements he had already made among the people. There was undoubtedly unwritten customary law already in existence by then.[5] Customs evolve over time and the imperial *yasa* probably had more legal content than mere tribal tradition. What is likely is that it was a body of case law built up from the imperial decrees or *yarlag* that were issued by Chinggis — and subsequent Khans — on an *ad hoc* basis. There is little differentiation between the words *yarlag* (a unique decree) and *yasa* (an alleged law). Juvaini uses the terms interchangeably. There certainly was something formal written down at the 1206 parliament or *huraltai*, probably at Chinggis' instruction. Whether it was a *Great Book of Yasas* (a formal body of legislation) or a general *yasa* (the beginning of a compilation of case by case legal decisions) can't be ascertained. But from it evolved a collection of customs, traditions and legal decisions. In short, we can only conclude that some sort of legal customary tradition did exist (referred to now simply as the *yasa*) but its exact form is not clear.

No copy of the alleged *Great Book of Yasas* survives, and any understanding of the *yasa* has to be constructed from fragments from a variety of sources, some Muslim, and various parts of Juvaini's *History*. However, Muslims in the Il-Khanate believed a book existed. Mahmud Amuli, writing in Il-Khan Oljeitu's reign, records that Chinggis Khan's 'precepts, maxims, and yasas were collected into a book'. Ibn Battuta, writing in the fourteenth century records:

> [Chinggis] had compiled a book of his laws, which is called by [the Mongols] the *Yasaq*, and they hold that if any [of the princes] contravenes the laws contained in this book his deposition is obligatory... If their sultan (that is Il-Khan) should have changed any one of those laws, their chiefs will rise up before him and say to him, 'You have changed this and changed that, and you have acted in such-and-such a manner and it is now obligatory to depose you.'[6]

The central idea of the *yasa* was that victory of the Mongols depended on unity of action, proper choice of leadership and bravery of each individual soldier. Gregor of Akanc, an Armenian cleric, writing in his *History of the Nation of the Archers*, portrays it as given by divine revelation:

> ... they [the Mongols] invoked the aid of God, the Creator of heaven and earth, and they made a great covenant with him

to abide by his commands.... These are the precepts of God which [an angel] imposed on them, and which they themselves call *yasa*. The first is: that ye love one another, second, do not commit adultery; do not steal; do not bear false witness; do not betray anyone. Respect the aged and the poor. If a transgressor of such be found among [the Mongols], the lawbreakers are to be put to death.[7]

The *yasa* enshrines religious tolerance

The *yasa* was a set of pragmatic ethical principles. With respect to religious policy, it expected tolerance of all religions and showed no preference to any. It demanded religious indifference. Juvaini summarises:

> Being the adherent of no religion and the follower of no creed, [Chinggis Khan] eschewed bigotry, and the preference of one faith to another, and the placing of some above others; rather he honoured and respected the learned and pious of every sect, recognising such conduct as the way to the court of God. And as he viewed the Muslims with the eye of respect, so also did he hold the Christians and idolaters (that is, worshippers of idols, namely Buddhists) in high esteem. As for his children and grandchildren, several of them have chosen a religion according to their inclination, some adopting Islam, others embracing Christianity, others selecting idolatry and others again cleaving to the ancient canon of their fathers (that is Shamanism).... But though they have adopted some religion they still for the most part avoid all show of fanaticism and do not swerve from the *yasa* of Chinggis Khan namely, to consider all sects as one and not to distinguish them from one another.[8]

Juvaini approved of Mongol religious tolerance. 'It is the *yasa* and custom of the Mongols that... they oppose no faith or religion — how can one speak of opposition? Rather they encourage them. They have exempted the most learned of every religion from every kind of occasional tax.'[9] Chepe, Chinggis' general during the Khara Khitai campaign (1217–1218), proclaimed to the locals the imperial decree of Chinggis that all people would have religious freedom, and that priests and laity of whatever religion would not be taxed.

This tolerance towards all religions was quite remarkable. The underlying political ideology of Chinggis was pragmatism: whatever worked was good. Or rather, whatever kept the Mongols in power, and the subordinate peoples quiet, was good. The Khans did not embrace or neglect any one particular religion out of doctrinal conviction. They were more interested in conquering and looting the nations. Religious policy therefore served the higher need to govern the conquered. If, by embracing Islam, the subjects were controllable, then Islam it should be. If Buddhism, then Buddhism. What really mattered to Chinggis and his successors was the nature of their call to conquer.

Chinggis claims divine right to conquer

Chinggis' foreign policy was messianic. The ideology that motivated him was his claimed divine right to conquer. Heaven (*munkh tenger*) itself had predestined him to rule the world. This doctrine allowed for the genocide of entire peoples. Cruelty and barbarism became a virtue. Juvaini calls Chinggis 'courageous, bloody and cruel. A just, resolute butcher'. Rashid quotes a *yarlag* of his: 'Let it be known to all emirs, aristocrats and to the people, that the Almighty gave us all the world from the east to the west. Those who show obedience to us will be saved, and so will their wives, children and relatives; but those who act otherwise will die, and so will their wives, children and relatives.'[10] Absolute obedience was expected and demanded.

This absolute obedience was held in tension with religious tolerance. To Chinggis, politics and religion were distinctly separate. A subject's personal religious convictions should not compromise his political allegiance. Priests of all religions were expected to say prayers on behalf of the Khan, and so, accordingly the empire would benefit. Therefore tax breaks and other privileges were not altruistic; they were conditional on all priests of all creeds praying for the welfare of the Khan.

This political obedience did have religious overtones, however. To obey the Khan was to obey *Munkh Tenger*. *Munkh Tenger* (literally 'eternal heaven'), was the highest deity in the Shamanist pantheon. The Mongols were completely adapted to the rigorous life of the vast steppe, and the *Tenger* (deities) they worshipped represented the powers of nature. The Shamans interceded with the divine pantheon on their behalf. What more was needed? Political pragmatism, driven by messianic conviction, was the mode of ruling. Religious conventions of conquered peoples were coincidental.

This initial messianic tone softened somewhat during the reign of subsequent Khans. Chinggis' son Joch (d.1227), from whose line the Golden Horde of Russia was to derive, opposed the mass extermination of conquered people. However, Joch's brother Ogedei, who was second of the Great Khans, and then Ogedei's son Guyuk, third of the Great Khans were both driven by this messiah complex. Then a shift to peaceful rule came. This went against the natural instinct of the Mongol aristocracy, and so the Khans had to curry the favour of the wealthy among the conquered peoples to ensure effective rule. This led to the *pax Mongolica*, the 'Mongolian peace', during which religious tolerance found full expression. When Kublai took the throne in the east as fifth and last of the Great Khans (1260), he shifted his capital from Karakorum to Da-tu (modern Beijing) and had to win the favour of the ruling Confucian bureaucracy to run his empire. In the west, the Il-Khans, descending from Hulegu, Kublai's brother, embraced the local religion to varying degrees, sometimes Islam, sometimes Nestorianism, to appease the local emirs, bishops and petty nobility.

Nestorianism finds a home through the back door

Nearly two centuries prior to the ascendancy of Chinggis Khan, the central Asian Turkic tribe of the Kerait converted *en masse* to Nestorian Christianity. Chinggis' immediate contact with Nestorianism was in his blood-bonded relationship with Toghrul, or Unc Khan of the Keraits. However, this relationship turned sour, and Chinggis defeated the tribe in 1204.

We have records of other pre-Mongol tribes of the central Asian steppe who were also converted wholly or partially to Nestorian Christianity: the Naiman and Merkit tribes being the most prominent. Like the Kerait, Chinggis conquered these tribes. In *The Secret History of the Mongols*, Temujin says in conversation with his ally Jurchedei, 'We finished off the Kereyit and plundered them. The most important nation being razed, the Naiman and the Merkit lost confidence.'[11] Chinggis found himself Khan over tribes that had had a Christian witness among them for several hundred years. As Chinggis built a bureaucracy to support his extending empire, it was members of these tribes in general, and the Kerait in particular, whom he appointed to positions of authority and influence. Nestorian Keraits became administrators, chancellors, ambassadors and generals throughout the empire, and Chinggis and subsequent Great Khans and Persian Il-Khans married Nestorian Kerait princesses. Thus Nestorian Christians came to play a key role in the fortunes of the Mongols and their empire.

Chinggis, although a Shamanist and worshipper of *Munkh Tenger*, was not above personal contact with the Christians. While contemplating vengeance on the Kharazim, he took himself away for three days and nights to a mountain where he had a dream. On the third night a monk dressed in black appeared and said there was nothing to fear and the proposed campaign would be successful. Chinggis then told this dream to one of the Nestorian Kerait women whom he had taken as wife. Her name was Obulgine, and she assured him that the monk was a bishop who occasionally visited her father.

Chinggis then appealed to the Uighur Christians who were dwelling at his *ordo* (encampment) to ask if they had any such bishop among them. They summoned Mar Denha, a Nestorian cleric, who was dressed similarly to the monk in the dream, but whose face was different. Mar Denha suggested it must have been one of the saints who visited Chinggis. After this, Chinggis apparently treated the Christians with special respect.[12]

However, Chinggis did not appoint Keraits to office because they were Christian. Ever the pragmatic leader, he appointed someone because they were the best person for the job. Kerait Nestorian women were taken as wives to ensure the ongoing allegiance of the Kerait to the Chinggis clan. Again, religious affiliation was coincidental; what counted was allegiance to the Khan.

This demand for complete allegiance gained Chinggis a war machine that established the biggest land empire the world has ever known. But death is no man's debtor and Chinggis died in August 1227 on the way back to the Mongol heartland after his war with the Hsi-Hsia in south China. He was sixty-six and had ruled twenty-two years as Great Khan. The scale of his conquests and the skill of his military leadership had been unprecedented. What he achieved in unifying his empire, organising his administration, and instigating legal traditions has not been surpassed. He showed astute broadmindedness in choosing his administrators and generals, making nationality or religious adherence secondary to skill and ability. His conquests checked the rise of Islam and re-established the Silk Road as a safe trading route with Europe.

How then did Nestorian Christianity fair under Chinggis? Given the policy of religious tolerance, Nestorian Christianity came to play an influential role in the Mongol empire. As long as subjects were obedient to the *yasa*, then credal adherence was one's own choice. In effect, Nestorian Christianity entered the Mongol empire through the back door.

The foreign media and the embassies had a feeding frenzy over the new law on the Relation of Religion and State. United Nations resolutions on freedom of religion were tossed around and eventually a small consortium of Democrats and Christians took the government to the constitutional court, on the grounds that parts of the law were unconstitutional.

'That's pretty brave for such a young church,' I commented to a Mongolian friend.

'Yes, but freedom of religion is at stake here,' she said indignantly. 'We Mongols were at our greatest when we respected each others' religions. We can't just deny that heritage of religious freedom we've received from Chinggis Khan.'

The constitutional court ordered three clauses to be rescinded. 'We're allowed to witness publicly still, but churches must be registered. Churches aren't allowed to meet in public halls. The state will control the number of clergy in any religion.'

I saw an immediate problem. All churches rented halls. All halls were owned by the state.

'Didn't your constitution of 1940 have a freedom of religion clause in it?' I asked, trying to explore how deep this freedom of religion really ran in Mongol thinking.

'Yes. That constitution is explicitly Communist, but Article 81 separates religion from the state and education system. Citizens of the Mongolian People's Republic had freedom of religion and also the right to distribute anti-religious propaganda. I think the government used the last bit more than it respected the first bit.'

I'd seen some of the press reports by now, both foreign and local, Christian and non-Christian. The Christian media was characteristically over-reactive. I'd also seen and digested an English translation of the law.

'Article 4.2 is interesting,' I suggested to my friend. 'It puts a high place on the unity of the Mongolian people, your historical and cultural traditions and your civilisation. I guess the legislators have seen Christianity as a threat to this, and that's why they want Buddhism as the official Mongolian religion.'

My friend was off hand. 'I don't know why they've given precedence to Buddhism. They don't seem to realise that Shamanism was the ancient Mongol religion. Anyway, Christianity should be an official religion too. It's certainly got a good case from an historical point of view.'

I flicked through the English translation I'd photocopied. 'I can live with Article 4.2,' I concluded. 'The challenge to the Christian church is to present Christ to the Mongolian people in Mongolian ways. Christianity in Mongolia must bring unity, not discord. It must be rooted historically and be seen to take on Mongol cultural forms.'

NOTES
1. Robert Michell and Nevill Forbes, trans., *The Chronicle of Novgorod: 1016–1471* (London: Camden Society, 1914), 64.
2. 'Ala-ad-Din 'Ata-Malik Juvaini, *The History of the World Conqueror*, trans. John Andrew Boyle (Manchester: Manchester University Press, 1958), 25.
3. P. Kahn, *The Secret History of the Mongols: The Origin of Chinghis Khan*. (San Francisco: North Point Press, 1984), 127,128. Also in U. Onon's version of *The Secret History: The History and the Life of Chinggis Khan* (Holland: E.J.Brill, 1990),112.
4. U. Onon, trans., *The History and the Life of Chinggis Khan* (Holland: E.J.Brill, 1990), 112.
5. A distinction should be made between Chinggis' alleged *yasa* or corpus of law, and the generic word *yasa* used in modern Mongolian, meaning 'customs and traditions'. Both words come from the same linguistic root, and works discussing Chinggis' *yasa* allude to a different spelling in the *mongol bichig* (the vertical Mongol script) by spelling it *yasaq*. The two English translations of *The Secret History*, Kahn (1984) and Onon (1990), both use the English word 'decree', without specifying the legal content; it may have been an unique precept (a *yarlag*) or part of a corpus of law (the *yasa*). For a detailed discussion see D.Morgan, 'The Great *Yasa* of Chingiz Khan', *Bulletin of the School of Oriental and Asian Studies* 49 (1986): 163–176.
6. Quoted in D.Morgan, 'The Great *Yasa* of Chingiz Khan', *Bulletin of the School of Oriental and Asian Studies* 49 (1986): 173.
7. Grigor of Akanc, *History of the Nation of the Archers*, eds. and trans. R.P.Blake and R.N. Frye, Harvard Journal of Asiatic Studies, 12 (1949): 291.
8. 'Ala-ad-Din 'Ata-Malik Juvaini, *The History of the World Conqueror*, trans. John Andrew Boyle (Manchester: Manchester University Press, 1958), 26.
9. 'Ala-ad-Din 'Ata-Malik Juvaini, *The History of the World Conqueror*, trans. John Andrew Boyle (Manchester: Manchester University Press, 1958), 16.
10. Grzegorz Leopold Seidler, *The Political Doctrine of the Mongols* (Lublin: Universitatis Mariae Curie-Sklodowska, 1960), 268.
11. U. Onon, trans., *The History and the Life of Chinggis Khan; The Secret History of the Mongols* (Leiden: E.J.Brill, 1990), 115.
12. Chinggis Khan married a daughter of Unc (Wang) Khan (the Kerait) called Wisulujin, or possibly Obulgine. This wife, being Kerait, was therefore probably a Nestorian Christian. See H.H. Howorth, 'The Northern Frontagers of China. Part VIII. Article IV: The Kirais and Prester John', *Journal of the Royal Asiatic Society* (1889): 392.

Chapter 7

Qadaq,
Scholar, Judge and Christian

'What Quadaq decides with my consent... shall remain unaltered into the most distant future.'
Chinggis Khan

I peered through the semi-gloom of the classroom, trying to read the writing on the blackboard. Learning to read *mongol bichig* was difficult enough without having the added burden of yet another power cut.

The winter of 1992–1993 was severe, with heavy snow in Ulaanbaatar and spring storms out on the steppe. Mongolia was struggling to make the transition from a centrally controlled economy to a market one. Democracy was in its infancy. Everything was rationed.

The power stations in the city were struggling, mainly due to the sudden lack of Russian engineers who were more interested in returning home to Russia than keeping the power stations going. Apparently, of the eight coal boilers in the main station, only one was working. We got letters from the British embassy outlining contingency plans if that last one died: there would be a civil emergency of huge proportions. There would not only be a lack of electricity, but also of hot water: everything would freeze and all the pipes would burst. Minus 35 degrees is not exactly the Bahamas. The embassy announced that it would want to evacuate us if the last boiler died.

Electricity was rationed and the hot water radiators cooled. We kept our down jackets on in language class. I could see my breath. There was enough to worry about that winter without tackling *mongol bichig* as well.

But my curiosity had got the better of me. Huge *mongol bichig* hoardings had appeared around the city and the children were learning it again at school. *Mongol bichig* simply means 'Mongolian writing': it is the vertical script in use before the communists rose to power, and the script still used in Inner Mongolia. In Ulaanbaatar, this script had taken a magnificent leap out of the University's history department and onto the streets.

Our language teacher had thrown the whole Cyrillic alphabet at us on the first day of class, printed and cursive, and expected us to be fluent in it the next day. Necessity is the mother of invention. We managed it. There was enough overlap with the Latin-English script to get on top of Mongol-Cyrillic relatively quickly. But *mongol bichig*? It looked more like a snail had fallen in the ink pot and slithered its way across the pages of the textbook in front of me.

'You read it top to bottom, left to right.' Our teacher was an authority on *mongol bichig*, and was in such demand that she had three part time jobs in three different institutions teaching it. The letters stopped dancing in front of me and slowly took on some meaning.

'N-o-m,' I declared. Three letters. The Mongol word for 'book'. Whew!

Our teacher obviously thought I'd now mastered this script. '*Ikh sain!* Very good. [Each] consonant has three forms depending on whether it is at the beginning or middle or end of the word. Don't forget the male and female vowels. And for the long vowels you have to put in a "g" in the middle of them.'

The fluorescent lights flickered. We cheered. I could see the board again. But my head was spinning.

Teacher carried on. ' "Ulaanbaatar", which has two long vowels, is spelt like this.... ' She carefully squiggled the word on the board, making sure the word's spine was perfectly vertical.

I had a go at spelling it out. 'U-l-a-g-a-n-b-a-g-a-t-o-r. That's nothing like how you say it!' I announced indignantly.

The more I got into this script the more it was like reading Chaucer's medieval English.

'It's an ancient script with lots of rules. What you read is not necessarily how you say the word. Chinggis Khan used *mongol bichig* to codify his laws and run his empire. He borrowed it from the Uighurs who had borrowed it from the Sogdians. We haven't been using it recently though. The Russian Communists introduced their Cyrillic script so that they could spread their propaganda more easily. *Mongol bichig* has been taught in the University only as a ceremonial script during the Communist era.'

The Chinese Communists hadn't suppressed the script as I'd noticed it on the Chinese yuan currency, and also on the plaques on the gates of the Mongolian embassy in Beijing.

Our teacher's brief history had one more point: 'I think *mongol bichig* originally came from Syria.'

From orphan to Grand Judge

During one of his campaigns against a neighbouring tribe, Chinggis came upon a boy lying on the roadside. Since his senior wife, Borte, was childless, and had long wished for a son, Chinggis sent the boy to her. Both *The Secret History* and Rashid give us the details, although Rashid's account is probably more reliable: '[Chinggis] picked up [the child] and sent it to Borte Fujin [with this message]: "Since you have always wanted a son, bring this one up as your own and take good care of him." When the foundling reached manhood, he was named Qadaq. He himself addressed Chinggis as 'father' and Borte as 'first mother'.[1]

Qadaq quickly proved his worth in both hunting (killing thirty gazelles single-handed in the middle of winter when he was fifteen), and protecting Chinggis' youngest son, Tolui, from bandits. On accession to the Khanate in 1206, Chinggis named Qadaq as a 'founder of the empire' when he issued this *yarlag*: 'To those who have contributed to the founding of the empire, I wish hereby to address my thanks and I shall appoint them as *chiliarchs* (commanders of a thousand men).'

However, Qadaq was unhappy about this reward and protested to Chinggis, implying that it was inadequate in recognising the true nature of his own allegiance to Chinggis.

Chinggis must have stood corrected: 'To you, my adopted younger brother... you shall be allotted the junior brother's share, that is two chiliarchs. Moreover, in recognition of your services, you shall be exempted from punishment for up to nine transgressions.' Chinggis then elevated him to Grand Judge: 'Divide up all the people into shares for the brothers; let no one violate your word. Put down brigandage throughout the entire empire and deal with all cases of fraud. Those that deserve death, have them killed; those that deserve punishment, have them punished.' Chinggis then ordered Qadaq to record all his decisions regarding judicial matters in a blue book, as we have noted already from *The Secret History*. Chinggis concludes: 'What Qadaq decides with my consent... shall remain unaltered into the most distant future.' Thus Qadaq, the orphan boy captured in battle, was eventually elevated to the position of Chief Legislator and Grand Judge of the Mongol Empire.

Nestorian Christianity among the Uighurs

One reason for this elevation was that Qadaq was literate: he was one of the first Mongols to master the Uighur script. The Uighurs were a Turkish tribe, originally from Lake Baikhal (north of modern Mongolia). Their grazing lands and capital were overrun by the Kirghiz, forcing them to migrate south into what is modern Xinjiang province of China where they proceeded to overrun the dominant Tibetans in the eighth century. The Uighurs were mainly Manicheans by religion, finding this Persian fire-religion at Chang-an when they attacked the city in 762. Their capital was Karakhoja, a large walled city, the ruins of which have been found near Turfan, Xinjiang province of modern China. However, although Manicheaism became widespread, they were also influenced by Nestorianism: their growth in power across central Asia brought them into contact with the numerous Nestorian communities.

Their adoption of Nestorian Christianity may well have been

due to the persecution received by Syrian Nestorians in Chang-an after an edict issued by the Tang emperor Wu Zong: 'As to the religions of foreign nations, let the men who teach them, as well as those of Da Qin (Nestorians) and Mu Hu Bi (Manicheans), amounting to 3000 persons, be required to resume the ways of ordinary life.' In effect, the edict ended the visible priesthood of both Nestorians and Manicheans. Both these groups then left Chang-an and moved west to the Chinese borderlands, into Uighur territories, where they taught their religions, and gained some success in converting the Uighurs. The Nestorian Stone may have been carved as a record of Christianity at the time of this departure.

Some historians are quite optimistic as to the extent of Christian influence among the Uighurs. One writes that by the second half of the eighth century the 'Christian Uighur Turks were all powerful in Eastern Asia and had their capital at Karakorum'.[2] Another concludes that the Uighurs 'appear to have been converted to Christianity at an early date and to have exerted a strong Christian influence for a very long period'.[3] Several European travellers through central Asia as late as the thirteenth century note the presence of Nestorians among the Uighurs.

The Uighurs adopt the Syriac script

Conversion to Nestorianism was extensive enough for the Uighurs to adopt a form of the Syriac script as their own. When Alopen and the Nestorians came to central Asia, they brought their Syriac Bibles with them, and it was the Syriac language in which Nestorian communities were taught. So if Uighur converts were to read the Bible, they had to learn Syriac. With subsequent Mongol influence extending well into Uighur territory, the natural choice of script for Chinggis to use for record-keeping was this Uighur/Syriac one. At some stage, the script rotated 180 degrees. With its adoption by the Mongols, it has evolved into the modern *mongol bichig* script of modern Mongolia.

As we have noted already, the Mongols were astute enough to recognise talent when they saw it, and exercised a pragmatic policy of adopting the best of the nations that they conquered. They learned from their enemies. Thus Qadaq, literate in the Uighur script and elevated to Grand Judge, was second only to Chinggis. Carpini, the first Western Christian sent by the Pope to the Mongols, met Qadaq in Karakorum in late 1245 and called him 'procurator of the whole empire'.

Qadaq as Christian in Chinggis' court

Qadaq was a Kerait Nestorian Christian, according to Juvaini. There were several Kerait Nestorians in Chinggis' administration, forming an elite group of educated Uighurs and Keraits (along with Turks and Chinese) all in high office. Of these, a number were Nestorian Christians, and this group had a magnificent opportunity to influence the whole of the Mongol empire and evangelise wider Asia.

Qadaq had the confidence of the Great Khans. He served under Ogedei and Guyuk, and Juvaini has much to say about his influence over Guyuk who was to become Great Khan in 1246:

Now Qadaq had been in attendance on him [Guyuk] since his childhood... and since he [Qadaq] was by religion a Christian, Guyuk too was brought up in that faith. Guyuk therefore went to great lengths in honouring the Christians and their priests, and for the most part too it was Christian physicians who were attached to his service. And because of the attendance of Qadaq... he naturally was prone to denounce the faith of Mohammed. The Emperor [Guyuk] had entrusted the binding and loosening, the tying and untying of affairs to Qadaq and Chinqai and made them responsible for good and evil, weal and woe. Consequently the cause of the Christians flourished during his reign.[4]

To be in this inner family circle of Chinggis reflects a character above reproach. Qadaq was incorruptible and was known for his keen sense of justice. Rashid believes that his judgements provided the whole basis for the judicial system of the Mongols in all their territories. He was also a highly skilled administrator, and Chinggis gave him powers over north China after the Mongols conquered it. Here he carried out a detailed census of the whole region. Qadaq also followed Chinggis on his western campaign, having personal responsibility for a range of military engagements throughout 1222. After Chinggis' death, Qadaq continued in service to Ogedei Khan who called him 'elder brother'. With this intimate relationship within Chinggis' own family, Qadaq was assigned to the endowment that went to Queen Soyo, a fellow Nestorian Christian, on the death of her husband, who was Chinggis' youngest son, Tolui.

Qadaq's influence in *The Secret History*

Qadaq's most enduring legacy may have been his work, *The Secret History of the Mongols*. This is the foundation document of Mongol culture and history. Although it is a plain mixture of legend and fact, it maintains a position in the collective Mongol psyche similar to the *Mahabharatha* in Indian folklore or *Morte d'Arthur* in English. Traditionally, *The Secret History* is said to have been composed by bards, storytellers and poets over a number of years, and therefore reads as a loose collection of myths, poems and camp-fire readings.

However, it reads as an epic poem. It is coherent and unified and seems to have the style of one author. It contains plot and theme and portrays the interconnections of the Chinggiside family as if the author knew them well. Names and dates are prolific and fairly accurate, suggesting first-hand experience. The author exalts Chinggis Khan to mythical status, but also portrays him as a comrade among equals, and all the episodes that Qadaq appears in are favourable to Qadaq, notably the dispute over the rewards that Chinggis had offered him at the 1206 *huraltai*. There is a bias towards the House of Tolui with which Qadaq was known to be sympathetic (namely Tolui's wife, Queen Soyo and her son Munkh).

The final copy of *The Secret History*, according to a note in the text, was completed at a *huraltai* on the Kerulen River in the 'seventh month of the Year of the Rat'. This would date it most likely as August 1228, at the *huraltai* which elected Ogedei as Great Khan. The text itself refers once to 'my father the Khan', referring to Chinggis. As there is nothing more in *The Secret History* after the life of Chinggis Khan, we could assume it was compiled and presented to Ogedei as a memorial to his father, and an epic to remind him in his new office of the heroes who had gone before him. Granted, there are folk tales which must certainly have been acquired around the campfire, but overall the evidence suggests a single, organised, author behind it. And Qadaq is the most likely candidate.

So the foundation document of the Mongols may have been written by a Christian.

I browsed the religious studies section of the University of Canterbury library in Christchurch, New Zealand, and eventually found a book of ancient Nestorian texts in Syriac. I was curious to find out exactly how similar *mongol bichig* was to the thirteenth-century Syriac which Qadaq used. I have to admit I was a bit sceptical. How comparable would the two scripts look after nearly 700 years?

I examined the Syriac text carefully. (It was nice to have some decent lighting.) The Syriac looked pretty similar to the *mongol bichig*. The text was horizontal, but I could easily recognise the shape of the letters. I turned the book so the text was vertical, like the *mongol bichig*. I stared long and hard. I'd studied the *mongol bichig* for about six months by now and knew enough about it to see the similarities were unmistakable.

The implications were astounding as I turned them over in

my mind: this *mongol bichig* script, which the Mongols were resurrecting from the graveyard of Communism, was the direct result of the introduction of the Syriac Bible into central Asia.

I did some more research, and when I returned to Mongolia, I delivered my findings to my students. I'd come across one more key fact by then.

'The Syriac language is a dialect of Aramaic,' I announced. I waited for the penny to drop, but there was silence.

I couldn't contain my enthusiasm and continued. 'Who is the world's most famous Aramaic speaker?' I was met with blank stares.

Then a hand at the back of the class nervously slunk into the air. The student offered a question as the answer.

'Jesus?'

NOTES

1. Rashid in P. Ratchnesvsky, 'Siqi Qutuq (ca. 1180 – ca 1260)' in de Rachewiltz, I., Hok-lam Chan, Hsiao Ch'i-ch'ing and Peter W. Geier (eds) *In the Service of the Khan: Eminent Personalities of the Early Mongol-Yuan Period (1200–1300).* (Wiesbaden: Harrossowitz Verlag, 1993): 76

2. Stewart, J. *Nestorian Missionary Enterprise; The Story of a Church on Fire* (Edinburgh: T and T Clark, 1928), 137 referring to H.H. Howorth, History of the Mongols; from the 9th to the 19th Century. (London: Burt Franklin, 1876), I/21.

3. Stewart, J. *Nestorian Missionary Enterprise; The Story of a Church on Fire* (Edinburgh: T and T Clark, 1928), 148.

4. Juvaini, 'Ala-ad-Din 'Ata-Malik, *The History of the World Conqueror*, trans. John Andrew Boyle (Manchester: Manchester University Press, 1958), 259.

Chapter 8

Chingay:
Christian Mediator and Statesman

'At the place we were summoned into the presence of the Emperor, and Chingay, the protonotary, wrote down our names.'

Jean de Plano Carpini

It was two in the morning and I couldn't sleep. The air conditioning was humming away, and jetlag had upset my biorhythms. I stood at the window of the hotel, fourteen storeys up, looking out over the spectacular lights of Singapore. There was so much electricity around that the city appeared eerie, as it might during a full moon anywhere else. A ship's horn sounded in the distance.

'Can't you sleep either?' Karen's question jolted me out of my thoughts.

'Just thinking,' I replied. 'Come here and have a look.'

I was intrigued by the incandescent outline of a Hindu temple nearby. 'How many religious places can you count?' I asked her as she pulled back the curtain. We'd been married three years and had done courses together in cross-cultural communication and read numerous books on the matter, getting ready for our first trip to Mongolia.

A cross was lit up on a nearby church below us, and I could see the myriad coloured lights of a Buddhist temple that followed the classic curves of a Chinese roof. The spire of a mosque seemed out of place, a tiny needle reflected in the glass walls of neighbouring tower blocks. We'd passed a number of little roadside shrines with incense burning at them earlier in the evening.

'Don't forget the temples to Mammon,' she suggested, counting up all the skyscrapers with neon designer names of banks, sports clothes, freight companies and soft drinks.

I love Singapore. It's fast, clean, colourful and exotic. It has always proved a pleasant surprise. If I'm travelling west to east, it's my introduction to the sights, sounds and smells of Asia. If I'm travelling east to west, it's my cultural air-lock that eases the transition back to my own Western ways. It is a revolving door; one in which I'm happy to whirl around.

All air-routes converge on Singapore. At least that is what Singapore Airlines would have us believe. Their inflight magazine diplayed a densely-packed radiating network, as if someone had splattered the page with a fountain pen. Not radiating outwards, but radiating inwards. Singapore is the fairy godmother that beckons the world's travellers to taste of the fruits of another place. It is a magic door.

'Seven,' she announced. I'd forgotten what the question was.

'I can see about seven religious places just from this window. It seems that the religions of the world have all converged here.'

Who was Chingay?

Qadaq's contemporary and colleague was a man called Chingay. Like Qadaq, Chingay was literate, went on to attain high rank among the Mongols, and was a Nestorian Christian. The main source that tells us of him is the *Yuan Shih*, or *History of the Yuan*. This is a document written by the Chinese Ming dynasty historians: the Chinese historians of each dynasty were commissioned to write a history of the dynasty before. However, we know some more about Chingay from Juvaini and also Carpini. No mention is made of him in *The Secret History*, which is very surprising considering the great height to which he eventually rose. If it is true that Qadaq wrote (or influenced the writing of) *The Secret History*, then it may be possible that he and Chingay had a falling out. This would explain the absence of Chingay's name.

Chingay's ethnic affiliation is debatable. He may have been Uighur, possibly Kerait, but probably Ongut. The Ongut were

Turkic-Mongols on the Chinese-Mongol borderlands within the northern bend of the Yellow River and were largely Nestorian Christians. They played a crucial role in mediating the relationships of the Chinese and the tribes of the central Asian steppe over the centuries, so it is probable that Chingay spoke Chinese. There is some evidence to suggest he may have been a travelling merchant and in this capacity gathered much intelligence about the rise of Temujin prior to Temujin's ordination as Chinggis Khan in 1206. His arrival at the court of Chinggis may well have been as an ambassador of the Ongguts. On the other hand, he could have been taken hostage by a warring party, as he is later recruited into Chinggis' bodyguard. (Chinggis usually recruited his bodyguard from hostages taken in war.)

Chingay's rise and influence

Under Chinggis, Chingay rose quickly. He served in military campaigns and by 1206 was a successful centurion. When Chinggis organised his administrative structure after the 1206 *huraltai*, Chingay was made Arbitrator, launching him on a ministerial career. His first duties were as an assistant to Qadaq (now Chief Judge), supervising the work of about sixty high officials and secretaries. He then rose to the position of Chancellor, with powers to appoint provincial governors. Chingay continued his military involvement in campaigns through to 1210 earning the 'golden tiger tablet' and the title of Chamberlain. In this role he ran Chinggis' domestic affairs, including his family affairs. His influence within the family is marked. Ogedei (Chinggis' son) later had Christian sympathies, and Guyuk (Chinggis' grandson) is said to have been a Nestorian Christian.

Chingay's responsibilties also meant he looked after the prisoners of war. The practice of the day was to take captives from their homeland and relocate them in a totally new place. Usually, if the captives were worth anything (metalworkers, tool makers, engineers, scribes, agriculturalists), they were moved near to the central government which could then use their skills. One of these settlements came under Chingay's governorship. Some time before 1222, he established a large settlement between the Khangai and Altai mountains as an agricultural base: it was called the 'Granary of Chingay' and acted as a supply centre for military campaigns, specifically for those against the Khwarzim about 1219. To establish an agricultural centre in such a remote area was a formidable task, but Chingay did it well, and inhabitants of the area today can trace their ancestry back to this colony.

Successes like these underlined Chinggis' high opinion of Chingay, and it seems they had a close and intimate relationship; on one occasion, Chinggis gave Chingay a horse, then in 1215 he gave him first rights to the spoils of the defeated Chin capital, Chengdu. Indeed, this imperial esteem for Chingay carried over into the reigns of both Ogedei and Guyuk.

Chingay's legacy

When Ogedei came to power, Chingay was made responsible for collecting revenue from the two richest provinces, China and Turkestan. Later military campaigns of Chinggis had cleaned out the treasury, and Ogedei's first task was to generate income and consolidate his own power while fending off bankruptcy. In effect, Ogedei turned to Chingay to reorganise his government, and supervise the lower administrative levels. Of Chinggis' administrators, Chingay was the first to be reappointed under Ogedei, and this shows the trust and esteem in which he was held.

In 1246, with the election of Guyuk to the Khanate, Chingay was appointed again as a senior administrator in a predominantly Nestorian-Christian government. Guyuk himself was sympathetic to Christianity, and Chingay had the chance to foster Christian expansion among the Mongol elite. Rashid, a Muslim, reports this with some distaste. Chingay resumed the role of Arbitrator, in charge of the day-to-day affairs of court; he had the role of Ombudsman, Adjutant and Deputy Principal all rolled into one. As well as running the affairs at home, his influence extended into the provinces, specifically China, Turkestan and Khorasan (modern eastern Iran and Afghanistan). Here he showed true skill as a mediator, instituting forms of local government rather than carrying on in the 'slash and burn' approach of Chinggis and Ogedei.

Chingay mediates between East and West — but is finally executed

As the effectual Minister of Internal Affairs, Chingay had the job of receiving foreign ambassadors. In August 1246, he received Pope Innocent IV's ambassador, the Franciscan Jean of Plano Carpini, at the *altan ordo*, the 'golden encampment' of the Khan, near Karakorum. This was the first of several Catholic-European embassies to penetrate Mongol central Asia. Carpini has left us a full account of his travels to the Khan's court. In his *History of the Mongols* he writes of this journey, the people he meets, something of the culture of the Mongols — including their military strength — and of the six months he lived among them.

When Pope Innocent IV and cardinals sent Carpini with a message for Guyuk, it was Chingay, the 'protonotary' (Carpini's word), who acted as secretary and mediator. He supervised Guyuk's reply, in the presence of Qadaq and Bala: it was first translated into Latin, phrase by phrase, then back-translated into Mongolian. A copy was also translated into 'Saracen', language of the Muslims (Persian), dated 'Jumada the second, 644' which equates to November 1246. Bearing responsibility for this translation was highly significant. He was directly influencing Europe's perception of the Mongols and the likelihood or otherwise of the Mongols converting to Catholic-Christianity.

Chingay's influence, power and prestige was surpassed only

by the Khan. Being a Nestorian-Christian, he had opportunity to promote the welfare of Christians, influence the Chinggiside family for the cause of Christ, and establish policies of central government that focused on order and just laws, rather than on punitive warfare. Together with Qadaq, these two Nestorian-Christians effectively ran the Mongol empire; once it had become established, they controlled its legal processes and internal affairs, and influenced its foreign policy.

After Guyuk died in 1248, possibly by poisoning, Chingay remained at court during the regency of Guyuk's widow Oghulgaimish (1248–1251). His role as administrator declined, but he continued to have extensive personal influence. This may have been his downfall. The line of succession had been shifted from Ogedei's house to his brother Tolui's house, and Munkh, Tolui's son and new Khan (r.1251–1259), had Chingay, now eighty-three years old, executed. It was all part of his general purge of all those associated with Ogedei's house. Chingay had had twelve sons by two wives, and these sons continued in their father's offices, ten of them going on to hold civil and military positions under Kublai during the Yuan dynasty of China. With this ongoing service to Kublai, Chingay's name was rehabilitated in gratitude, but he was never granted a posthumous title.

I woke up with a start and realised the telephone was ringing.

'Wake up call sir.' I think that's what the voice said. It was in a thick Chinese accent.

I looked at the luminous numbers on the clock: 5am. I'd told the bell boy 5.20am. We needed every bit of sleep we could get. I hated catching the 8am flight from Singapore to Beijing.

'We can get our Mongolian visas tomorrow. We're going to have the rest of the day in Beijing to go exploring,' I said excitedly to Karen as we zipped along the motorway to Singapore's Changi airport. An orange sun was emerging from behind the haze of dust and smog. The boats on the harbour were hooting at each other. I took a deep breath of the mixture of diesel

fumes, frangipani, salt spray, spices and bougainvillea that
wafted on the morning breeze. Being born in India, I felt right
at home in Asia. Karen wasn't so sure of herself.

'I'm a Kiwi. And I grew up in South America. I think differently, I eat differently and I do things differently. Don't forget
I'm new to Asia,' she reminded me.

Chapter 9

Soyo-bekh,
Christian Queen and Mother

*'Furthermore, in the management of her household
and in the ceremonial of her court, she laid for
kinsmen and stranger such a foundation as the
khans of the world had not been capable of.'*

Juvaini

I spent a whole language lesson learning how to make a clicking sound. I tried to analyse it: your tongue is lightly placed
against the top teeth, then you inhale quickly. When I tried to
do it, my language teacher and the other three students in the
class wept with hysterical laughter. I guess I sounded something like a cross between a strangled chicken and a deflating
tyre.

This sound meant 'yes'. I'd heard it a lot on the streets of
Ulaanbaatar. Its equivalent in English was 'a-ha' as one would
say over and over as you chatted on the telephone. Narantuya,
our teacher, was determined she'd lower my language to the
colloquial.

'Now we'll learn the Mongol slang for "no",' she announced.

This sound was similar, but different. I watched her mouth
(or rather her jaw) closely while she demonstrated. She stuck
her jaw out a little, pursed her lips, and from deep within the
lower realms of her throat she made a scraping sound by inhaling a short bit of air. This time it was my turn to enjoy a good
chuckle watching (and listening) to my classmate having a go.
He sounded like a frog with asthma.

I reckon I pretty well mastered those two sounds that day,
after about two hours' practice, and the lesson drifted off onto
other things. Narantuya had a great habit of digressing. In fact
all our Mongolian language teachers meandered off the set lesson at the slightest bit of prompting. We usually got back to our
lesson eventually; something about employment opportunities
for women, that day.

'In Mongolia we have a genuine 50:50 gender balance in all employment,' Narantuya said. I didn't doubt this for a minute. More than half our language teachers were women. I put it down to one of the achievements of Communism.

Equality for women of nobility

In imperial times, women had equality with men both in economic responsibilities and — among the nobility — in political life. A man's wife may well have ridden next to him in war as an equal, and widows were redeemed by brothers or step-sons.

Polygamy was the norm, and in each Khan's *ordo* there were likely to be a few Nestorian wives. Chinggis married the Nestorian Keraits Ibaka-bekh, niece of Unc Khan, and also Obulgine, a daughter of Unc Khan. Tourakina, wife of Ogedei Khan, may also have been a Nestorian Christian. Widowed queens acted as regents until the next *huraltai* when the subsequent Khan was elected. Through the Chinggiside dynasty, women proved to be wise counsellors and skilful leaders, especially during their regency. On the death of a Khan, if his chief queen was a Nestorian Kerait, the Mongol empire was run by a Christian woman until the next *huraltai*.

Soyo-bekh — a Christian queen[1]

One woman left a deep impression on her contemporaries and received high accolades for her public Christian commitment. This was Soyo, daughter of Jagambu, niece of Unc-Khan and wife of Tolui, Chinggis' son. She was the mother of Hulegu (first of the Il-Khans of Persia), Munkh (fourth Great Khan), Kublai (fifth Great Khan), and Arik-boke. Such was her public Christian presence that Juvaini assigns a whole chapter to her. Juvaini arrived at Karakorum a year after she died, and although he didn't meet her, his account of her is based on fresh second-hand reports. Rubruck, Franciscan ambassador to the Khans, says she was a Christian. Another eyewitness records a conversation with Hulegu: 'He conversed with me at length upon the events of his life and childhood and upon his mother, who was a Christian.' Her compassion was evident from early in her career when she sent condolences and gifts to Oghul-gaimish in 1248 at the death of her husband Guyuk Khan.

The fact that Soyo was a Christian was not lost on the Chinese Ming chroniclers either. After her death in 1252, her image was preserved in the *Monastery of the Faith of the Cross* in Gansu province, an area where there had been a large number of Nestorians as early as the T'ang dynasty. The *Yuan Shih* records:

> On the wu-yin day of the ninth month, the first year of T'ien-li [1328]... the Emperor commanded... the Yeh-li-k'o-wen [Nestorians] to perform the Buddhist ritual [ie religious ritual] at the Shrine Palace of Hsien-yi Chuang-Sheng Huang-hou [Queen Soyo].

And again:

> On the ping-shen day of the third month, the first year of Chih-yuan [1335], the ministers Chung-shu-sheng reported: 'Now the mother of Emperor Shih Tsu [Kublai], Pieh-chi ['bekh' ie Soyo-bekh] T'ai-hou, is worshipped in the shih-tze ssu [temple of the cross] of Kan-chou Lu, Gansu province.[2]

Her image was later transported to Da-tu (modern Beijing) and placed in a hall consecrated to the spirits of deceased princesses.

Was Soyo a manipulator or outstanding leader?

Queen Soyo wielded tremendous political power, and she used this for the welfare of the empire, and for the Christian religion. Carpini notes: 'Among the Tartars this lady is most renowned... and more powerful than anyone else except Bati [of the Golden Horde].'³ Juvaini observed her as having the 'greatest authority' in the *huraltai* at the election of Guyuk in 1246, and also records that the Khan 'commanded that as long as he lived, affairs of state should be administered in accordance with the counsel of Soyo-bekh'.

Queen Soyo was a highly-skilled leader and diplomat. She was behind the process that moved the line of succession from the House of Ogedei to the House of Tolui, her husband. When Tolui died, his brother Ogedei, reigning Khan at the time, wanted to wed her to his youngest son Guyuk, according to Mongol custom. Soyo managed to sidestep this without offending anyone. She manoeuvred herself so well that when Guyuk ascended the throne, he gave her the responsibility of distributing 500 wagon loads of war-loot as a mark of his respect. If she had married him, this would have meant the future of the empire was in Ogedei's house, thus excluding her own sons. By the time Guyuk died, she had cultivated enough good will that it was a *fait accompli* that the succession would move to her sons. Some portray her as a blatant manipulator for this.⁴

Juvaini has given us a less harsh and more realistic opinion:

As for Soyo-bekh, she had won favour on all sides by bestowing gifts and presents upon her family and kindred and dispensing largesse to troops and strangers and so rendered all subject to her will and planted love and affection in everyone's heart and soul, so that when the death of Guyuk Khan occurred, most men were agreed and of one mind as to the entrusting of the keys of the Khanate to her son, Munkh Khan.

Juvaini explicitly links Queen Soyo's leadership skills with the *yasa* of her father-in-law, Chinggis Khan:

As for her control and management of her sons... whenever by reason of a death they awaited the accession of a new khan, she would allow no change or alteration of the ancient ordinances or *yasa*. So it was that when Guyuk Khan was raised to the Khanate, all were put to shame save only Soyobekh and her sons, who had not swerved a hair's breadth from the law, and this because of her great wisdom, self-discipline and consideration.

Her particular desire was to nurture her sons in the legal traditions of the *yasa* and groom them for the Khanate. Three of them were to fulfil this dream:

Now in the management and education of all her sons, in the administration of affairs of state, in the maintenance of dignity and prestige and in the execution of business, Soyobekh, by the nicety of her judgement and discrimination, constructed such a basis — and for the strengthening of these edifices laid such a foundation — that no [man] would have been capable of the like, or could have dealt with these matters with the like brilliance.[5]

Kublai's respect for his mother is clearly evident. His initial education was under her guidance, and, although eventually throwing his lot in with Buddhism, he maintained an empathy towards Christians throughout his reign. The *Yuan Shih* records that Kublai built her a 'Chapel of the Number 10' in Da-tu.[6] The pictogram '+' in Chinese is the number 10, so the name of the chapel could be translated as 'The Chapel of the Cross'.

Juvaini notes her political influence:

In any business which the Khan undertook, he used first to consult with Soyo-bekh and would suffer no change of whatever she recommended. The ambassadors too held her in great honour; and the dependants of her Court in nearest and farthest East and West were distinguished by the dignity and protection they enjoyed; and because of her zealous concern for each of them individually their lives were contented and carefree. And the tax-gatherers... and the army, for fear of her punishment and discipline, were fain to deal equitably with the people. And whenever there was a *hural-tai* or assembly of the princes, and there was great elegance, and decoration, she was distinguished above them all with respect both to her retinue and to her troops.

Queen Soyo, though a Christian beyond doubt, also promoted the welfare of those of other religions in her domain due to her adherence to the *yasa*. The fact that Juvaini was so conciliatory towards her is remarkable. He records:

Her hand was ever open in benefaction, and although she was a follower and devotee of the religion of Jesus she would bestow alms and presents upon imams and sheikhs and strove also to revive the sacred observance of the faith of Mohammed. And the token and proof of this statement is that she gave 1000 silver balish that a [Muslim]college might be built in Bokhara.

Regarding her own sons, she allowed Hulegu to be educated by a Nestorian tutor and Kublai by a Chinese Buddhist tutor. This religious tolerance had its consequences: Hulegu became sympathetic with Nestorianism and Kublai eventually imported Buddhism from Tibet.

For a time, then, the Mongol empire had a gifted Christian woman in an influential position of power. She commanded the respect of her subjects and her fame extended internationally. She was a skilled administrator and, largely due to her insistence on the adhesion to the *yasa*, the empire held together during the intrigue following Ogedei's death (1241). She maintained order and propriety in the kingdom by enforcing the correct use of pasture lands and prompt payment of taxes. Her decisions were binding as law and there was no dissent. It was due to her leadership that the Mongol military kept fit and battle-ready and free from dissension. There can be little doubt that a great Christian woman lived and influenced an empire. Juvaini concludes: 'Furthermore, in the management of her household and in the ceremonial of her court she laid for kinsmen and stranger such a foundation as the khans of the world had not been capable of.'

Kutuktei, a second Christian queen (and her tragic death)

Part of Soyo's prudence was the marriage of her son Munkh to a Nestorian called Kutuktei. The Franciscan traveller Rubruck calls Kutuktei a Christian. He could not however bring himself to believe Nestorian claims that Munkh, then Kutuktei, had been baptised:

> The following day [after Munkh had allegedly been baptised], all the Nestorian priests assembled before daybreak at the chapel; and they sang solemn Matins, and put on their vestments and prepared incense. While they were waiting in the court before the church, the chief wife, by name Cotota Caten (Kutuktei-hatan)... entered the chapel with a number of other ladies and her eldest son Baltu and her other little children; and they prostrated, placing their foreheads on the ground after the Nestorian custom, and then they touched all the statues with their right hand, always kissing the hand afterwards; and then they proffered their right hand to all present in the church, for this is the custom of Nestorians on entering church. After this, when it was broad daylight, she began to take off her head-dress... and I saw her bare head. She thereupon ordered us to leave, and as we were going out I saw a silver bowl being brought. Whether they baptised her or not I do not know.[7]

Kutuktei was a Kerait, and it is likely that what Rubruck

observed was indeed her baptism. After this ceremony Rubruck was impressed with the Christian behaviour of the queen: 'The Khan... then left and his wife stayed behind and distributed gifts to all the Christians present.' However, he comments in disgust at her subsequent behaviour: 'then the drinks were brought... and the lady, holding a full goblet in her hand, knelt down and asked a blessing... then the lady, now drunk, got into a cart... and she went her way.'

Rubruck, being Catholic, was predisposed to find fault in the Nestorian scheme of things, and in this case is likely to have observed a mere cultural practice. Being a time of celebration, the ceremony would have finished with drinking of *airag*, fermented mare's milk; the verdict of drunkenness was hasty considering the Mongol capacity to drink *airag*. Elsewhere, Rubruck again relates her Christian qualities: 'At Lent, the chief wife, Kutuktei, fasted that week with all her suite; and each day she came to our oratory and gave food to the priests and other Christians.'[8]

The evidence points to Kutuktei being more than just Christian in name. During her lifetime, the Nestorian presence at Karakorum was strong enough to warrant building a church at which she was in the habit of worshipping. Until this time, the chapel had been a tent. The site of this church appears on the historical maps of Karakorum which the schoolchildren in Year 4 and 5 use today in Mongolia.

Kutuktei's life ended sadly. She gave birth to a daughter, for whom the Buddhist priests predicted good health and a long life, but the baby died when she was three days old. The priests blamed the nanny, saying she was a witch, who had taken control of the child. Kutuktei executed the nanny, and for this, her husband Munkh Khan executed her.

'I'm impressed by the achievements of some of the women in Mongolia,' I said to Narantuya at the end of the lesson. 'You've got many women in very high positions in both government and university.'

She did her click-inhale affirming my statement. 'The opportunities are there,' she said. 'I hold this job, plus another part-time job, and I'm doing a Masters degree at the University at the same time.' She alluded to needing the right connections to get into the degree programme.

'But,' she said, 'it's not real equal opportunity. I get up at 6am, spend half an hour on the bus to start work at 8am in my first job. I then come directly here for the afternoon teaching session with you. From 5 until 9 each evening I'm at the university. Then I have to go home and do all the washing, cleaning, cooking. And then there's lesson preparation for the next day. Most nights I don't get to bed before midnight.'

'What about your husband?' I asked naively. 'Does he work?'

'Him?' she said disparagingly. 'He's tried a few trading trips. You know, go down to Beijing and buy some down jackets and sell them here in Ulaanbaatar. Now he mainly sits around with his mates drinking. He's supposed to be looking after the kids, but they basically fend for themselves when I'm not around. Many Mongol men follow a similar pattern.'

I had suspected something like this from observing some Mongol men, so it wasn't surprising to hear it confirmed. The Mongol men seem caught straddling the chasm between the job security of Communist days and the very liberal entrepreneurial business climate since 1990. I had learned in orientation during my first few weeks in Mongolia that it was the women who controlled the purse strings. Certainly Narantuya both earned the money and controlled it.

'The Mongol men?' she mused. 'They love three things. Vodka, their horse...'. She paused. 'And their mother.'

NOTES
1. The term 'bekh' simply implies royalty. Soyo is an abbreviation which I have chosen to use for convenience. Her full name is Soyorgachtani-bekh.
2. In Sechin Jagchid, 'Why the Mongolian Khans Adopted Tibetan Buddhism as their Faith', *Essays in Mongolian Studies* (USA: Brigham Young University, 1988), 87.

3. C. Dawson, ed., *Mission to Asia; Narratives and Letters of the Franciscan Missionaries in Mongolia and China in the 13th and 14th Centuries*, trans. a nun of Stanbrook Abbey (NY: Harper & Row, 1966), 26.

4. Michael Prawdin, *The Mongol Empire, its Rise and Legacy*, trans. Eden and Cedar Paul. 2nd edition. (NY: The Free Press, 1967), 292 .

5. 'Ala-ad-Din 'Ata-Malik Juvaini, *The History of the World Conqueror*, trans. John Andrew Boyle (Manchester: Manchester University Press, 1958). All subsequent quotes from Juvaini are from pp 550–552.

6. *Yuan Shih* (Peking: Zhong hua shu ju, 1976), chapter 38.

7. C. Dawson, ed., *Mission to Asia; Narratives and Letters of the Franciscan Missionaries in Mongolia and China in the 13th and 14th Centuries*, trans. a nun of Stanbrook Abbey (NY: Harper & Row, 1966), 162.

8. C. Dawson, ed., *Mission to Asia; Narratives and Letters of the Franciscan Missionaries in Mongolia and China in the 13th and 14th Centuries*, trans. a nun of Stanbrook Abbey (NY: Harper & Row, 1966), 172.

Chapter 10

Kublai Khan,

Last of the Great Khans

'Following my example, all my nobility will then in like manner receive baptism, and for this will be imitated by my subjects in general; so that the Christians of these parts will exceed in number those who inhabit your own country.'

Kublai Khan

In Xanadu did Kublai Khan,
A stately pleasure dome decree:
Where Alph, the sacred river, ran
Through caverns measureless to man
Down to a sunless sea.[1]

Anna picked us up at 9.30am. Singapore Airlines had given us a 'stopover holiday' and this entitled us to a guided tour of Tiananmen Square and the Forbidden City, two of the big tourist attractions in Beijing, absolutely free. Anna was a student at Beijing University and guiding tourists was a summer job for a bit of pocket money. And she got to practise her English.

Half of China seemed to be milling around Tiananmen Square that Sunday. It was the great recreational activity for families, much like wandering aimlessly around shopping malls. But even with so many people, I could feel the immensity of the place. The roar of the traffic as it circled around the outside added to the general chaos.

Anna had obviously learned a party-line monologue outlining all the glories of the various buildings around the square. The suppression of the student protests of 4 June 1989 was noticeably absent from her patter. Armed guards forbade anyone from going up onto the Martyrs' Monument in the middle of the square. The queue outside Mao's mausoleum snaked around for about a kilometre. I was glad I gave my allegiance to a resurrected saviour and not a dead one.

Mongol Emperors of Yuan China

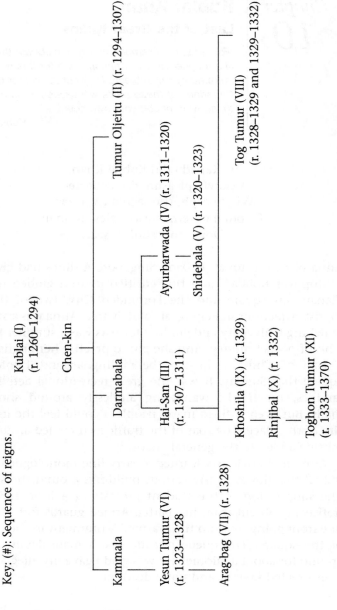

Key: (#): Sequence of reigns.

Kublai (I)
(r. 1260–1294)

Chen-kin

Kammala

Darmabala

Tumur Oljeitu (II) (r. 1294–1307)

Yesun Tumur (VI)
(r. 1323–1328)

Arag-bag (VII) (r. 1328)

Hai-San (III)
(r. 1307–1311)

Ayurbarwada (IV) (r. 1311–1320)

Shidebala (V) (r. 1320–1323)

Khoshila (IX) (r. 1329)

Rinjibal (X) (r. 1332)

Toghon Tumur (XI)
(r. 1333–1370)

Tog Tumur (VIII)
(r. 1328–1329 and 1329–1332)

We had Anjali our daughter, then eighteen months old, in her pushchair. She's blue eyed and blonde. And very cute.

'Take picture?' A small child, all trussed up in ribbons and white frilly dress, was thrust into my face. I looked at Anna for a cue, but she said nothing.

'Sure,' I replied.

That was my main mistake for the day. Within seconds, a gaggle of mums and their toddlers were vying for photos with our daughter. They pushed their children forward, then grandma squeezed the kids together and dad would take the photo. This lasted for about ten minutes. I'm sure our daughter's portrait now graces the photo albums of several dozen Chinese families. When the crowd reached about two hundred, I decided it was time to leave.

'I guess they don't see too many foreign families in Beijing. Mainly businessmen?' I suggested to Anna as we elbowed a hasty retreat. I had grown up in India and the one thing I detested as a child was inquisitive people coming up and pinching my cheeks. I knew how Anjali must be feeling and I felt very protective.

'Let's go to the Forbidden City now.' Anna took control.

I was really looking forward to this. Here we were, in transit in Beijing, and on our first trip to Mongolia. The Forbidden City was the first really Mongol thing to see. I had read in my Lonely Planet guide that the Forbidden City, as it is today, was built by the Ming emperors. However, Kublai Khan had chosen the site and laid out the essential plan for it.

I reminded Anna of Beijing's Mongol heritage before she started off on her monologue again. 'Chinggis Khan razed Beijing in 1215 didn't he? That was the end of the Jurchen empire. In 1264 Kublai shifted the Mongol capital here from Changdu, near Dolon-noor in Inner Mongolia. We have a poem in English about Kublai's capital in Changdu.'

Kublai flirts with Christianity

Kublai Khan was the fifth and last of the Great Khans, reigning from 1260 to 1294, for the first twenty years from Karakorum in the Mongol steppe heartland, then shifting his capital to Da-tu (Beijing) as first of the Yuan Emperors in China. Like his forefathers, Kublai was well exposed to Christianity.

His mother, Queen Soyo, was a Kerait Nestorian, and Kublai became well acquainted with her Nestorian Christianity, and was favourable towards Nestorians in general. He respected Christian holidays and the Bible. Marco Polo, the Venetian who travelled to Kublai's China and lived there for many years, records:

> being aware that the Easter festival was one of our principal solemnities, he commanded all the Christians to attend him, and to bring with them their Book, which contains the four Gospels of the Evangelists. After causing it to be repeatedly perfumed with incense, in a ceremonious manner, he devoutly kissed it, and directed that the same should be done by all his nobles who were present. This was his usual practice upon each of the principal Christian festivals, such as Easter and Christmas.[2]

Kublai's sympathy with Nestorian-Christianity also showed in practical government policies. He sent a *yarlag*, or decree, to vassal states ordering his governors to free all Christians from unequal servitude and taxes and to treat them with honour and reverence. He appointed a Nestorian Christian called An-t'ung (Anthony) as prime minister, and promoted another Nestorian, Ai-sie, to the office of Western Astronomy and Medicine in 1263. Mar Sargius, Nestorian Patriarch who ruled over the province of Gansu in the years 1278–1280, was appointed to an office in Kublai's household, and went on to build a number of Nestorian monasteries.

In 1289 Kublai set up the *Ch'ung-fu-sze*, a government ministry in charge of overseeing Christian affairs. The *Yuan Shih* records: 'The *Ch'ung-fu-sze* has the management of the sacrifices and offering in the temples of the cross belonging to *Ma Ha-si* (Bishops) and *Lie-pan Ye-li-ko-wen* (Christians)'.[3] This government ministry made sure that the 'temples of the cross' (the churches) were observing their religious and civil duties and teaching Nestorian Christians to respect Kublai's *yarlag*.

However, it would be unwise to assume that Kublai deliberately chose Christians for his key posts. He appointed administrators who could do their job well. Thus, even though he remained anti-Muslim for much of his life, he also appointed Muslims — undogmatic ones — to high administrative roles. Kublai allowed both Nestorian and Catholic practice in his empire, but little can be determined about the influence of Christian administrators for the cause of Christianity. Ai-sie, a Christian with knowledge of medicine and astronomy, was chief of the *Ch'ung-fu-sze* for six years, and must have had some influence. But his department oversaw all foreign Nestorians in the empire, not just Mongol Nestorians. So this would not have impinged on the psyche or culture of the ruling Mongols.

An unusual invitation

Another instance of Kublai's apparent open endorsement of Christianity was his invitation to the Pope:

> to send 100 persons well skilled in your law, who being confronted with the idolaters (ie Buddhists) shall have power to coerce them, and showing that they themselves are endowed with similar art.... When I am witness of this, I shall place them and their religion under an interdict, and allow myself to be baptised. Following my example, all my nobility will then in like manner receive baptism, and this will be imitated by my subjects in general; so that the Christians of these parts will exceed in number those who inhabit your own country.[4]

Here is perhaps an unparalleled invitation for Christianity to come unhindered to China. A window of opportunity suddenly opened for Europe to send '100 persons' as missionaries to Kublai's China. Would Europe oblige?

Kublai became acquainted with Catholic Europe mainly through hearing of the journeys of the Franciscans Carpini, then Rubruck, but then at first hand by meeting Nicolo and Matteo Polo who visited his court in 1267. It was Nicolo and Matteo who returned to Europe with Kublai's invitation, having been officially elevated to the status of ambassadors for the Khan and carrying his *paiza* (passport). The European reply was feeble. Pope Gregory 10 (r.1271–1276) sent two Dominican friars who turned back in Armenia when they encountered some warfare. Nicolo and Matteo then returned to China, this time with their nephew Marco who became famous for his long stay in Yuan China from 1271 to 1295.

To say that Catholic Europe missed out on evangelising the Mongol Empire would be an understatement. Here was the opportunity of the millennium: at least 100 missionaries could have poured into central Asia, all formally invited, and all supported by the government. Invitations like that today are unheard of. There was probably about a thirty-year period during the early years of Kublai's reign in which the empire could have embraced Christianity as its official religion.

Much has been made of this invitation, but it would be naive to accept it at face value. The Polos are the only ones who record it: it does not appear in any Chinese or Mongolian sources and therefore can't be verified. The Polos may have fabricated it somewhat to give to European readers what they might like to hear. 'Christian', 'Western' and 'European' were synonymous terms to Kublai. Ever since the days of Chinggis, the Nestorians had been in demand in the Mongol court as they proved able administrators, physicians, scribes and technicians. Kublai wanted their skills, not necessarily their religion. It is unlikely that Kublai could have been aware of the subtle differences between the Nestorians in his empire, and the Catholicism of the Polos.

Kublai may have wanted to recruit more foreign administrators. He was wary of the Confuscian bureaucracy he had inherited and had a policy of placing foreigners in key civil posts to control the Chinese. On the other hand, he was interested in the miraculous powers that Christians from Europe could perform to outdo the miraculous workings of the Buddhist lamas. So the invitation is more complex than first appears. However, Polo is in no doubt that Kublai had a genuine interest in Christianity despite being clearly pluralistic in his practice. Polo concludes: '... it must be evident that if the Pope had sent out persons duly qualified to preach the gospel, the grand khan would have embraced Christianity, for which, it is certainly known, he had a strong predilection.'

Kublai the pragmatic pluralist

Kublai never explicitly declared himself for Christianity and continued to patronise whatever religious festival was happening at the time. 'I do honour and show respect to all the four [religions], and invoke to my aid whichever among them is in truth supreme in heaven.' Marco Polo records his statement: 'There are four great Prophets who are worshipped by the different classes of mankind. The Christians regard Jesus Christ as their divinity; the Saracens, Mahomet; the Jews, Moses; and the idolaters, Sogomombar-kan [the Buddha], the most eminent among their idols.'

Within Kublai's borders Buddhists, Taoists, Muslims, Christians, Confucians and Jews all had the freedom to practise their religions. He set up government ministries for Buddhism, Daoism, Islam and Confucianism as well as Christianity. Jews and Manichaeans were tolerated but had no official government ministry to order their affairs.

Like his grandfather Chinggis, Kublai treated religion as a political matter. He was conforming to the *yasa*, or official decrees. He expressed on one occasion his annoyance with the obligation placed on Muslims by the Koran to wage holy war against infidels; a doctrine that could potentially ferment rebellion within his borders. The priority was obedience to the Khan: how an individual worshipped God was inconsequential; all religions were varieties of the one religion, all gods the representation of one God. 'If one only prays to Eternal Heaven [*munkh tenger*] and thinks about it in a befitting manner, is that not the same as if one had become a Christian?' Kublai allowed Mongols to become Christians as long as their religion did not compromise their political allegiance to himself.

Kublai imports Tibetan-Buddhism.

Later in his reign, Kublai publicly showed a strong favour for lamaism, the Tibetan form of Buddhism. His interest in this had started as early as 1242 when the Buddhist monk Yin Chien preached Buddhism to him and won his sympathy. Kublai later invited the Tibetan lama Phags-pa to his empire, and was most impressed by him, giving him the title 'Teacher of the Realm'. His favour of lamaism then became explicit. He invested a lot of money in temple building throughout his realm and in Tibet. On accession to the throne, Kublai had had a ceremonial reception of the relics of the Buddha which had been sent by the Raja of Ceylon. Other religions, especially Daoism and Islam, fell victim periodically to his sympathy for Buddhism.

Lamaism grew under Kublai, despite the constraints of the *yasa*. However, even though he explicitly favoured Buddhism by the end of his rule, it would be unwise to assume this was from doctrinal conviction. Again, political pragmatism was the reason. Acquiring the religious allegiance of Tibet meant he did not have to conquer it. Unity of religion meant unity of empire. It also meant that the Confucian bureaucracy was subordinate to foreign policies, and their own distinctly Chinese culture would not become dominant.

In short, Kublai held to a strong ideal of pragmatic government throughout his life. Whatever worked was good. From a religious perspective, this allowed practical freedom. Hence lama Phags-pa enjoyed Kublai's patronage, and Marco Polo regarded him as sympathetic towards Christianity. It meant that Christians had the freedom to live in Kublai's China and to meet together in Christian 'temples of the cross'. It meant also that the Franciscan John of Montecorvino, resident in Da-tu between 1294 and 1328, could get on and translate the New Testament and *Psalms* into Mongolian. It meant that Christians, both Nestorian and Catholic, periodically enjoyed imperial favour. In 1330, the Archbishop of Soltania noted that there were more than 30,000 Nestorian Christians in Cathay (ie China) who were 'rich, with very handsome and devoutly ordered churches and crosses and images in honour of God and the saints. They hold sundry offices under the... Emperor and have great privileges from him'.[5] This number cannot be verified, but the plurality afforded by the *yasa* meant a large number of Nestorian Christians enjoyed the freedom to meet and worship together during Kublai's reign.

Successors of Kublai Khan were all lamaists including grandson Tumur (r.1294–1307) and great grandson Khaishan (r.1307–1311). Khaishan invited the translation of the Buddhist canon of Scripture into Mongolian, and some Christian lands and temples were taken over by the Buddhists.

One can only dream of what may have been if Kublai's invitation had been fulfilled, whatever his intentions in making it.

Nayan's rebellion

In Kublai's twilight years, there were two insurrections in the empire, one from his long-term rival Khaidu who ruled central Asia, and the other from Nayan, a distant relative who held territories north of Da-tu in Manchuria. Nayan had become alarmed at Kublai's estrangement from his nomadic heritage and at how he had adopted Chinese ways. Marco Polo reveals that Nayan had 'privately undergone the ceremony of baptism, but never made open profession of Christianity'. During his insurrection he bore the sign of the cross on his banners and employed a large number of Nestorian soldiers in his army. Nayan's uprising was put down swiftly by Kublai, and Nayan was taken prisoner and executed in 1288, much to the delight of the Muslims and Jews.

However, Kublai did not hold Christianity *per se* responsible for the rebellion, and reprimanded Muslim and Jewish taunts:

> If the cross of Christ has not proved advantageous to the party of Nayan, the effect has been consistent with reason and justice, inasmuch as he was a rebel and a traitor to his lord, and to such wretches it could not afford its protection. Let none therefore presume to charge with injustice the God of the Christians, who is Himself the perfection of goodness and of justice.[6]

Kublai interpreted Nayan's rebellion as political rather than religious. Nayan's religion was of no matter to Kublai, and Kublai continued to invite Christians to take key administrative and army posts.

The Forbidden City's Meridian gate was absolutely chock-a-block with tour buses, vendors, cars and pedestrians. This must be where the other half of China was. We got out of our taxi with our blonde, blue-eyed, eighteen-month-old crowd puller. We were tempted to give her some phenergan to put her off to sleep so she wouldn't have to go through with all the poking and prodding.

Anna started on her monologue, most of which was lost on me. It was enough to stand in the place and hear the echoes and imagine the pageantry. I thought of the film *The Last Emperor*. The palace (now officially a museum) was strangely sterile; it lacked a heart and emotion.

'Take picture?'

'Let's keep moving,' I said to Anna.

We started off on a slow trot. Karen cursed the cobblestones as she tried to negotiate the pram. We hoped the grand historical significance of the place would detract further mothers from noticing Anjali.

Not so. Crowds parted and stared as we briskly plunged forward. Mothers pointed, cameras clicked.

The magnificence of the place was lost on us. We were in survival mode.

'I think she's too easily reached,' I said to Karen. 'I'll take her out of the pushchair and put her on my shoulders.'

'Make sure she doesn't run off,' Karen warned, as I stood her first on the ground.

I could just imagine trying to find her again in this rabbit warren of buildings! I saw in my mind Pu-yi, the last emperor as a boy running through the corridors of the palace. I hoisted Anjali up onto my shoulders out of harm's way, confident that she was now completely safe.

Anna tried to keep up. 'You walk very fast,' she said. 'There are nice gardens at the end. We rest there.' I'm not sure what dynasty Anna was up to in her explanation.

We were following the general flow of people down the main axis of the complex. At the Hall of Supreme Harmony we joined the back of the crowd to gawk at the splendour inside.

The man in front of me glanced back. 'Take picture?'

I signalled not. He tried anyway.

I peeled off and hid behind a pillar. This wasn't going to deter him. Cute foreign girl riding high on daddy's shoulders was the photographic prize of the day, obviously. Much more important than the ghosts of past emperors and the mystique of a thousand concubines and eunuchs.

He lined up a shot on the left side of the pillar. I shuffled right.

He peek-a-booed on the right side. I shuffled left. The Hall was obviously wrongly named. I didn't feel supremely harmonious at all. He tried it twice more. Anjali got motion sick.

Anna and Karen had retreated away from the crowd. I contemplated hiding in a nearby gilt-bronze vat until closing time.

An hour-and-a-half later, we burst out of the Gate of Martial Spirit like two people suddenly getting unstuck after jamming in a narrow door. The noise, fumes and general mayhem of Beijing traffic hit us. This gate was well named.

'You people walk fast. I never go through Forbidden City so fast before.' Anna was disappointed she wasn't able to deliver her full tourist speech for us. 'We now must wait. Driver not expecting us for half an hour. Ice cream?'

That sounded like an excellent idea. I chose a black-bean ice cream, mainly to show Anna that I was not totally put off her country despite having just seen the pinnacle of Chinese culture in record time.

We slurped our ice creams and watched the people exiting. Black-bean ice cream is different, but interesting. I decided we needed a memento of this grand occasion too. I marshalled Karen and Anjali together and gave my camera to Anna.

'Take picture?'

NOTES

1. W. Empson and D. Pirie, *Coleridge's Verse: A Selection* (London: Faber and Faber, 1972) 177.
2. Marco Polo, *The Travels of Marco Polo*, ed. E.Rhys (London: J.M. Dent & Sons Ltd, 1908), 158.
3. Palladius, 'Traces of Christianity in Mongolia and China in the 13th Century: drawn from Chinese Sources', *Chinese Recorder* 6 (1875), 107. See also A.C. Moule, *Christians in China before the Year 1550* (London: SPCK, 1930) 225ff which has a more detailed account of the *Yuan Shih's* record than Palladius.
4. Marco Polo, *The Travels of Marco Polo*, ed. E.Rhys (London: J.M. Dent & Sons Ltd, 1908), 160.
5. Henry Yule, trans. and ed., *Cathay and the Way Thither; Being a Collection of Medieval Notices of China*. 2nd ed., rev. H.Cordier (Nendeln/Liechtenstein: Kraus Reprint Ltd., 1967), 3:102.
6. Marco Polo, *The Travels of Marco Polo* (London: J.M. Dent & Sons Ltd, 1908), 158.

Part **3**

The Il-Khanate

Chormagan, Simeon and Ichikadei,
Novices in International Relationships

'The arrival of Rabban-ata [Simeon] brought much relief to the Christians... Before the coming of the Mongols it had been forbidden so much as to pronounce the name of Christ.'
Kirakos of Ganja

The words 'Outer Mongolia' conjure up images of desperate barrenness in the furthest-flung steppes of central Asia to which one is banished by friends in jest. I was anxious about the potential clash of cultures: a white middle-class couple from a small island nation in the South Pacific going to live in a country of huge expansive grassland and blue sky, in a central Asian city where the average annual temperature is –3° celsius. Some friends thought us odd when we left New Zealand in August 1992.

I was obviously a curiosity to at least one Ulaanbaatar taxi driver too. His questions reflected a naivety born of isolation, but also a winsome longing of better things to come.

'Is life difficult for you here in Mongolia?'

Not wanting to raise a rich-West poor-East dichotomy, I reply, 'Last winter there wasn't much food on the shelves, but I think it's getting better.' This draws an approving grunt.

'Where do you come from?' These questions are easy. Book one, lesson one at language school.

'New Zealand. (Pause) Do you know where New Zealand is?' I had discovered most Mongolians have a pretty good idea of world geography. Our language teacher had informed us that New Zealand was a fascist country.

'Near Finland.'

I gasp and mimic in Mongolian my LAMP loop tape, 'New

Zealand is three small islands in the Pacific Ocean. It has three million people and seventy-five million sheep.'

The taxi driver, taking his eyes off the road and hands off the wheel, wildly gesticulates about the number of sheep, making comparisons with the total number of livestock in Mongolia (twenty-four million) and the land space (size of Western Europe). I make a mental note not to foist agricultural statistics upon Ulaanbaatar taxi drivers, especially when following delapidated trolley busses.

'So what do you do?' On to lesson two.

'I teach English,' I reply, and mention the name of the college.

'Do they pay you in *tugruks*?' I knew that question would eventually come. I reply truthfully in the affirmative.

'But teachers get paid so little!' he exclaims, expecting me to reveal my monthly salary.

'It's enough,' I lie. In 1993 foreigners had to pay rent, utilities and international travel all in hard currency. I didn't dare try to explain. That would be about lesson fifteen.

'Do you like Mongolia?' Silly question really as you have to say 'yes'.

'Winter was very cold, but I'm really enjoying my first summer.' This triggers a monologue about the glories of the steppe and the wonderful life of freedom and plenty that the nomads enjoy. I suspect some truth is homogenised with a hefty injection of Communist propaganda. I make quick click-like inhaling sounds to show that I agree with his appraisal. I think he was impressed with my colloquial Mongolian.

Whether I liked it or not, I was an ambassador for my country. And every Ulaanbaatar taxi driver I chatted with was an ambassador for his. As we drove around the city together, we were in a momentary cross-cultural interactive bubble.

Simeon arrives in Chormagan's domain

After the death of Chinggis Khan, the Mongol empire split into a number of smaller khanates, each ruled by a descendent of Chinggis. In the Persian Khanate, the Mongol conquerors found themselves interacting with Eastern Christians (mainly Nestorians) and European Catholics. Mongol generals and governors had to negotiate alliances and treaties with European Crusaders, and at times these generals were sympathetic to Christianity. Chormagan was the first of these generals to show favour towards Christians. From 1231 to 1241 he commanded the Khwarizmian Khanate in the centre-west. We know that he had two Nestorian brothers.

During his generalship he received a Syrian Christian called Simeon, sent by Ogedei Khan. Simeon was a Doctor of Philosophy, and a permanent resident at Karakorum. He had gained the trust and confidence of Ogedei Khan, and persuaded him to be more lenient on the Christians in Mongol domains. He had reminded the Khan that Christians of Armenia, Georgia and Asia Minor had served him faithfully and always paid their tribute on time. Simeon had impressed Ogedei with his learning and character, and as a consequence received the title *ata* which means 'father'. Ogedei sent Simeon to Armenia in 1241 as administrator of Christian affairs. When Simeon arrived in Chormagan's territory, he was acting as courier of Ogedei's *yarlag*; this forbade the massacre of disarmed Christian communities which had accepted Mongol authority. Kirakos of Ganja (an Armenian chronicler) records:

> the arrival of Simeon brought much relief to the Christians, and saved them from death and servitude. He [Simeon] built churches in Muslim towns where, before the coming of the Mongols, it had been forbidden so much as to pronounce the name of Christ, notably in Tabriz and Nakhichevan. He built churches, erected crosses, caused the gong to be sounded night and day, and the dead to be buried with the

reading of the Gospel, with crosses, candles, and chanting. Even the Tartar generals gave him presents.[1]

Simeon acted as a mediator between the Christians of Armenia, Georgia and Albania who had up to then endured attacks by the Mongols. On his arrival, persecutions stopped and Christians were given freedom to worship. As a consequence, many of the Mongols of the occupying forces were baptised, which led to false rumours in Europe that the Mongols as a nation had embraced Christianity. From this time on, when Christians were persecuted, it was not the result of anti-Christian policies, but because of problems with local Muslim clerics and petty bureaucrats. The Christians in the western provinces faired reasonably well with these three powerful patrons: Simeon as Ogedei's *chargé d'affaires*, Chormagan as general, and ultimately with the backing of Ogedei himself.

European-Mongol dialogue has a shaky start

In 1241, Chormagan became dumb (possibly due to paralysis) and was replaced by Baiju in 1242. Baiju was supreme commander of the Mongol forces in Persia, representing the interests of Ogedei's successor, Guyuk Khan. Baiju was later joined by Ichikadei as Governor of Persia. This trio — Chormagan, then Baiju, then Ichikadei — reveals a growing willingness to interact with Catholic-Christian Europe, rather then attempting to over-run it.

News in Europe was confusing: Europe was anxious about the reported atrocities of the Mongols. But news of Mongol conversions to Christianity added some substance to the hope that Europe might even be able to convert Mongols to Catholicism. By the time Ichikadei was appointed Governor of Persia, there was frequent postal communication between Europe and the Persian Mongols.

Chormagan had been sympathetic to Christianity and listened to Simeon. Baiju was less sympathetic. Pope Innocent IV was concerned and sent five Dominicans to Baiju's *ordo*, on 24 May 1247, to exhort the Mongols to cease their massacres and submit to his spiritual authority. These ambassadors refused to genuflect three times in front of Baiju, as was the Mongol custom. Baiju was so furious he nearly had them executed, but for the intervention of his wife. Christianity, at least the European Catholic version, had not made a good start. Little distinction, if any, was made between European Catholicism and Syrian Nestorian Christianity. Christians were subsequently mocked, accused of idolatry (specifically of worshipping wood and stone; probably a reference to the cross) and thought of as dogs.

A few weeks after the visit of the papal embassy, Ichikadei arrived at Baiju's *ordo*, sent by Guyuk Khan. Together, Baiju as military commander and Ichikadei as civil governor controlled Persia. Ichikadei found an icy stand-off between Baiju and the European envoys. Ichikadei knew the contents of the letter penned six months earlier in November 1246 by Guyuk to the Pope and sent via Carpini. In response to the embassy, he and Baiju wrote a similar letter, reiterating the Mongol divine right to rule, demanding the Pope come and pay homage to the Khan and failing this, saying that he would be treated as an enemy. Two months after they arrived, the papal embassy was released to return to Rome accompanied by two Mongol envoys, Aibeg (possibly a Uighur) and Sargis, probably a Nestorian Christian. Pope Innocent IV received them well and gave them a long audience, and sent a reply back to Baiju which arrived on 28 November 1248.

Ichikadei and King Louis IX

Earlier that same year, Ichikadei had learned that the French King Louis IX was in Cyprus preparing for a crusade against the Mamalukes of Egypt. He saw here a window of opportunity to foster closer relationships. He chose two Nestorian Christians by the names of David and Markus to go to Nicosia, Cyprus in May and relay letters of introduction.

Ichikadei presented a sympathetic Christian mood to King Louis. His choice of Nestorian envoys was diplomatic and his letter full of Christian rhetoric. In it he explains that the Great Khan Guyuk had entrusted himself to liberate the Persian Christians from their servitude to the Muslims so that they could worship God without hindrance. The letter contains assurances that the Great Khan intended to protect all Christians, namely Latin, Greek Armenian, Nestorian and Jacobite. King Louis was naturally disbelieving at this claim that Christianity had spread throughout the Mongol tribes, and asked why Ascelin's embassy had had such a poor reception by Baiju. David and Markus explained that Baiju was not a Christian and was surrounded by Muslim advisers.

Louis was impressed and in response sent an embassy on 27 January 1249 made up of three Dominicans: Andre de Longjumeau, his brother Guillaume and Jean de Carcassone, who accompanied David and Markus back to Mosul, Ichikadei's provincial capital. On arrival, Louis' ambassadors were sent on to the Khan's *ordo* in Karakorum to take their array of gifts from Louis to Guyuk Khan. These included a portable chapel of gold-edged scarlet embroidered with scenes from the life of Christ, a letter of joy assuming ongoing conversions among the Mongols, and a piece of 'the true cross' (the Crusaders did a grand trade in alleged relics). On arrival at the Khan's *ordo* at Karakorum, the three Dominicans found that Guyuk had died and that his widow Oghul-gaimish was now regent. They returned to Louis, then in Caesarea, in April 1251.

Mixed motives and half truths

What is to be made of this curious exchange of embassies? Was Ichikadei representing a genuine expression of Mongol Christianity? There was certainly truth in the fact that Guyuk was sympathetic to Christianity and Persia itself was well populated with Eastern Christians. There was some truth in the content to Ichikadei's letters to Louis. But why the sudden opening of dialogue with Louis, considering the contempt shown for the embassy from the Pope?

The Mongols were willing to work with Christian Europe against the Muslims at this time. Mongol opinion of Islam was very low, oscillating from extreme contempt (as shown explicitly by Kublai later in China) to mere tolerance. But nothing as open as an embrace of Christianity was ever on the Mongol agenda. Very simply, Ichikadei was trying to foster an alliance with Louis' crusaders so that the Mongols could take Jerusalem. Later, he himself could then turn on Europe. The interest in Jerusalem was strong, and was part of Kublai's motivation to endorse the journey of Markus and Sauma, two Mongol Nestorian-Christians in 1278. When William of Rubruck visited Munkh's court in 1254, sent by King Louis, Rubruck had become alarmed at the Mongol interest in France: 'They began to ask a great many questions about the Kingdom of France, whether there were many sheep and oxen and horses there, as if they were about to march in at once and take everything'.[2]

Ichikadei's letter to Louis was indescribably exaggerated. He simply wanted in the long term to form an alliance to capture Jerusalem. He may have even been trying to recruit an ally to capture Baghdad (which Hulegu successfully did ten years later). These political exchanges were full of mixed motives and half truths. Although Ichikadei was 'Guyuk's confidential adviser', after Guyuk's death he quickly fell from grace, as the royal line moved to the house of Tolui. Ichikadei was executed by Munkh Khan on the grounds that he had overstepped his brief and added words and conditions of his own in the letter to Louis.

Certain rules were now in place. The *yasa* dictated tolerance of all religions, and the Christians naturally benefited. The Khans themselves, specifically Ogedei and Guyuk showed some sympathy towards Christianity and gave licence to their administrators and generals to act well towards them. An official portfolio of the Administration of Christian Affairs was established, first filled by Simeon. The Mongols' exposure to

Christianity had been only through Nestorianism, and it is to their credit that they did not distinguish between the various Christian sects of Eastern Christianity, if they had in fact recognised any differences.

Two significant events occurred during this time. First, Nestorianism was starting to return to its birthplace in Mongol dress, after a 500-year sojourn in central Asia. Secondly, Catholic Europe had begun to dialogue with the Mongols. Despite its being fraught with gross misunderstandings and offence, the contact had been made.

Before I got out of the taxi, the driver had a couple more questions for me.

'Do you have camels in New Zealand?'

I can see it now: bactrians to take you over those famous South Island mountain tracks. One hump for you, one hump for the gear. His last question really sent me spinning.

'Do you milk your horses in New Zealand?' The assumption was that every country has horses. And that we drink the mares' milk.

I said, 'Yes we have camels. In zoos.' He couldn't get his mind round this.

'And yes we have horses too. We don't milk them, we race them.' I knew he was thinking of the long twenty-kilometre horse races that the children enter in the summer Naadam festival. I hadn't the heart to try to explain that we raced our horses nowhere in particular, just around in circles. The cultural gap had widened considerably in the last two minutes.

I paid him and we exchanged a hearty farewell: *'za, bayartai'*.

As I stood on the curb watching him drive away, I couldn't help chuckling. I could just imagine a Cambridge stable milking their million-dollar mares. Imagine trying to catch one to get the cups on!

NOTES

1. Kirakos of Ganja (an Armenian chronicler) in René Grousset, *The Empire of the Steppes: A History of Central Asia* trans. Naomi Walford (USA: Rutgers University Press, 1970), 348.
2. C. Dawson, ed., *Mission to Asia; Narratives and Letters of the Franciscan Missionaries in Mongolia and China in the 13th and 14th Centuries*, trans. a nun of Stanbrook Abbey (NY: Harper & Row, 1966), 156.

Chapter 12

Dokuz-hatan,
Peacemaker and Arbitrator

'The princess was brought up in the Christianity professed by the Kerait nation to which she belonged, and she constantly protected her fellow believers: it was through her influence that [her husband] Hulegu was induced to show so much favour to the Christians.'

Rashid ad-Din

I waited for Tuya at the Chinese shop on the corner in front of the college where I used to teach English. Ulaanbaatar hadn't changed much since I left seven months earlier in August 1996. I was back in Mongolia for three weeks to be consultant to a variety of educational endeavours, but this evening I was going to her home group. Tuya had asked me to lead the Bible study.

Tuya is a woman of about thirty who had been a Christian believer since 1992. I'd had the privilege of baptising her in 1993, and then witnessed her rapid spiritual growth since. She had good English and had secured a very well-paid job with a foreign company.

We greeted with the customary exchanges

'Are you well?'

'Yes, I'm well. And you?'

'I'm well. How is your health?'

'Fine. Yours?'

'Fine. How is your work?'

'Fine. Yours?'

'Fine. How is your family?'

'Fine. Yours?'

'Fine. How is your husband?'

'He still drinks.'

We wandered up past the new Tibetan Buddhist temple dominating the hillside to the old Russian military barracks

Il-Khans of Persia and their Christian Queens

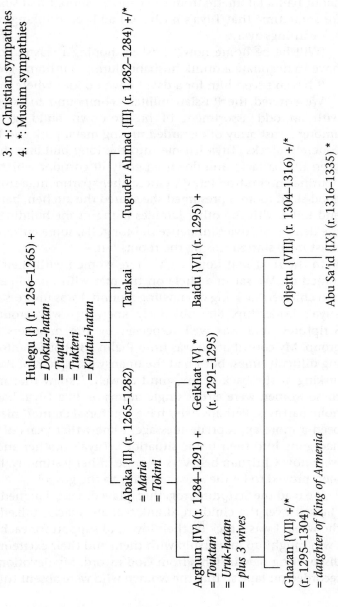

Key:
1. *Italics*: Christian queens.
2. {#}: Sequence of Il-Khans
3. +: Christian sympathies
4. *: Muslim sympathies

Hulegu [I] (r. 1256–1265) +
= *Dokuz-hatan*
= *Tuquti*
= *Tukteni*
= *Khutui-hatan*

Tarakai

Tuguder Ahmad [III] (r. 1282–1284) +/*

Abaka [II] (r. 1265–1282)
= *Maria*
= *Tokini*

Geikhat {V} *
(r. 1291–1295)

Baidu {VI} (r. 1295) +

Arghun {IV} (r. 1284–1291) +
= *Touktan*
= *Uruk-hatan*
= plus 3 wives

Ghazan {VII} +/*
(r. 1295–1304)
= *daughter of King of Armenia*

Oljeitu {VIII} (r. 1304–1316) +/*

Abu Sa'id [IX] (r. 1316–1335) *

about half a kilometre from the Chinese shop. I had suspected for some time that Tuya's husband had been drinking most of her earnings away.

'Will he be home now?' I asked, hoping I wasn't going to have to negotiate a drunk husband during our home group.

'I haven't seen him for a day. I have no idea where he is.'

We entered the Russian military compound to be greeted with an odd assortment of broken-down buildings sitting among a vast array of discarded rusting metal junk and broken concrete blocks. Tuya led me into the long building that had been the barracks and down a poorly lit corridor which smelt of urine and mutton fat. We entered her apartment, a single but good-sized room. I presumed she shared the kitchen, bathroom and toilet with the other families living in the building. With the demise of Soviet influence in Mongolia, some entrepreneur must have started leasing the rooms out.

In the next half hour, eight more women with their babies joined us. We sat in a circle on the mat with our Bibles open and children suckling or crawling around. I was impressed with Tuya's leadership. She obviously knew her way around the Scriptures, and was well respected by the members of the group. My contribution was from Psalm 23 about comfort during difficult times, but I had the unanswered pleas of Psalm 22 lurking at the back of my mind as well. I knew that most of these women were either single mums or, like Tuya, had alcoholic partners. Perhaps 'why have you forsaken me?' may have been a more appropriate message. I knew that years of prayer had gone into their home situations. Tuya's mother and sister were now Christian believers because of her testimony, but the men proved to be the most resistant to the gospel.

We read the Scriptures together, prayed, sang, laughed, cried, clucked over the children, drank tea, ate snacks, talked about the week. I was struck by their love and support for each other. I was caught up in worship with them and their excitement on discovering new insights from God's word. My devotional was recorded on tape so that the women who were absent this week could listen to it later. I was profoundly moved by their sincerity and humility.

_____

Swift rise of a Christian queen

Like Soyo, Dokuz-hatan was a Nestorian Kerait queen. She was the wife of Hulegu (brother of Munkh and Kublai, and first Il-Khan of Persia). Rashid tells us that she was 'Hulegu's principle wife... the daughter of Iku, son of Wang [Unc] Khan. She had been his father's wife'.[1] Dokuz-hatan was a subordinate wife of Hulegu's father, and was therefore his stepmother. According to Mongol custom, when a man died, his wives became the property of the eldest son, except for the son's own mother. So Hulegu inherited Dokuz-hatan as his wife on the death of Tolui in 1233.[2] Hulegu already had several wives, but when he received and married Dokuz-hatan during his campaign to Persia, she retained pre-eminence in his harem because she was his father's widow. Hulegu in effect acquired a Kerait Nestorian wife by default. Dokuz-hatan's swift rise to a position of influence was to bring much good for the church in Persia under the Mongols.

There is no doubt that Dokuz-hatan was a practising Christian. Gregor of Akanc writes: 'his [Hulegu's] blessed wife Dokuz-hatan was good in every way, and was compassionate to the poor and needy. She very much loved all Christians, Armenians and Syrians, so that her tent was a church, and a sounder travelled with her, and many Armenian and Syrian priests.'[3] Rashid writes of her in a similar way: 'as the Kerait had long ago embraced Christianity, Dokuz-hatan made it her constant care to protect Christians, and throughout her lifetime they prospered... and at the gate of her *ordo* there was always a chapel, where bells were rung.'[4] Out of Christian charity, she interceded on behalf of conquered peoples for leniency from Hulegu on several occasions. She undertook the role of peacemaker and arbitrator, and people came to her to appeal for clemency.

Dokuz had the confidence of Vartan, an Armenian monk. Before Hulegu died, she talked with him about whether mass should be said for the souls of the dead. He counselled not, but advised distribution of charity instead. She also consulted him regarding the succession, and he recommended Abaka be enthroned according to Hulegu's wishes. When Hulegu Il-Khan and his queen died within a short time, Bar Hebraeus records that all the world mourned:

> At the beginning of Lent died Hulegu, whose wisdom, magnanimity, and great exploits have no parallel; and in the summer following, his faithful queen Dokuz-hatan also quitted this world. By the disappearance of these two... protectors of the Christian faith, the Christians of the whole world have been plunged into sorrow and mourning.[5]

St Martin, a contemporary of Bar Hebreaus, uses even more lofty language:

> The great and pious king, the master of the world, the hope of the Christians, Hulegu Khan, died in the year 1265, and was soon followed by his excellent wife, Dokuz-hatan. The Lord knows that they were scarcely inferior to Constantine and his mother Helena. As Hulegu loved the Christians, all nations which professed the true faith obeyed him willingly.[6]

Queen Dokuz had a unique opportunity to influence her husband in favour of Christianity. Of her, Rashid writes:

> it was through her influence that Hulegu was induced to show so much favour to the Christians, who, profiting by this period of prosperity, built churches in all the provinces of his dominions. At the entrance of the *ordo* of Dokuz-hatan, there was always a church whence the sound of bells could be heard.[7]

Munkh too had respected her wisdom and had instructed his brother Hulegu to consult her often. Rashid: 'To please his princess [Dokuz-hatan], Hulegu heaped favours upon [the Christians] and gave them every token of his regard... so that all over his realm new churches were continually being built. Dokuz-hatan was much attached to the Christians, who during her life were in a flourishing condition. Hulegu favoured the Christians in consequence all over his empire.'[8] Vartan adds:

In 1264, the Il-Khan Hulegu summoned us..... When we were admitted into his presence, we were excused from bending the knee and prostrating ourselves according to Tartar etiquette, since Christians bow only to God. They bade us bless the wine and received it at our hands.... After we were seated, the brethren with me sang hymns. The Il-Khan said to me, 'These monks have come from everywhere to visit me and bless me. This is proof that God is inclined in my favour.'[9]

Dokuz shapes a legacy

Dokuz' legacy was far-reaching. Rashid observed: 'This princess was brought up in the Christianity professed by the Kerait nation to which she belonged, and she constantly protected her fellow believers.'[10] Vartan continues:

she hoped to see Christianity increase in lustre, and its every advance is to be attributed to her... the Mongols of Persia carried with them a canvas tent in the shape of a church. The rattle called the faithful to prayer. The offices of Mass were celebrated every day by priests and deacons. Here ecclesiastics drawn from among Christians of every language could live in tranquility. Having come to ask for peace, they obtained it, and returned home with gifts.[11]

When Hulegu sacked Baghdad in 1258, he spared the

Christian quarter because of Dokuz. Kirakos of Ganja, the Armenian chronicler records the incident: 'At the capture of Baghdad, Hulegu's wife Dokuz-hatan, who was a Nestorian, spoke on behalf of the Christians... and interceded for their lives. Hulegu spared them and allowed them to keep all their possessions.' [12] Vartan confirms this in saying that at the time of the assault on Baghdad, the Christians shut themselves up in a church at the order of the Nestorian patriarch Makikha 2, and the Mongols spared the church and the Christians in it. Afterwards, Hulegu gave one of the newly conquered Caliph's palaces to Makikha.

Dokuz stood in the line of a Kerait tribal succession which had started early in the eleventh century. Two and a half centuries later, at the death of Hulegu and Dokuz in 1265, this Nestorian faith was still active and Dokuz received these high accolades. Hers was no isolated commitment to Christianity. Her brother Sarijeh has been called the King George of Nestorian Onguts. Her niece was also a wife of Hulegu and a 'devoted' Nestorian Christian. Her cousin was Queen Soyo, Hulegu's mother, and so also her mother-in-law.

The Il-Khanate queens and the *yasa*

One of Hulegu's subordinate wives was the Nestorian Khutui-hatan. She mothered Abaka (who reigned 1265–1282 as second Il-Khan after Hulegu died), and Tuguder Ahmad (who reigned as third of the Il-Khans: 1282–1284). Bar Hebraeus calls her a 'Great Queen' who re-instigated Christian ceremonies and gave the Christians confidence within their Islamic environment. These Christian wives must have had a good influence on Hulegu for he asks for another, this time from the Emperor of Byzantium. The emperor Michael 8 Paleologus sent his own daughter Maria. [13] On her journey to the Khan's court, Hulegu died, but Maria continued on her way, and was pledged to Abaka, his successor. Vartan records that Maria wished Abaka to be baptised before she married him, which started the rumour in Europe that he was baptised. One contemporary claims that the patriarch of Antioch and other bishops first baptised him, and then married him to Maria. This does not mean that Abaka had become a Christian. However, it put Maria, a Greek Christian, in an influential position, not only in court but also in the life of Baidu her nephew-in-law who later became the sixth Il-Khan, though he reigned for less than a year (April – October 1295). They related to each other as mother and foster-son.

Abaka's son Arghun was fourth Il-Khan of Persia (r.1284–1291). His sister, a Christian, married the king of Georgia. He had five Christian queens: at least three were publicly active Christians.

So Kerait Nestorian princesses played influential roles in the Great Khanate and in the Persian Il-Khanate in the west. In the east, during the Yuan dynasty, Kublai took the kingdom into Buddhism, and apart from the personal influence of his mother Queen Soyo, and intermarriage with the Nestorian Ongut tribe (see Chapter 21), Nestorian influence was limited. In the west however, due to the return of Nestorianism to its homeland, the Il-Khans were much more aware of Christianity as a religion and even a political force.

The Muslim and Eastern Christian subjects within the Il-Khanate were probably unaware of the *yasa*. Some Il-Khans openly sympathised with Christianity, others with Islam. The detached indifference demanded by the *yasa* was not as easily seen in Persia where the battle lines of Islam-Christian bickering were very clear. It was among the Mongol nobility themselves that the *yasa* remained a compelling doctrine. When Tuguder Ahmed openly declared himself to be a Muslim, his mother appealed to the Grand Khan Kublai on the basis of the *yasa*. He was furious that she had gone over his authority and threatened the life of a Nestorian ambassador from Kublai's court for allowing it. His life was spared, again on the basis of the religious tolerance demanded by the *yasa*.

After Tuya's homegroup had finished, I stepped outside into the early spring chill, with the warmth of good fellowship in my heart. Tuya and I lingered at the gate.

'I think you led the group very well, Tuya,' I offered, not quite knowing what to say. 'You're like the shepherd in Psalm 23.'

'Well I try to encourage them all to contribute. Next week we will meet in someone else's home. We all take turns.'

I knew this was not as easy as it sounds. The mixture within a modern Mongolian family could be a hazardous brew: Buddhist mother, disillusioned-Communist father, Shamanist grandparents, cynical Gen-x siblings. The extended family usually all shared the same dwelling.

'And what about your husband?' I enquired.

She muttered something about keeping on praying, but I could see the pain in her eyes.

I suddenly felt I really had had little to contribute except for some meagre thoughts from a Psalm. It was these Mongolian Christians who had taught me something of perseverance and joy in the face of suffering and unanswered prayer. I had experienced blessing in a group that had been led by a mature Mongolian believer at whose feet I had sat, and I pledged to continue to pray for the salvation of the men.

We said our customary farewells, and I picked my way through the rubble and out into the street. Tuya would return to the rhythm of a working week, and I would return to New Zealand. I am richer for visiting that homegroup, and I will always remember that on Friday nights a touch of grace can be experienced in that home in the old Russian barracks.

NOTES

1. Rashid in H.H. Howorth, *History of the Mongols; from the 9th to the 19th Century* (London: Burt Franklin, 1876), 1: 542.
2. H.H. Howorth, *History of the Mongols; from the 9th to the 19th Century* (London: Burt Franklin, 1876), 3: 216, footnote 3 explains this custom in detail, noting that Juvaini, Bar Hebraeus, Rubruck, Carpini and Marco Polo all confirm observing it.
3. Gregor of Akanc, 'History of the Nation of the Archers', eds. and trans. R.P. Blake R.N. Frye, *Harvard Journal of Asiatic Studies*, 12 (1949): 341.

4. Rashid al-Din in René Grousset, *The Empire of the Steppes: A History of Central Asia*, trans. Naomi Walford (USA: Rutgers University Press, 1970), 357.
5. Bar-Hebraeus in Regis Evariste Huc, *Christianity in China, Tartary and Thibet*. (London: Longman, Brown, Green, Longmans, and Roberts, 1857), 1:276.
6. Saint Martin in Regis Evariste Huc, *Christianity in China, Tartary and Thibet*. (London: Longman, Brown, Green, Longmans, and Roberts, 1857), 1:276, footnote.
7. Rashid al-Din in Regis Evariste Huc, Regis Evariste Huc, *Christianity in China, Tartary and Thibet*. (London: Longman, Brown, Green, Longmans, and Roberts, 1857), 1:275.
8. Rashid al-Din in René Grousset, *The Empire of the Steppes: A History of Central Asia*, trans. Naomi Walford (USA: Rutgers University Press, 1970), 357.
9. René Grousset, *The Empire of the Steppes: A History of Central Asia*, trans. Naomi Walford (USA: Rutgers University Press, 1970), 358.
10. Rashid al-Din in Regis Evariste Huc, *Christianity in China, Tartary and Thibet*. (London: Longman, Brown, Green, Longmans, and Roberts, 1857), 1:275.
11. Vartan in René Grousset, *The Empire of the Steppes: A History of Central Asia*, trans. Naomi Walford (USA: Rutgers University Press, 1970), 357, 358.
12. René Grousset, *The Empire of the Steppes: A History of Central Asia*, trans. Naomi Walford (USA: Rutgers University Press, 1970), 356.
13. Maria's name is often hyphenated with the Greek title '-despina' which means 'princess'.

Hulegu Il-Khan,
How Nestorian Christianity Returned to Persia

'Hulegu Khan was of a great mind and great soul, just, and quite learned. He was a great shedder of blood, but he slew only the wicked and his enemies, and not the good or righteous. He loved the Christian folk more than the infidels.'

Gregor of Akanc

'These are appalling,' I declared. 'There's nothing accurate about them at all.'

My colleague looked over my shoulder at the magazine cuttings spread across my desk.

'I guess the Christian media loves to romanticise about Mongolia,' he suggested. 'You have to admit, Mongolia is flavour of the month with some mission agencies and churches. Every summer we've had dozens of short-term mission teams come through Ulaanbaatar. They all take their pictures and videos and they write these articles when they get back home.'

'But these all give the impression that Christianity is absolutely new to Mongolia.' This was a common view and was born out of ignorance of Mongolian history. 'Here, read these.' I handed him a selection.

'Evangelist Sammy Tippit conducts the "first outdoor crusade" in Mongolia.'[1] He summarised it slowly as he scanned the article.

'Here's some more.' I pushed them under his nose and he flicked through them.

'Mongolia is hearing the gospel preached for the first time.'[2]

'The first Mongolian believer gave her life to Jesus less than five years ago.'[3]

'For the first time, Mongolians are receiving some books of the Old Testament in their own language.'[4]

'These just simply aren't true,' I said indignantly. 'There were Christian missionaries preaching on these streets of Ulaanbaatar as recently as 1924, before the Communists took over. Besides, the Mongols have been doing "outdoor crusades" well before Sammy Tippit ever came here. I went to Darhan with a team in September 1992, within a month of arriving in Mongolia. We showed the *Jesus* film and a Mongol evangelist preached. There were decisions for Christ and a homegroup was planted. I was the only foreigner there.'

'So are you suggesting that the first churches in 1991 were not the first?'

'Exactly. These articles imply that no Mongol had ever heard the gospel or responded to it before 1991. The first Mongolian became a Christian in the eleventh century, not five years ago. And the Old Testament — there was a full Mongolian Old Testament printed in 1840.'

'I see your point. Maybe you're right,' he conceded. 'The Christian popular media loves to dish up a diet that feeds the romantic notions of supporters in the sending countries.'

Hulegu sacks Baghdad

Hulegu started moving his armies into the vicinity of Baghdad in November 1257. A Naiman Nestorian and general called Kitbuqa led the division that took the city the following February. Hulegu also had Georgian (ie Eastern Orthodox) auxiliaries in his army. Baghdad fell in February 1258.

Gregor of Akanc records the event: 'When the Mongols arrived on the spot they took at once the great and famous city of Baghdad, filled with many people and rare treasures, and countless gold and silver and pearls.'[5] Rashid reckons 800,000 were killed in the ensuing mayhem.

The Christians of Syria and Persia were elated with the Mongol capture of Baghdad. Nestorians, Syrian Jacobites and Armenians all saw it as avenging the ills of oppressed

Christendom, in the light of Islamic persecution. With such a large and visible Nestorian presence in his armies, and the fact that Hulegu himself had been raised as a Nestorian by his mother, the arrival of the Mongol armies meant the return of Nestorianism to its original homeland, six hundred years after Alopen and the first Syrian monks had gone to China.

Hulegu shows more Christian sympathies ...

Hulegu now had an empire to run, and his subjects were a mixture of Christians and Muslims. At times he appeared personally committed to Christianity. He took Allepo and Damascus, but it was Jerusalem that was the real prize: 'Hulegu Khan hearing [that the city of Jerusalem and the Holy Sepulchre of Christ had remained in the hands of the Arabs] went against the city of Jerusalem and took it. He himself entered the Church of the Holy Resurrection and prostrated himself before the Holy Sepulchre.'[6]

Haithon, King of Armenia, maintains that Hulegu always intended to return Jerusalem to the Christians. However, Hulegu didn't hold these three towns for long, and the Egyptians allied with French knights took them back again.

The Georgian Chronicle records further overt Christian sympathies. The Catholicos Nicoloz approached Hulegu about the protection of various monasteries in Georgia. Hulegu gave him a *yarlag* ensuring the monasteries' protection, assigned him an overseer, and made two gold jewelled crosses for the Catholics.

Hulegu never became a Christian but remained a Buddhist throughout his life, being a devotee of the future Buddha Maitreya in particular. Because there were no Buddhists in his kingdom apart from his own compatriots, it was natural that he leaned towards the Christianity of his mother and wife. Their tempering of matters had profound consequence, as we have seen, and the Christians benefited. Hulegu admitted to Vartan that his sympathy with Christianity had begun to create a rift between himself and his cousins in the Russian and Turkestan

Khanates. Hulegu and Dokuz were deeply mourned in death. One historian suggests they were murdered by Muslim conspirators: 'The great and pious king, the master of the world, the hope and stay of the Christians, Hulegu Khan, died.... He was soon followed by his respected wife, Dokuz-hatan. They were both poisoned by the crafty Sahib Khoja.'[7]

... but retains a true commitment to the *yasa*

Hulegu was a Mongol, great-grandson of Chinggis and a brutal military campaigner just like his forefathers. He cared nothing for dogma, following the *yasa* which demanded political expediency over religious bias. He had a Nestorian general, a Buddhist general and a Shamanist general. As others before him, he appointed the best person for the job, no matter what their religious affiliation.

The Christians were not distinguished when the Mongols swept through towns in sorties or punitive military exercises. For example, in Takrit the Christians appealed to Hulegu for clemency but got butchered along with Arab Muslims due to a conspiracy reported by an Arab to Hulegu that the Christians had killed many Muslims themselves and appropriated their property. In keeping with his commitment to the *yasa*, on consolidating his victories, Hulegu issued a *yarlag* allowing every religious sect to proclaim its faith openly and under the protection of his government.

Kitbuk abuses religious freedom

Freedom to practise one's religion can lead to excess. Although enjoying some degree of protection by Hulegu, the Christians in Persia sometimes flaunted this before the Muslims. Hulegu's 'most trusted general', the Nestorian Kitbuk, was a loose canon when it came to relationships with the Muslims.

Kitbuk 'loved Christians' and 'belonged to the race of the three kings who went to worship our Saviour at his nativity'.[8]

His tribal origin seemed of no consequence to Bar Hebraeus. (He was Naiman or possibly Kerait.) He was a very successful general who eventually controlled all of Mongol Syria and Mongol Palestine on behalf of Hulegu. He also took the Islamic fortress of Maimundiz in 1256, and with Hulegu destroyed the Assassin sect once and for all in the same year. In a quasi-Christian alliance with Bohemund VI of Antioch (r.1251–1268) and King Hayton I of Lesser Armenia, Kitbuk was responsible for capturing Damascus.

Kitbuk's true Christian sympathies were shown after the fall of Damascus. The local Syriac and Greek Christians of Damascus received a *yarlag* of Hulegu's guaranteeing them protection and freedom of expression which was a welcome reprieve from Muslim oppression. But this they flaunted to the local Muslim population. They offended Muslim sensibilities by drinking publicly during the Islamic festival of Ramadan, spilling wine in the streets and on the Muslims' clothes, compelling Muslims to stand while they sang Psalms and carried the cross through the streets, and harassing those who refused. The Muslims complained to Kitbuk. He, however, did not intervene, and allowed the local Christians to 'deconsecrate' an old Byzantine church building which had been used as a mosque, in effect returning the building to the Christians. Kitbuk's endorsement of Christian behaviour was evident, as throughout he maintained a relationship with all the local Christian leaders, visiting all the churches of the different Christian sects in the city.

In 1259 Hulegu was recalled to Karakorum for a *huraltai* to elect a new Khan as Munkh had been killed in battle. He left the Il-Khanate in the charge of Kitbuk. This proved Kitbuk's undoing. He was defeated and killed by the Mamaluke Sultan of Egypt at Ain Jalut on the plain of Tiberius in 1260. This was the first defeat the Mongols had suffered from the days of Chinggis and spelled the beginning of the end of Mongol dominance in Persia.

We gathered up all the news clippings and put them back in my file. I was determined that my colleague was going to get a more accurate picture.

'You see, there were Christians among the Mongols in the thirteenth century. They were the result of the Nestorian mission to central Asia which Alopen started. The gospel had arrived from Syria originally. Many of the Mongols were Christians. When the Mongols over-ran Syria and Persia six hundred years later, Nestorian Christianity returned to its homeland, but in Mongol dress. This was a full-circle event.'

We left the office and went outside. A deep eerie yellow light surrounded us. 'I hate these spring dust storms,' I muttered. I knew that within minutes, the sands of the Gobi desert would be trying to strip my epidermis from me and infiltrate mouth, ear and nostril. But my colleague's mind was still mulling over those articles.

'So...' he started.

The storm hit us and we doubled over into it. Hail, snow, dust and debris pummelled us.

'So, we're not really planting the church in Mongolia for the first time, then are we?' he shouted at me over the wind. 'We're re-planting the church in Mongolia.'

NOTES
1. *Christianity Today* (July 19, 1993): 53.
2. *Christianity Today* (May 17, 1993): 90.
3. *March for Jesus*, (Christchurch. Feb. 1995)
4. 'Mongolian First' *Word at Work* (Winter, 1995): 5
5. Grigor of Akanc, History of the Nation of the Archers , eds. and trans. R.P.Blake and R.N. Frye, *Harvard Journal of Asiatic Studies*, 12 (1949): 333, 337.
6. Grigor of Akanc, History of the Nation of the Archers , eds. and trans. R.P.Blake and R.N. Frye, *Harvard Journal of Asiatic Studies*, 12 (1949): 349.
7. H.H. Howorth, *History of the Mongols: From the 9th to the 19th Century* (London: Burt Franklin, 1876), 3:210.
8. H.H. Howorth, *History of the Mongols: From the 9th to the 19th Century* (London: Burt Franklin, 1876), 3:150.

Arghun Il-Khan,
Eclectic King of Persia

'By the power of Almighty God. Under the auspices of Khan Arghun, our word [to] the King of France, by the envoy, Mar Bar Sauma Sakhora. You have told us you will set out to join us when the Il-khan's troops begin their march towards Egypt.... If you keep your word and send your troops at the time fixed, and God favours our undertaking, then when we have taken Jerusalem from these people, we will make it over to you.'

Arghun Il-Khan

At our most strategic points of communication, language often lets us down. My first sermon in Mongolian proved for me to be a huge psychological hurdle. Forty hours preparation for thirty-two minutes delivery. And I practised at home in front of the mirror. Full volume too. One of the neighbours from three storeys below us came to investigate.

My opening line was a disclaimer for sounding like a two-year old.

'Bagsh-aa!' said one young man afterwards, 'Never mind. Next time you'll sound like a three-year old, then the next time like a four-year old, then the next time....' I understood it as a hearty affirmation that there would indeed be a next time.

Karen and I eventually got our preparation time down to about five hours for a half-hour Bible study for our homegroup on Saturday afternoons. They always seemed to grasp such deep theological truths so quickly. Well at least they always said they understood. I suspect they were being polite: if the truth be known, they probably didn't understand anything of the shredded language we gave them.

'I think Joseph was sold into slavery because he was a bad man.' Unravelling a Buddhist worldview of karma and replacing it with a more biblical worldview is always a delicate process.

'Do you have mantras in Christianity?' This question came from Baterden, one of my language teachers, during class one day.

'No,' I replied. 'I neither have to get God's attention nor earn any merit.' I then stammered my way through the gospel with very imprecise grammar, offset I hope by my enthusiasm for the moment.

'Do you believe in Buddha then?' I finally concluded.

'Whatever,' he mused. 'For seventy years we've been told that God is irrelevant. I don't know what to believe any more.'

Arghun Il-Khan's Christian sympathies

Arghun Il-Khan, fourth of the Mongol Il-Khans of Persia, rose to power by dethroning his uncle, Tuguder Ahmed (r.1282–1284). Tuguder had been an ineffectual Khan whose reign lasted only two years. He had oscillated in his policies and antagonised his subjects; the Muslims would not trust him, the Christians abhorred him, and the kings of Armenia and Georgia would not submit to him. The Great Khan Kublai threatened him at one point for wandering from the footsteps of Chinggis Khan. So Arghun, his nephew, revolted against him, captured him and beheaded him in front of his own army, justifying this by accusing him of abandoning the ancient *yasa* of the Mongols and embracing Islam, which none of his forefathers had done.

Like Hulegu, Arghun had public Christian sympathies, and like Hulegu, his mother had been a Nestorian Christian. Arghun had at least five queens who were Christians: Touktan, Dathani-hatan, Anichohamini, Elegag, and Uruk-hatan. We know that both Elegag and Touktan had been baptised, according to a letter that Arghun sent to Pope Honorius 4 (r.1285–1287) in 1287. Pope Nicholas 4 (r.1288–1292), hearing of the Christian faith of Arghun's wives, wrote to them individually to commend them. Arghun also had a sister who was a Christian and who married the king of Georgia.

Arghun wrote to the Pope and the king of England in 1291, and among other things, told them that his wife Uruk-hatan was a Christian. The Pope replied directly to Uruk-hatan, expressing gratitude that he had heard she was a Christian, and urging her good influence on her sons. These sons were Ghazan, later seventh of the Il-Khans (r.1295–1304), who married the daughter of the king of Armenia, and Oljeitu, eighth of the Il-Khans (r.1304–1316), whom Uruk-hatan baptised with the Christian name Nicholas, in honour of the Pope. Uruk-hatan had a small chapel at her *ordo* where she employed a Christian priest to conduct regular services in her presence. Hetoum II, king of Armenia (reigning from 1289), confirmed that she had been a Christian 'all her life', although he may only have known this second hand.[1] Uruk-hatan stood in a long Christian line: she was a great-granddaughter of Unc-Khan of the Keraits.

Some reports of Christian sympathies among the wives of Arghun, and the Pope's assessment of their Christian faith may have been based on misinformation, or at least exaggerated information. All the Persian Il-Khans courted the favours of the European Popes and monarchs in the hope of an alliance with the European Crusaders to pincer the Muslims who had reoccupied the Holy Land. It was no secret that the Mongols wanted to take Jerusalem from the Egyptian Mamalukes. So Arghun's correspondence may have exaggerated the Christian faith of his queens, knowing that this was what Europe wanted to hear.   However, King Hetoum II of Armenia independently confirms that the queens were Christian. Arghun himself was in a line of Khans who had all taken Christian wives: Arghun's father Abaka had married Maria, daughter of Michael VIII Paleologus, Emperor of Byzantium (r.1261–1282); Arghun's grandfather Hulegu had inherited Dokuz-hatan as his wife, and later, Arghun's son Ghazan was to marry the daughter of the Christian king of Armenia.

Muslim-Christian friction

The tensions in the Il-Khanate surrounding Arghun's *coup d'e-tat* were due to the friction between Islam and Eastern Christianity. Hulegu had been sympathetic to Nestorian Christianity, then Abaka, his successor, had oscillated between Islam and Christianity. Tuguder however, had bent to the will of his Muslim subjects and openly converted to Islam. Arghun, on the other hand, had the sympathy of the Mongol Nestorians, and it may well have been because of Nestorian units in his army that he was able to effect a swift and decisive coup. These 'Christian' army units were very evident, decorating standards and arms with the cross. The Great Khan Kublai immediately endorsed the coup, possibly because of its anti-Islamic agenda.

Arghun was not merely anti-Islamic; he was openly pro-Christian. He wanted to take Jerusalem again so that he could be baptised there. He restored the churches that his father Abaka had built and which his uncle had destroyed. The kings of Armenia and Georgia renewed their patronage and he opened a correspondence with Christian Europe. He even went as far as having a coin struck during his reign which had on one side a representation of the Holy Sepulchre in Jerusalem and on the other the words 'In the name of the Father, the Son and the Holy Ghost'.[2]

Arghun corresponds with Europe

Arghun and Christian Europe exchanged a veritable volume of correspondence. Arghun started this with a letter to Pope Honorius IV in 1285. Although some parts of the letter are unclear, there is allusion to the protection that Mongols had always given to Christians. He reminds the Pope of the favours that Hulegu and Abaka gave to Christians (exemptions from taxes and freedom to meet and worship) and promises that the Christians will have their fortunes restored which were taken under Tuguder, even apologising for his uncle's apostasy. The letter also suggests an alliance with Christian Europe to attack the Muslims, and promises part of Egypt to Europe after Arghun has taken it.

The Pope's reply was favourable and so Arghun sent an embassy to Europe in 1287 to cultivate the goodwill of the European princes. He chose Rabban Sauma as his ambassador, a Mongol-Nestorian originally from Kublai's China who had arrived in Persia on pilgrimage to Jerusalem, and who was good with languages. This embassy led to more letters being sent to the European princes expressing sympathy with the Christian West, and in which Arghun declares himself an enemy of Islam and Egypt. He tried explicitly to ally himself with Christian Europe against the Mamaluke Egyptians by letter in 1289 to King Philip the Fair of France.

The extraordinary tone of this correspondence would suggest that all of the Mongol realms were openly Christian, which was not true. In spite of his obvious Christian sympathies, Arghun was a religious eclectic. In bringing a genuine Mongol legal corrective to the backsliding policies of his uncle, Arghun had to show his allegiance to the *yasa*. This was imperative in light of the rebuke that Kublai had given to his uncle. In theory Arghun still gave his allegiance to the Great Khan Kublai. In practice he was free to rule as he chose and so structured his court like his fathers before him, placing the best person in the job because of skill, rather than religious or ethnic affiliation. There were Muslim advisers, a Jewish vizier, and at least ten European Christian interpreters among his courtiers. The Nestorian patriarch (and fellow Mongol) Mar Yaballaha III was a close friend most of Arghun's reign.

How Islam was to win through

Arghun's correctives were not so much from doctrinal conviction, as in effect a pendulum swing. His letters to Europe were more to do with currying favour than stimulating genuine religious intercourse. He wanted the Seljuk Turks out of Asia Minor, the Turcomans out of Aleppo, and he wanted to plunder Damascus. To this end, an alliance with Europe against the Egyptian Mamalukes was a priority. Even though his family heritage was Nestorian, he was something of a fence-sitter. He needed to rule a domain of assertive Muslims; he had an army of Mongol Nestorians; and he wanted to ally himself with Catholic Europe for his own gain. Of all the Persian Il-Khans, he was probably the most eager for an alliance with Christian Europe, but the power of his Muslim subjects was growing, and his successors had to give in more and more to their demands.

Arghun's reign is a paradigm for the Il-Khans in general. The *yasa* ruled that political pragmatism was to be accompanied by religious indifference. So any religious sympathies for either Islam or Christianity in any of the Il-Khans were really to appease their Persian subjects. One Khan would be pro-Islamic, another pro-Christian, depending on which way the political winds were blowing. In essence, all remained sympathetic to the ancient Mongol Shamanism, and some even flirted with imposing Buddhism on Persia. Christian marriages were undertaken to win (and keep) the allegiance of subordinate princes. Mongol dialogue with Europe was motivated by the desire to acquire military intelligence and alliances. Arghun was an eclectic, and the religious pendulum swung widely.

Ironically, it was due to the *yasa* that the Mongols lost their virility in Persia. A primitive sort of 'messianism' or divine right to rule had motivated Chinggis. It was God-ordained that he would conquer the world. His was a divine cause, a sense of destiny dictated by eternal heaven. This was well lost by the time the Il-Khanate had run its course in Persia. Religious pluralism meant there was no single cause for the Mongols to contend. So instead of their subjects becoming Mongol-Shamanists, the Mongols allowed themselves to be absorbed into the Islamic Persian culture around them. Nestorianism, in the early years of the Il-Khanate had been a religious bed-partner with Mongol Shamanism: the Mongols were familiar with it, their queens and their Kerait and Naiman allies were adherents of it. Both religions had coexisted side by side for three hundred years. The Mongols never went home to their central Asian heartland like they did at the fall of the Yuan empire in China. They came to Persia, they conquered it, settled down, and were absorbed into it. Despite such open Christian sympathies among some of the Mongols, in the end, Islam won because Mongol pluralism allowed it to continue to be the dominant religion of the region.

Baterden, my language teacher, seemed to be really floundering. The official religion of the last seventy odd years had been Marxist atheism. With new religious freedom, there was an honest and genuine search for truth among some of the Mongols I knew. Baterden's winsomeness betrayed the disconnectedness around me: Communism had collapsed, Buddhism didn't provide satisfactory answers, and he knew so little of the ancient Mongol Shamanism that it really wasn't a viable option. And now he found he had Christian students.

I felt out of my depth as I had rather quickly exhausted my own linguistic capabilities. I thought it best for the Holy Spirit to take over, so gave him a New Testament.

Questions of religious allegiance often got mixed up with other things.

'If America is a Christian country, how come they all kill each other?' This question came from a student in English class this time. I figured she'd been watching too many American cop dramas on TV.

This time I stammer forth in Monglish, a survival hybrid of Mongolian and English. My main concern was to try to disengage the notion that a country could be 'Christian'. And I suggested to her that the Eastern Bloc hadn't exactly been a paradigm of righteous living over the last seventy years. I'd found myself a month earlier apologising for the Crusades of all things. She ended the conversation by rejoicing in the fact that Hong Kong was going to 'be free' in 1997. I suppose it depends on which side of the colonial fence you make your fortune.

Our first two years in Mongolia were finished and we were to return to New Zealand for a break. It was June 1994, and Karen was expecting our second child. We'd seen phenomenal growth in the Christian church. Our church had started with a hundred members in October 1992 and we had planted numerous daughter churches in the countryside. Some Sundays we had about four hundred in the congregation. All up, the Mongolian church was about three thousand strong by the middle of 1994. The Mongols were getting connected again: first with God, and with each other.

'Will you come back?' asked our young friends at church.

'One bright and sunny day.' I mimicked their flippant way of disclaiming any responsibility for what may or may not happen in the near or distant future.

'Good,' they replied. 'When you return, you will have two children. Karen will be a quarter of the way to receiving the state prize of glorious motherhood!'

NOTES

1. Hetoum in Regis Evariste Huc, *Christianity in China, Tartary, and Thibet*. (London: Longman, Brown, Green, Longmans, and Roberts, 1857), 1:310, footnote. Hetoum II reigned thrice: 1289–1293, 1294–1297, 1299–1307. See T.S.R. Boase, ed., *The Cilician Kingdom of Armenia* (Edinburgh and London: Scottish Academic Press, 1978), 25.
2. Regis Evariste Huc, *Christianity in China, Tartary, and Thibet*. (London: Longman, Brown, Green, Longmans, and Roberts, 1857), 1:296.

Chapter 15

Mark and Sauma,
Mongol Christian Ambassadors to the West

'And on that day, a very large number of people were gathered in order to see how the ambassador of the Mongols celebrated the Eucharist. And when they had seen, they rejoiced and said, "The language is different, but the use is the same."'
Sauma before Pope Nicholas IV and
the cardinals in Rome

I was usually the last to know what was happening in our Mongolian church. This was rarely surprising because of the language barrier. I struggled to get to grips with the fast discussion between fourteen Mongol leaders; plus there was a bit of Korean thrown in to keep the Korean pastor informed. And I could never get to all the church leadership meetings anyway. They'd start about 5pm and usually last until midnight.

One evening I did figure out what was going on. After a meal of those ubiquitous steamed dumplings or *buudz*, we all sat back and planned the summer evangelism trips. I was amazed.

'I think this year we should make it our aim to send a team to every one of Mongolia's provinces: there are eighteen *aimags* in total,' one of the leaders suggested. We spread a map of the country out in front of us. 'Each team should be about three or four people. We need to hire a *jaran yus* for each team.' I recognised the Mongolian word for the number sixty-nine. This referred to the year in which the common Russian jeep was manufactured; everyone referred to them as 'sixty-nines'.

We all gazed at the map. Eighteen provinces was a lot of provinces. Mongolia was the size of Western Europe and had only 2.5 million people in it, a quarter of whom were in Ulaanbaatar, right outside our door. The rest of the population were nomads. Nomads had a tendency to move. I wondered where we'd find anyone else.

I was overwhelmed by my lack of faith, so chipped in. 'What have we done so far? Can someone fill me in, please?'

'Of course.' Ganbat held the portfolio of evangelism. 'Last summer we sent teams over the northern border to Buriatia in Russia. They're a Mongol tribe. We also sent a team down to Hohot, the capital city of Inner Mongolia, in China. Then teams went out to the western *aimags* to the Khazaks. They're Muslims and their language is a bit different. Those were strategically focused visits. Now we need to ensure that there is a church planted in every *aimag* centre. I think that should be our goal this summer.'

My mouth dropped. I sat there in stunned humility. In New Zealand we'd had the gospel for 150 years and I hadn't seen any systematic evangelistic programme that even approximated what this Mongolian church was doing. This church was barely three years old, and it was already sending evangelistic teams to other countries.

On a mountain near Da-tu

In a cave in the mountains west of Da-tu, during the reign of Kublai Khan, a Nestorian monk called Rabban Sauma established himself as an ascetic, and attracted a small following of disciples. Sauma had been born about 1225 of Nestorian-Christian parents and, having shunned a bride at age twenty-three, had been ordained as a Nestorian monk by the Metropolitan of Da-tu, Mar George, taking the title Rabban, signifying ordination.

One of Sauma's disciples was a Nestorian monk, Rabban Mark. Mark was born in the Ongut town of Koshang in north China in 1245, the son of an archdeacon of the Nestorian church. He had been ordained as a Nestorian priest in Da-tu by Mar George's successor, Mar Nestorius.

Bar Hebreaus believes these two monks to have been Uighurs by ethnic origin. They were both Mongols in as much as the

Uighur and Ongut had been overrun by the Mongols from the days of Chinggis, sixty or so years previously.

Mark and Sauma travel to Persia

Some time in the 1260s, after Mark had joined Sauma at his cave, Mark persuaded Sauma to go with him on a religious pilgrimage to Jerusalem and the Holy Land, and perhaps bring back some religious relics. They set off in 1278 along the tedious and dangerous Silk Road, and arrived at Mosul (just north of Baghdad), having enjoyed the hospitality of Nestorian Christians in modern-day Gansu province on the way. During this arduous journey, they had carried Kublai's *paiza*, the Khan's official passport to free travel, made of engraved silver and hung around the neck.

If Kublai favoured the journey by affording them official *paiza*, what had he hoped for? By endorsing an openly religious pilgrimage of two Christian kinsmen to Jerusalem, did this express his commitment to Christianity *per se*, or was it to foster good political links with his cousins now ruling Persia, and perhaps even curry favour with the European kings and popes? The journey could also acquire vital intelligence about Jerusalem for a future conquest. All of these are possibilities.

One novel answer to Kublai's motivation has been suggested: 'they [Mark and Sauma] had simply received a commission from the emperor Kublai, on account of the Christian ladies of the palace, who were very numerous.'[1] In other words, it was the Nestorian women, perhaps even Kublai's mother, Queen Soyo, who had encouraged him to support the journey. This may well be the case, as the Mongol Nestorian wives were influential throughout the reigns of all the Khans.

Mark is ordained near Baghdad

After resting in Mosul, Mark and Sauma set off again for Jerusalem. However, they were blocked from getting to the

Holy Land by the Muslim Turks, and therefore stopped at Maragha. Here they presented themselves to the Nestorian patriarch of the city, Mar Denha.

Mar Denha (r.1265–1281) was one of two key figures who dominated the political and religious ethos of Persia at that time. The other was the Mongol Il-Khan Abaka (r.1265–1282). Both saw Mark and Sauma's arrival as a fortuitous event: here were two Mongol pilgrims from the Grand Khan Kublai whom they could send back to Kublai as official ambassadors. Mar Denha, along with twenty-four Nestorian bishops, then ordained Mark as Catholicos of China and gave him the title Yaballaha III. This happened in Ctesiphon/Seleucia, the Nestorian centre, near Baghdad. Consequently Abaka issued a *yarlag* for the Christians of Baghdad to accept him as their Catholicos. Mark then consecrated his former teacher Sauma as Bishop of Uighuria, and Mar Denha appointed Sauma as Visitor General of the Churches.

In 1281 Mark, now Yaballaha III, set out for China, to become its metropolitan bishop. A full circle had been completed. Syrian Nestorians who had come to central Asia in the seventh century had now given over leadership of the church to a Mongol in the thirteenth century. The whole of the Nestorian Christian church in Asia was now destined to be under Mongol leadership. Mark's parish was from Mesopotamia in the west to the China Sea in the east.

But this high ordeal was short lived. The way to China was blocked by war, and he had to return to Maragha. On his return, he found that Mar Denha had died. A year later, Abaka Il-Khan also died. Although Mark was young and not at great ease with the Syrian language, the bishops took hold of this new opportunity to elevate a Mongol as head of the church. Because he could speak the language of the Mongol overlords, in theory his election would ideally be for the benefit of the whole church. Thus he was elected to Catholicos of the East in the same year; his new parish consisted of the whole of the territories of the Eastern Church.

Sauma is sent to Europe

In 1287, Arghun Il-Khan asked Mar Yaballaha III for an ambassador whom he could send to Europe. Yaballaha nominated his
old friend and teacher, Sauma. Sauma was sixty years old by
this stage, but still a good choice for the job: he was Mongol
and he knew 'the Frankish language' and so could communicate with the Europeans with minimal help from translators.
Arghun wanted to negotiate a Mongol alliance with Christian
Europe against the Muslim Marmaluke Egypt, if the European
Pope and monarchs could raise another crusade. Sauma was
given *paiza*, letters and presents for the princes of Europe, and
took with him Saabadin, a fellow Nestorian monk.

He went first to Constantinople, then sailed for Naples
(where he saw Mount Vesuvius erupting), then went on to
Rome. In Rome, he was received initially by the college of cardinals as Pope Honorius IV had died on 3 April, just prior to his
arrival. In the absence of a pope, Cardinal Jerome of Ascoli led
a council of twelve cardinals in questioning him. Sauma got
exasperated by this: 'I did not come from distant countries to
discuss, or learn about the faith, but to venerate the Pope, to
see the relics of the saints and to bring letters from my Khan
and Patriarch.'[2] He reported that the Nestorian fathers had
evangelised the 'countries of the Mongols, Turks and Chinese
and taught them the gospel'; that 'many of the sons of the
Mongol kings and queens have been baptised and confess
Christ'; and that 'there are many [among the Mongols] who are
believers'. Sauma also relayed to the college that the 'king of
the Mongols, who is joined in the bond of friendship with the
Catholicos, has the desire to take Palestine and the countries of
Syria, and he demands from you help to take Jerusalem'.[3]
Whether Sauma was referring to Arghun or Kublai as 'king' is
not clear. The cardinals then demanded from him his creed,
which they approved.

After visiting Rome, Rabban Sauma journeyed on horseback
to Tuscany and then Genoa where the Genoese received him

well: the Genoese wanted a solid alliance with the Mongols to secure the trade routes. Sauma then went on to Paris arriving in September 1287. Here he was received by King Philip the Fair. From Paris he travelled on to Bordeaux in Gascony and met the 'king of Angeleterre', Edward 1, who had possessions in France and happened to be there at the time. King Edward seems very moved by the meeting: 'We have taken the sign of the Cross and we have no other preoccupation but this. My heart is overwhelmed to learn that Arghun Khan thinks as I do.'[4] Edward even received the sacrament of communion from Sauma: a Mongol Christian giving an English king communion!

On his return in 1288, Rabban Sauma went through Rome again and had an audience with the newly elected Pope Nicholas IV, formerly Cardinal Jerome of Ascoli whom he had met on his first visit. Sauma was allowed to celebrate the Eucharist. 'And on that day a very large number of people were gathered together to see how the ambassador of the Mongols celebrated the Eucharist. And when they had seen they rejoiced and said, "The language is different, but the use is the same."'[5] This is a remarkable event in the history of the church: a Nestorian, that is Eastern Orthodox Christian, celebrating the Eucharist before the (Catholic) Pope in Rome, where the Pope and the cardinals acknowledge that essentially there is no difference in the celebration! Alas it proved only a fleeting glimpse at potential for unity.

Christianity in the public arena

Considering that the Catholic West had always considered the Nestorian East as heretical, this celebration of mass was a major step back from the enmity expressed by Carpini and Rubruck, the first two ambassadors sent by Pope Innocent to the Great Khans. Did the Curia actually know whom Sauma represented? Had the translators done a good job? We'll never know the precise dynamics of that occasion, but it is beyond question remarkable. Perhaps the Roman Curia did know with whom they were talking; maybe the Prester John rumours had been real after all!

Arghun was so pleased with the results of Sauma's embassy that he allowed him to pitch his collapsible chapel tent next to his own *ordo* as a mark of his esteem. The English King Edward 1 had been helpful, the French King Philip was open to keep talking, and Pope Nicholas had given Sauma reply letters for both Arghun and Yaballaha. These letters were a mixed bag: Nicholas told Arghun to get baptised and outlined for Yaballaha some errors in his theology. However, the seeming openness to dialogue on the part of the Europeans never amounted to more than agreement in principle, and the proposed crusade never happened. The Mongols soon abandoned hope of an alliance and turned to support the Muslims a few years after the fall of Acre.

This realignment with Islam led to persecution of the Christians and Yaballaha died a hunted man in 1317, aged seventy-two. He had been Patriarch at Baghdad for thirty-six years. After Arghun's reign, Yaballaha had continued to wield influence at court and to protect Christians from Muslim persecution over seven successive Mongol Il-Khans. Bar Hebreaus writes of him: 'although he was too little versed in doctrine and in the Syriac tongue, he was nevertheless of a naturally good disposition, endowed with the fear of God, and showed much charity to us and our people.'[6]

'How did it go?' I cornered Bayaraa after church one Sunday in August. 'How was your evangelism trip in the countryside?'

'*Mash ikh sain*. It was terrific. We left a small housegroup of believers behind. One of the new Christians will come to Ulaanbaatar next month for some teaching and training.'

'So what happened?' I was really curious.

'When we got to the *aimag* centre, we tried to find someone with a VCR so we could show the *Jesus* video,' Bayaraa started.

This was a common strategy for evangelism. The *Jesus* film has had a huge distribution in Mongolia.

He continued, 'We wandered around the streets asking everyone, and soon a bunch of kids were trailing us, and one of them suggested that the local TV station may have a VCR we could borrow one evening.'

The need of a steady supply of electricity crossed my mind, but I didn't say anything.

'So we went to the local TV station, and introduced ourselves and told the director about the *Jesus* film. We asked him if we could borrow their VCR and show the video in the town hall that night.'

'So what happened?' I asked.

'He said, "Ah well, if it's such a fantastic movie like you say, why don't we show it on state-wide television tonight instead"!'

NOTES

1. Paul Pelliot, 'Christianity in Central Asia in the Middle Ages', Journal of the Central Asian Society 17:311.
2. A. Bryer, 'Edward I and the Mongols', History Today XIV (October, 1964), 700.
3. E.A.Wallis Budge, trans., The Monks of Kublai Khan, Emperor of China: Life and Travels of Rabban Sawma and Markos (London: Religious Tract Soc. 1928), 174.
4. A. Bryer, 'Edward I and the Mongols', History Today XIV (October, 1964), 700.
5. E.A.Wallis Budge, trans., The Monks of Kublai Khan, Emperor of China: Life and Travels of Rabban Sawma and Markos (London: Religious Tract Soc. 1928), 190.
6. H.H. Howorth, History of the Mongols: From the 9th to the 19th Century (London: Burt Franklin, 1876), 3:283.

Part **4**

Medieval Europe and the Mongols

Pope Innocent IV and Ramon Lull,
the European Response to the Mongol Threat

'... thus we may be able to learn the languages of the adversaries of God; and that our learned men, by preaching to them and teaching them, may by the sword of truth overcome their falsehoods and restore to God a people as an acceptable offering, and may convert our foes and his to friends.'

Ramon Lull in his appeal to
the University of Paris

When I arrived at Buyant Ukhaa international airport, just outside of Ulaanbaatar, I didn't know a word of Mongolian. In fact, I had never even heard any. Ever. I'd searched in vain for language books or tapes, but found nothing.

And the second language of Mongolia was Russian. Sink or swim was the only option. So we swam. Sometimes we nearly drowned.

On our second day in Mongolia we hired a language helper, and dived into learning the language. We had our greetings worked out by the end of that day.

'Hello, my name is Hugh. I come from New Zealand. I'm learning your language. This is all I can say. Goodbye.' In August 1992, the people visiting the Sansar Service Centre in eastern Ulaanbaatar had to endure this monologue from this strange new foreigner. Once they realised I wasn't Russian, we all had a few good laughs.

By the third day, we had our numbers from one to ten worked out. Batdorj was an excellent source of information.

'Here, I bought ten eggs,' I announced to Karen at the end of the day, proud of my achievement of not only finding some eggs, but buying them unassisted.

'I asked for a dozen.' she replied casually.

'Yeah, I know. But I can only count to ten!'

By the end of the first week we were doing all our shopping on our own. I even attempted a visit to the hairdressers. Unbeknown to me, 'wind' and 'beard' differed only by one consonant.

'*Sain bain uu*,' I greeted the hairdresser. 'I'd like you to cut some wind.'

'*Yu genee?*' she looked at me blankly. 'What did you say?'

'I said I'd like you to vacuum my beard.'

I left the shop feeling very pleased with my language abilities, ready to take on anyone.

The Mongols' arrival in Europe

The Mongols wreaked havoc in Eastern Europe. For the main part, the Europeans had no idea who they were and understood their arrival as divine castigation. The Russian *Chronicle of Novgorod* records:

> The same year [1224], for our sins, unknown tribes came, of whom no one exactly knows who they are, nor whence they came out, nor what their language is, nor of what race they are, nor what their faith is; but they call them Tartars.... God alone knows who they are. We have heard that they have captured many countries, slaughtered a quantity of the godless... and scattered others, who all died, killed thus by the wrath of God.[1]

Batu, Khan of the Golden Horde, and grandson of Chinggis, was behind the Mongol push into Europe. He was totally impartial to the Europeans, killing and pillaging without thought to creed or reason. Juvaini writes of him: 'he was a king who inclined towards no faith or religion: he recognised only the belief in God and was blindly attached to no sect or creed.'

Juvaini says he had no problem destroying 'large nations professing the Christian faith'. Batu Khan desolated the valley of the Danube, advancing to within three kilometres of Vienna 'where they slaughtered many Christians'.

Pope Innocent IV decides to send embassies to the Mongols

Vienna was too close for comfort for the Europeans and so at the Council of Lyons in 1245, the Mongol threat was on the agenda. The pope of the day was Innocent IV, an Italian from Genoa who was in the process of trying to wrestle temporal power from the Holy Roman Emperor Frederick II whom he had excommunicated. Both political and ecclesiastical power were his. These days were tumultuous. It was this Innocent who sanctioned the inquisition, unleashing a wave of zealous prosecutors throughout Europe to hunt down alleged heresy, blasphemy, sorcery, alchemy, sacrilege, sodomy and magic.

Thus the Mongol threat came at a very inconvenient time for Innocent personally. Caught up in internal European affairs, he now had to deal with a foreign policy crisis. Europe had been procrastinating over the Mongols. Disagreements between the European princes were rife: perhaps the Mongol threat would provide a distraction for the feuding nobles; there is nothing like a common enemy to unite a nation, or a continent. Added to this, Innocent was confused about the identity of the Mongols: could Batu be Prester John himself? Perhaps an alliance could be negotiated and both he and Prester John could have a united crusade against the Muslims?

Innocent was appalled at Batu's devastation in Eastern Europe and this was his primary motive for calling the Council of Lyons: Christian unity and defence against the Mongols. However, rather than confronting the Mongols (could he have mustered an effective army from the sparring European princes?), he chose a conciliatory strategy: the Council made the decision to send embassies to them.

A century of embassies

Innocent chose to recruit his ambassadors from the newly-founded Franciscan and Dominican orders. He initially sent two embassies: the first (1245) was made up of three Franciscans-Benedict of Poland, Laurence of Portugal and Jean de Plano Carpini who went east into Mongol heartland. The second (1247) was made up of four Dominicans-Anselm of Lombardy, Simon of St Quentin, Alberic and Alexander, who were sent to Persia with letters from Innocent to the camp of Batu Khan, and with the instruction to 'make diligent inquiry into the manners and customs of the Tartars'.

The ambassadors were expected to achieve spiritual and political goals. They were to find out information: the who, why, when, where of the Mongol armies. They were also to propagate the Christian religion and the 'Christian civilisation'. Innocent thought that the Mongols would renounce their barbaric ways and adopt a humane character as soon as they were converted to Christianity. When they were converted they would then naturally take the welfare of the Christian nations to heart. Thus the ambassadors were briefed to 'entreat them to shed no more Christian blood and to be converted to the true faith'.

This strategy was both innovative and naive. It was new in that Innocent sought to find out who the Mongols were: he wanted to open a dialogue with them. It was naive in that he presumed they would dialogue on his terms. Innocent knew nothing about what motivated the Mongols' drive for world dominance. He knew nothing of the Mongol language, culture or religion. When the Mongols received the ambassadors' letters, the Khan perceived the Pope's requests as a threat. Not surprisingly, the ambassadors were perceived as spies.

The Council of Lyons spawned a number of papal embassies to the Mongols over subsequent years. In fact it is legitimate to talk about a 'Franciscan mission to the Mongols', although some Dominicans were also recruited, and the Polo brothers' two journeys (1260–1269; 1271–1295) were not technically 'missionary journeys'. A total of nine were sent, starting with Carpini's in 1245, and spanning exactly one hundred years. The last was that of John of Marignolli in 1346. The originals of some of their letters are still stored in the Vatican library today.

Ramon Lull: his strategy and passion

Ramon Lull, born about 1235 and a native of Majorca, put forward a more strategic agenda for the evangelisation of the Mongols. He was a man ahead of his time.

Lull had gargantuan evangelistic zeal coupled with an over-active mind and a down-to-earth practical cheek that gained him a hearing among princes, popes and academics. He was trained as a courtier, and after conversion to Christ, felt called by God to bear Christian ideals before the kings and princes he served. He resolved to do three things: to write apologetic books, to work to found missionary colleges, and to lay down his life as a missionary martyr. He decided to travel around the courts of Europe and beg princes to send out missionaries, especially to the Muslims and the Mongols. He would also petition for the establishing of colleges where Europeans could learn theology and study the languages of these peoples. He believed learning the language should be a pre-requisite for any missionary endeavour.

To this end, he persuaded King James to found a college at Miramar on the north-western slopes of Majorca as a training centre for missionaries. Lull also appealed to the University of Paris:

> Ye see reverend fathers and masters, how great a peril hangs over the whole Church of God... unless your wisdom and devotion... opposes the impetuous torrent of the Tartars. Thus conscience stings me and compels me to come to you... Here in Paris... there would be founded a faculty for

Arabic, Tartar and Greek studies. Thus we may be able to learn the languages of the adversaries of God; and that our learned men, by preaching to them and teaching them, may by the sword of the truth overcome their falsehoods and restore to God a people as an acceptable offering, and may convert our foes and His to friends.[2]

Lull was ahead of his time in insisting missionaries learn the languages of their future hearers. And he was well advanced in wanting to write an apologetic to convince the Muslim and Mongol of the truth claims of Christianity. He believed he had developed a semi-mathematical 'art' by which he could supply infallible answers to questions of theology, metaphysics and natural science. His written works to this end are immense.

> A science I have found that's new,
> whereby comes knowledge of the true,
> and falsehood's followers grow few,
> Infidels now their creeds will rue —
> [Mongol, Muhammadan] and Jew —
> For God therewith did me imbue.[3]

Lull made three trips to Muslim north Africa where he taught a strictly rational apologetic and condemned Islam as wrong; needless to say, he was nearly lynched for his efforts.

His apologetic *The Book of the Tartar and the Christian*, on the conversion of the Mongols, is a narrative embodying a theological debate. In it a Mongol anxious about his own soul is drawn into discussion with a hermit, Blanquerna. The hermit asserts that faith can be understood. When the hermit explains to him a Psalm and the service of the Eucharist, the Mongol begins to feel the 'grace of the Holy Spirit coming to him'. The dénouement is that grace has supplied faith to a person first given understanding to receive it. 'Blessed be the Lord God Almighty,' cries the Mongol, 'and blessed be all his works, and blessed be the time and place wherein I found Blanquerna [the hermit].' In conclusion, Blanquerna instructs the Mongol to return home 'and preach Christ... for the good of all men'.[4]

Disappointingly, *The Book of the Tartar and the Christian* is not written with the Mongols as the target audience, but for theologians and academics for whom the conversion of the Mongols was the subject of periodic discussion. Lull was keen to mobilise Rome for evangelism so he went straight to the papal court with his *Petition for the Conversion of the Heathen*, written in 1294. In this he proposes that a tithe be levied on the whole of the church's wealth, and this be assigned to crusades and missionary work, 'till the Holy Land is conquered and the whole world won for Christ'. This work also makes clear his thinking that the best people to evangelise the Mongols are those who already have the language and who have lived among them.

Ever the imaginative thinker, he put forward the idea that one cardinal be commissioned to travel around Europe recruiting missionaries, ordained and lay, who would be trained in theology and in preaching and taught the languages of the world. And he had an even more radical plan: that foreign language schools be set up in Mongol territory.

Lull had a practical concern that Europe should not be overrun by Mongol armies. Initially advocating a pacifist lifestyle, his writings show a gradual move to endorsing a crusade to win back the Holy Land. He is a typical medieval cleric in that he viewed the kingdom of God as territorial: Christendom was Christian Europe, both religious and political.

In his book *Five Wise Men*, representatives from four different Christian traditions (Latin, Greek, Nestorian and Jacobite) debate which way the Mongols will jump when it comes to conversion: will Asia be converted to Islam, Buddhism or Christianity? Lull sees the answer in strictly doctrinal terms; logically presented Christian apologetic must surely win in the end by the sheer force of air-tight argument.

Lull had a genuine spiritual concern for the Mongols. His evangelistic strategy was the first case of an actual concrete plan to dialogue with the Mongols on their terms, by learning their language. This was sophisticated thinking for his day.

His passion for missions was filled with realism as to cost: 'missionaries will convert the world by preaching, but also through the shedding of tears and blood and with great labour, and through a bitter death.'[5] This would prove the case for himself. He achieved the martyrs' crown in Tunis, north Africa in late 1315, aged eighty-four, after proclaiming loudly, before a hostile crowd, the gospel message to which he had committed his life.

———————

I was absolutely convinced that to communicate effectively I had to have a good handle on the Mongolian language. I loathed preaching through translators, so I enrolled at language school and made it a top priority.

'*Bagsh-aa*,' I asked my language teacher one warm summer day. The sky was deep blue and the carpet of summer flowers beckoned. 'Could we please have our lesson outside, inside the sun?'

'Inside the sun?'she prompted.

'Yes,' I replied, not realising I'd muddled my post-positions already. 'Outside, in a tree.'

It got worse when I started to preach.

'Please turn with me to the book of Exhibition. It's the last book of the Bible.'

I took the wise step of rehearsing language before important events.

'Kiss my boots,' I announced one day. What I wanted to say was 'please sew-up my boots.' It's just as well I had the presence of mind to check my verbs with Karen before leaving the house to see the cobbler that day.

Our language helper retired from our employ, possibly in exasperation. We hired a part-time nanny, mainly to look after our now two-year-old daughter while we were at language school, but she helped out a bit around the house too.

Ten minutes to one in the afternoon was always a mad panic. Our nanny would arrive, Karen would then deliver instructions for the afternoon, all in broken Mongolian, and then we had to tear out of the door to catch the language school bus.

'When you finish the dishes, please wash the nappies in the bucket.' Karen had got this sentence worked out perfectly, and used it often. But she hadn't realised that the verbs 'to wash' and 'to drink' sounded very similar.

She'd been saying it all week before the penny dropped.

'When you finish the dishes, please drink the nappies in the bucket.' The thought of it made me feel ill.

The curious part of this was that our nanny usually just said 'za,' one of those all-purpose words simply meaning 'OK'.

NOTES

1. Robert Michell and Nevill Forbes, trans., *The Chronicle of Novgorod: 1016–1471* (London: Camden Society, 1914), 64.
2. M. Broomhall, ed. *The Chinese Empire: A General and Missionary Survey*. (London: Morgan and Scott/China Inland Mission, 1907), 7.
3. E. Allison Peers, *Fool of Love: The Life of Ramon Lull*. (London: SCM Press, 1946), 33.
4. E. Allison Peers, *Ramon Lull: A Biography*. (New York: Burt Franklin, 1929), 199.
5. A.J.Broomhall, *Hudson Taylor and China's Open Century: Barbarians at the Gates; Book 1*. (England: Hodder and Stoughton, 1981), 52.

Chapter 17

John of Carpini and Guyuk Khan,
Strangers or Brothers?

'Thou thyself... come at once to serve and wait upon us! At that time I shall recognise your submission. If you do not observe God's command, and if you ignore my command, I shall know you as my enemy.'

Guyuk Khan to Pope Innocent IV

The Western saddle is made of leather and is designed to be sat upon. Not so the Mongolian. The Mongolian saddle is a formidable piece of equipment. It is designed more as a brace with a high front and back so that the rider can stand upright while his horse gallops beneath him. This is essential if you're chasing gazelle on the steppe or riding into battle. The rider has to be steady if he's going to get a good shot. If you tried to sit in a Mongolian saddle, it would be very painful. It's made of wood.

Naadam is the annual summer festival of the 'three manly sports': wrestling, archery and horse racing. For three days in July, Ulaanbaatar bursts into colourful life with thousands of people milling around the streets eating ice-cream, candy floss and taking pictures of each other. Heroes are made in the wrestling ring and veterans reassert their archery skills. The festival is long looked forward to after the freezing months of winter. Spring rains and hot sun bring the dormant grasslands and riverbeds to life.

'Come on, we'll take you out to see the horse racing,' Battsetseg announced one Naadam. This suited us fine as we would better understand if we had a guide.

We weaved our way in her car out to Yarmag, the grassland area south of Ulaanbaatar which was covered with hundreds of tents and thousands of horses. Men on horses were whooping their way between the cars. We bounced along, caught up in the flow in only one direction: to the horse racing.

'The race has different age groups, starting with the children,' Bat-tsetseg explained. 'The riders can be as young as six or seven, boys or girls. Race officials lead them about twenty kilometres out of town and then they just race back across country. First one home is the winner.'

Carpini's background

The decision at the Council of Lyons was somehow to contain the Mongol threat to Europe, and John of Carpini was to lead the first European embassy to the court of the Mongol Khan. Perhaps the Mongol Khan could be dissuaded from invading Christian lands, and maybe even embrace Christianity?

John was from the plane of Carpini, about twenty kilometres from Perugia, or modern-day Pian la Magione in Italy. It was near to Assisi, the home of St Francis, and Carpini grew up to be a close disciple of St Francis. Having joined the Franciscan order, he became a very zealous monk, founding friaries in at least six different parts of Europe.

With this sort of track record, he was a natural choice. Innocent believed Carpini and the friars who travelled with him were 'men proved by years of regular observance and well versed in Holy Scripture... following the humility of the Saviour'.[1] They left Lyons on Easter Day 1245, and Carpini was not to return to Europe for another two years. Two other monks accompanied him, and though these travelling companions appear to have been replaced on the way, not able to manage the journey, the party finally reached the Mongol outposts on the banks of the Dnieper River (in modern Russia). Carpini handed over the Pope's letters, but no translator was available, so the Mongol general sent the ambassadors on to Batu, Khan of the Golden Horde. This involved another five weeks of hard riding until they arrived at Batu's *ordo* on the banks of the Volga River. Batu in turn sent them on to the Grand Khan at Karakorum.

Carpini arrives at Karakorum

A very odd sight this must have been. Carpini, short and rotund and sixty-five, had only a donkey to travel on. The Mongol escort pushed them hard: 'we started at dawn and journeyed until night without a meal, and many a time we arrived so late that we did not eat that night but were given in the morning the food we should have eaten the previous evening.' The journey took them only five months. And because the first part was taken during Lent of 1246, Carpini was fasting. 'During the whole of that Lent our food had been nothing but millet with water and salt, and it was the same on other fast days, and we had nothing to drink except snow melted in a kettle.' They arrived gaunt and exhausted, 'and so weak we could hardly ride', on 22 July 1246, at the royal *shar ordo* or yellow encampment, near Karakorum. Here they found that the Grand Khan Ogedei had died five years previously, and that his son Guyuk would not receive them because he had not yet officially been elected as Khan. Guyuk sent Carpini to his mother, Ogedei's wife Tourakina-hatan who was acting as regent. Carpini stayed a total of four months, until November, during which time he witnessed the enthronement of Guyuk, third of the Great Khans. He kept a record of his journey and his time at the Mongol court, and we have it today as *History of the Mongols*.

Carpini delivered two letters from Pope Innocent IV to Guyuk Khan. Initially the Mongols had some difficulty finding translators for the letters, but eventually, due to the high number of foreigners living in Karakorum (there were many artisans and technicians captured in war, as well as several thousand princes come to pay homage at the enthronement), translations were able to be made from the Latin into Mongol, Russian and Arabic. The first letter was basically an introduction of

Carpini. The Khan was to listen closely to Carpini so he could 'come to acknowledge Jesus Christ... and worship His glorious Name'. This letter also contained a basic exposition of Christian doctrine. The second letter was a demand to end Mongol devastation of Christian lands suggesting that the Mongols had aroused the wrath of God for their 'many and grievous offences' and so 'to make fully known to us through these same Friars what moved you to destroy other nations and what your intentions are for the future'.

Guyuk was in no hurry to reply and Carpini and his companion Benedict had a chance to look around. They found at Karakorum Georgians who 'use the Greek version of Holy Scripture and have crosses on their camps and their carts. They follow the Greek rites in divine worship among the Tartars.' They also noted that there were Nestorians in the Khan's actual household.

Guyuk Khan replies

Guyuk's reply to the Pope was relayed to Carpini through Chingay and Qadaq, the Nestorian administrators whom we have already met. 'On St Martin's day we were again summoned, and Qadaq, Chingay and Bala, the aforementioned secretaries, came to us and translated the letter for us word by word.' Guyuk understandably was not impressed with Innocent's presumption.

Guyuk's reply, still stored in the Vatican archives today, is a mixture of puzzlement and threat, theology and politics: 'You have... said that supplication and prayer have been offered by you, that I might find a good entry into baptism. This prayer of thine I have not understood.' Neither could Guyuk fathom Innocent's request to halt the devastation of so-called Christian lands: 'These words of thine I have also not understood. The eternal God has slain and annihilated these lands and peoples because they have [not] adhered to Chinggis Khan [who had] been sent to make known God's command. How could anybody seize or kill by his own power contrary to the command of God? From the rising of the sun to its setting, all the lands have been made subject to me. Who could do this contrary to the command of God?'

Guyuk was driven by a divine call and disputed Innocent's assumption of the same. He was unimpressed with Innocent's claimed intimacy with God: 'how knowest thou whom God absolves, in truth to whom he shows mercy? How dost thou know that such words as thou speakest are with God's sanction?' Guyuk finishes his letter with a threat: 'Now you should say with a sincere heart: 'I will submit and serve you.' Thou thyself, at the head of all the Princes, come at once to serve and wait upon us! At that time I shall recognise your submission. If you do not observe God's command, and if you ignore my command, I shall know you as my enemy.... If you do otherwise, God knows what I know.'

The *History of the Mongols*

Carpini's *History of the Mongols* is a travelogue that doubles as a report to Innocent and a warning to Europe. Carpini had got a pretty good idea of the storm about to be unleashed on Europe. He describes at length the land, culture, religion, history and habits of the Mongols, then describes their tactics in war, and reminds the reader of the devastation that they had already wreaked on their foes. 'The Lord Pope... wanted to learn the truth about the desire and intention of the Tartars... then if by chance they made a sudden attack they would not find the Christian people unprepared.' Carpini was very clear about the Mongols' intentions: 'It is the intention of the Tartars to bring the whole world into subjection if they can.... Since there is no country on earth which they fear with the exception of Christendom, they are preparing to make war on us.' Carpini then makes recommendations as to how to defend Europe against the Mongols, something that the Council of Lyons wanted to know: 'we write to you to put you on your guard.'

Carpini's strategy was to attack under united leadership before the Mongols arrived: 'If Christians wish to save themselves, their country and Christendom, then ought kings, princes, barons and rulers of countries to assemble and by common consent send men to fight against the Tartars before they begin to spread over the land... for troops of Tartars search out the inhabitants everywhere and slaughter them.' The rest of the *History* is anecdotes of his journey and a description of Karakorum and the enthronement of Guyuk.

Was this first European embassy successful? Yes and no. It failed on two counts: Guyuk did not become a Christian, nor did it do much to assuage further Mongol expansion. Certainly no military alliance was formed with the Mongols against the Muslims. It was a success, however, in that Europe was sufficiently forewarned about the Mongols' intentions. Carpini had been ambassador, postman, evangelist and spy all rolled into one.

Was Guyuk Khan a Christian?

Guyuk may have been more sympathetic towards Christianity than his threatening letter to Innocent IV may at first suggest. He was surrounded by Nestorians: his two chief administrators, Chingay and Qadaq were Nestorians. They mediated Carpini's relationship to Guyuk. Guyuk also had Nestorian physicians at his court, and his chief governor in Persia and Armenia was Ichikadei, also a Nestorian. Carpini tells us that the Christians of Guyuk's household said they believed Guyuk would imminently become a Christian because he himself supported Christian priests. In addition he always had a chapel near his tent and he allowed the Christians to sing openly and in public.

Juvaini too had much to say about Guyuk's sympathies with Christianity. 'Now Qadaq had been in attendance on him [Guyuk] since his childhood; and since he [Qadaq] was by religion a Christian, Guyuk too was brought up in faith, therefore went to great lengths in honouring the Christians and their priests…. Consequently the cause of the Christians flourished during his reign.'[2]

Was Guyuk a Christian? Juvaini, a Muslim, implies he was. If so, then he certainly had no visible love for the Western-Roman Church. The Christians (Greeks and Nestorians) at Karakorum told Carpini that Guyuk was 'very intelligent and extremely shrewd, and most serious and grave in his manner. He is never seen to laugh for a light cause nor to indulge in any frivolity.' It seems then that Guyuk would have been astute enough to recognise the dynamics of Nestorian/Catholic bickering. He certainly understood Innocent's letters as offers of submission: 'Thou, who art the great Pope, together with all the Princes, come in person to serve us. At that time I shall make known all the commands of the *yasa*.' Did Guyuk see the possibility of bringing Catholic Europe in under Nestorian overlordship much like Innocent wanted to bring the Nestorian 'realm of Prester John' under Catholic overlordship?

At this point, definitions become confusing. William of Rubruck, who led the second European embassy to the Khan, was headstrong, sectarian and a staunch defender of the Catholic faith. Anyone non-Catholic was suspect. For him 'Nestorian' meant heretic at worst, or pagan at best and Nestorians were rumour-mongers and liars:

> among these pasture lands was a Nestorian… a lord of all the people called Naimans, who were Nestorian Christians. He set himself up as king and the Nestorians called him King John, and they used to tell of him ten times more than the truth. For the Nestorians coming from these parts do this kind of thing — out of nothing they make a great rumour. This accounts for their spreading the story that Sartaq was a Christian, also Mongke Khan and Guyuk Khan, just because they pay greater respect to Christians than to other people. And yet the truth is they are not Christians. So in the same way the great tale of this King John went abroad. Now I

passed through his pasture lands and nobody knew anything about him with the exception of a few Nestorians.

According to Rubruck, Guyuk Khan (and others he mentions) weren't Christians because they weren't Catholics. Guyuk may well have been a Nestorian, on account of his open sympathies with Nestorians in Karakorum. Guyuk's mother Tourakina was either a Naiman or a Kerait and hence probably Nestorian. This certainly leaves us with the likelihood that Guyuk may have been baptised Nestorian as an infant.

Were Carpini and Guyuk strangers or Christian brothers? Thousands of miles divided their homelands, and two extremely different cultures separated their ability to communicate effectively. Both knew they were going to clash on the battlefields of eastern Europe at some stage. Did they have a common faith without realising it? Were they Christian brothers without knowing it? This is a question that has to remain open. Both had politics on their mind. The ever-pragmatic Mongol Khan, ruled by the religious indifference dictated by the Mongol *yasa*, subordinated personal religious sympathies to the task of running his vast empire.

I was jammed up the front against the ropes between two horses who were nuzzling my ears. I made a mental note not to come on foot again. Sitting on horseback was obviously the better way to see the end of the race. Some kind lady had grabbed our two children and plonked them up on her horse with her. They would have a better view. We were about four horses deep. The men at the back were standing on their horses' backs, all craning to see the end of the race. I must remember to get the children back after the race!

I ducked under the ropes, crawled along the grass towards the finish line, and hoped that no custodian would accost me.

One did. 'Hey, get back behind the ropes!'

I conveniently forgot all my Mongolian language, and

waved my huge telephoto lens at him. 'Tourist,' I said in English. 'Take picture?'

A yell went up and distracted him. Everyone was looking at the first riders coming over the knoll of the hill. And they kept coming like a line of ants in the distance. A cloud of dust curled upwards. I lay down in the grass and focused. I could feel the ground shaking.

And then they came thundering through. After twenty kilometres I was amazed that the finishers were so close. About six crossed the finishing line within seconds of each other. Dust, heat, sweat and fatigue swirled around me. Riders from the outside of the spectators peeled off to go around and congratulate the winners.

More horses came through. The rumble was deafening and the dust got up my nostrils and in my eyes. I gave up clicking the camera and paused to take it all in.

'I'm glad I don't have to fight them in battle,' I muttered to myself. And these were only kids. Imagine the men, all dressed up in their leather armour, yelling and screaming and shooting arrows at you! To have such an awesome firepower bearing down on you would have been incredible. I felt a tinge of fear. How on earth was I going to find my way back to the car? And the kids?

I stood up. By now horses were going in every direction as the well-ordered ranks of spectators broke up. Horses were weaving in and out of people running to congratulate the riders. The safest thing was to stand still. A rider thundered towards me and swerved so close I could see the fire in the horse's eyes and feel the foam from its nostrils. The stirrup brushed me and I spun around and staggered. I was glad the archers were over at the stadium and these guys had left their weapons at home, seven hundred years ago.

'No wonder the Europeans were terrified of the Mongols,' I offered to Bat-tsetseg after she had rescued me. She'd managed to extract Karen from the crowd and persuade the lady to give us back our daughters. I was relieved to see everyone again. Bat-tsetseg had come across some long-lost very distant cousin from the neighbouring *aimag* for Naadam, and we were now enjoying the ceremonial three nips of vodka in her cousin's tent. It was reassuring to see the horses tied up, their reins hooked over a long line, much like a washing line we'd have at home. The horses stomped their hooves and swished their tails against the flies.

The host passed his snuff bottle around. *Airag*, the fermented mare's milk followed and someone offered to take my four-year-old daughter for a ride on one of the horses. I swallowed hard, knowing that this could possibly be embarrassing. I hadn't taught her to ride yet.

They lifted her into the saddle. I winced. She looked fine.

'Better stick to walking,' I suggested.

NOTES
1. C. Dawson, ed. *Mission to Asia; Narratives and Letters of the Franciscan Missionaries in Mongolia and China in the 13th and 14th Centuries*. Translated by a nun of Stanbrook Abbey. (NY: Harper & Row, 1966), 75. All subsequent quotes are from Dawson.
2. Juvaini, 'Ala-ad-Din 'Ata-Malik, *The History of the World Conqueror*, trans. John Andrew Boyle (Manchester: Manchester University Press, 1958) 259.

Chapter	**William of Rubruck,**
18	**Zealous Franciscan Evangelist**

'... and when I come among them [the Mongols], I really felt as if I were entering some other world.'
William of Rubruck

Tsagaan Sar or 'White moon/month' is the lunar new year festival in February each year. Traditionally, you visit relatives and older friends, take them gifts and wish them a happy new year. Officially there are about three days of holiday, but the whole of Mongolia grinds to a standstill for about a fortnight.

On our first *Tsagaan Sar* in the winter of 1993, we made the unfortunate mistake of visiting more than one friend on the same day. It was all about quantities of food; *buudz* to be precise.

'Before-noon' or 'after-noon' is about as accurate as one can get with appointment times in Mongolia. This year we had been invited 'after-noon' to Chimgee's house. Being clock-conscious Westerners, we showed up for lunch at 12.30. This would allow us plenty of time, we thought, before our next engagement at 6pm. We'd learned to pace ourselves a bit.

Chimgee had gone to a lot of trouble. Coleslaw, pickles, potato salad ('capital salad' they called it) and a platter of cold meats were all spread out before us on the coffee table. In the middle was the back half of a sheep, roasted, but now cold, complete with fatty tail the size of a football, draped over a layered stack of flat deep-fried breads; all this was about half a metre high and the stack was impregnated with hundreds of hard lollies.

Chimgee brought in *su-tai tsai* or milk-tea, and then the *buudz* followed (Karen and I were expected to eat the whole bowl of about twenty-five between us). Then the three nips of vodka to toast the new year. Then as many slices of cold mutton as we could eat. Then a bowl of warm camel's milk. Then more 'capital salad'.

All this time they'd left the TV on, and Chimgee's son had insisted on channel-surfing. Not at all a very conducive environment for stimulating conversation, but I thought I'd give it a go.

'Enkhay. Are you studying *mongol bichig* at school?' I asked.

'I'm studying.' The mongol affirmative was very rarely a simple 'yes'. It was often the main verb repeated back to you. Or that inhaling-click sound.

'I can read *mongol bichig* too,' I announced proudly. 'Well, maybe just a little bit.'

I had got his attention. 'Bet you can't read this,' he said, handing me a newly published coffee-table book.

'Ulaanbaatar: Mongolia's Capital City.' I had fortunately bought a copy myself the week before. He seemed a likeable young lad. About eight. 'What else are you studying?'

He turned the TV off. (I was relieved: there is only so much Cartoon Network, CNN news repeats, and Communist propaganda reruns you can watch during an afternoon.) Enkhay rummaged around in a cupboard and pulled out a pile of books.

'*Mongol bichig*, maths, writing, geography, science.' He flicked through his books.

'And history.'

Rubruck's desire to meet the Mongols

When William of Rubruck read Carpini's account of his travel to the court of Guyuk Khan, he decided he would go and preach to the Mongols himself, and also offer some pastoral care to German captives he'd heard were among them. There were rumours circulating that Sartaq, a Mongol general stationed on the borders of Eastern Europe, was a Christian, and with the Prester John legend always whispering in the background, Rubruck was curious to know the truth.

Unlike Carpini, Rubruck was not a papal ambassador, but he

was a confidant of the French King Louis IX (later canonised as St Louis) who officially endorsed his mission by sending with him a letter to the Khan, but never expecting Rubruck himself to travel as far east as Karakorum itself. On his return from Mongolia, Rubruck wrote a report to King Louis, and it is this report which is the primary source of what follows. Rubruck is quite clear that his initial intent was solely evangelistic, not political. Addressing King Louis on his return: 'I had stated publicly in a sermon in St Sophia [in Constantinople] on Palm Sunday [13 April 1253] that I was not your envoy nor anyone else's, but that I was going among these unbelievers in accordance with our Rule [of the Franciscans].'[1]

William was a Flemish from Rubruck, now in French Flanders, near the village of Cassel. Very little is known about him (including his birthdate and year of death), except that which he reveals about himself in his own writings. Like Carpini, he was a Franciscan friar, self-confessedly short and overweight, but zealous for his order. Rubruck's journey to the Khan's court was between April 1253 and August 1255, and in July 1994, this journey was commemorated in the north of France: the town of Rubruck became the sister town of Bulgan, a provincial capital north-west of Ulaanbaatar.

The first significant Mongol encampment Rubruck came across was where he met Sartaq and he notes: 'now concerning Sartaq, whether he believes in Christ or not, I know not. This I am sure of, that he will not be called a Christian... he has about him certain Nestorian Priests.' Rubruck had concluded that Sartaq was non-Catholic, therefore not a Christian. As Sartaq had around him Nestorian priests, it is possible he had Nestorian-Christian sympathies. Coiac, Rubruck's Nestorian guide, says, 'do not say that our master [Sartaq]is a Christian, for he is not a Christian but a Mongol'. Rubruck interprets this as a misunderstanding of the word 'Christian', thinking it to be the name of a nation, or confusing it with the continent of Europe. Sartaq did take an interest in the variety of religious paraphernalia that Rubruck had with him but then sent him on to Batu Khan, who promptly sent him on to the Grand Khan Munkh, whose *ordo* was about ten days' ride from Karakorum.

Rubruck's *Report to King Louis*

Rubruck's *Report to King Louis* is longer and more detailed than Carpini's *History*. He had excellent powers of observation and records events and places in meticulous detail, and often quite critically. Of special note are his observations of the various religions represented at the Khan's court. He is amazed at the number of Nestorians whom he met on his journey, and at both the Khan's court and Karakorum. He is completely puzzled by Buddhism: Rubruck was the first European to observe and record anything to do with Buddhism. The Khan who received Rubruck was Munkh, fourth of the Great Khans (r.1251–1259), son of the Nestorian Queen Soyo who had manipulated the line of succession after Guyuk's death so that her sons would attain to the Khanate.

Rubruck arrived at the Khan's *shar ordo* near Karakorum in late December 1253. At his first audience in early January, he asked for permission to remain in his territories to teach the Christian religion. Munkh initially permitted only two months' residence, but Rubruck ended up staying for six. Rubruck immediately notes a strong Nestorian presence all around, and records it all in detail:

> I saw facing the *ordo* towards the east, distant from it twice as far as one can shoot with a cross-bow, a building with a little cross on top. Thereupon greatly rejoicing, for I presumed that it had something to do with the Christian religion, I boldly went in and found an altar most beautifully decorated.... An Armenian monk was sitting there... and the monk stood up and prayed with us. We told him the reason of our coming and he began to encourage us greatly, saying that we were to speak out boldly for we were the ambassadors of God, Who is greater than any man.

Not only were there Armenians, but Rubruck records that he found 'a large crowd of Christians there — Hungarians, Alans, Ruthenians, Georgians...', a Christian from Damascus and a cleric from Acre. He even found a compatriot, William Buchier from Paris, the silversmith who made the famous *airag* fountain, now depicted on Mongolian tugruk banknotes. Buchier's wife was Hungarian, and their son ended up being a better translator for Rubruck than the one assigned him. There was also a man called Basil from England.

Munkh Khan: sympathetic to Christians?

Like his cousin Guyuk, Munkh seemed to favour the Nestorians in his court. He had appointed Nestorian administrators and the most powerful position in the realm was held by a Nestorian Christian, Chief Secretary Bolgai, 'whose advice is followed in almost all matters'. Rubruck also noted that Munkh had a Nestorian interpreter, 'but I was ignorant of the fact that he was a Christian'.

Like Guyuk, there were rumours that Munkh had converted to Christianity, or at least was about to. The Armenian monk told Rubruck one day that he was about to baptise Munkh:

The day of the Epiphany (6 January) was approaching and the Armenian monk, Sergius by name, told me that he was going to baptise Munkh Khan on the day of the feast. I begged him to do all in his power to enable me to be present so that I could bear witness of what I had actually seen, and he promised he would. The day of the feast arrived and the monk did not send for me, but at midday I was summoned to the court, and I saw the monk coming away from there with some priests, and he had his cross and the priests a thurible and a gospel book.... On these [feast] days the Christian priests come first with their paraphernalia, and they pray for him and bless his cup; when they retire, the Saracen (Muslim) priests come and do likewise; they are followed by the pagan priests (Buddhist) who do the same. The monk told me that the Khan only believes in the Christians; however, he wishes them all to come and pray for him. But he was lying, for he [Munkh] does not believe in any of them... yet they all follow his court like flies honey, and he gives to them all and they all think they enjoy his special favour and they all prophesy good fortune for him.

Rubruck considered that Sergius had lied to him about baptising Munkh, but other Nestorians were adamant it had happened. Rubruck remained highly sceptical: '[Sergius] was covered with confusion at the lie he had told me, and so I did not wish to oblige him to talk about the matter. Some of the Nestorians wanted to assure me that the Khan had been baptised; I said to them that I would never believe it nor tell anyone else, seeing I had not witnessed it.' The day after Munkh's alleged baptism, a similar ritual was undertaken for his wife Kutuktei at which a number of Munkh's children were also present. Again, Rubruck was unable to observe the actual alleged baptism, and remained sceptical.

Some historians have been quick to pronounce Munkh a Christian: one uncritically declares that 'two of Soyo's sons, though not Kublai, became Christians'.[2] These would have been Hulegu, Munkh or Arik Boke. On one occasion Munkh did ask both Rubruck and the Nestorian monks to pray to lessen the cold and the wind, for the sake of the animals, after a storm had been blowing for two days. The storm died down after this prayer. Munkh Khan also attended Nestorian services, other than the one in which he was allegedly baptised.

It would be unwise to declare Munkh a Christian when he was merely following the *yasa*. The rumours may well have been fuelled by Nestorians at Karakorum passing on their observations to other Nestorian merchants as they came and went. That Munkh (and Guyuk before him) flirted with Christianity added grist to the Prester John rumour mill.

Munkh's interest in Christianity was non-commital.

Rubruck records that after his alleged baptism, Munkh entered the Nestorian church at Karakorum, where he 'had our books, the Bible and the breviary taken to him and he made a diligent enquiry as to the meaning of the pictures. The Nestorians answered him as well as they could, for our interpreter had not come in with us. The first time also that I had been in his presence I had carried the Bible before me, and he had had it brought to him and had had a good look at it.' 'Having a good look' was about all the commitment that Munkh showed.

Rubruck's disappointment

Rubruck was naturally disappointed with his own efforts to convert Munkh. That Rubruck even considered the possibility of Munkh's conversion seems a touch arrogant. In his *Report*, he mentions the Mongols' superstitions regarding astrology and witchcraft, their fear of eclipses, and the role of divination (using the charred shoulder blades of sheep) in setting the dates of military campaigns. Rubruck was frustrated that the Shamans seemed more powerful: 'Had I had the power of Moses to work miracles, perhaps I could have convinced him.'

All up, by the time Rubruck wrote his *Report* to Louis, he had not been impressed with the Nestorians he met on his journey through Mongol lands. The dominant peoples across the steppe had been Uighurs, and Rubruck records that there were Nestorian Christians in all Uighur towns he visited. He records that Nestorian moral behaviour was lax, with immorality and drunkenness. Rubruck thinks the Nestorians were despicable, but is fairly consolatory towards the other Christians he met: regarding *airag*, the fermented mare's milk: 'they [the other Eastern Christians] wish strictly to observe their law, and do not drink it. They even no longer consider themselves Christians after they have drunk it and their priests reconcile them as if they had denied the faith of Christ.'

On returning to Europe, Rubruck delivered a letter from Munkh to King Louis, the gist of which he summarises in his

James Gilmour

Yong He Gong Tibetan Buddhist temple, in modern-day Beijing.
James Gilmour wintered here to have contact with Mongol pilgrims and
learn the Mongolian language.

Eva French deep in
conversation in
September 1936.
Away from Western time
pressures, she could
address 'the great
questions of the road'.

'Three women of the Gobi' (chapter 43). The trio and Topsy (second left) over tea back in England.

Erecting a *ger*, the Mongol nomad's tent home.
After the floorboards are laid, lattice and ribbing are lashed together,
then covered with felt and canvas.

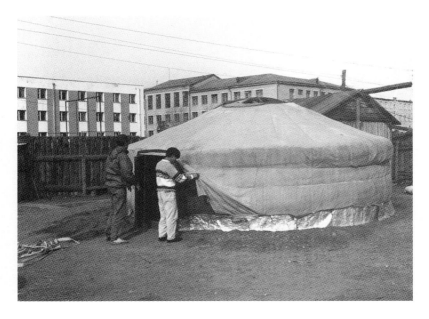

Obos, or cairns of rocks and offerings, which are situated at high places and passes. Travellers place propitiatory offerings to the spirits here, and prayer flags to gain merit.

Naadam, the main summer festival, features horse-racing, archery and wrestling.

The Mongol steppe: nomads and their livestock still graze the pastures of their ancestors.

Report. The threatening tone of it sounds somewhat like Guyuk's letter to Innocent IV via Carpini: 'if you are willing to obey us, you should send your envoys to us: in that way we shall be sure whether you wish to be at peace with us or at war. If, on hearing and understanding the order of the everlasting God, you are unwilling to observe it or to place any trust in it, and you make war on us, how can we know what will happen? He who has made easy what was hard, and brought near what was far distant, the everlasting God — he knows.'[3]

Misplaced zeal

Rubruck was motivated by evangelistic zeal, but Munkh understood his visit as essentially political. Rubruck had protested clearly that he was not an ambassador (and had therefore no right to represent King Louis officially), knowing as he said this that false ambassadors were punishable by death. Rubruck was emphatic that Louis' original letter to Sartaq was as one Christian brother to another, thinking that Sartaq was a Christian. Things were also complicated by the Armenian monk Sergius who 'told Munkh Khan that if he would become a Christian the whole world would come under his sway'. Rubruck was alarmed by this comment, especially as Munkh seemed to take a close interest in France itself: 'They began to ask a great many questions about the Kingdom of France, whether there were many sheep and oxen and horses there, as if they were about to march in at once and take everything.'

Rubruck baptised only six people while in Karakorum, and Munkh or any in his household were not among them. Rubruck's evangelistic technique did not endear him to many of the Mongols. He had said to Batu prior to going on to Karakorum, that unless Batu became a Christian he would be unable to possess the things of heaven. Batu apparently took offence at this and James of Iseo writes the following:

When Friar William, who had been sent with his letter by the lord king of France, appeared before the great king of the Tartars, he began to press on him the Christian faith, saying that the Tartar — and every infidel — would perish eternally and be condemned to everlasting fire. He [the King] replied as one surprised at the stance he had taken in seeking to attract him to the Christian faith. 'The nurse,' he said, 'begins first to let drops of milk fall into the child's mouth, so that the sweet taste may encourage the child to suck; only next does she offer him the nipple. Thus you should have first persuaded us in simple and reasonable fashion, as this teaching seems to us to be altogether foreign. Yet you threatened us at once with everlasting punishment.' The word came through the king of Armenia that the religious who had gone about it differently found favour with the king of the Tartars.[4]

Rubruck pushed the favours he'd enjoyed with Munkh Khan too far. Munkh had arranged a unique inter-religious debate, which Rubruck tells of in his *Report*, but Rubruck's arrogance and assertiveness angered Munkh, and Munkh dismissed him from Karakorum: 'You have stayed here a long time; it is my wish that you go back.' Rubruck appealed a final time that he may return and offer pastoral care to the 'poor slaves of yours at Bolat [who] speak our language'. Munkh said yes to this and had the final word: 'You have a long journey ahead; recruit your strength with food, so that you may reach your own country in good health.'

'Can I look through your historical atlas?' I asked Enkhay. He plonked himself next to me on the divan. Karen and Chimgee were looking through the family photo albums. I sipped my *sutai tsai*.

'You can look,' he replied. 'That's the atlas we use in class four and five.'

I started flicking through the book. 'Can you tell me about all these maps?' I could see for myself they were about military movements, economic productivity, locations of important historical monuments and the like, but the language practice would be good for me.

He explained everything in great detail, proud to show off how much he'd learned of his own national history. I was impressed. Chimgee brought in another plate of *buudz*.

'Tell me about this one,' I said. It was a diagram of a square encampment of some sort.

'Oh that's Karakorum. Ogedei Khan built walls and fortifications. It had just been a tent city before that. If you went to Karakorum today, you'd see something of what's left, although I think Erdenzuu, the nearby lamasery has used most of the stonework.'

'What's this here?' I asked gazing at the page. An odd symbol had caught my eye, located in an inner courtyard within the confines of the ancient wall.

'*Medekh-gui*'. Enkhay shrugged his shoulders. 'I don't know.'

He looked at the key.

'It says it's where a Nestorian church used to be.'

NOTES
1. P. Jackson and D. Morgan, eds. *The Mission of Friar William of Rubruck*. (London: The Hakluyt Society, 1990), 66.
2. Gordon H. Chapman, 'Christianity Comes to Asia', in *The Church in Asia*. ed. D.E. Hoke (Chicago: Moody Press, 1975), 199.
3. P. Jackson and D. Morgan, eds. *The Mission of Friar William of Rubruck*. (London: The Hakluyt Society, 1990), 250.
4. P. Jackson and D. Morgan, eds. *The Mission of Friar William of Rubruck*. (London: The Hakluyt Society, 1990), 282.

Munkh Khan,
Arbitrator in Inter-religious Debate

*'...just as God has given the hand several fingers,
so he has given mankind several paths.'*

Munkh Khan

On 12 September 1997 the Dalai Lama came to speak at the Anglican Cathedral in Christchurch, New Zealand. At first I was rather puzzled. Here was a god-king-reincarnation of the Tibetan god Chenresi, head of a Tantric religious system, and object of devotion for millions worldwide. I went to hear him with three questions in mind: What was he saying to the West? Why did New Zealanders want to hear him? Why should a Buddhist god-king be speaking in a Christian cathedral?

I estimated the crowd in Cathedral Square at about 1,500. It was a motley cross-section ranging from the business-suited to the multiple ear-ringed. I asked myself if this crowd would show up for the Archbishop of Canterbury or the Pope? Probably not. I settled for the TV relay outside, as the cathedral itself was packed. I noticed the Wizard, Christchurch's eclectic self-appointed pseudo-prophet, well positioned in all his unique regalia. I was accosted to accept some pamphlet advertising the imminent arrival of a must-hear Hindu guru. Nobody took much notice of anyone else. We were there to see and hear His Holiness.

My first impression was of a man who was short, bent over and incessantly smiling. Not a bad posture for a Nobel peace prize winner, I thought: a symbiosis of happiness and humility. However, the irony started to dawn on me as I positioned myself for the procession that would pass within half a metre of me in the cathedral foyer. The instructions to visitors on the wall read: 'Remember that this is the House of God and a House of Prayer.' There had been Communion and Bible studies in the cathedral earlier in the day. The song at the Maori welcome had been 'How Great Thou Art'. I had the feeling something didn't quite gel. A Buddhist god-king speaking in the 'House of God'?

He entered the building, ever smiling, to be greeted by the dean. In his speech, the dean welcomed him as a peacemaker. A welcome from the heart of the people of Christchurch should be in the heart of the city, her cathedral, he said. As a Nobel peace prize winner, the Dalai Lama could teach us about peace and reconciliation with respect to The Treaty of Waitangi (1840), the founding document of modern New Zealand, the meaning of which is still hotly debated. The dean was very clear that this event was a civic event, not an inter-faith worship event. We had gathered together to celebrate kindness, commitment to peace, justice, mutual respect and non-violence, he said. The mutual respect and dialogue of living faiths is important: 'our media are unaccustomed to interpreting inter-faith conversations.'

Munkh calls for an inter-religious debate

By the time of Rubruck's visit to Karakorum, the town had become an international cosmopolitan centre. It had also become a pluralistic religious marketplace with Nestorians, Buddhists, Manichaeans, Muslims, Daoists and Shamans.

With such a concentration of priests in the town, a good deal of theological sniping was inevitable, some of which was caused by Rubruck, it seems. After a day in which Rubruck had engaged the Khan's cup-bearer and a number of Muslims in theological debate, Munkh sent some scribes to him who said, 'Our master sends us to you and he says, "Here you are, Christians, Saracens (ie Muslims) and *tuins* (ie Daoists, but probably all idol-worshippers), and each one of you declares that his law is the best and his... book the truest." He therefore wishes you all to meet together and hold a conference and each one is to write down what he says so that he can know the truth.'[1] Munkh could not fathom why the priests of the different religions kept arguing. To Rubruck he had said:

> To you God has given the Scriptures and you Christians do not observe them. You do not find in the Scriptures... that one man ought to abuse another, do you? So then, God has given you the Scriptures, and you do not observe them; whereas to us He has given soothsayers (ie Shamans), and we do as they tell us and live in peace.[2]

Rubruck was naturally delighted at Munkh's invitation and understood it as an expression of God's hand at work. A flurry of doctrinal statements were made by interested parties over the next few days which culminated in Munkh calling for a public inter-religious debate.

Representatives from the religions were summoned and three judges were put up by Munkh: a Christian, a Muslim and a *tuin*. Munkh declared: 'This is the decree of Munkh and let none dare to say that the decree of God is otherwise. He decrees that no one shall dare to speak words of contention or abuse to another, and no one is to cause a disturbance such as would hinder these proceedings, on pain of death.'[3] And so 31 May 1254 saw the world's first attempt at formal inter-religious dialogue.

The theological bickering that had been going on in Karakorum was symptomatic of deeper fundamental changes that were taking place among the religions of the central Asian steppe. Islamic records of this period claim that Munkh was on the verge of converting to Islam. Ten years previously, his cousin Godan had become a patron of the Sakya school of Tibetan Buddhism, and only three years previously, Munkh had appointed Buddhists to his own court. A contemporary Buddhist tract outlines that the Buddhists and Daoists were having a violent controversy just prior to the arrival of Rubruck, and had taken their complaints to the Khan, their representatives arriving at Munkh's *ordo* in the autumn of 1256, soon after the debate.

The writer of the tract says that the first round of the debate was so much in favour of the Buddhists, that the Daoist did not bother to appear again for the second round. Munkh settled this debate in a fashion in line with the *yasa*:

> The Sine-shing say that the Daoist teaching is the highest, the Sew-ts'ai, that Confucianism is the first, the Tie-sie, honouring Mi-shi-ho, trust the celestial abodes; and the Ta-shi-man, praying to heaven, thank it for its gracious deeds. If all these religions are thoroughly studied, not one can be compared to Buddhism... As the fingers with regard to the palm, from which they grow, so are all the other religions with regard to Buddhism.[4]

The religion 'Tie-sie' is Christianity which honours the 'Mi-shi-ho' or Messiah. Thus to Munkh, as it was to his forefathers, different religions were merely similar expressions of a universal truth. None should therefore be given priority, least of all Christianity (although the author of the tract would like to think that Munkh was sympathetic to Buddhism at the time).

To Rubruck, religious doctrine was an either/or phenomenon. One could not hold to two logically disparate creeds at once. Rubruck expected a winner, and certainly portrays monotheism coming off better than polytheism. To the Mongol, however, there was no contradiction, and Munkh remains uncommitted. In a pragmatic political move, Munkh dismissed Rubruck after the debate, sending him back to Europe via Batu's *ordo* with a letter to King Louis demanding he come in person to pay him homage.

What was really happening at the debate?

When we ask the question 'was Munkh (or Guyuk before him, for that matter) a Christian?' Or 'were the Khans sympathetic to Christianity?' we are naturally asking them from within a Western worldview. The answer to the first question is 'no' and to the second 'generally yes'. At no point in the history of the Mongols did the Khans exclusively sympathise with Christianity or consciously endorse a Christian agenda. The *yasa* dictated to all Khans a policy of pan-religious sympathy. Religious pluralism was enshrined in law and tradition. But was this policy adhered to merely because of the need for political expediency? Were the Khans truly political pragmatists? On the one hand, they were. But on a deeper level, the *yasa* was essentially a policy derived from a deeply held shamanistic worldview.

Munkh's inter-religious debate at Karakorum reflected the Mongols' true agenda. Rubruck was both participant in and recorder of the debate, and his record gives us the first detailed account of the interfacing of the world's great religions on the central Asian steppe. Rubruck understood the debate to be convened so that Munkh could decide for himself which religion was true.

However, from the start, the debate was plagued by equivocations, vagueness and ambiguity. How could Rubruck have hoped to make sense of the subtleties of the doctrines of Buddhism, for example, considering that he knew nothing of Buddhist doctrine, and nothing of its linguistic complexities. And he would have to work through young Buchier junior, his translator. Confusion and misunderstanding were unavoidable.

The debate was a rowdy one, with monotheists (Nestorians and Muslims) oddly siding together against the polytheists. No converts to Christianity were made from it. No one said, 'I believe; I want to become a Christian,' as Rubruck thought should happen.

With the ascendancy of Buddhism at the time, the ancient Mongol Shamanism was trying to find ways to accommodate it. The simple folk-Shamanism of the Mongols was feeling the pressure of the more sophisticated Buddhism. 'Camouflaged in the borrowed trappings of other religions, Mongol folk religion [that is, Shamanism] became virtually indistinguishable from that from which it sought to defend itself [that is, Buddhism].'[5]

To be a Mongol was to be a Shamanist (although it is very doubtful that a Mongol would have understood his Shamanism in a systematic doctrinal sort of way). Shamanism was a folk religion, uncomplicated and practical.

With the arrival of Catholicism and Buddhism within a decade of each other, the Mongols were in a predicament. How could Shamanism be preserved, yet Buddhism and Catholicism be accommodated? Buddhism seemed less threatening than the dogma of Christianity, therefore Shamanism had a better chance of surviving with Buddhism. Munkh did not declare a winner of the debate, but rather outlined his own theology to Rubruck: 'But as God gave different fingers to the hand, so has He given different ways to men.'[6]

To run a vast multi-religious empire, Munkh had to formulate a policy that preserved an essential 'Mongol-ness' in view of the tendency of the Mongols to lose their conquering virility when they settled down among their sedentary foes. He had called the debate, not so much to establish religious truth, but to determine which one of these new religions would best be able to coexist peacefully with Mongol Shamanism. There was an inclusivity that Munkh was looking for: some way of reconciling the *yasa* with the need to keep Mongol Shamanism alive.

Fu-yu, the Buddhist delegate, therefore won the debate on behalf of Buddhism because it was 'psychologically reassuring; Buddhism did not appear to pose the same threat that Christianity did'. Buddhism got the upper hand because, unlike Christians who wanted to convert the Khans, the Buddhists wanted to convert the gods of Shamanism to Buddhism, much like Buddhism had done to the ancient Tibetan religion of Bon. Fu-yu's strategy was more a gentle syncretism; he wanted to 'dim the light' of Buddhism. On the other hand, Rubruck was thinking in 'exclusive' categories: the Khan should be converted to Christianity and forsake all other religions. Rubruck wanted not to 'dim the light', but show the full glory of God.[7] Munkh expelled Rubruck from Karakorum after the debate, more for Rubruck's arrogance than for supposed inferiority of doctrine.

Munkh's hidden agenda: protecting Shamanism

Munkh favoured Buddhism to protect Shamanism. And here we have a paradigm for all future Khans. They never really gave up their Shamanism, and any perceived concessions to Christianity must be understood in the light of their essential Shamanistic worldview. In the House of Kublai, it was relatively easy to continue in lamaistic Buddhism, as Tibet was a vassal state. In the House of Hulegu though, the dominant religion was Islam. Like Christianity, Islam was an exclusive religion. That the Il-Khans were paradoxical in their religious policies was symptomatic of this search for inclusive categories. Ironically, the Il-Khans often courted Nestorian Christianity, not because of any perceived truth in it, but because of its familiarity within the Nestorian heritage they brought with them from central Asia. If Islam continued to threaten a break-up of their realm, inclusive solace could be found in a familiar religion, Nestorian Christianity. So the *yasa* gave the religio-political breathing space for each Khan to choose a religious affiliation that allowed for the ongoing practice of Shamanism.

Munkh rejected Catholicism because it was exclusive. It was a threat to Shamanism and therefore a threat to Mongol identity. The Mongols accepted lamaistic Buddhism as a self-defence strategy to preserve their own Shamanism. This also explains the oscillating religious practice of the Persian Il-Khans. In the absence of a local expression of Buddhism, they constantly struggled to endorse the local religion that least threatened their own Shamanism and hence their own identity. Because the choice was limited to only two exclusive religions, Islam and Christianity, the Mongol identity was eventually lost, and so the Il-Khanate fizzled and in the end was absorbed into the more dominant Islam.

Rubruck was expelled from Karakorum for wanting to show

the glory of God and demanding personal immediate conversion to Catholicism. He had, as it were, come to Munkh's *ordo* with 'both guns blazing'. This threatened Mongol Shamanism and hence Mongol identity. But Nestorianism had made sufficient inroads into the Mongol psyche not to be a threat to Mongol identity over a period of fifty odd years since Chinggis had over-run the Keraits.

I positioned myself outside by the multi-console TV relay. His Holiness the Dalai Lama said he felt a warm and open feeling in the diversity of faith that was meeting in the cathedral. 'Our humanity unites us; we all experience the same in life.' 'Everyone wants happiness and not suffering,' he continued. This is the unique feature and quality of each religion. The desire for the release from suffering showed that 'our common effort and experiences bind religions together'. He proceeded to amplify this with the analogy of the fingers on the hand. The hand was religion, and each finger had a different purpose.

He stopped short, however, of explicitly saying that in effect all religions, being 'on the same hand', were essentially one, each having different functions. But that implication was clear. 'The spirit of pluralism is coming; this is a very healthy sign.' The way to contribute to this harmony was through dialogue and self-effort, which leads to mutual understanding, and so to minimising personal and international conflict.

To illustrate this, he meandered off on a philosophical discourse on the inherent harmony there is in the multi-religious ethos of democratic India. At this I was incredulous, having lived in India for twelve years. Intersectarian harmony was something I saw very little of. The papers had dozens of stories every day telling of just the opposite: Hindu killing Muslim, Sikh killing Hindu, this temple razed, that holy place desecrated.

But, to his credit, His Holiness did give five clear practical ways that people can 'increase harmony'. Theologians of different religions should meet together to discuss similarities and differences. There should be meetings of religious practitioners, to 'exchange deeper spiritual experiences' which would lead to appreciation and respect for each other. The Dalai Lama himself had spent time with a Trappist monk to this end. 'There should be no more 'we and they''. And we should go on religious pilgrimage to the holy places of each other's religions.' He himself had visited Jerusalem 'as a pilgrim'. People of different religions should 'pray together; if not, then meditate together. This will increase the field of harmony'. There should be meeting of the heads of different religions. For example the Dalai Lama and the Pope. Lastly, there should be more co-operation between different religions. At this point, the Dalai Lama acknowledged that this was really Bishop Desmond Tutu's idea: 'Tutu is a good friend.' An example would be working together in a civil defence emergency.

And so his speech ended. The crowd had shown genuine interest and certainly identified with his jovialness and genuine humanity. The Mayor of Christchurch, Vicky Buck, thanked him for his 'incredibly powerful message'.

As a Christian, what was I to make of this visit? I observed it to be classic Buddhism, dressed up for the West.

There was no recognition that one person's religion may have tenets of belief that are exclusive of another person's religion. His five-point plan to increase harmony was admirable but unrealistic, as it is built on the assumption that through dialogue there can be found a middle way of compromise which will lead to greater harmony and less suffering. Both Christians and a Buddhists agree that the core issue in the world today is suffering, but they don't agree on the way to resolve that suffering.

Buddhist doctrine was plainly evident. The Dalai Lama was asked: 'When you reach final enlightenment, what will become of the Dalai Lama and the institution?' His reply was essentially Buddhist, revealing a worldview encompassing reincarnation: 'I am only a beginner. I don't know... it will take several eons to do. There is no hurry.' Reincarnation and resurrection are two completely different phenomena. Both have undergirding views of humankind that are at odds with each other. Sin is another example. The Dalai Lama said that 'religious faith and basic good human quality is separate. Religious faith comes later... compassion and affection are there at birth.' In other words, a person is born inherently good. However, Christian doctrine pronounces humankind separated from goodness when born. Goodness is something given to us by the merits of Christ alone. On salvation: Humanity's problems cannot be solved 'from outside' but the 'ultimate answer is found within ourselves'. This is the exact opposite of Christian doctrine. Because humanity's fall from grace has been so devastating, not even the smallest amount of goodness within can save us. That is why there must be a rescue 'from outside', namely through the merits of Christ.

But these are only three examples. I had overheard someone in the square say, 'Buddhism has a lot in common with the Christian thing, really.' I couldn't actually see where the overlap was.

However, I really liked what the Dalai Lama said at the end of his speech. In summarising, he drew our attention to the importance of respect at grass roots for the different religions. He rightly appealed to everyone to be in practice what you claim to believe, no matter which religion you follow: 'Be consistent.' The religion that you choose to follow must manifest itself throughout daily life, and if so, then eventually you will gain 'deeper values'. In other words, practise what you preach. And as you put into practice what your faith teaches you, so you will grow in faith. Echoes of the letter of James, I thought.

And what did I observe of the New Zealand audience? People come to hear a Nobel peace prize winner? Possibly. People come to hear yet another esoteric voice in the wilderness of postmodernity? Probably.

The venue? Well, everyone said it was just a civic event. But it was definitely a religious event as well. It was an 'inter-faith conversation'. There were religious leaders on the podium. It was held in a Christian cathedral. The Dalai Lama's speech was religious through and through. No Christian leader would ever get that type of air-space in the central temple of any city in Tibet. The Mayor said there was 'no other venue big enough'.

And me? I did two things. I sat in the empty cathedral afterwards and pondered the banners that hung on the columns. They depicted the fruit of the Spirit. The other thing I did was to go and buy the Dalai Lama's autobiography.

NOTES

1. C. Dawson, ed., *Mission to Asia; Narratives and Letters of the Franciscan Missionaries in Mongolia and China in the 13th and 14th Centuries*, trans. a nun of Stanbrook Abbey (NY: Harper & Row, 1966), 189.

2. P. Jackson and D. Morgan, eds. *The Mission of Friar William of Rubruck*. (London: The Hakluyt Society, 1990), 237.

3. C. Dawson, ed., *Mission to Asia; Narratives and Letters of the Franciscan Missionaries in Mongolia and China in the 13th and 14th Centuries*, trans. a nun of Stanbrook Abbey (NY: Harper & Row, 1966), 191.

4. Palladius, 'Traces of Christianity in Mongolia and China in the 13th Century: drawn from Chinese Sources', *Chinese Recorder* 6 (1875): 105.

5. Richard Fox Young, 'Deus unus or Dei plures sunt? The Function of Inclusivism in the Buddhist Defense of Mongol Folk Religion Against William of Rubruck (1254)', *Journal of Ecumenical Studies* 26 (Winter, 1989): 103. It should be noted that lamaistic Buddhism amongst the Mongols during Munkh's reign was only incidental. It was not formally endorsed until the reign of Kublai, and even then did not take hold until after the 15th century. See W. Heissig *The Religions of Mongolia*, trans. by G. Samuel (London: Routledge & Kegan Paul, 1980), chapter 1.

6. C. Dawson, ed., *Mission to Asia; Narratives and Letters of the Franciscan Missionaries in Mongolia and China in the 13th and 14th Centuries*, trans. a nun of Stanbrook Abbey (NY: Harper & Row, 1966), 195.

7. Richard Fox Young, 'Deus unus or Dei plures sunt? The Function of Inclusivism in the Buddhist Defense of Mongol Folk Religion Against William of Rubruck (1254)', *Journal of Ecumenical Studies* 26 (Winter, 1989): 130.

Chapter 20

John of Montecorvino,
First Catholic Bishop and Bible Translator in Mongol-China

'I have an adequate knowledge of the Tartar language script... and now I have translated... the whole of the New Testament and the Psalter.'
John of Montecorvino

It's March 1997 and I'm teaching a seven-lecture course to forty students on the history of Christianity among the Mongols. I start with the arrival of Syrian Christians in central Asia in the seventh century, look at the conversion of the Keraits and other pre-Mongol tribes, and we sift through the religious policies of the Great Khans and discover that several of them had Christian wives. We examine in detail the Franciscan mission to the Mongol Empire. I tell them that the first Mongolian New Testament was translated in 1305 in Beijing by a Franciscan father called John of Montecorvino.

'*Bagsh-aa*,' a student near the front interjects. 'Are you telling us that this *Shin Geree* is not the first Mongolian Bible?' She holds up the book in question. It is unmistakable with its bright golden sunset cover. 'I understood that this New Testament had been translated and printed by 1990 and was stockpiled in Hong Kong. When Mongolia opened in 1990, it was all ready to ship here. That was certainly God's timing, wasn't it?'

'Absolutely. You need to realise that it was the first modern Mongolian Bible in popular, idiomatic Khalka dialect. But it wasn't the first Mongolian Bible,' I replied. 'There was a full Bible done in 1840 as well. The New Testament of that was revised in 1952. The script is in *mongol bichig*. You can still buy it from the Hong Kong Bible Society. There seems no reason to doubt that Montecorvino's New Testament and Psalms was the first. It wouldn't have been mass printed. If there were copies made, they would've been made by hand.'

'I have a copy here,' Tuvshee called out.

'What? Of Montecorvino's New Testament?' someone asked.

'No. The 1952 revision.'

Over morning tea we all passed the book around. Tuvshee explained. 'They used this in Inner Mongolia. A friend sent it up to me from Hong Kong. The language is older than *Shin Geree* and quite different in some places. It also uses different key terminology.'

Personal background

Carpini and Rubruck had so opened the way for further missions that the Pope now sent numerous missionaries eastwards. The Mongols never delivered on their threat to Western Europe, and during the second half of the thirteenth century, the popes felt secure enough to commission envoys to the Mongols, capitalising on the zeal of the newly-formed Franciscan and Dominican orders. These missions mainly focused on the common borders: most went to Eastern European lands and to Persia.

John, of Montecorvino in southern Italy, was one of these missionaries and had been sent as an official papal ambassador to Constantinople as well as Armenia and Persia. All up he spent ten years in missionary service for his Franciscan order (which he had joined in 1272) in Persia and surrounds. Montecorvino and his colleagues returned to Italy in early 1289 with letters to the Pope from King Hethum II of Armenia. On his return he reported that an Isola of Pisa had gained great rapport among the Mongols. Pope Nicholas IV, encouraged by this report, commissioned Montecorvino to take a letter, dated 15 July 1289, to all the patriarchs and princes of the East.

On arrival in Persia, Arghun Il-Khan, arguably pro-Christian, sent Montecorvino on to the Mongol capital, by then Da-tu (now Beijing). In effect, Montecorvino became the first

Catholic missionary to Mongol-China, arriving in Da-tu in 1294.

Montecorvino arrives in China

The year he arrived, the Great Khan Kublai had died. Montecorvino was received by Temur Oljeitu Khan, Kublai's grandson and second of the Yuan Khans (r.1294–1307). Montecorvino saw himself as 'legate and envoy of the Roman Apostolic See'. We know of his endeavours in Da-tu because he wrote two letters to Europe which we have today. They display a man devoted to his task, living a simple, even naive life, but yet with an apostolic conviction and constancy of character. His letters were desperate in their appeals for more help in the great task of evangelising Mongol-China.

Montecorvino's first letter home to Europe was from India, while en route to China. His second letter (and first from China) is dated 8 January 1305: 'I departed from Tabriz [in Persia] in 1291 and entered India... for thirteen months. My fellow traveller was Brother Nicholas of Pistoia... who died there. And going on further, I reached Cathay, the kingdom of the Emperor of the Tartars.'

Montecorvino received a polite but indifferent response from the Khan on arrival: 'I summoned the Emperor himself to receive the Catholic faith of Our Lord Jesus Christ with the letters of the Lord Pope, but he was too far gone in idolatry. Nevertheless he behaves very generously to the Christians and it is now the twelfth year that I have been with him.'

On arrival, Montecorvino quickly discovered that he was on someone else's patch: 'The Nestorians, who call themselves Christians, but behave in a very unchristian manner, have grown so strong in these parts that they did not allow any Christian of another rite to have any place of worship, however small, nor to preach any doctrine but their own.'

Montecorvino's first five years in Da-tu were dominated by conflict with the Nestorians:

... the aforesaid Nestorians both directly and by the bribery of others have brought most grievous persecutions upon me, declaring that I was not sent by the Lord Pope, but that I was a spy, a magician and a deceiver of men. And after some time they produced more false witnesses, saying that another messenger had been sent with a great treasure to the Emperor and that I had murdered him in India and made away with his gifts. And this intrigue lasted about five years, so that I was often brought to judgement, and in danger of a shameful death.

Temur Oljeitu Khan must have intervened at some stage for Montecorvino goes on to write: 'but at last, by God's ordering, the emperor came to know my innocence and the nature of my accusers, by the confession of some of them, and he sent them into exile with their wives and children.'[1]

Montecorvino attempts a Bible translation

Montecorvino's achievements in Da-tu were formidable considering the opposition he received from the Nestorians and the lack of support from Europe. His letter continues:

I have built a church in the city of [Da-tu]... and this I completed six years ago and I also made a tower and put three bells in it. Moreover I have baptised about 6,000 persons there up to the present, according to my reckoning. And if it had not been for the aforesaid slanders I might have baptised 30,000 more, for I am constantly baptising.

He adopted a curious evangelistic strategy:

I have purchased... forty boys of the sons of the pagans, between seven and eleven years old, who as yet knew no religion. Here I baptised them and taught them Latin and our rite, and I wrote for them about thirty Psalters and hymnaries and two breviaries by which eleven boys now know the office. And they keep choir and say office as in a convent whether I am there or not. And several of them write Psalters and other suitable things... I ring the bells for all the Hours and sing the divine office with a choir of 'sucklings and infants'... but we sing by rote because we have no books with the notes.

Temur Oljeitu Khan must have shown some interest in this: 'The Lord Emperor takes much delight in their singing.' The church was within earshot of the Khan's palace.

Most remarkably, Montecorvino tells the Pope that he has learned the language and attempted a Bible translation: 'I have an adequate knowledge of the Tartar language and script... and now I have translated into that language and script the whole of the New Testament and the Psalter and have had it written in beautiful characters.' Montecorvino's knowledge of the Mongol language was more than academic translation, and he enjoyed the freedom to preach on the street: 'I bear witness to the Law of Christ and read and preach openly and in public.'

He wrote again a year later in February 1306. This second letter from China has a note of melancholy in it, and one gets the impression that he is winding down and in need of rejuvenation.

I have thought that you may well wonder why you have never received letters from me who have dwelt so long in such a distant land. But I have wondered no less that never until this year have I received letters or good wishes from any Brother or friend, so that it seemed to me that no one remembered me, especially as I heard that rumours of my death had reached you.

He goes on to say he is relieved to hear through some means that his first letter got through. Then he gives news of the building of another church and takes great delight in its significance: 'The Lord Khan can hear our voices in his chamber, and this is told as a wonder far and wide among the nations, and will count for much according to the disposition and fulfilment of God's mercy.' New missionaries were sent in 1309 with instructions from the new Pope, Clement V, to consecrate Montecorvino as bishop of Khanbaliq (that is Da-tu). In 1313 he was elevated to the rank of archbishop. With these new priests, Montecorvino was able to extend the Catholic mission, travelling extensively up onto the Mongolian plateau and also down the coast. He went on to create dioceses in Hangchou, Yangchou and Chuanchou (Zayton).

Montecorvino: an innovative pioneer

John of Montecorvino stands beside Carpini and Rubruck in his pioneering effort to bring the gospel to the Mongols. Carpini and Rubruck opened the way by not only initiating a dialogue with the Mongols but also awakening Europe to the potential of sending further missionaries. Unlike his forebears, Montecorvino was able to stay on in Mongol territory and settle down. He lived his life out in Da-tu, dying there in 1328.

Montecorvino was innovative in his strategy. He recognised the need to think in Mongol categories, to learn the language and attempt to translate part of the Bible into it. He was applying, probably unconsciously, the radical agenda that Lull had first expounded to the universities of Europe: that to win the Mongols, missionaries would have to learn their language and do so by living among them. Montecorvino achieved the remarkable feat of being the first to translate the New Testament into Mongolian. He would have done this in the *mongol bichig* script, or more precisely in the Uighur script that Chinggis had borrowed from the Kerait-Nestorian and Uighur bureaucrats in his court. The translation would not have been mass-produced on a printing press: at best, there may have been one or two manuscript copies, transcribed by Montecorvino's choir boys. No modern copies exist: one manuscript was discovered a century later and is mentioned in a Chinese source.

From his letters, one might think that Montecorvino spent most of his time constructing church buildings. This was true. Who were they for and why such big building projects? It is unlikely that large numbers of Mongols converted to Catholic-Christianity; Kublai had formally introduced Tibetan Buddhism into his kingdom immediately prior to the arrival of Montecorvino. Neither is there any explicit reference to the Nestorians in Da-tu being Mongols. We do know that, like the Khans before him, Kublai had relocated captured peoples, and employed foreigners to do the key administrative jobs. Hence in Da-tu there was a very large Alan community, originally imported from Georgia as mercenaries in Kublai's army. The Alans were Eastern Christians, a sect under the general Eastern Church umbrella much like the Nestorians. Montecorvino took on pastoral care of the Alans by default. The church building programme may well have been for the Alan community. Brother Peregrine, originally a travelling partner with Montecorvino and later bishop of Zayton writes: 'there are good Christians, called Alans, 30,000 of whom are in the great king's pay, and these men with their families come to Brother John [that is Montecorvino]; and he preaches to them and encourages them.' Similarly, Montecorvino picked up the pastoral care of the Armenians in Da-tu. Peregrine continues: 'the other Christian peoples... have followed Brother John, especially the Armenians who are now building for themselves a remarkable church.'[2]

Montecorvino had a sacramental theology of mission. The mere presence of the church of God in a location was testimony in itself. Singing in Latin, building churches, baptising and conducting mass, were for Montecorvino signs of the coming of God into a place and therefore legitimate forms of mission. For him Christian worship was Christian witness.

But his strategy was more profound than this. He preached 'openly in public' and engaged in translation: in modern language he did street evangelism and tract and gospel distribution. And like modern times, some of his worst opposition came from other Christians. There was no love lost between the Nestorians and Montecorvino and the other handful of Franciscan fathers who were to follow. It was chiefly in response to the Nestorian opposition, perhaps for his own pastoral nourishment, that he desperately appealed for reinforcements from Europe: 'Again I say that had it not been for the aforesaid slanders, great results might have followed. If I had even two or three fellow [helpers], perhaps the Emperor... might have been baptised. I beg for some brethren to come, if any are willing, to do so.' It is only too common still today that lack of co-operation among Christians, and indeed slander, is a prime reason for the stalling of the spread of the gospel.

Some effort was made to send missionaries to assist Montecorvino. Not all made it through to China. Those who did stayed for life and achieved some success in the new bishoprics in China, notably in Zayton. Montecorvino spent a total of thirty years in Da-tu, the first twelve with no help or even any news from Europe. He single-handedly established the presence of Catholicism in the world's mightiest empire of the day.

———

The following Saturday I deliver a shortened public seminar open to all. Seventy show up. I'm encouraged. I share the day with a colleague who leads the afternoon session and challenges us regarding indigenisation of the Mongolian church. I had spent two hours that week with Mongolian leaders listening to them explain their vision for the church.

'What do you mean by wanting a uniquely "Mongolian" church?' I had asked them.

'To be truly Mongolian, we believe the church needs to be led by Mongolians. The time of up-front foreign leadership is over. We should be encouraging our musicians to be writing

Mongolian worship songs. We also should be self-supporting as a church.'

I'd been encouraged by their answer. I believed that all missionaries should be aiming to work themselves out of a job eventually. These were the same leaders who had organised evangelism teams to every province of Mongolia and had sent mission teams to Russia and Inner Mongolia already. And the modern Mongolian church was barely seven years old!

In the Saturday seminar we explored possible ways of expressing our Christian faith in a uniquely Mongolian way.

One foreigner observed: 'I notice that the Mongolians put their hats on during important occasions. Should we not wear hats then when administering communion?' This idea was radically new to most and generated some interesting discussion.

Another noted: 'Mongolians love proverbs, and the language is rich in them. I've noticed that some of them are very similar to the Proverbs in the Bible. Can we use these to open doors for evangelism?'

Good healthy discussion followed. As I listened, it started to dawn on me that to understand our history and culture is to understand our identity. Who I am as an individual Christian is determined somewhat by where we've come from as a Christian community. Knowing that people have gone before me who have planted seed and cultivated its growth instils in me a tremendous feeling of gratitude to God and appreciation for the work already done.

'*Bagsh-aa*.' I snapped out of my thoughts and focused on the questioner in the audience.

'God has worked among our people for centuries already. I'm humbled to think that God's word was in our own language 700 years ago. I am now not ashamed to be a Mongol and a Christian. I am encouraged to express my faith according to the customs of my people.'

NOTES

1. C. Dawson, ed., *Mission to Asia; Narratives and Letters of the Franciscan Missionaries in Mongolia and China in the 13th and 14th Centuries*, trans. a nun of Stanbrook Abbey (NY: Harper & Row, 1966), 225.

2. *The Letter of Brother Peregrine, Bishop of Zayton* in C. Dawson, ed., *Mission to Asia; Narratives and Letters of the Franciscan Missionaries in Mongolia and China in the 13th and 14th Centuries*, trans. a nun of Stanbrook Abbey (NY: Harper & Row, 1966), 232.

| Chapter 21 | **King George of the Onguts,** **A Christian Mongol King and His Tribe** |

> 'A certain king of these parts... attached himself to me in the first year that I came here, and was converted by me to the truth of the true Catholic faith. He brought a great part of his people to the true Catholic faith.'
>
> John of Montecorvino, referring to King George of the Onguts

I was intrigued by the Mongol naming system. I recognised several Tibetan names: Dorj, Myagmar, Davaa. Other than these, the names were all double-barrelled.

'Flower' and 'Ray/beam' were common among the women. 'Golden-flower', 'Strong-flower', 'Sun-flower', 'Golden-ray', 'Moon-beam', and other variations.

'Hero', 'strong' and 'light' were common among the men. 'Strong-hero', 'Golden-light' and the like.

The names were quite easy to recognise in a sentence. The problem arose when nicknames were used, and most people had one. Usually either half of their name was shortened. For example, 'Strong-flower' (Bat-tsetseg) became simply 'Tsetsegee'. 'Bayar-Magnai' became 'Bayaraa' or 'Magnai' or 'Baika'.

There wasn't a big pool of names. At any one time in Mongolia, I probably knew about four or five people with exactly the same name.

I asked my language teacher one day to explain some more.

'What about family names? How do you know what the connections are between the families?'

'Well we don't have a family name like you have in English,' my teacher replied. 'For official documents we write the name of the father and then the person. It reads something like

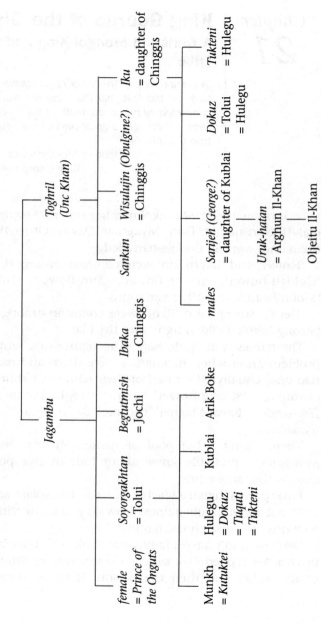

Intermarriage of the Kerait/Onguts and Chinggiside Mongols

Key: *Italic script:* Nestorian Kerait and Onguts.
Normal script: Chinggisides

Jagambu

female
= Prince of
the Onguts

Soyorgakhtan
= Tolui

Begtutmish
= Jochi

Ibaka
= Chinggis

Hulegu
= *Dokuz*
= *Tuquti*
= *Tukteni*

Kublai

Arik Boke

Munkh
= *Kutuktei*

Toghril
(Unc Khan)

Sankun

Wisulujin (Obulgine?)
= Chinggis

Iku
= daughter
of Chinggis

males

Sarijeh (George?)
= daughter of Kublai

Dokuz
= Tolui
= Hulegu

Tukteni
= Hulegu

Uruk-hatan
= Arghun Il-Khan

Oljeitu Il-Khan

"Bayar-magnai's Enkh-tuya" or "Enkh-tuya who belongs to Bayar-magnai".'

I struggled with addressing my superiors with only one name. 'Do you not have a formal name system like 'Mr Smith' or 'Mrs Jones?' I asked.

The answer was simple. 'No. We use only one name. You call your teacher by one name only.'

This to me was a bit bizarre and took some getting used to.

'What about these other names?' I asked. 'Like "In-bish" and "Ner-gui"?' Literally translated these names meant 'Not-This' and 'No-Name'. I'd already met one or two people with these names, and I was intrigued.

My teacher shuffled nervously. 'Sometimes we don't name our children until they are past three years old. This is because we believe that once a child is named, then an evil spirit can latch on to that name and harm the child. If a child is referred to as 'Ner-gui', then we will confuse the evil spirit and it will leave. You'll find that someone with this name will actually have a normal Mongolian name as well, but it isn't used until after childhood.'

I was rather taken aback with the superstition and also pondered the immense psychological damage that must happen when a child grows up being called 'Not-this' or 'No-name'.

The Onguts and King George

One tribe that had converted to Nestorianism as a whole by the time of Kublai's reign was the Onguts. This was a Turkic-Mongol people living in the Ordos region within and north of the great northern bend of the Yellow River. Their territory commanded the main trade route from China to Mongolia and so the Onguts were influential in the cultural, religious and political interchanges between the two countries. In John of Montecorvino's second letter (1305) he writes:

A certain king of these parts, of the sect of the Nestorian Christians, who was of the family of that great king who was called Prester John, attached himself to me in the first year that I came here. And was converted by me to the truth of the true Catholic faith. And he took minor orders [ie became a Franciscan] and served my Mass wearing the sacred vestments, so that the other Nestorians accused him of apostasy. Nevertheless he brought a great part of his people to the true Catholic faith, and he built a fine church with royal generosity in honour of God, the Holy Trinity and the Lord Pope, and called it according to my name 'the Roman church'. This King George departed to the Lord a true Christian, leaving a son and heir in the cradle, who is now nine years old. But his brothers who were perverse in the errors of Nestorius perverted all those whom King George had converted and brought them back to their former state of schism. And because I was alone and unable to leave the Emperor the Khan, I could not visit that church, which is distant twenty days journey. Nevertheless if a few helpers and fellow workers were to come, I hope in God that all could be restored for I still hold the grant of the late King George.[1]

Here then is a Nestorian Mongol tribe with a Khan called George, who, according to Montecorvino, was a descendent of Unc-Khan, the Kerait Khan whom we have said is our most likely candidate for the title of Prester John. Together with a large portion of his tribe, King George converted to Catholicism under Montecorvino's influence, but after the death of King George some time around 1298 or 1299, tribal leaders, possibly under the leadership of George's blood brothers, persuaded the tribe back to Nestorianism.

It is reasonable to claim that this tribe had directly descended from Toghril, or Unc Khan the Kerait king. The name 'Unc' or Ong is the singular form of the tribal name, and 'Ongut' (or 'Ongghud') is the plural. In other words, they were the 'Unc-Mongols' who had descended from the Kerait 'Unc-Khan'. Nestorian crosses from the eleventh to the fourteenth centuries have been excavated from graves in the Ordos region, and Nestorian Christian names were common among them (for example, Simeon, Paul, John, Jacob and Luke). Mark, who became Nestorian Patriarch Yaballaha III, was probably an Ongut.

As a Nestorian tribe, their bishops held temporal and spiritual power which is probably the reason that Europe thought them to be descendants of Prester John. But the connections with the Chinggisides is more substantial than this. In gratitude for helping him defeat the Naimans, Chinggis decreed that future generations born to Unc-Khan, that is the Onguts, would marry into the Mongol nobility and so become imperial sons-in-law.

More connections between families

Rashid identifies two sons of Unc Khan called Sankun and Iku. Iku had a son called Sarijeh, that is, Unc Khan's grandson. The name 'George' may be a corruption of the word 'Sarijeh'. It is difficult to transcribe Mongolian names that have been written in Roman script without seeing the original name written in *mongol bichig*. Sarijeh may well be pronounced more like 'Sharja' (shar meaning 'yellow') hence 'Georg-a'. Alternatively, 'George' may be a corruption of the common Tibetan name 'Dorj'. Marco Polo mentions this George as well: 'The king of the province... is of the lineage of Prester John, George by name, and he holds the land under the Great Khan.... It is a custom... that these kings of the lineage of Prester John always obtain to wife either daughters of the Great Khan or other princesses of his family.'[2]

King George was the son-in-law of Kublai. Two of George's sisters were married to Hulegu Khan, first of the Il-Khans of Persia. These were Dokuz-hatan and Tukteni-hatan. It is known that Dokuz was a Nestorian, but there is no mention of the religion of Tukteni. It would be reasonable to assume that she was Nestorian at least in name due to her Kerait pedigree.

The Secret History tells of a brother of Unc Khan called Jagambu,[3] who had three daughters Ibaka, Begtutmish and Soyo.[4] These three Kerait sisters married into the Chinggiside family: Ibaka married Chinggis himself (although he later gave her to one of his lieutenants, Jurchedei), Begtutmish married Jochi (Chinggis' eldest son), and Soyo married Tolui, Chinggis' youngest son. Rubruck mistakenly surmises that Soyo was the daughter of Unc Khan, but The Secret History specifically names her as niece of Unc-Khan, and this is confirmed by Juvaini, who had lived among the Mongols longer than Rubruck.[5] The Secret History also states that Soyo was given by Chinggis to Tolui after the final submission of the Kerait.[6] This was to start the process of Kerait assimilation into the Mongol tribe. That the Kerait gained legitimacy as truly Mongol is recognised by the fact that Soyo became the mother of Munkh (fourth Great Khan), Kublai (fifth Great Khan), and Hulegu (first of the Il-Khans of Persia).

The above genealogy is rather simplistic and has some gaps. The Chinese Yuan Shih, or History of the Yuan outlines further relationships between the Chinggisides and the Onguts that are interesting but can be confusing. The Ongut chief who assisted the Chinggisides against the Naimans was Alaqush-tagin (not Unc-Khan) according to the Yuan Shih. After this magnanimous gesture Alaqush-tagin was assassinated by rival members of his tribe, but his wife escaped with a son (Chinese name: Po-yao-ho) to Yuncheng. When Chinggis attacked Yuncheng, he wanted to restore the Ongut nobility to their rightful place as an act of gratitude for service rendered.

Po-yao-ho went with Chinggis to fight the Khwarizm (1219), and on returning was given Chinggis' own daughter Alaghai-bekh in marriage. When Po-yao-ho died, Alaghai-bekh ruled the Onguts for a time as regent. Having no children of her own, she mothered Po-yao-ho's three sons by concubines as her own. The first two of these married Chinggiside princesses: Kunbuqa married Yelmish (*Yeh-li-mi-shih* in Chinese), daughter of Guyuk Khan, and Ai-buqa married Yurak (*Yueh-lieh* in Chinese), daughter of Kublai Khan. Ai-buqa and Yurak had a son they named George (*K'uo-li-chi-ssu*), who first married Qutadmish (*Hu-ta-ti-mi-shih*), daughter of Kublai's son Chen-kin, then married Ayamish (*Ai-ya-shih-li*), Tumur Khan's daughter.[7]

There are problems in establishing the genealogy exactly. The Mongol record in *The Secret History* and the Chinese record in the *Yuan Shih* are irreconcilable at several points. Marco Polo believed King George was sixth in line from Prester John (Unc Khan). The main problem is that the Mongol naming system incorporates double-barrelled names, where either half may be used. To add to this, either half of the name may be shortened to a nickname, giving any one person the possibility of five names. The incorporation of titles into the name creates further confusion. And terms like 'daughter' or 'son' tend to be used generically to mean 'descendant'. The Ongut connections with the Chinggiside family are definitely there, if confusing at points.

George and the Onguts embrace Catholicism

George's conversion to Catholicism was a breakthrough for Montecorvino's mission. The Kerait had converted en masse to Nestorianism at the beginning of the eleventh century, and here now were their descendants, the Onguts, still Nestorian two centuries later. As the original Unc-Khan led the Keraits into Nestorianism, so his descendant King George led the Onguts from Nestorianism into Catholicism. It was another 'people movement'. Apart from building a church, George adopted the Franciscan order and assisted Montecorvino at Da-tu. Montecorvino was frustrated at his own inability to give good pastoral care to George and the Onguts due to the distance they were from Da-tu. Perhaps George advised Montecorvino with his translation of the New Testament and Psalms, and even used it among his own people. Montecorvino saw George as an intimate colleague, and was devastated when he died. That George had named his son John (*Tchou-ngan* in Chinese) in Montecorvino's honour bears witness to their close relationship.

Montecorvino's colleague, Brother Peregrine, wrote to the Pope and among other things, gives good testimony to Montecorvino's ministry to George and the Onguts: 'For as to that King George, it is certain that Montecorvino converted him completely and worthily to the true faith, though previously George had mingled with the Nestorians. And the King himself [that is, George] in one day converted several thousands of his people. And had he lived, we should indeed have subdued his whole people and kingdom to Christ, and a change might even have been wrought with the Great Khan.'[8]

Archaeologists discover Olon Sum

Montecorvino's letter mentions George building a church. The ruins of this church are situated at an archaeological site called Olon-sum ('Many Temples') about twenty kilometres north of Pailingmiao, in Inner Mongolia. This 1000m by 600m enclosure was discovered in 1929 by Houang Wen-pi, a member of Sven Hedin's expedition in north-west China, and in 1932 Owen Lattimore found many stone pillars there with Nestorian crosses on them.

In 1937 the Japanese scholar Egami suggested that a Catholic church was among the ancient structures and that this town had been the capital of the Onguts. Later excavations in 1938 revealed the base of a Gothic chapel, the corner stone of which had a Christian cross superimposed on a Buddhist lotus blossom. This confirmed Egami's hypothesis. In total, two churches, one Catholic, the other Nestorian, and numerous tombstones with Nestorian crosses have been found at the site. It is reasonable to conclude that this was the church that George built, probably in 1292. Certainly it was a Nestorian centre, probably the Ongut capital of Kosang that Sauma mentions, and which Mark was originally from. Egami suggests that the tomb of George is near Olon-sum, 'about one kilometre east of the city walls'.[9]

Christianity and the demise of the Mongols in China

That Nestorianism had so permeated the Chinggiside family by intermarriage with the Kerait and Ongut tribes is evidence again of the tolerance which the *yasa* afforded. That subsequent Yuan Khans accommodated the two forms of Christianity, Nestorianism and Catholicism, also bears witness to this. The doctrinal difference between the two Christian sects was of no consequence to them.

Although Catholicism gained a foothold in Da-tu and further down the coast, Nestorianism held strong in the hinterland. Kosang (Olon Sum) was probably the centre of this Nestorianism. The intermarriage of the Onguts and the Chinggisides ensured that the Onguts remained political allies of the Chinggisides. Nestorianism had great influence among the tribes of modern-day Gansu as well as the Onguts. This visible and active presence of Christianity must have been resented by the subsequent Ming who sought to erase it along with the Mongols.

The Khans after Kublai became more sinocised and lost their original nomadic warring spirit. With this decline in their essential mongol-ness came a decline in their allegiance to their own Chinggiside heritage. Nestorianism faired better than Catholicism in the long term. During the Yuan Khanate, Nestorianism had been better established before the Catholics arrived in China. Also, because of intermarriage, Nestorianism was more familiar to the Chinggisides.

When the Ming conquerors pushed the Mongols back to their steppe lands in 1368 to 1370, they saw the Onguts as political, if not religious allies of the Chinggiside Mongols and therefore their enemies. Hence the razing of Olon Sum and the end of a unique Christian dynastic succession. The Ming saw Nestorianism as a religion foreign to China intimately associated with the Mongols, such that when the Ming pushed out the Mongols, Nestorianism (and Catholicism) went with it. In essence, the Ming understood Christianity to be a Mongol religion.

After the fall of Yuan, the Mongols retreated to their steppe hinterland, where they became subject to the Manchus until finally gaining independence over five hundred years later in 1911.

———————

I found this lack of interconnectedness in the Mongolian naming system quite confusing to start with. I wanted to pigeonhole everyone and sort out their relationships in my mind. In New Zealand, where everyone is a migrant from somewhere else, our genealogy is important. I could trace my family back eight generations to the Shetland Islands, and could name the ship they came on to New Zealand.

But the Mongols all knew who they were related to. It was me who was the foreigner.

'Tell me about the titles that you do have,' I asked in class one day. I'd noticed that the parents all called their children *khuu* which I knew meant 'son'. I'd also noticed that I kept making mistakes in trying to guess the sex of a child. All the children had long hair done up in a fancy ribbon. There was no way to tell at first glance if a child was male or female. Again, I guessed it was something to do with fooling the evil spirits.

'*Khuu* must mean either boy or girl, right? It would be like "child" in English,' I suggested.

My teacher agreed, making that odd inhaled clicking sound. '*Duu* is another word like it. It means a younger sibling, either male or female.'

That title had been really confusing. Only the day before, a friend had introduced her *duu* to us. I had never realised she had a *duu*. When I explored the relationship some more, I discovered that the *duu* was a third cousin twice removed. Age, I guess, was the main defining parameter.

Akh for older brother, and *Ekhch* for older sister were more precise.

My teacher explained some more. 'Everyone will have a title after their name. It designates their relationship to you, or their status in society. Because you are a teacher, the Mongols will call you Hugh-*bagsh*; literally Hugh-the-teacher.'

My family name was obviously inconsequential. In our church, I noticed that Karen's title changed depending on her role. Normally, she was 'Karen-*ekhch*', or 'Karen-our-older-sister'. If she taught a Sunday school lesson or led a homegroup, she would temporarily become 'Karen-*bagsh*' or 'Karen-the-teacher'.

I felt nervous having the title of 'Hugh-*bagsh*'. I really didn't want to promote a pedestal mentality, and so I set out to lower my title. I thought 'Hugh-*akh*' would sit better: 'Hugh-our-older-brother' was more in accord with the Christian doctrine of the priesthood of all believers. With close Mongol friends, I was pleased it eventually caught on.

Not so my three-year-old daughter who told me one day: 'Daddy, your name isn't Hugh Bagsh. It's Hugh Kemp!'

NOTES

1. C. Dawson, ed., *Mission to Asia; Narratives and Letters of the Franciscan Missionaries in Mongolia and China in the 13th and 14th Centuries*, trans. a nun of Stanbrook Abbey (NY: Harper & Row, 1966), 225.

2. H.H. Howorth, 'The Northern Frontagers of China. Part VIII. Article IV: The Kirais and Prester John', *Journal of the Royal Asiatic Society* (1889): 424.

3. U. Onon, trans. *The History and the Life of Chinggis Khan; The Secret History of the Mongols* (Leiden: E.J.Brill, 1990), 91.

4. See also René Grousset, *The Empire of the Steppes: A History of Central Asia*, trans. Naomi Walford (USA: Rutgers University Press, 1970), 583, footnote 78.

5. 'Ala-ad-Din 'Ata-Malik Juvaini, *The History of the World Conqueror*, trans. John Andrew Boyle (Manchester: Manchester University Press, 1958), 550,

6. U. Onon, trans., *The History and the Life of Chinggis Khan; The Secret History of the Mongols* (Leiden: E.J.Brill, 1990), 91.

7. Grousset has based his genealogy on the Yuan Shih, the text of which is more readily available in A.C. Moule, *Christians in China before the Year 1550* (London: SPCK, 1930), 234–236.

8. C. Dawson, ed., *Mission to Asia; Narratives and Letters of the Franciscan Missionaries in*

Mongolia and China in the 13th and 14th Centuries, trans. a nun of Stanbrook Abbey (NY: Harper & Row, 1966), 232.

9. Namio Egami, 'Olon-sume et la découverte de l'église catholique romaine de Jean de Montecorvino', *Journal Asiatique* 240 (1952): 166.

Chapter 22

Odoric of Pordenone and John of Marignolli,

Last Catholic Missionaries to a Dying Empire

'We [Franciscans] have a place of abode appointed out for us in the emperor's court, and are enjoined to go and bestow our blessing upon him. And I enquired of certain courtiers concerning the number of persons pertaining to the emperor's court. They answered me... the Christians also were eight in number.'

Odoric of Pordenone

'Where are the turnips?' I asked Markus. 'All I can see are weeds!'

I didn't think this first harvest at Khurkhree was going to be much. Khurkhree meant 'Waterfalls', an unusual name considering that we were standing in a semi-desert area of south-western Mongolia. It was a huge wide open valley with jagged mountains in the near distance. I guessed the water in the irrigation channels came from a spring higher up. Apart from the vivid emerald green of this twenty-hectare vegetable plot, there was not a tree in sight. And it was hot. Very hot.

Markus was an agronomist from Switzerland and in charge of reviving an old irrigation system which the Russians had originally started, but they had begun going home in 1990 and things had fallen into disrepair. The residual cluster of Mongolian families struggled to keep the site productive due to a combination of lack of skill, inter-family bickering, laziness and a general disinterestedness in vegetables in the first place.

We rummaged through the knee-high nettles and other weeds. Markus showed me which leaves belonged to the turnips underneath. Five Mongol men had come with us out to the site. They were mildly excited about the potential harvest.

Nomads kept moving, so learning to cultivate a vegetable plot would be a lifetime process.

'It's just enough to get the water here and the seedlings in rows. Weeding is next year's lesson,' he replied.

Getting some vegetables into the Mongolian diet was imperative. They lived off boiled mutton, dairy products and sweets. Gertrud, Markus' wife and graduate in home sciences, taught the women how to cook the vegetables.

Markus stood up and pointed at the fencing: 'We had to go down to the Chinese border to buy all those fence posts. The fencing is electric. Runs off a solar panel. It's to keep the horses and camels out.'

We got about ten good sacks of turnips. Not too bad at all for the first harvest. The men bundled them onto the trailer and we bounced our way in our Russian 'sixty-nine' jeep eight hours back to Altai, the *aimag* centre.

'What else have you planted at Khurkhree?' I asked Markus as we unloaded the sacks at the local grocery shop.

'Carrots, onions, beetroot, potatoes. We have a few experimental plots. Plus we're aiming at seed stock as well. All the original seed came from overseas. A container load of seed was sent to the project last year.'

Odoric of Pordenone

John of Montecorvino had single-handedly set up a Catholic mission to Mongol-ruled China. In answer to his pleas for help, a handful of other Franciscans followed. The last two Franciscan missionaries to Mongol China were Odoric of Pordenone and John of Marignolli. Both had a sojourn in Datu and recognised the spadework that Montecorvino had put in, and both commented not only on the extent of the Nestorian presence in Mongol-China, but also of its demise.

Odoric left Europe for the east in 1318, and travelled extensively throughout Asia. He went to China by boat via Ceylon, but returned to Europe via the Silk Road. He spent several years at the church that Montecorvino founded in Da-tu:

> I, Friar Odoric, was present in person for the space of three years, and was often at the banquets, for we Minor Friars [ie the Franciscans] have a place of abode appointed out for us in the emperor's court, and are enjoined to go and bestow our blessing upon him. And I inquired of certain courtiers concerning the number of persons pertaining to the emperor's court. They answered me... the Christians also were eight in number, together with one Saracen.[1]

He also observed Montecorvino's influence as he travelled through China: he found Franciscan communities in Fujian, Hangzhou and Yangzhou provinces. He reports that the Franciscans in Zayton had two residences there.

Odoric comments on the Christian interest shown by the Khan, Yesun Temur (r.1323–1328): 'Upon a certain time when he [the Khan] was coming towards Khanbaliq, or Da-tu, the fame of his approach being published, a bishop of ours, with certain of our Minorite Friars and myself, went two days journey to meet him... and we put a cross upon wood... and began to sing... and when we came near to him, he veiled his hat... doing reverence to the cross.' According to another translator: 'he removed his head-dress... and bowed in reverence before the cross. The bishop pronounced his blessing and the grand khan kissed the cross with great devotion.'[2] Odoric reports that in this entourage of the Khan were 'certain of his barons, which had been converted to the faith by friars of our order, being at the same time in his army'.

Odoric's zeal for the propagation of the gospel drove him inland from Da-tu, going through the Wall into Mongol heartland where he discovered communities of Nestorians. He claims that he persuaded many to convert to Catholicism: he was unimpressed by their lax morals in particular. He also relates that he baptised 'a great number of infidels' during his journey in central Asia.

Odoric's writings were an immediate hit in Europe on his return in 1328, being more popular than Marco Polo's works. He died in Italy, his native country, in 1331.

John of Marignolli: the last papal ambassador

John of Marignolli (sometimes referred to as John of Florence) was also an Italian Franciscan. Born about 1290, his travels to east Asia were between 1338 and 1353, sent by Pope Benedict XII (r.1334–1342). He was the last papal ambassador to the Mongol Khan's court. On the way to China he paid pastoral calls on several Christian communities across central Asia.

Like Odoric before him, Marignolli spent several years in Da-tu, arriving in May or June of 1342. The reigning Khan, Toghon Temur (r.1333–1370), the eleventh and final Khan in the House of Kublai, received him that August. Marignolli made a grand entrance with incense burning, a retinue of thirty-two and gifts of warhorses from Europe.

On arrival in Khanbaliq, Marignolli was quick to observe the legacy of Montecorvino. The Franciscans had a cathedral church 'immediately adjoining the palace, with a proper residence for the Archbishop, and other churches in the city besides, and they have bells too, and all the clergy have their subsistence from the Emperor's table in the most honourable manner'. Marignolli travelled down to Zayton to the Franciscan houses there and observed 'three very fine churches, passing rich and elegant'.[3]

Marignolli left China in December 1347. Arriving back at the Pope's court at Avignon in 1353, he claimed, 'we made a great harvest of souls in that empire.' He brought with him letters from Toghon Temur expressing esteem for Christianity, and declaring that all Christians in his empire give allegiance to the Pope (now Innocent VI). These letters also asked for more missionaries. That request proved ironical, for Toghon Temur was to be the last of the Mongol Khans to rule China. The Ming Chinese had already started to foment revolution, and Toghon Temur retains the dubious honour of having been chased out of China back to the Mongol steppes. In these dying gasps of a once-magnificent empire, any vestiges of Christianity disappeared completely.

Christianity on the central Asian steppe at the end of the Yuan dynasty: a summary

In essence, Christianity came into the Mongol consciousness through the back door. The Nestorian Kerait tribe proved influential through well-placed bureaucrats, generals and queens. They gave protection to the persecuted, influenced official policy in favour of Christians, and in the case of the queens, directed the line of succession and groomed future Khans. The Nestorian church had royal patronage from time to time which allowed for its growth. And Franciscan missionaries had relative freedom to move and preach in Mongol realms. But did Christianity take root among the Mongols as a unique exclusive phenomenon? Was conversion genuine? Or was there a prevailing plurastic atmosphere that demanded a syncretistic absorption of whatever Christian sect was in town?

Some key Mongol princes were attracted by Christian doctrine rather than religious or political expediency. Nestorianism was widespread enough among the Mongol nobility such that Chinese Ming historians thought the Mongols were Christians. Rumours abounded in Europe of the conversion of Khans and princes. But the picture remains misty. Among the Great Khans, the House of Kublai and the House of Hulegu, there were many foreigners serving in the courts, many of them Christian. The wishful thinking of European travellers fuelled rumours in Europe, and even the vast numbers of Nestorians in Yuan China were probably more foreign than Mongol.

The religious dynamics of the Mongols in their empire were

a unique blend of Shamanism, Nestorianism and an emergent Tibetan-Buddhism in the homelands. In Persia, the Mongols had to interact with Islam, and further west, the Golden Horde interacted with Russian Orthodox Christianity. But originally the first Christian expression the Mongols encountered was Nestorian which they discovered when they conquered the Kerait.

Why the Mongols embraced Nestorianism

The Mongols embraced Nestorianism for several reasons.

First, to be Kerait was to be Nestorian
The Kerait had converted en masse to Christianity in the first decades of the eleventh century and Nestorianism had become the 'state religion'. Being the official tribal religion, it may well have lost an evangelistic drive and therefore been less threatening to Mongol Shamanism than was Catholicism. Rubruck is scathing about the Nestorians' lack of Christian graces on his travels through central Asia and while resident at Karakorum.

Secondly, the Kerait Nestorians had converted from Shamanism themselves
Shamanism was the dominant religious worldview of the central Asian steppe. By the time Chinggis conquered the Kerait, Shamanism and Christianity had made room for each other. The Khans absorbed Nestorian Christianity: they took Kerait wives and employed Keraits in their courts. Likewise, when Kublai ruled China, he inherited a large Nestorian population in the hinterland. Nestorianism had been well ensconced in central Asia and China before the Mongols rose to power. It was not a new import, whereas Western European Catholicism was.

Thirdly, Nestorianism had gained respect among the Mongols before Catholicism arrived

Nestorian governors, queens and generals all proved able rulers. Nestorianism was an Asian phenomenon. In one sense it became an indigenous religion of central Asia from the seventh century. Similarly, these Asian Christians had brought their writing with them, which the Sogdians, then Uighurs had adopted. Chinggis adapted this writing to form the basis of record-keeping and communication in his empire. His administrative networks were the direct result of Nestorian literacy. Their script has since evolved into *mongol bichig* which is still used in Mongolia today. In contrast, Catholicism was a religion that had come from 'over there'; Europe was seen as a potential enemy, good only for the grasslands she could offer to the Mongol horses, a small garden on the edges of a huge empire. Why then should the Mongols embrace the religion of their soon-to-be-conquered subordinates?

Fourthly, Nestorianism had the internal fortitude to last the distance in central Asia

It had weathered many a persecution in its early days as it was rejected from Palestine in the fifth century, and indeed it was persecution that pushed it eastwards along the Silk Road in the sixth and seventh centuries. It endured waves of persecution during the T'ang dynasty of China, declined, then made a comeback. Because it was cut off periodically from its sending source of Syria, it had to rely on its own resilience to persevere. The Nestorian centres in central Asia rarely saw their patriarch or metropolitan visit to offer pastoral care because of the distance and the periodic outbreaks of war that blocked the Silk Road. Nestorianism had no other option but to adapt quickly in order to survive.

Catholicism however tried to get established while the Mongols were at the height of power. They did not need the Catholics during the Great Khanate, and during the Il-Khanate, their links with Catholic Europe mainly had a political agenda.

That Carpini and Rubruck had first come to ascertain the military strength of the Mongols was not lost on Guyuk or Munkh. Meeting two European Catholic spies did not encourage the Mongols to embrace their religion. So from the beginning, Catholicism asserted itself from a position of weakness while the Mongols were in a position of strength.

The *yasa* rules on

Odoric's first impressions of China were amazement at the diversity of peoples: Chinese, Mongol, Buddhist, Nestorian and Muslim. He admired Mongol administration: 'the fact that so many different races are able to live together peaceably under the control of a single power seems to me one of the greatest wonders of the world.'[4] That all could live together in China is testimony of the efficacy of the *yasa*. As long as each people gave their allegiance to the Khan and were law-abiding citizens, each was free to practise the religion of their choice.

Chinggis' *yasa* was the prevailing ideology of the Mongols. Enshrined in this was the ethic of religious tolerance. This expressed itself in Munkh's criterion of inclusiveness during the inter-religious debate he arbitrated. The influence of the *yasa* has reached down through the centuries to affect the lives of modern Mongols. With the fall of Communism, lamaistic Buddhism now has the freedom to rebuild itself and present a uniquely post-Communist face in the twenty-first century. What is evident is not only a renewed practice of Buddhism, but the resurrection of ancient Shamanistic rituals. Indeed, sometimes the two are indistinguishable. In awarding Buddhism the free run of his people, Munkh effectively protected the ancient Shamanism. The conduit of this protection was the *yasa*.

The *yasa* also afforded to Christianity the freedom to expand. However, a 'critical mass' was never reached in Christian witness in central Asia. Lost opportunities abound, the most obvious being the poor response to Kublai's invitation to send a hundred Christian teachers from Europe. For Christian witness today, evangelists can rightly appeal to the principles enshrined in the *yasa* to claim the freedom to move and preach. However, to ensure that Christianity regains its place in Mongol thinking, it must be expressed in culturally appropriate ways that will be recognised by the Mongol, and so attract the Mongol to the gospel of Christ.

Markus' agricultural project in Gobi-Altai worked well, considering the odds stacked against it. I had nabbed some of the seed from that shipping container. Markus was keen for people to experiment with small garden plots around the city. I was tired of vitamin pills. Karen wanted fresh lettuce. So we thought we'd give a garden plot a go.

We started with silverbeet in window boxes in the bedroom. It didn't fit the decor of the room, but it was nice to have fresh silverbeet. We mentioned to a friend that we had access to seed.

'My father-in-law lives in Sharkhad in a *ger*. I'm sure he'll let you plant something out in his *hasha*,' Chimgee told us.

Ulaanbaatar is surrounded by suburbs of *gers*, the round white tents. Because the residents are semi-permanent, a rabbit warren of *hashas* or fenced compounds has grown up over the years. Enterprising families keep chickens or the odd sheep or goat in their *hasha*, and some grow spring onions commercially, judging from the odd garden plot you can sometimes see.

Sharkhad, or 'Yellow Rock' was about half an hour's ride on the bus outside Ulaanbaatar. To make the garden plot work, I knew I'd have to go out there at least every weekend and possibly once or twice during the week. It was going to be a huge commitment. We were a bit idealistic that summer: we thought that pottering around a vegetable plot while the kids paddled in the irrigation channels and sunbathed on the grass banks with sheep and cattle lowing in the distance would be a nice way to spend the season.

Sharkhad was windswept and dusty. The soil was exceedingly poor. And I just couldn't get there regularly to tend to the plot. Neither could I guarantee an adequate water supply.

'Could you make sure it gets watered every day,' I asked Chimgee's brother-in-law who was living in the second *ger* in the *hasha*.

'*Zugeer*,' he said. 'It's not a problem. I'll haul the water up from the creek down there in this jerry can.'

This seemed satisfactory enough. A colleague of mine living in Murun in north-west Mongolia had trained his Alsatian dog to take a bridle and pull a trolley with a water can on it. I hoped my new friend was as innovative.

He wasn't, and the harvest was embarrassingly pitiful. I had figured that the garden would need about six cans, twice a day. That was a lot of work. I never was convinced he watered the plot sufficiently. They kept whatever carrots and turnips there were, and we took all the leafy vegetables. The lettuces never hearted and some fungus got into the cauliflower.

On my last bus ride back from Sharkhad that summer, I got to thinking about my vegetable plot. It was a good metaphor for the history of Christianity in Mongolia. The gospel seed had come from overseas, but the soil was poor, the garden was irregularly tended, and the watering was erratic. When that hot wind blew through Sharkhad, it battered the seedlings and sucked what little moisture there was out of the ground. The seedlings never got the strong start they needed. They never got to that critical point of strength; they never really 'hardened up' into mature vegetables.

NOTES
1. M. Komroff, *Contemporaries of Marco Polo*. (London: J.Cape, 1928), 245.
2. R. Grousset, *The Empire of the Steppes: A History of Central Asia* (USA: Rutgers University Press, 1970), 317.
3. H. Yule, trans. and ed. *Cathay and the Way Thither; Being a Collection of Medieval Notices of China*. 2nd edition. Rev. H. Cordier. (Nendeln/Liechtenstein: Kraus Reprint Ltd., 1967), 229.
4. R. Grousset, *The Empire of the Steppes: A History of Central Asia* (USA: Rutgers University Press, 1970), 316.

Section 2

Eighteenth to Twenty-first Centuries

Part **5**

The Moravians

Chapter 23

The Moravian Brethren,
Mission to the Torgut Mongols

'I have but one passion... 'tis He, 'tis only He. To seek for souls, souls, in order that Jesus may receive those who love Him. That is my work.'

Count Zinzendorf

I first heard of the Moravians through a fellow student. I was in Mussoorie, India at the time, a hill-station town about 300 kilometres north of Delhi in the foothills of the Himalayas. I was a dorm parent for junior boys at Woodstock International School. Thespal Kundan and I were both doing a Theological Education by Extension course.

Thespal was a Ladhaki from Leh in north-east Kashmir. When I knew him, he was teaching at The Moravian Institute in Rajpur, near Mussoorie.

'Moravian missionaries planted our church last century.' I had invited him for a cup of *chai* and sweets after our tutorial. I could never pass Omi's sweet shop in the Landour bazaar without indulging myself.

'So who are the Moravians?' I asked. I was curious, knowing that Ladhakh was a Tibetan Buddhist region in north India. I didn't realise it at the time, but an indigenous Christian church among the Tibetans was very rare.

A shop-boy plonked down our two cups of hot *chai* on the table. 'Are the *gulab jamuns* fresh?' I asked. Freshness was the guiding principle when buying Indian sweets. Flies, heat, dust and grime quickly accumulated on anything sitting around in shop windows. *Gulab jamuns* are small dumplings soaked in rose-water syrup. They're nauseatingly sweet. I love them.

'They're still warm,' he replied.

'Two each,' I ordered.

Thespal continued: 'A count by the name of Zinzendorf in Europe started the Moravians from a group of Protestant refugees who had found sanctuary on his estate in the eighteenth century. They were called the Unity of the Brethren to start with.'

The boy returned with the *gulab jamuns*. I'd once eaten eighteen *gulab jamuns* in an afternoon, sitting in a tea shop after a long hike in the Himalayas. We'd planned our menu poorly and had eaten a lot of unleavened *chapattis* and peanut butter. My hiking partner and I had craved something sweet all that week. I think he ate about twenty-five.

'Zinzendorf was passionate about mission. Plus he wanted to see the end to all the religious bickering that had been going on in Europe. Some call him the father of the ecumenical movement. The Moravians had a huge mission agenda. They sent out one missionary for every sixty home members. I think in the West today, the ratio is more like one in five thousand.'

The Moravian Brethren

The Moravians were the spiritual descendants of Jan Hus (1374–1415). Hus was a Czech who wrote and preached for personal piety and purity of life. In pre-Reformation Europe, he was brave in promoting an evangelical view of Scripture as authoritative in the church. He also taught that clergy were unable to offer forgiveness of sin, and that this could come only from God. Hus was condemned by Rome as a heretic and burned at the stake, but in 1457, some of his supporters organised themselves into the Unity of the Brethren. These Brethren stressed the unique authority of the Bible (as opposed to the authority of the Catholic Church). They differed in the celebration of communion from the Roman mass, and they promoted disciplined Christian living. For these things they were harassed and suppressed by the dominant Roman church, and suffered greatly during the Thirty Years War (1618–1648).

Brethren refugees from the war survived and grouped themselves from 1722 under the leadership of Nikolaus Ludwig

Count von Zinzendorf (1700–1760). They were joined by the German pietist movement, and numbers of Protestant sympathisers, including Lutherans, Reformed, Separatists and Anabaptists. Together they became what we now know as the Moravian Brethren. The name came from the original homeland of the movement, that is Moravia, south-east of modern Prague in the Czech Republic, bordering Austria. These Moravian Brethren never intended becoming a denomination, but saw their role as bringing leaven to existing Protestant churches. The movement had to adopt a formal structure to survive, and it did so along evangelical pietist lines. This base became the centre for a worldwide missionary movement.

Count Zinzendorf was a passionate visionary for Christian unity. He sent out expeditions to establish where efforts should be concentrated. His first missionaries to the lower Volga were Conrad Lange, Zechariah Hirschel and Michael Kund between 1742 and 1748, but they never made it, as Russian authorities accused them of spying and they languished in a gaol in St Petersburg for five years. However, Empress Catherine II (r.1768–1776) was openly sympathetic to the spread of Christianity, and allowed the Moravians to send enough German settlers to the lower Volga to establish a Christian colony, which they called Sarepta. Thus was born the Moravian mission to the Kalmucks: Sarepta was right in the heart of Kalmuck grazing lands.

Who were the Kalmucks?

The Kalmucks were Torgut Mongols. On the lower reaches of the Volga River, before it empties into the Caspian Sea, a tribe of Mongols appeared in 1630. The chief of this tribe and his six sons had crossed the Ural Mountains with 25,000 troops and simply subdued the tribes of the Russian steppe. They plundered the villages and tried to conquer Astrakhan on the mouth of the Volga. Failing in this, they settled in the hinterland. These were the Torguts, and they were to be followed by other Mongol tribes.

Despite sporadic warring with the Zungars, who now dominated the Mongolian steppe, the Torgut maintained much of their previous culture, including their Shamanism, some vestiges of Buddhism, and their Mongol language. But the Russians did not remain accommodating to this foreign group, and between 1725 and 1770 they harassed the Torguts. Tensions mounted as the Torguts lobbied for more independence, while the Russians tried to appoint the Torgut leadership themselves. In between periodic oaths to the Russian Tsar, the Torguts pillaged Russian villages. The Tsar was tolerant at first, if for no other reason than the Torguts also helped defend the southern border from the Muslims. But then Russian patience ran out, and Empress Elizabeth encircled the Volga steppe with fortresses and increased Russian colonisation of the area.

The Torguts understood these actions to mean that the Russians wanted to make them sedentary house-dwellers. Naturally they were alarmed. It was rumoured that there was vacant land in the fertile steppes of western China, and a return 'home' sounded attractive. They were separated from things Buddhist, and there was a threat that the Russians wanted to force them to become Christians according to the Orthodox tradition, and bring them under the rule of Dorbet-Mongols who had become Orthodox Christians and been partly Europeanised. A persuasive orator, Obush Khan, summoned the tribes to 'return home' and several hundred thousand started migrating eastward again.

Under normal conditions the whole tribe could have left on the same night. The Volga had frozen over, and those pitched on the western side of the river could simply cross the ice and join those on the eastern bank. However, a terrible storm broke up the ice on the night of 4 January 1771, as the migration was just getting underway, and it became impossible to get across. The inhabitants of some 15,000 Mongol tents were unable to move with the rest of their people. It was this 'left behind' tribe that became known as the 'Kalmucks', this name coming from a Turkish/Mongol word meaning 'those who remained behind'.

Work among the Kalmucks proved slow and difficult, producing little fruit. The Moravians managed to baptise only one convert to Christianity between the mission's start in 1764 and the end of the century. In fact the mission was abandoned in 1800 due to the inability of the Moravians to persuade the Kalmucks to turn from their Lamaism to the gospel of Jesus Christ.

The Moravians try again: the planting of the first Mongolian Protestant church

However, the British and Foreign Bible Society (BFBS), which had started a branch in St Petersburg, made an attempt to reopen the mission in 1815, with Tsar Alexander 1's approval. The work was initiated by Isaak Schmidt, whose story we pick up again later. A small Kalmuck congregation was formed at Sarepta, under the leadership of a man called Sodnom, a Torgut Mongol, who had also persuaded his brother to become a Christian. And so the first Protestant Mongol church was born. This congregation enjoyed an active presence for seven years. In 1818 it numbered twenty-three adults. In 1821, tribal authorities expelled them from the Khoshote horde and they were forced to relocate to the opposite bank of the Volga.

This congregation attracted the attention of the Russian authorities also. Russian law said that all converts had to be baptised into the Russian Orthodox Church: the Moravians were told they had to surrender their converts. This they did, but it proved the death knell of the mission and the Moravians withdrew from Sarepta for good in 1822.

H.A. Zwick, one of the Moravian missionaries writes:

The question what was to become of the exiles who had settled near Sarepta was decided in 1823. On the 12th of October in that year, fifteen Kalmucks of the Dorbet horde, headed by a Lama priest, made a plundering expedition upon their believing (that is, Christian) countrymen; one of them named Lurum escaped with difficulty. Nothing remained for the oppressed but to put themselves under the Russian protection at Zaritzin. Sodnom and his brother were baptised there into the Orthodox Greek Church, and so ended the efforts of the Sarepta Brothers for the conversion of the Kalmucks.[1]

However, the Moravian influence had not merely been limited to this small congregation. The number of Kalmuck men who were nominally Christian may have reached as many as 12,000. The Russian authorities were certainly threatened by their presence and transplanted them north to the area of Samara, and south to the city of Stavropol, just north of the Caucasus mountains. In Stavropol, the Russians tried to russify them and make them sedentary by building them churches, schools and houses. Orthodox priests continued some work among these Kalmucks but without much success, and it seems that the Kalmuck Christians remained Christian only in name, perhaps to avoid Russian military service.

The return of the Torguts

Between thirty and sixty thousand people left the Volga steppe on 5 January 1771, under the leadership of Obush Khan. Their departure was abrupt and final, leaving their burning home-steads behind. They received the protection of the Manchurian emperor Chien-Lung and were allowed to settle on the banks of the River Ili, between Xinjiang province and Kazakhstan, and also just north of the modern province of Gansu. Why the Manchurians welcomed them back is a mystery. Perhaps by allowing them only the grazing lands on the far western border, the Chinese emperor wanted the Torguts 'out of sight and out of mind'.

Their return to Mongol central Asia was for religious reasons.

Oppression from the Muscovite princes and the Orthodox Church, as well as growing serfdom under Muslim overlords around the Caspian Sea all contributed to this. The solution seemed simple enough: return to the land of Lamaism where they would be able to practise their own religion.

Although they had an optimistic and enthusiastic departure, their numbers dwindled en route. They had to travel some 3800 kilometres across central Asian steppe and desert. Thousands died from cold, heat or famine, and they were constantly harassed by the Russian cavalry. Millions of livestock perished, and when this bedraggled ragtag assortment of wanderers arrived on the borders of China, they numbered barely a third of the original number with only a handful of horses and camels.

There is a certain irony at this point. The Torguts were fleeing from growing constraints from both Russian authorities and the Orthodox Church. But when they arrived in the Ili valley, they found another form of Christianity. The Franciscans had established a Christian centre called Ily-Ballik there from as early as the fourteenth century, during the decline of the Mongol Yuan dynasty. They had built a magnificent church. Furthermore, Ili later became the Gulag of China, to which criminals were banished and to which Chinese Christians who refused to apostasise were also sent.

Mildred Cable (see Chapter 43), noted in 1929 that the Torgut Mongols (whom she calls 'Kalmucks') were well established in the area and the surrounding Altai mountains and were pursuing their ancient nomadic ways of cattle-ranging and were practising Lamaism.[2] What became of the Franciscan mission isn't known, but the modern CICM order of the Catholic Church had 300 Catholic members in five sub-stations in the area by 1920. This number must have included Torguts. George Hunter, another CIM missionary who worked out of Urumqi between 1908 and 1946, records making contact with Torgut Mongols in the area, and some professing conversion to Christ.

We sat at Omi's for some time talking, and I had another three plates of *gulab jamuns*. I watched the cook making the next batch of *barfi*, a white milk-based sweet. He was sitting cross-legged on a slightly raised earthen platform that was discoloured by decades of grime. A huge wok sat atop an opening over an enclosed wood fire that drew air in from the street.

He was at the front of the shop, and I'm sure that his theatrical style of cooking was to attract more patrons. He liberally attacked the simmering broth of milk and sugar with a metre-long ladle, mixing, stirring, and on every fourth move, he raised the ladle to shoulder height and poured the contents back into the wok with great to-do. All this among wafting clouds of steam and flies.

He was short and fat, dressed in a singlet and wrap-around *lungi*, and sweating profusely. He wiped his brow with his hand and flicked the sweat into the milk.

'Oh well, at least it's cooked,' I thought. Thespal sipped his *chai*.

Then the cook blew his nose. No handkerchief, but Indian style: block the side of one nostril with the thumb, and with the index finger twist the nose so the other nostril is pointing in the direction you desire, then blow. Do the same for the other nostril. At least he had the sense to aim into the aisle.

Then he wiped his brow again (with the same hand), and flicked the sweat into the wok.

Thespal interrupted my gaze. 'The Moravians sent missionaries to the Mongols. They had some success with a tribe in Russia, and so they wanted to send some to real Mongol territory. Those missionaries tried to get to Mongolia by way of India but couldn't get through Tibet. They just stayed and planted a church in Ladhakh instead.'

The sweetmaker blew his nose again, and flicked more sweat into the boiling milk. I felt a wave of nausea pass over me.

It was getting on a bit, and I had to be back at school for my dorm-parenting duties after the boys' classes finished. It was good to have heard something of the Moravian story. We said our farewells till the following week, and I paid the man at the front desk.

'*Sahib*,' he said as he handed me my change. '*Barfi* is very fresh. It is made now, only. Would you like to be trying some?'

NOTES
1. Quoted in H.H. Howorth, *History of the Mongols; From the 9th to the 19th Century* (London: Burt Franklin, 1876), 1:679.
2. M.Cable, F.Houghton, R.Kilgour, A.Mcleish, R.W. Sturt and O.Wyon., *The Challenge of Central Asia* (London: World Dominion Press, 1929), 47.

Chapter 24

Isaak Jakob Schmidt,
Merchant, Scholar and Bible Translator

'Commissioned by the Ministers of the Interior, and National Education, I have examined this version of Genesis in Mongolian and have found it consonant with the various Protestant versions; as such I recommend it for publication.'

I.J. Schmidt, censor for the Russian authorities, referring to the LMS Bible translation

I'd never seen a *ger* being set up or taken down. Bold informed me that he'd be shifting his *ger*; his relatives were coming from the countryside and he needed to fit another ger into his *hasha*. The surrounding hills of Ulaanbaatar were quilted with a patchwork of compounds, with several tents in each one. Did I want to come and see how to set up a Mongol tent in his compound?

'I'll come,' I replied enthusiastically. 'May I bring a friend? She's a professional photographer who arrives tomorrow and is doing a promotional video on Mongolia.'

'Of course,' Bold replied.

Darla was planning to go to Afghanistan long-term to make health education videos for rural development programmes, but the war there had delayed those plans. My agency was making good use of her professional skills doing promo videos throughout Asia.

We showed up at the *hasha* just as Bold and two others were starting to take the outer white canvas cover off the *ger*. Darla was armed with photographic paraphernalia. I took the opportunity to bring my camera too.

Juggling cameras, we found the whole process fascinating.

It took exactly half an hour to dismantel the *ger*. After the outside cover was removed, the inner felt layers were stripped back to reveal a lattice framework with about seventy roof ribbings reaching up from the lattice walls to the *tawn*, the round window structure that is held up by two wooden pillars. This skeletal structure was tied together with odd pieces of twine. The whole lot was designed to fit on the backs of two or three camels, or in the back of a truck or utility van today.

Bold stopped while the others tore up the wooden floor pieces. 'The *ger* has quite precise spatial arrangements,' he said. 'Men's side is west, women's is east. The door always faces south. Because it's round, and only has one window in the *tawn*, it acts like a big sundial.'

I was fascinated. 'How do you mean?'

'All *gers* face south. When the sun rises in the east, it shines on the man's bed through the *tawn* window. In the afternoon, it shines on the woman's bed.'

The Mongols' casual disregard for precise time now made sense. When we'd asked friends what time we should arrive for meals, they merely said 'in the afternoon'.

Bold got back to work. 'Can you come and help with the floor? This is the most important part.'

The first modern Mongol language Bible portions

The 'left-behind' Kalmucks remained on the western bank of the Volga River in the area now known as Krasnoarmeiisk which is part of modern Volgograd. It was here that the German Moravians had established their colony called Sarepta. It was also here, thousands of miles from their original homelands, that Moravian missionaries attempted the first modern Bible translation for a Mongol people.

These first attempts at Bible translation are referred to in a letter by a Reverend C.F. Gregor, minister of the congregation at Sarepta for the British and Foreign Bible Society (BFBS), dated in 1807. He writes that a couple of his Moravian colleagues had attempted to write some Bible harmonies and paraphrases.[1] One of these was Conrad Neitz, 'who for forty years had been qualifying himself for a Kalmuck version'. Encouraged by a grant of £60 from the BFBS in response to Gregor's letter, the Moravians decided to undertake a more ambitious translation programme and enlisted the help of Isaak Jakob Schmidt.

Schmidt was a Moravian Dutchman, born in Amsterdam, who at the time had business interests in the Sarepta colony. He went on to devote his life to the study of Mongol language and culture and later became a senior member of the Russian Council of State and a member of the Russian Academy of Sciences. Schmidt went on to compile a Mongolian grammar and a Mongolian-German-Russian dictionary.

Neitz may have translated the first Kalmuck Scripture portions, but it was Schmidt who started a full translation of a Gospel, that of *Matthew* in 1809. The BFBS reported in 1812 that it was ready for printing but it was not printed until 1815. The delay was caused by Napoleon's attack on Moscow. Schmidt and others in the BFBS had to evacuate Moscow in September 1812, and relocate to St Petersburg. It has been suggested that Schmidt's first manuscript of *Matthew* was left behind and was consumed in the flames of the fires that swept through Moscow during the battle. If this was the case, then Schmidt would have had to re-write the whole manuscript and this would account for the three-year delay.

A more likely scenario for the delay is that there was no Kalmuck type. The original £60 had been donated for the cutting of a Kalmuck type, but due to inevitable delays caused by war, Schmidt records that the font was not ready until mid-1814. The print run of *Matthew* was 3000 and these were circulated free of charge among the Khoshote horde of the Kalmucks located about 225 kilometres from Sarepta, by two of the Sarepta brethren, Schill and Hubner. By the time of Tumen's death in 1816, the whole print run was in circulation. This Gospel of *Matthew* proved to be the seed from which the first Mongol church grew.

The Kalmuck Gospel of Matthew stimulates a Buriat New Testament translation

Perhaps the most significant aspect of this endeavour was that it provided the impetus to translate into another Mongolian dialect, namely Buriat-Mongol. Robert Pinkerton and John Paterson were the two men with this idea. Pinkerton was a Scottish missionary who had been working in the Scottish colony at Karass, but by 1811 had taken up residence in Moscow. He was an avid promoter of the work of the Bible Society. He met Paterson, another Scotsman, in 1812. Paterson was the driving force behind setting up the Russian Bible Society in January 1813, based in St Petersburg.

In 1814 both these men were in England on Bible Society business and in the course of their travels opened a dialogue with the London Missionary Society (LMS) about staffing a mission station in Irkutsk, on the shores of Lake Baikal, western Siberia, to gain access into the Buriat Mongol area. Both parties saw the potential for Christian work among the Buriat Mongols and the LMS commissioned two missionaries, Edward Stallybrass and Cornelius Rahmn to go to Irkutsk and to research the potential for ongoing work in that region. Meanwhile Schmidt continued with the Kalmuck New Testament in light of the good reception that *Matthew* had had in Sarepta.

Schmidt's Kalmuck New Testament was his *magnum opus*, and was printed in 1827 by the BFBS in St Petersburg. Disappointingly, it never made it into circulation. The Russian authorities, perhaps because of the pressures from the Orthodox Church, confiscated the whole print run. Negotiations followed between the BFBS and the Russian authorities to try to buy back the books, but the Russian authorities would not be persuaded. There was no further work done in the Kalmuck for another sixty years until a Russian academic named Alexis Pozdneev printed his own translation of the four Gospels in Kalmuck-Mongol in 1887.

Alexis Pozdneev

Pozdneev was a Russian Mongolist of high standing, excelling in archaeology as well as translation work. He was later to become the chief Russian archaeologist at Karakorum during digs in 1898. In the summer of 1887, he travelled to Sarepta, a place with which he was well acquainted, to test his translation of the four Gospels. He took with him two hundred Gospels and a manuscript copy of *Acts*. He was well received and his work was 'heartily welcomed' by the Bishop of Astrakhan, the chief inspector and guardian of the Kalmuck tribes. His welcome was endorsed by the Orthodox Church, the ecclesiastical seminary and by the Kalmuck schools. Pozdneev read his *Acts* in several Kalmuck camps, where it received 'favourable criticism' from a number of Buddhist priests, who 'listened earnestly'. Pozdneev visited the area three more times subsequent to this to have his translations checked.

Pozdneev was assisted by a Kalmuck named Dordzhe Kutuseff, and together they went on to translate *Romans* to *Revelation*. Their four Gospels may have been a revision of Schmidt's, but no substantial evidence connecting the works of the two men has been uncovered. Nevertheless, a full New Testament, attributed solely to Pozdneev, was published by the BFBS in Shanghai in 1894. Schmidt's New Testament was reprinted in 1895/6 in Shanghai also. Why two Kalmuck translations were printed within two years of each other is not clear. It may well have been the same printing project and Pozdneev may have been drawing on Schmidt's work. Whatever the details, the Kalmuks were the first tribe of Mongols to have the four Gospels available to them in their own language.

Of all the translation work that had gone on among the Kalmucks, the BFBS records a total of 35,600 Gospels or other parts of Scripture printed by 1904.[2]

The floor of the *ger* comprised twelve sections, each about a metre square and each piece unique. The outer pieces had a curved edge to get the overall round shape. The ground first had to be cleared of odd rocks and levelled, and then the sections could be manoeuvred into position. It was like doing a large-scale jigsaw puzzle. A fire plate had to go under where the stove would be. None of the pieces were marked in any special way, but Bold seemed familiar enough with how they should join together.

Bold took this part of the construction seriously. He was all concentration. We got just about the whole floor down, and then he told us to tear it up and make some minor adjustment, then put it back down again. That happened four times. It was just as well we didn't have to shift a *ger* every day.

Bold must have been reading my thoughts. He kicked the last piece into place and stomped it down. 'Not all *gers* have floors. Just the city ones that don't get moved very often. In the countryside, the nomads lay down a whole lot of sheepskins on the bare ground.'

That seemed quite attractive, having taken the last two hours to do what seemed at first to be quite an elementary procedure.

'You have to get the floor absolutely right,' Bold explained. 'It's like the foundations of a building. If you don't get the foundations right, the building will collapse. If you don't get the floor of the *ger* right, the walls and roof above it will all blow away if a winter gale comes up.'

I thought he was being over dramatic. However, when I did get out into the countryside later, the nomads had piled up about a half metre of dirt all around the outside of their *ger* to stop the wind getting in underneath. Over the top they strung a number of ropes with heavy things tied to the end of them to keep the whole *ger* down. The engine block of a wrecked 'sixty-nine' jeep seemed quite popular for this. I could only imagine the types of gales that must blow up.

Once Bold was happy with the floor, the rest of the *ger* was easy. All up it took half an hour to collapse it and three hours to put it up again, two hours of which was getting the floor right.

'Did you get lots of good footage?' I asked Darla as we packed up.

'Yes, that was great. Can you thank them very much on my behalf,' she replied.

'*Ikh bayarlalaa*,' I called as we headed out onto the street to find a taxi home.

An old black Moskovich pulled up and we piled in. I asked the driver to take us to Sansar. I had learned in language school that week that *sansar* was the Mongol word for 'outer space'. I guessed they named the suburb Sansar because it was on a hill.

'He took ages getting those floor boards right,' Darla commented.

'Yes, I've been thinking,' I said. 'The early missionaries to the Mongols, or to anywhere for that matter, usually start with a Bible translation. I think it's like putting up a *ger*. The foundations have got to be right before you can build anything else. We can never afford to rush the foundations.'

'Putting up that *ger* took time, and it was a team effort,' Darla added. 'I guess it pays not to rush a Bible translation; and I guess it should be a team effort, if the whole church is going to use it.'

We arrived in Sansar and I directed the driver to our building. In the years immediately after the Communist system broke down in Mongolia, the government still put all the foreigners in the same building. Our flat had one lounge and one bedroom. This was called a 'two room' apartment. In the long winter months ahead, I could see us getting on each other's nerves all jammed into such a tiny space. There were 125 apartments in our building.

I had also learned in language school that week that the word for 'foreigner' was literally 'outside person', or 'alien'.

I understood now why the taxi drivers chuckled when I

asked them to take me home. All the 'aliens' lived together in 'outer space'.

NOTES
1. C.R. Bawden,'The English Missionaries in Siberia and their translation of the Bible into Mongolian', Mongolian Studies 6, (1980) 5–39.
2. William Canton, A History of the British and Foreign Bible Society, Vol. 5, (London: John Murray, 1910), 430.

Chapter 25

Edward Pagell, Henry Augustus Jaeschke and William Augustus Heyde,
Moravian missionaries to an inaccessible Mongolia

*'We thank God for sending so many brethren from
Moravian provinces abroad to... encourage and
inspire us.... We need to be renewed as He
renewed our spiritual forefathers in Herrnhut in
1722.... Let us obey Him so that the dedication
and faith of our European and Ladakhi
predecessors might live on in us and grow into a
mighty strength so that the very mountains in
which we live are moved.... May His Spirit move in
us.'[1]*

Thespal Kundan, principal of The Moravian
Institute in Rajpur, north India, at the time of the
Moravian Church's centenary (1885–1985)

Ian and Elizabeth Kemp write:

The 13,000-foot mountain pass into Leh in north India is
often blocked with snow through the winter and right up to
early June, so when we went there in 1983, we had to fly. Our
first impression was of the airport reception lounge: it was an
old army nissen hut. Thespal greeted us and took us to our
lodgings, a guest house run by his parents-in-law, Dr and Mrs
Sonam, who treated us with great kindness, providing most of
our meals for the next five days. Thespal was to be our guide
and interpreter throughout, taking us around the town, to the
old palace, to Buddhist temples and for outings up the Indus
river valley.

Although not large in area, Ladakh boasts some of the highest mountains and passes in the world. These bleak and barren
mountains tower menacingly over deep valleys hiding small
villages. Industrious villagers, helped by the trusty and sturdy

dzo (a cold weather beast with a cow mother and a yak father) turn these dark valleys into productive fertile ones. When the snow melts in May, the valleys burst into life with apple, pear and apricot blossoms, while the people tend their rock-walled terraces of cabbages, cauliflowers, potatoes and peas.

'The most thoroughly Tibetan culture you'll find outside Tibet,' said the tourist brochures — and so we found it to be. We observed the people to be sturdily built, with rosy faces and cheerful expressions; the children had chubby cheeks; the old people were very wrinkled. The dress is mainly of the Tibetan style — heavy coats buttoned down the side with a sash belt; both men and women wear a 'top' hat or *gonda*, heavily coated with sheep fat, presumably to keep out melting snow, but with little protection against the freezing winter blasts. Turquoise and other precious stones bejewelled many garments.

We motored up the Indus further to Thiksay where we climbed to the 550-year-old monastery which covers a whole hilltop. Here we saw through two small temples where we found an 'obrary' containing the wrapped bundles of 180 books of scriptures, murals, greasy floors, torn cushions and unlit gloominess. A monk was leading a dozen twelve-year-old novices through chants and the copying of scriptures. A relatively new building contained a magnificently painted Buddha amid detailed colourful murals depicting many scenes from Buddha's life. Lamas politely showed us around, while the small boys in training sneaked a glance up from their slates to study the foreigners.

As we passed through different villages, we noticed that they all had a few things in common: a *choten*, or small white stupa, a *mane* wall, with Tibetan religious writing on it, and more often than not, a *gompa*, where the lamas and their novices live. It seems that in the early days *gompas* were built on the trade routes so they could offer rest and sanctuary to travellers. On our tour around this huge valley, we noticed some signs of Islam amid the strong Tibetan-Buddhist culture. Thespal then took us to a little Moravian church which had but five families, and a total congregation of thirty. This church, the larger one in Leh, and another associated with a school in Rajpur, are the only Moravian churches in India.

The Moravians try to establish a mission in Buriatia

The Moravian brethren at Sarepta had to hand over their small group of converts to the Russian Orthodox Church, and the Torguts who returned to western China were absorbed into the Franciscan mission in Ily. However the Moravians did not give up on the Mongols.

Dr Karl Frederich August Gutzlaff (1803–1851) challenged them to keep their vision alive. Gutzlaff was visiting Europe in 1850, promoting mission awareness and the spiritual needs of the Chinese, having been involved in a good number of energetic mission enterprises in China, including the translation of the Mandarin Bible. He persuaded the Moravian mission at Herrnhut to build on their Kalmuck mission by considering a mission to Mongolia itself.

Thomas Stallybrass, son of Edward Stallybrass, one of the initial LMS Buriatia missionaries, was available to return to Buriatia where he had been born. The LMS had established a mission in Buriatia, the area east of Lake Baikal and north of the modern Mongolian/Russian border, from 1817, but it had been shut down by Russian imperial decree in 1840. Perhaps the Moravians could build on this work and gather together the converts the mission had made. Thomas was keen to return, and in preparation he trained in medicine and acquired some parish experience. On hearing that Gutzlaff was in Europe, he got in touch with him and together they agreed that it made sense to approach Mongolia from the north again, building on the previous work of the LMS in Buriatia.

However, Herrnhut overlooked Thomas Stallybrass (for reasons that are unclear) and appointed Edward Pagell and Augustus William Heyde in 1853 to open a mission in Buriatia to the Mongols. Pagell had trained as a worker in marble and Heyde as a metal-worker. Although from artisan backgrounds, they did well in academic pursuits, studying Mongolian in 1851–1852 from H.A. Zwick, a leading Moravian scholar who had written a Mongolian grammar. They also studied rudimentary medicine with a doctor in Berlin, and Heyde learned English from a pharmacy student in Herrnhut.

Russian Imperial policy had not changed since the LMS was ordered to stop work in Buriatia, however, and the Russian authorities never issued their visas for Buriatia. Herrnhut then decided on an alternate route, this time from the south via India and Tibet.

Pagell and Heyde reached Shimla, north India, in 1854. They had travelled from Calcutta up the Ganges, through Kulu and Ladakh towards the Tibetan border, hoping to be awarded transit visas so they could continue on across Tibet to Mongolia. They had been led to believe that Mongolia was not too far distant by a misinformed Dr Prochnow, a German working for the Anglican CMS in Kotgarh, near Shimla. He had pointed out that Mongolian caravans daily passed his place, and so Mongolia could not be too far away. However, access into Tibet was denied. After three years of constant appeal to the Tibetan authorities, they made the decision in 1857 to commence work where they were while they waited and prayed for the closed door to open. Using Shimla as their base, they continued their study of English, Hindustani, Mongolian and Tibetan.[2] Dr Prochnow had been wrong about the 'Mongolian caravans'. They turned out to be Tibetan.

The Moravian mission's dream of getting to Buriatia was never realised, but a Tibetan mission was started instead. Kyelang, near the Kulu-Manali hill-station in north India was the first site selected, then Poo, south-east of Kyelang in the upper reaches of the Sutlej river valley. The aim was to start Christian mission activity in the Indo-Tibetan border regions until Tibet opened.

The third centre selected was Ladakh, a fortnight's journey

north of Kyelang. Ladhakh had been an independent mountain kingdom until 1834 when the Hindu Raja of Jammu and Kashmir conquered it, and ultimately it came under the rule of British India.

Three years after they arrived in Kyelang, Pagell and Heyde were joined by a German from Niesky called Henry Augustus Jaeschke. He had been appointed superintendent of the mission with a special commission to study Tibetan and begin translation work. After he had settled in, they decided that they all needed wives and so the mission board in Hurrnhut duly sent three out by ship to Calcutta. Arranged marriages were not unusual for that day: it was not uncommon for the Moravians, and it was the norm for India. Pagell married Friederike Machtle in September 1859, and then Heyde and Jaeschke conducted each other's wedding ceremonies in November: Heyde married Maria Hartmann, and Jaeschke married Emilie Rosenhauer. Pagell and Friederike died in Poo within twelve days of each other of typhus, in 1883, after a solid thirty years of work among the Tibetans. Heyde and Maria continued working together among the Tibetans for forty-five years, never returning to Europe until their retirement.

After their marriages, Jaeschke put his phenomenal intellect to work. He was a man of immense linguistic capabilities. He had studied Polish and Hungarian at school, then while studying theology had learned Greek, graduating top of the class. On commencing a teaching career, he learned Danish in his spare time. During a summer holiday in Sweden he picked up Swedish. Czech, Sanskrit, Persian and Arabic were also part of his repertoire, so on arrival in India, he came by Hindustani and Urdu quickly. Presumably he picked up English on the ship to India, so when he reached India in 1856 he had a good working knowledge of twelve languages. He used to keep his diary in seven languages! He was also a brilliant mathematician and musician.

Jaeschke set himself the task of learning the Tibetan language and committed himself to the Tibetan people for twenty-six years. He was not only the first European to master Tibetan, but he also started translating the Tibetan Bible, wrote a Tibetan grammar, a Tibetan-German dictionary, a Tibetan-English dictionary, and Bible stories in Tibetan. A harmonisation of the Gospels, a hymn book, a liturgy, a catechism and several school textbooks were also the results of his prolific career. People of such linguistic brilliance are rare.

The legacy of the Moravian mission to the Mongols

The Moravian missionaries were denied access to Buriat-Mongolia via Russia, then via Tibet, and the Ladhaki church was the direct result. Efforts from the initial station at Kyelang spread through the Himalayan foothills, and Leh, Ladhakh became the centre from 1885. This was mainly because the original Christians in Kyelang had been Ladhakhi refugees after Ladhakh had fallen to the Maharajah of Jammu and Kashmir. Being outside the cultural pressures of Kyelang, conversion was less of an obstacle for them. Slowly they moved back to Ladhakh. Heyde had made frequent tours of Ladhakh in the 1860s and 1870s and by the 1880s, many of the Kyelang Ladhakhis were planning on returning home. In the winter of 1882–1883, Heyde negotiated with the British Joint Commissioner, and with the persuasion of Lord Ripon, the British Viceroy, the Maharajah of Jammu and Kashmir was persuaded to allow a resident missionary in Leh. This was to be Friedrich A. Redslob, a linguistics student of Jaeschke.

The mission stations at Poo and Kyelang disappeared almost instantly when the missionaries pulled out. By the 1940s the Ladhakhi Christians were insisting that changes had to be made which invested more decision-making with them, rather than with the missionaries. An innovative Christian by the name of Dorje, who was a skilful self-taught engineer, organised the people of Leh to build an airstrip and bridges during the tensions with Pakistan which led up to partition, and so was able to open up access for more military defence and future trade and tourism. In 1950, after partition, Norman and Mary Driver, the resident missionaries who had stayed on, were joined by Pierre and Catherine Vittoz. These would be the last European missionaries to serve there. Eliyah Thsetan Phuntsog, a Ladhaki Christian who had been involved in local politics, joined the mission leadership as an equal in 1951. The Drivers left in 1952 and Phuntsog and the Vittozes worked together to make the transition from European leadership to a genuine Ladhakhi leadership.

In 1955 the Ladhakh church joined the Church of North India and the Vittozes left the following year to continue work on the Tibetan Bible translation, based in Mussoorie, Uttar Pradesh, India. Phuntsog and another younger Ladhakhi Christian, Yonathan Paljor were ordained, and the church became truly self-dependent.

Phuntsog went to Mussoorie to help the Vittozes with the Tibetan translation and found that the area was filling up with Tibetan refugees following the Dalai Lama's hasty exit from Tibet in 1959. In 1961 he helped settle Tibetan refugees in Rajpur, near Dehra Dun, 5,000 feet below Mussoorie where the Himalayas rise up out of the plains of north India. With a grant from the Moravian Church and some assistance from The Evangelical Alliance Mission (TEAM), small-scale cottage industries were started and a small medical dispensary began. In 1963, Phuntsog's daughter, Mrs Zhidey Kundan, started an open-air school for a dozen Tibetan children.

From these small beginnings, the Moravian Institute of Rajpur grew. Phontsog ran it until 1971 and died suddenly of a heart attack in 1973. The school was then run by members of his family: Mrs Sungkil Phontsog, his widow, led the board of management, and Obed Kundan, his son-in-law, administered the school from 1972. Another son-in-law, Stephen Hishey, was principal from 1977 to 1980, and he was succeeded by a grandson, Thespal Kundan, who was in leadership during the Moravian church's centenary celebrations in 1985.

What if Jaeschke, Pagell and Heyde had reached Mongolia,

as was the Moravian Board of Mission's intention? We are left only with our imagination as to what the Moravian Mongol mission may have become if Jaeschke's mind and skills had been harnessed there.

The Moravians were the first Protestant missionaries to attempt to evangelise a Mongol tribe. They also formed the first missionary endeavour to the Mongols since John of Marignolli had visited the Franciscan missions in Da-tu and Zayton in China in the fourteenth century. There may have been little success in the number of converts, but the New Testament was translated into Kalmuck-Mongol, and of this, the Gospels got into circulation. A small and hardy Kalmuck-Mongol church was established for a short time. Ministry to the Kalmuck-Mongols created the impetus for the Buriat-Mongol Bible translation, and for the establishment of the LMS mission to the Mongols in Buriatia. In short, in wanting to build on the work set up by the LMS missionaries in Buriatia, the Moravians attempted to send missionaries to Mongolia. But their inability to access Mongolia either from the north through Russia or from the south through India and Tibet meant that they devoted themselves to the establishment of the church in Ladhakh.

The modern Mongolian church should always be appreciative that their loss was Ladhakh's gain.

———————

Ian and Elizabeth Kemp continue:

On Sunday, we went to the worship service at the main Moravian church in Leh. Thespal preached in English, Urdu and Ladhakhi, phrase by phrase to accommodate us tourists and a contingency of visiting Indian soldiers. We were about sixty altogether. The church was on an old mission compound where several Christian families were living, and there was a small primary school adjacent. An inscription at the gate read, 'Bruder Gemeinde Unitas Fratrum Hernhutt — founded 1888' linking this church to its missionary past. Later in the week we joined the Christians at their weekly prayer meeting held in a home on the mission compound. About fourteen were present, huddling together in a poorly lit room (electricity comes on daily only between 7.30pm and 11.30pm). An elderly retired pastor led this meeting. He read from the Tibetan New Testament, then made a few comments. We sang a hymn and several people prayed. The meeting was followed by tea and a catch-up on the events of the week. We learned that the local Christian community numbered about 150 in total.

Compare this small outpost of Christ's Church amidst the towering and craggy mountains of this remote spot with the great cathedrals of the bustling metropolises of the world. God is honoured in the huge cities, and in the isolated corners of his world. And who is to say which is the more precious in his eyes?

NOTES

1. Kundan, Thespal, 'The Moravian Church in India after 1985' in *The Himalayan Mission: Moravian Church Centenary, 1885–1985, Leh, Ladakh, India.* ed. John Bray (Publisher unstated) 78,79.
2. A.W. Marston, *The Great Closed Land: A Plea for Tibet* (London: S.W.Partridge and Co.) 76.

Part **6**

The London Missionary Society

Edward Stallybrass and Cornelius Rahmn,

First LMS Missionaries to the Buriat-Mongols

'As the union of Christians of various denominations... it is declared to be a Fundamental Principle of the Missionary Society that its design is not to send Presbyterianism, Independency, Episcopacy, or any other form of Church Order and government... but [to send] the glorious gospel of the blessed God, to the heathen.'

Plan and Constitution of the London
Missionary Society

I gazed out the window of the aeroplane down at the grey city emerging from behind some low hills in the distance. The shadows of low fluffy clouds gave a blotched appearance to the whole of the Ulaanbaatar valley. We banked steeply and immediately below me, at about 500 metres I could see clusters of *gers*, flocks of sheep and stone circular enclosures. It was August and the best time of the year to arrive in Mongolia. Everything was deep green.

That first flight into Ulaanbaatar I still remember well. What stood out was that there were no fences anywhere on the grassland. Emerging out of a Communist economy, the state owned everything. If there was no private ownership of land, then I guessed there was nothing to fence.

We were met by a young man who bundled us into two unlikely Ladas and we rattled and banged our way the sixteen kilometres into the city. I noticed there were no fences around any of the buildings either.

'Did you have a good flight?' Bayaraa asked me in broken English, quite oblivious to the numerous potholes, wandering pedestrians, the odd goat and the fact that we were travelling about eighty kph in a car that wasn't fit for more than a quarter of the speed.

'Yes thanks. Singapore Airlines gave us a first-class luggage allowance on an economy ticket to Beijing. That's why we brought so much stuff with us. The Mongolian airline MIAT wouldn't extend us the favour, so we had to upgrade to first class. It was cheaper than staying another night in Beijing.' This was a trick I fast cottoned on to when travelling with a family. On one occasion a few years later, we travelled with 180 kgs of checked luggage, courtesy of Korean Airlines.

We had no idea what sort of accommodation Bayaraa had organised for us. We had been planning for eight months to come to Mongolia, and had read every book we could find in New Zealand (which wasn't a lot). We'd gone up and down the length of New Zealand telling people about Mongolia and our sense that God had called us there. Our mission wanted someone there to start exploring strategic opportunities for further partners to come, and also to check out how to get a united Christian agency registered with the government. It seemed a better use of resources if a dozen interested mission agencies partnered together under one umbrella, rather than all coming independently. Our immediate aim was to survive the ride in from the airport.

'This is it,' Bayaraa announced as we pulled into an alley way. Karen exhaled. I looked up at the building and counted five storeys and eight stairwells. 'You're in the eighth stairwell, fourth floor, apartment 123. These guys will help you up with the luggage.' Three young men appeared from somewhere.

Double doors to the stairwell flapped and banged as we made several trips up and down those stairs. The stairwell smelt of mutton, urine, wet wool and cold concrete, all mixed together. The doorway to 123 was double, and had four locks in it.

The apartment had one room, a tiny kitchen and a bathroom. And it was filthy.

'We got the key for it only this morning,' Bayaraa said apologetically, interpreting my open mouth as an expression of horror. 'If there's anything you need, just let me know.'

I thanked him genuinely for all his trouble, and for the friendly welcome at the airport. The door closed and we were on our own. Karen burst into tears. I squashed a cockroach.

Beginnings of the LMS

In the closing years of the eighteenth century, the great evangelical awakening spawned several mission agencies: the Baptist Missionary Society (1792), the Church Missionary Society (1799), and the Wesleyan Methodist Missionary Society (1818). The London Missionary Society was founded in September 1795, sparked initially by a letter from the Baptist missionary to Indian Bengal, William Carey. Carey wrote to John Ryland of Bristol, then minister of Broadmead Church and President of the Baptist College, describing his first six weeks in Bengal. Ryland immediately gathered together a group of six evangelical clergy friends, mainly of the Independent churches, to hear it read.

These clergy were already well schooled in the missionary needs, and the Rev. Dr David Bogue, Independent minister, and head of the Missionary Academy at Gosport, formulated a statement on the missionary need and obligation of the church addressed *To the Evangelical Dissenters who Practise Infant Baptism*. The appeal was published in an evangelical magazine and immediately drew together a core group of likeminded Episcopalians, Methodists, Presbyterians and Independents. A new society was decided upon and at its inaugural address in 1795, Thomas Haweis declared, 'the petty distinctions among us, of names and forms, the diversities of administrations and modes of Church Order, we agree, shall this day be merged in the greater, nobler, and characteristic name of Christians.'[1] In the following year, the Plan and Constitution of the Society included this declaration:

As the union of Christians of various denominations... it is declared to be a *Fundamental Principle* of the Missionary Society that its design is not to send Presbyterianism, Independency, Episcopacy, or any other form of Church Order and Government... but [to send] the glorious Gospel of the blessed God, to the heathen... and that it shall be left to the minds of the persons whom God may call... to assume for themselves such form of Church Government as to them shall appear most agreeable to the Word of God.[2]

The aim of this new society, The London Missionary Society, was not so much to be inter-denominational, as to be non-denominational. Criticism has been levelled at it such that it was committed to a view of evangelism unrelated to the church. This was not the intention of the founders, and Alexander Waugh, the final drafter of the *Fundamental Principle* was a staunch Presbyterian and a stickler for correct church order. The underlying conviction was the union of word and Spirit. The Holy Spirit must be free to move as he so wishes on the one hand, but on the other, missionaries associated with the Society must be well grounded in biblical truth. Waugh, on hearing a sermon preached at its annual general meeting on the Holy Spirit, said, 'I am always afraid when I hear any minister speak on the influences of the Spirit without appealing to the Word of God.... I know not where a man will land who goes to sea without chart or compass.... Let all the evidences of the Holy Spirit's influence be decided by the Word of God.'[3]

The LMS was founded then as a thoroughly evangelical society. Missionaries were free to carry on their endeavours and establish churches with order and government 'agreeable to the Word of God'. A further development of the policy occurred following Henry Venn's memoranda on *Native Church Organisation*. He wrote in 1851 that churches should become 'self-supporting, self-governing and self-propagating'. This phrase became the *locus classicus* of much mission organisation and is influential up to the modern era. The LMS adopted the phrase as official policy.

Famous people such as Robert Morrison of China, John Williams of the South Seas, and David Livingstone of Africa were all LMS missionaries. The LMS was the first Protestant mission agency to enter China in 1807, mainly supported by the Congregational Churches of Great Britain and Australia. Its mission to the Mongols was in two phases: the first was between 1817 and 1840 with a work at Selenginsk, Buriatia, a little north of the modern Mongolian-Russian border. The major achievement of this mission was the first full Mongolian language Bible. The second phase of the mission was from 1871 to 1902 and is dominated by the name of James Gilmour (1843–1891). Not much fruit was born from Gilmour's work, but his is a tale of unfailing commitment to the cause, and an inspiration for deeper consecration to God.

Connections to the Moravian Kalmuck mission

Subsidiaries of the Russian Bible Society sprang up throughout Russia, including one in Irkutsk. Its influence in eastern Siberia was profound enough for copies of Schmidt's Kalmuck *Matthew's Gospel* to be sent to the Buriat Mongols for their appraisal. The reaction was so favourable that they took up a collection of 11,000 roubles, the equivalent then of 550 pounds of silver, so that this Kalmuck *Matthew* (and preferably the whole New Testament) could be translated and printed in their own Buriat-Mongol dialect.

This money was sent to the Russian Bible Society in St Petersburg and two helpers were commissioned to follow the project to its completion, arriving in St Petersburg in December 1817, to work with Schmidt. This Kalmuck-Irkutsk Bible Society connection was the link that stimulated the LMS to look seriously at the possibilities of setting up a mission in Buriatia. It was deemed a strategic location as it would lead, so it was thought, to access into China from the north, and hence supplement the work of the LMS on the Chinese coast.

Edward and Sarah Stallybrass with Cornelius and Betty Rahmn were the first recruits. They began work among the Buriat Mongols in 1817, initially in Irkutsk.

Edward and Sarah Stallybrass: beginnings of the Buriatia mission

Edward Stallybrass was an Englishman from Royston, Hertfordshire, and one of nine children. His father, William Stallybrass was a deacon of the Congregational Church. Edward studied for the ministry at Homerton College, then in east London, but which later moved to Cambridge. He studied Latin, Greek and Hebrew, which put him in good stead for future translation work. While waiting placement, the LMS encouraged him to learn French, German and Russian.

Stallybrass was thoroughly evangelical in conviction. On his application to the LMS he wrote:

> about the seventeenth year of my life, the blessed Spirit of God applied to my mind, in a saving way, the great truths of the Gospel; at which time I was led to see my own lost and fallen state as a sinner in the sight of God; the impossibility of being justified in the sight of God, except by the righteousness of the Lord Jesus Christ; the importance of immediate application to, and implicit reliance on him as the only Saviour from the wrath to come.

The rest of his application reads like one of the early creeds. His motivation for mission work was because of the 'comparatively small number of persons who appear disposed to engage in... [missionary exertions]'. His strategy for his own involvement in missions was simple: 'the plan which is adopted for enlightening the heathen, by the translation of the Scriptures and the preaching of the gospel, appears to me to be the most likely... to promote that most desirable end.'[4]

In August 1816, Edward became engaged to Sarah Robinson. In October of the same year, the LMS announced that his field would be Irkutsk, and that they were to sail for Europe in three weeks time. However, a severe European winter that year froze the Baltic Sea ports early and they couldn't sail for St Petersburg, leaving time for an unhurried wedding on 5 March 1817.

Sarah was a 'charming young woman', and a zealot. She was earnest in her self-discipline and piety and unfailing in her self-castigation against sin. She was a restless energetic whirlwind. Faithful to the work in Buriatia, the mission, and the call of her husband, she was a woman of vision and commitment. She had considerable physical stamina, enduring the long cold midwinter sled trip to Irkutsk from St Petersburg while pregnant. Edward wrote of her once that 'she possessed great compassion for the temporal, and much greater for the spiritual miseries of men.... She eagerly desired to see greater facilites opened up for staying the spiritual plague'. Perhaps her evangelical piety was too narrow at times, which lent itself to pride and social snobbishness (and friction with the wives of the other missionaries in the LMS Mongol mission). Sarah's unbounding energy drove her to her death in 1833, burned out at the young age of forty-four. Edward wrote of her from Buriatia: 'Many of the poor by whom we are surrounded will, I doubt not, deeply and sincerely lament her loss.'

Trials of sickness

Edward and Sarah's first colleagues were Cornelius and Betty Rahmn. Cornelius was born in Gothenburg, Sweden in 1785. He was educated at the University of Lund, Sweden, where his father insisted he studied law. Cornelius didn't have a heart for law and eventually pursued a career in the church, although the Russian campaigns against Finland and Sweden in the early

1800s tempted him to follow his father's career in the army. Cornelius was ordained at the age of twenty-five and became chaplain in an artillery division until he joined the LMS. By this time he had acquired a well-rounded education and gained much life experience. He had studied Latin, Greek and Hebrew, and could also converse in German and French. His English was adequate, but not fluent. He was a member of the Swedish church and he had good contacts with Independents and Moravians. It was the story of the Moravian mission to Greenland that sparked his call into missions, and throughout his life, the Moravians remained an inspiration to him.

Like Edward Stallybrass, Cornelius Rahmn was a good choice for the beginning of the Mongol mission in Buriatia. With his foundation in languages and experience in Christian ministry, he was a natural choice, especially for translation and education work. His personal Mongolian Bible is in the Royal Library, Stockholm.

Permission to start the LMS mission in Buriatia was given to Edward and Cornelius personally by Tsar Alexander I in St Petersburg in 1817. Together they travelled across the vast expanse of central Russia: Edward and Sarah Stallybrass (now pregnant), with Cornelius and Betty Rahmn and their young daughter Hanna. They arrived in Irkutsk on 26 March 1818. Tsar Alexander I had assigned a grant of land for the mission and given a gift of 7,000 roubles for the construction of buildings.[5] Edward and Cornelius soon decided that Irkutsk was not a good location for the mission due to the lack of Mongols in the city and after sixteen months made the decision to shift further south-east into genuine Buriat territory, to a settlement called Selenginsk. Here they made their homes in the Siberian style of log cabin corked with moss.

The mission in Buriatia made a good start. It was well staffed with theologically trained and highly motivated personnel. The LMS demanded that mission work would be based on the word of God, and evangelism would be its main reason for existence. However the stresses and strains of living in a totally new environment so completely isolated from their homes meant that the personality barbs soon showed themselves. Betty Rahmn's health became a real set-back. She was a hypochondriac, and often clashed with Sarah Stallybrass. Edward worked with Cornelius, but had no time for Betty. Her emotional instability meant she demanded constant attention. Her periodic hysteria put strain on Cornelius who vented his frustrations on the Stallybrasses. The Rahmns left Irkutsk on medical advice in 1819 but continued to make a contribution at Sarepta among the Kalmuck Mongols until 1823. Cornelius was deeply frustrated with this move. He mustered enthusiasm for his new field in Sarepta, but again was dragged down by Betty. They moved on to Astrakhan 'on account of the debilitated and nervous state of his wife', and finally went home to Sweden. Ironically, Betty lived to the age of sixty-nine, dying in 1847, outliving both Sarah Stallybrass and Edward's second wife Charlotte (née Ellah).

Karen set to cleaning our new apartment. I assessed the future: there was a small bench-top hotplate, a tap (which leaked), two single beds (with linen surprisingly): but the stop-cock on the toilet wouldn't shut off; there was no toilet lid.

I flicked a cockroach off the bench in the kitchen. 'I hope the rest of our airfreight doesn't come just yet,' I said. We had sent three barrels and a trunk separately. 'There'd be nowhere to put it!'

We were in that apartment for a month until we shifted to another in the same building, but twice the size: it had two rooms. This new apartment, we discovered, had a very poor water supply. Our airfrieght arrived the day we were to shift.

We settled in and went exploring. We hired a language helper and plunged into the community. Anjali, our daughter, played outside and we made friends. We went shopping and we stood in food queues. We travelled by bus and we bought *samar*, pine nuts, from the kids on the street. By the end of the first month, we had a reasonable handle on survival language and started looking for ways to place a team of future personnel.

'I've met a handful of other foreign Christians here,' Karen said one day. 'Not many. Everyone is new. We're all in this together.'

'Getting a good grasp of this language has got to be top priority,' I said. 'We've also got to build a good relationship with the government if we can. Russian won't remain the second language for long. All the Russians are going home. I've been accosted by so many people to teach them English. I think it's a real need.'

I looked out from our apartment window past the city to the green steppe beyond. I got to thinking about those fences again. Or lack of them. We had come to Mongolia with the good news of the gospel of Jesus Christ. We ourselves were going to look for opportunities in education. And there didn't seem to be many fences blocking us. In 1992, once you got over the initial shocks, Mongolia was an open, unbroken field of opportunities.

NOTES
1. Norman Goodall, A History of the London Missionary Society: 1895–1945 (London: Oxford University Press, 1954), 3.
2. Norman Goodall, A History of the London Missionary Society: 1895–1945 (London: Oxford University Press, 1954), 3.
3. Norman Goodall, A History of the London Missionary Society: 1895–1945 (London: Oxford University Press, 1954), 4.
4. C.R. Bawden, Shamans, Lamas, and Evangelicals: The English Missionaries in Siberia (London: Routledge and Kegan Paul, 1985), 64 .
5. Frans Larson, Larson, Duke of Mongolia (Boston: Little, Brown, and Co., 1930), 263.

William Swan, Robert Yuille and John Abercrombie,
Shackled by Conflict

'I desire to promote the glory of God in the conversion of sinners.'

William Swan

The doorbell rang and I welcomed in two young Mongolian women: one I recognised as Tuya, a leader at church. Karen invited them in and gave them tea. Tuya introduced her friend, Togsoo, and we chatted for an hour. Then we finally arrived at the reason for their visit.

'Togsoo's been a Christian for two weeks. She's part of my home group. She's from Dundgov province and is studying at the university.' Togsoo was a long way from home. Dundgov meant 'Middle Gobi' and was half way between Ulaanbaatar and China, a very solid day's driving at least.

Tuya continued. 'Togsoo has been living with her uncle, but he just died, and she has no other relative to live with in Ulaanbaatar. She's going to fly home to Dundgov tomorrow.' Togsoo shifted uneasily with the attention.

Then the bombshell dropped. 'I was wondering if Togsoo may be able to live with you for a while?'

Karen and I excused ourselves and had a hurried conference in the kitchen. We agreed it was a good idea.

Karen took over. 'Togsoo can live with us for the rest of the semester and then we'll review it. It's important that she gets some good Christian discipleship. It's also important that as a woman she gets every opportunity she can to better her status. It's not going to be easy with two cultures living under the one roof, but we'll give it a go.'

Togsoo stayed with us for three months. She was studying Tai Kwon Do, a Korean martial art. What relevance that had for a Mongol nomad completely alluded me. After Christmas we decided that it was time for her to return to her home. We had a tearful farewell and she caught the bus out to the airport.

About four hours later there was a knock on the door. It was Togsoo.

'The flight's been postponed. Can I stay another night?'

That last night with Togsoo was the best we'd had during those three months, and in hindsight was a divine appointment.

'Are there any Christians in Dundgov that you can have some fellowship with?' I asked.

'None,' Togsoo replied. 'I'm the only Christian I know of. My family is Buddhist.'

I imagined the flack she might face. 'It could be tough. Remember to read your Bible every day and keep up your habit of prayer. Ask for God's help every day. I'll talk to Tuya and see if our church can send a team to Mandalgov, the *aimag* capital in the summer. You look out for them'.

We prayed together and we gave her a few extra copies of Luke's Gospel to give to family and friends.

'There's something I want to tell you.' Togsoo went all thoughtful. 'I've been keeping a diary. I recorded every day what it was like living with you.'

Karen nearly fell off her chair. I knew that Karen had struggled with the inevitable culture clashes; they'd spent a lot of time at home together. Togsoo was admitting that she'd recorded every minor detail: how we related to each other as a married couple, how we were bringing up our daughter, how we greeted our guests, what patterns of life we kept to, and the likes. I suspected the diary must look like something out of the inquisition, a notebook of the sins of commission and omission. I imagined all the raw details of life with the Kemps were recorded therein.

Togsoo seemed oblivious to our embarrassment and continued. 'When I arrive back in Madalgov tomorrow, it will be difficult for me to live as a Christian. Plus I don't know if I'll be able to get a job.' (That didn't surprise me. I couldn't see too many opportunities with a half-completed certificate in teaching Tai Kwon Do.) 'My family will put pressure on me to marry and have kids.'

A tear trickled down her face. 'I kept this daily diary for a reason. When I start my own family, I want it to be a Christian family, just like yours.'

William and Hannah Swan

William Swan joined Edward and Sarah Stallybrass at the Selinginsk mission in 1819, as a replacement for Cornelius and Betty Rahmn. Like Stallybrass, Swan had a good handle on Latin and Greek which he had learned at school. Swan had studied at the University of Edinburgh for a year and then become apprenticed to a lawyer. He picked up financial management skills by working for three and a half years as an accountant. During this time he did further studies in maths, logic and law. For two further years he studied at the Theological Academy at Glasgow attending courses in Latin, Greek and Hebrew. He also knew some French. He was articulate, intelligent, clear-headed, socially polished and had an instinct for diplomacy. He often acted as the liaison between the London Missionary Society and the Russian government; the London directors implicitly trusted his judgements.

William Swan had wanted to go to China initially, to work in Bible translation. On his application to the LMS, William wrote, 'I desire to promote the glory of God in the conversion of sinners.'[1] He outlined his motivation in four points: devotion to work, unremitting diligence, noble faithfulness and courage, and a dependence upon God to give success. He would not be distracted in his duty; both he and Edward had the potential to become renowned in a new field of scholarship, but they rejected this temptation and solely committed themselves to their mission duty.

William went out to Buriatia as a batchelor but found himself at his new station at Ona in need of some company. He therefore married Hannah Cullen during a return trip to Scotland in 1832. William and Hannah returned to Buriatia, but they had a delay of a year in St Petersburg, due to some irregularities in the Bible translation procedures of the mission. On arriving back in Buriatia, Hannah threw herself into the work of the mission with the same zeal as the Stallybrasses and her husband William. She opened a small school at Ona from 1837. She outlived William and returned to Scotland where she wrote several works on Mongolia.

Robert Yuille: odd man out

Robert Yuille and William Swan had two things in common. They were both born in 1791, and both were Scotsmen, but there the similarities end. Yuille was the 'odd man out', the non-academic, non-achiever and the socially-different loner. From the start, there was disparity between Yuille and his colleagues. Robert Yuille came from a working-class background, having grown up in Glasgow where he worked as a weaver until the age of thirty, and then in manufacturing. He had enough initiative to get himself out of the grime of industrial Glasgow, and managed to achieve some success in part-time studies at the university. After acceptance by the LMS he went on to study at the missionary seminary at Gosport.

Robert's religious background was Antiburgher, a group that broke away from the established Church of Scotland in 1735. He had little interest in Christianity as a young boy, but when his mother died, he became more open to spiritual things. He records his own conversion: 'after [two sermons which I heard], I resolved to remain no longer a presumptuous or a luke-warm sinner, but to make an open avowal of my attachment to Christ'. He left the Antiburghers and joined an Independent Congregation, under the influence of Ralph Wardlaw, an avid supporter of the LMS. This patronage by Wardlaw masked deficiencies in Yuille's character that the LMS subsequently overlooked. It is odd that the directors of the LMS failed to recognise his false humility, conceit, lack of integrity and self-interest in his initial correspondence with the Society.

Yuille never fitted into the Buriat mission and sparks flew with John Abercrombie the printer, and also with Edward Stallybrass, the more senior of his colleagues. Yuille took much credit for translation done by Rintsin, one of the mission academy's Buriat graduates. In their correspondence with the LMS, both Edward and William paint a poor picture of Robert's intellectual capabilities; as far as they were concerned, he was ignorant and incompetent. At times he defied agreed procedures, acted independently and deliberately disobeyed directives from the LMS directors in London. Edward had initially asked the LMS directors for single missionaries to replace Cornelius and Betty Rahmn, recognising that to shift the mission from Irkutsk to Selenginsk would require the commitment of missionaries unencumbered by family responsibilities.

Yuille had applied to the mission as a single man, then, in defiance of the mission, announced his engagement to Martha Cowie just before being sent to Buriatia. The mission promptly cancelled his appointment due to his impertinence, but then reinstated him (and now Martha). This was plainly an error of judgement, for the Yuilles' appointment permanently crippled the mission. Robert Yuille was eventually expelled from the LMS, but even so, refused to leave Buriatia. The Society then just ignored him, and there is no further record of him in Society annual reports after the mid-1830s.

John Abercrombie, the printer

The fourth member of the LMS mission in Buriatia was John Abercrombie. He was a native of the Caucasus. Scottish settlers in Karass had in 1806 received permission from the Russian Imperial government to ransom slaves from neighbouring tribes. A Dr John Abercrombie of Edinburgh, one of the Scottish settlers, ransomed a young Cabardian lad called

Teeona. Teeona took the name of his redeemer and trained as a printer. He also learned to speak Scots, Russian and a couple of local languages. He went on to do some Bible work in the Caucasus and became known in St Petersburg. In 1827, Abercrombie left Karass and worked as printer for the Basel missionaries in Shusha, who stopped printing in 1833 at which time William Swan discovered him. He and his family then joined the Buriatia mission.

The disagreements with Yuille had forced the Stallybrasses, Swans and Yuilles to separate to three different locations in the hinterland around Selenginsk. The press was originally located at Yuille's station at Selenginsk, but due to Yuille's abuse of it, Stallybrass moved it to his own station on the River Khodon. Abercrombie and his family arrived at Selinginsk early 1834 to start printing *Genesis*, and he was assisted by two young Buriats.[2]

Travelling: a strategy of the LMS Buriatia mission

The work of the mission was essentially threefold: itinerant evangelism among the local Buriat population, the establishment of schools, and the translation of the Bible. We will look at the Bible translation in Chapter 28, for this was the major legacy of the mission, and is worthy of separate treatment.

The LMS missionaries quickly saw the potential of travelling as a strategy of contact with the Buriat Mongols for several reasons.

- The Buriats were nomads, and they needed to shift their livestock between their winter and summer pastures.
- Nomads tend to avoid sedentary dwellings.
- The missionaries wanted to get away from a Russian environment. Edward decided to place the Selenginsk mission station on the other side of the river from the town, to distance themselves from the Russian presence. If contact with Buriats was to be made, it had to be genuine and

untainted by any association with Russians. The religious milieu of the area meant that the LMS missionaries had actively to engage the Buriat in religious debate.

- Lama temples were dotted throughout the region: the LMS missionaries had to go to them as the lamas were unlikely to come to the mission station.

In 1820 Edward was enthusiastic about the prospects of an itinerant work. He writes:

We intend to continue our journeys among them [the Buriats] as [we did] last summer; this is advantageous and desirable, not merely as it gives us an opportunity of distributing books, but also for the opportunity of conversing with the people and knowing more of them — I rejoice in our prospects.[3]

They distributed Gospels and tracts that they themselves had written, but the content of the tracts was inappropriate. They were written in linear logic in an argument genre. For example, the truth of Christ's claims to divinity were evidenced by his miracles. This did not impress the local lamas, as their own religion provided ample examples of miracles. Alternatively, they would engage in debate over idols, again, in a rhetorical linear-logical approach. Robert Yuille relates one episode that went like this:

Robert: (to a tent-full of Buriats) 'Who is your chief God?'
Buriats: 'Shigomony'
R: 'What sort of god is he?'
B: 'There is no greater God than he, for he knows every thing.'
R: 'If your God Shigomony knows everything, he must know that we are in this tent and that we are talking about him.'
B: 'Yes.'

R: (directing his question to one man) 'He must know that you are one of the ferrymen last summer on the Temnik River?'

B: 'Yes.'

R: 'He must know that the ice now on the river must pre vent you from crossing it?'

B: 'Yes.'

R: 'Well then, my friend, Shigomony must know all the evil that you have done, and all the evil that is in your heart.'

The Buriat man remains silent.

R: 'This must be so, for he knows everything. Where then is Shigomony? In that chest there? (pointing to a chest in which an idol probably was stored) When do you take him out? During the White Month, when the lamas come and pray?'

The Buriats in the tent remain silent.

R: 'You cannot put a man in that chest, therefore Shigomony must be less than a man. You could not put a dog in there, therefore Shigomony must be less than a dog. You could not even put a mouse in there, for it would either eat its way out or die. Therefore your god must be less than a mouse!'

The Buriats in the tent remain silent.

R: 'My friend, you are quite mistaken about your god Shigomony; but let me tell you what I think. Your lamas deceive you... you fear Shigomony and bow to him, when you might as well do it to the ashes from the fire — if you give Shigomony to me I shall burn him in the fire, and you shall find that we shall sleep as soundly tonight, and rise as well in the morning without him, as with him

The Buriats still remain silent, but Robert declares that they wondered at his boldness and presumption.

Certainly a full frontal attack on their god and the lamas did not endear Robert (or Edward and William if they debated in a similar fashion) to favour with the locals.

Their strategy ran into many problems. It was physically difficult to make contact with nomads, and to establish an ongoing relationship with any one person or family. The missionaries tried to visit two or three times, but the nomads remained elusive. When contact was made, the men were often drunk, especially in spring when the *airag* was plentiful. When sober, religion was relegated to a specialty topic of the lamas and the common man had little interest in it. Apart from the overt Buddhist lamas' presence, the underlying Shamanistic worldview threw up some theological problems. On hearing the basic Christian doctrine, for example, that man has only one soul, the Buriats laughed it off as an impossibility. Explicit opposition from Buddhist lamas, and even by the Orthodox Russian Church was experienced. If access to a tent was gained, apart from the alcohol, the missionaries had to contend with an underlying culture of gambling, along with a host of other vices, including sexual. Occasionally, the travelling ministry was accompanied by some distribution of medicines.

Some converts were made and the strategy was picked up by one or two Buriat men. As late as 1839, a convert by the name of Shagdur, who also taught in one of the mission's schools, was undertaking long evangelistic journeys to remote areas. In the 1830s the mission was involved more in education and translation, and the initial surge of travelling had become now only occasional. It is disappointing that the potential for Buriat Christians like Shagdur to get out among his own people was not captialised on.

Educating the Buriats

Establishing schools among the Buriat was a natural and appropriate strategy of evangelism. Literacy was the sole domain of the lamas and chieftains (*zaisans*), and so if common people were to read the Bible then missionaries would have to teach him how. The missionaries first started elementary schools in their own homes, and then they established a seminary (called 'The Academy') for promising students. The main objectives were twofold: first to bring the light of knowledge to the people, and secondly to train the more able students to be teachers and evangelists. Education removed prejudices and opened the mind to new ideas. It was pre-evangelism. Ultimately, the missionaries wanted to plant a church among the Buriats, and education would be the vehicle towards this end.

But like the strategy of an itinerant ministry, formal education ran into several problems. Parents saw little reason to send their children to school; children were needed at home to tend the livestock. Accommodation for students from distant locations meant that some sort of boarding option had to be provided. The lamas stirred up opposition as their position of power was naturally threatened. There was a fear too that Buriat children would become English children. Also, the local Russian political scene was changing, with Russian educational policy demanding that the Buriats learn Russian, as part of the Russian attempt to integrate the Buriats into Russian society. Some of the missionaries' own eccentricities worked against them too. They would not interact with the local Buriat on a Sunday (being a Sabbath rest), so inquirers that came on a Sunday were turned away. This was not a wise policy as nomads would be unlikely to return. Nevertheless, small beginnings were made and converts like Shagdur and Rintsin, who both studied at The Academy, went on to higher things.

In 1826, the Academy, located at Selenginsk, had fourteen students aged between eleven and twenty-six. The curriculum was Mongolian, Russian, Latin, Greek and English grammar; arithmetic, geometry, trigonometry, algebra, geography, history, composition, translation and logic. One can't help wondering at the appropriateness of such a curriculum for nomadic Buriat children. Eight dropped out. Three small schools were started at the three different station sites after the missionaries split up in 1828, and they included both boys and girls.

Numbers varied from ten to thirteen in the Stallybrass' school at Khodon, including, in 1834, four or five girls. The Stallybrass children joined in the teaching at this school: Sarah Stallybrass jnr taught the girls and women, and the two elder boys, Thomas and William, assisted with the more able boys. In the Ona school, there were twenty-five students in 1839 under the guidance of the Swans.

The ultimate aim of the three schools (Selenginsk, Khodon and Ona) was to produce evangelists. The Bible was used as a text book, Christian songs were taught, and essays on spiritual themes were set. Some small success was gained, the most famous graduate of The Academy being the Buriat scholar Rintsin who went on to be a leader in the development of the intellectual life of the Buriat nation. Rintsin was a 'secular' success, and the missionaries were disappointed that no great amount of 'spiritual' success was achieved. Some names have been left for us: Shagdur, Badma, Wangdang, Jigjit, Tarba and Rinchindorj. The last turned against the mission in the late 1830s, and Tarba, being quite a capable student went on to become chief *taisha*, but fell from office in 1852. The others went on to join the Russian Orthodox Church.

It was three years later and we'd lost contact with Togsoo. She'd been swallowed up in the vast expanse of middle-Gobi and the idiosyncrasies of Mongol Post. We had received one letter with a photo.

'Do you want to come to Dundgov with me?' The question came from Gerald, an American vet. 'I have to go down to a *ger* west of Mandalgov and deliver a whole lot of vaccinations for a member of the Herders' Association.'

'That'll be great. Any chance of doing something else on the way?' I asked and then told him about Togsoo. 'I'd love to locate her and encourage her in her Christian faith.' It was a very long shot even attempting to find her. Which horizon would we start looking on?

Early June was a good time to travel. Not too hot or cold. Not wet and boggy.

The 'sixty-nine' pulled up outside our apartment. Karen had made up a large box of children's clothing, teddy bears and other domestic paraphernalia for Togsoo's new baby. In my bag were new editions of Old Testament books that had just been published. I threw my gear in the back on top of the odd assortment of vet stuff and said *Sain bain uu* to the driver.

'Where's the translator?' I asked Gerald as we pulled away.

'You're it,' he replied and grinned at me.

Ten hours later we bounced into Mandalgov. How the driver ever found his way amazes me to this day. We followed the telegraph poles for some way, then he just navigated by instinct. There was no road as such, only a route. We lost it only once. I'd heard of drivers getting distracted by passing herds of gazelles or wanting to go off to shoot wolves. Our driver was remarkably restrained, stopping only three times to drink *su-tai tsai* in *gers* that we passed.

'I've only got this photo.' I showed the tatty black and white to Gerald. We went through Mandalgov and it was only on the way back that we had some time to look for Togsoo. 'I'll try at the post office to start with.'

After much explaining and gesticulating to the lady at the post office, the word 'Tai Kwon Do' triggered a response.

'Yes. I know her. She's Demberel's daughter. She used to teach Tai Kwon Do here. She lives out in Guravan uul *som*, about two hours east of here.' My heart sank. 'But her uncle works upstairs. I'll ring him.'

Togsoo's uncle must have persuaded his boss to let him off work for the rest of the day.

He greeted me enthusiastically. '*Sain bain uu*. Togsoo has told us all about you. Thank you for looking after her in Ulaanbaatar. She's not in Guravan uul just now. She's gone to help her father with the livestock over the summer. I'll take you there.' I was very relieved on two counts: that the first Buddhist relative was pleased to see me, and that we were in fact going to meet Togsoo.

Demberel's encampment was about an hour north of Mandalgov, on a route parallel to the main route back to Ulaanbaatar. Summer rain hadn't arrived yet, and the grass was struggling to push through the fine desert gravel. Ragged, thin and moulting camels casually looked up as we passed, their humps sagging at the end of a long cold winter.

We pulled into Demberel's encampment in a huge cloud of dust. There was no way that Togsoo would have known we were coming. She stood up from milking the goats and just stared at the sixty-nine. I suppose we all looked like martians, covered from head to toe in dust.

Once the penny dropped, the welcome was overwhelming. They cooked food, showed us the animals, talked about the past year, and thanked me again for looking after Togsoo during her studies in Ulaanbaatar. I clucked over Togsoo's baby (the father was in Mandalgov) and gave her the box of gifts. I gave her the Old Testament booklets. She assured me that she was reading her Bible every day and that her family had not given her much opposition.

'There's a small group of Christians in Mandalgov now,' she volunteered. 'When I can, I go along to the meetings. I usually have to borrow a horse to get in from Guravan uul.'

Gerald was very pleased to have met the family. 'It's a real pleasure to be able to bring some encouragement to a Christian so far away from regular fellowship and teaching. There's a real ministry just wandering around the steppe here contacting the nomads and living life with them and telling them about Jesus.'

Before leaving, Demberel gave us a formal Mongolian greeting complete with blue *hatag* and milk. This was a Shamanistic ritual. I knew I was expected to flick the milk with my fourth finger to the four points of the compass, and appease the spirits that dwelt there.

Flicking the milk, I said in very poor Mongolian: 'Thanks be to the Lord of the universe who created the four points of the compass, who made this beautiful land. Thanks be for Jesus who came to die for our sins and give us new life through his resurrection. Thanks be that his Spirit now lives in Togsoo and we ask that his Spirit will come into the whole of this family.'

We said our farewells. I didn't know if I'd see Togsoo again. I promised that I'd pray for her and her baby.

We drove off east and the driver, by some miracle, found the main track north to Ulaanbaatar again.

'I was really impressed by your handling of that last ceremony with the blue scarf,' said Gerald. 'How did you know what to say when you were flicking the milk?'

'I didn't know what to say,' I replied. 'If I'd known the right words, I probably wouldn't have said them anyway because of all the Shamanistic content. I thought it was a good opportunity to give them some good Christian content. So I made it all up.'

NOTES

1. Charles R. Bawden, *Shamans, Lamas, and Evangelicals: The English Missionaries in Siberia* (London: Routledge and Kegan Paul, 1985), 86.
2. Charles R. Bawden, 'The English Missionaries in Siberia and their Translation of the Bible into Mongolian', *Mongolian Studies* 6 (1980), 24.
3. Charles R. Bawden, *Shamans, Lamas, and Evangelicals: The English Missionaries in Siberia* (London: Routledge and Kegan Paul, 1985), 237.

Chapter 28

Alexander I
and Nicholas I
Russian Tsars who influenced the
LMS Buriatia Mission

*'We have discovered the pearl of a devout heart.
We are fully and firmly resolved to receive the
doctrine of the saving God, Jesus Christ... after the
conviction we have obtained of the truth of the
Word of God... We must abide by this doctrine.'*
Batma and Nomtu

Hidehiro, my Japanese colleague, opened a box which he had
placed on the coffee table in front of him.

'I've photocopied Stallybrass' and Swan's Bible for you,' he
announced.

I couldn't believe my ears. I didn't think that any manuscripts still survived. I tore open the box and stared at a huge
pile of A4 sheets of *mongol bichig* text.

'Where did you get this?' I asked incredulously.

'I found it in Japan. There's only one copy in Japan. I think
there are probably four manuscript copies worldwide. This is
both Old and New Testament. The Old Testament never got
into circulation, but here it is. I photocopied it all for you.'

I stroked the top page lovingly. 'I'm learning *mongol bichig* at
language school, but I don't think I'll ever be able to read this.
It's written in quite a formal style. I think that most Mongols
here in Ulaanbaatar wouldn't be able to read it either.'

Hidehiro filled in some gaps. 'Yes, and the choice of vocabulary is different too. The modern Mongolian New Testament,
Shin Geree, uses different words for the key Christian concepts.'

I was very aware of the language debate among the expat
Christians in Ulaanbaatar. It had usually generated more heat
than light.

'I've got something else for you.' Hidehiro handed me three

computer disks. 'Last year this whole volume of Stallybrass' and Swan's was transcribed into the Cyrillic text. It's here on these disks. You can copy them if you like.'

High ideals

There had been high expectations for the London Missionary Society's work in Buriatia. Robert Pinkerton and John Paterson, prime movers behind the mission, had promised the LMS that Irkutsk and its neighbouring countryside could become one of the most important missionary stations in the world. Strategically, it was ideal. The Buriats would first be converted, then other neighbouring Siberian tribes would follow. From the north, the Christian gospel could then penetrate south into Mongolia where the Khalka tribe would be converted, and so further south even to Beijing. Ultimately, the whole of China could be reached from this northern Christian base.

However, within twenty-five years of its closure, writers were dismissing the mission as of no consequence. By 1915, the only significant achievement had been the translation of the Bible. A very distorted picture was being painted, ignoring two decades of preaching, teaching and travel. In some mission histories, the London Missionary Society is not even acknowledged: 'No actual attempt to evangelise the Mongols was, however, made till the coming of James Gilmour in 1870.'[1] A morbid fascination arose as to the mission's alleged failure.

Why was this? Why did the mission 'fail'?

Reform and suppression: two Russian tsars

It seems that Russia was chosen because of the potential for state patronage. Tsar Alexander I brought many correctives to a legacy of corruption and mismanagement from previous reigns of Russian monarchs. He was a handsome, strong, humane and optimistic emperor who tried to instigate reform at several levels. Alexander freed up many land laws, allowing even serfs to purchase land on which they worked. In 1801 he issued a decree allowing merchants and state peasants to buy land, where this had been a privilege of only the nobility before. Alexander also repealed laws prohibiting the importation of foreign books, and also allowed private ownership of printing presses. His main achievement was an overhaul of the education system, establishing many different types of schools throughout Russia, including three new universities. However, this drive for reform was also his undoing. He was intoxicated by the challenge of magnificent schemes, but then didn't have the skills to carry them through to completion.

It took Napoleon's attack on Moscow in 1812 to bring Alexander back to reality. The burning of Moscow precipitated a personal spiritual crisis and he turned to reading the Bible daily and praying regularly. After pushing Napoleon all the way back to Paris, he became something of a mystic, embracing the teachings of a French prophetess. He endorsed a 'universal religion', with hints of Quaker and Moravian teaching. After returning from France, he gave his sole attention to the efforts of the Russian Bible Society. His spiritual fervour drove him to extremes, both politically and spiritually.

The permission granted to the LMS to establish the Buriatia Mission was due directly to Alexander and his personal spiritual sympathies. He and Prince Golitsyn of Irkutsk were both favourable toward the LMS translation work, even supporting it personally on occasions. However, it would not be right to view the initial favour granted to the Selenginsk Mission by Tsar Alexander I as exceptional. It rode on the back of his nationwide reforms.

However, for the LMS to be courting Alexander's favour proved to be short-sighted. If the state changed its mind, then there would be no more mission. This is exactly what happened. In 1825, Alexander's younger brother, Nicholas I, succeeded him.

Nicholas I (r.1825–1855) has been described variously as the 'personification of classic autocracy' and the 'emperor who froze Russia for thirty years'. He was 'infinitely majestic, determined and powerful, hard as stone and relentless as fate'.[2] His strong one-man rule was driven by military fascination and fear. He would strike quickly at things he hated, whether people, ideas or countries. Being Alexander's junior by nineteen years, he grew up during the Napoleonic wars. This influenced his 'Official Nationality' policy which was introduced in 1833 and had three parts: Autocracy, Nationality and Orthodoxy.

Autocracy was that of the emperor; he was the father of the nation. Nationality was the duty of the commoner to uphold the order of the motherland. Orthodoxy was the endorsement of the Russian Orthodox Church as the ultimate source of ideals and ethics that bound society together. Where Alexander had flirted with reforms, Nicholas swung the pendulum to extreme conservatism. Nicholas was suspicious of all independent initiatives, opposing creative thinking, and barring all common participation in local politics.

When Nicholas came to power, he quickly over-ruled much of Alexander's reforms, centralising government and curbing the dissemination of all foreign and liberal ideas. In his Official Nationality policy he promoted 'Russification', and it is within this overall national return to conservative politics that the Selenginsk Mission was closed. The mission was interpreted as a small outpost of England disseminating non-Russian and non-Orthodox ideas. Its very existence was due to the whim of Russian emperors, and ultimately it got caught up in circumstances greater than itself.

Further hurdles for the London Missionary Society

The LMS missionaries had to deal with further hurdles. It could take up to six months for a letter to return to England from southern Siberia, so major policy decisions which had to be endorsed by the LMS directors were slow in coming. Even local communication was exceedingly difficult with few formed roads, no telegraph system and irregular postal services.

This isolation compounded the interpersonal strife in the mission. We have already mentioned the neurotic behaviour of Robert Yuille. Sarah Stallybrass too was idiosyncratic. When the missionaries separated, they were located up to three days' ride from each other, making communication on such projects as Bible translation even more difficult.

Local Russian government officials were suspicious of motives and contemptuous of the missionaries' desire to work with the Buriats. Why should anyone really care about the despised Buriats? Religious reasons were deemed insufficient motivation. Surely what lay behind their staying power was political, or so the Russian governors were tempted to think. Any Buriat converts naturally remained close to the missionaries while they were being taught the faith, and this led to the accusation of 'going over to England'. By the time the missionaries were evicted from Buriatia, Russian authorities in Irkutsk were monitoring all their movements, contacts and mail. There must, they thought, be some ulterior motive. Were they English spies? Or perhaps commercial spies, monitoring Russian/Chinese trade through Kiachta on the Russian/Mongol border?

Mistrust also arose among the Buriats. Their worldview was Shamanist and, at the time, Buddhism was growing in influence. More than half the people were Buddhist lamas, and the rest of the population was nomadic. They were a naturally passive and unemotional people. For an Englishman to travel half way around the world to teach them a new religion did not make sense.

Opposition came from the local Russian Orthodox Church too. When a powerful, intelligent and influential Buriat, who had opposed the missionaries, resolved to become a Christian, the Orthodox Church became defensive and shut the mission station down. Indecisive Russian administrators in Irkutsk, coupled with an ambitious new archbishop from 1838 presented new local opposition. Ironically the Orthodox Church inherited the few converts that LMS missionaries had made, and soon afterwards started a mission to the Buriat itself.

Was the LMS mission a grand failure?

Was the legacy of the LMS the grand failure for which it has been criticised? Records list three major achievements.

First, the LMS introduced formal education for the Buriats. They established The Academy built on Alexander's official policy of new educational endeavours across Russia. In a small way, the intellectual life of a few Buriats was enhanced, and perhaps even a national Buriat consciousness was a result, although this would be hard to measure.

Secondly, the LMS regards its missionaries' long trips in the hinterland as significant. These missionaries were the first Europeans to get a good view of Mongolian life and culture. Gilmour writes of Hannah Swan: 'turning her back on so many things and friends that were dear to her, she set her face towards Siberia, and... so mixed with the people, and so applied herself to the acquisition of the language, that not only could she speak it well among the natives, but could read and write it so as to be able to conduct a correspondence in it upwards of a quarter of a century after the missionaries had left the country.'[3] The level of proficiency of language and culture attained by the missionaries should not be downplayed. They were competent in the Buriat environment. Their itinerant efforts could be described as 'seed sowing'. A good number of tracts and Gospel portions were scattered across the Buriat hinterland. Larson, about a hundred years later, records finding some literature in the *gers* of the nomads in northern Mongolia: 'I have several times found copies of the Bible in the translation of these Selenginsk missionaries in Mongol tents pitched at various places on the plateau, the book sharing the sacred place on the family altar with the holy books of Buddhist faith from Tibet.'[4] Granted, some literature was taken to make cigarette papers and to start the fires in the *gers*, but some Buriats were converted.

Thirdly, the Bible was translated into the Buriat-Mongol language. This was the main achievement of the mission. Even if their converts were never baptised, and no formal church other than home meetings in missionaries' houses was ever established, the LMS workers in Buriatia must be credited with the translation of the first full Mongolian Bible.

The first Mongolian Bible

Isaak Schmidt started work on the Buriat New Testament because of the interest shown by the Buriats in Irkutsk after they read his Kalmuck *Gospel of Matthew*. Badma and Nomtu, two Buriat *zaisans* or petty nobles, were enlisted to help him in St Petersburg. The translation proved effective, at least in the lives of these two *zaisans*. They wrote from St Petersburg to the Governor back in Irkutsk:

> We have discovered the pearl of a devout heart. We are fully and firmly resolved to receive the doctrine of the saving God, Jesus Christ. Although we are not yet acquainted with the manners and usage of His religion, and when we return home should find no teacher upon whose breast we could lean our head, neither any house of God, yet after the conviction we have obtained of the truth of the Word of God, we can no longer endure the want of it; we must abide by this doctrine.[5]

Badma was baptised shortly before his death and entered the Orthodox Church; this must have been his testimony. Nomtu proved himself an ineffective translator. He had been unable to learn Russian, was intemperate and given to occasional violence. He was, in essence, a drunkard.

The LMS missionaries had a problem when they started their translation: should they start with the New or Old Testament, and at what level should they pitch it? Literacy was the sole privilege of lamas and *zaisans* who did not condescend to read religious literature in the vernacular. Holy scriptures had to be written in 'holy' language, if they were to be read at all. They chose to pitch their translation in the high form and it was this translation, the so-called 'Literary Version', that became the standard Mongolian Bible for a hundred or so years.

Stallybrass and Swan started translating *Genesis* in 1823 and the full Old Testament was finished in 1840. Schmidt had already been working on the New Testament. There had been some unhappiness about Schmidt's translation, but as he sat on the Russian Academy of Sciences, and had to approve all translation work before the Russian Imperial licence to print would be issued, this was the prudent course of action.

Stallybrass and Swan worked from the Hebrew and co-opted two Buriat scholars to help them: Kichi Bomnia worked with them for eight years (1823–1831), and Vemxchi Zavem for four (1836–1840). Alongside this, the missionaries distributed tracts and parts of Scripture as these were printed.

The translation was threatened by a turn of events that no one could have predicted when the mission was ordered to close down. In 1841, Tsar Nicholas I ordered the press to stop and the three missionaries were forbidden to teach religion. As the imperial decree did not expel them, the missionaries lodged an appeal to stay on and finish their last book, *Ezekiel*, so they could publish a fully bound Old Testament. The appeal succeeded, but permission to circulate the Old Testament was denied. Wary of the change of imperial policies, the LMS closed down the whole project in Buriatia. The New Testament too was nearly finished at the time of the suppression order.

All was not lost by the closure of the Mission. Printing continued in England sponsored by the British and Foreign Bible Society, but the greatest challenge now was the lack of Mongolian type. Manchu type was borrowed for the first print. It was usable, but not the best. Eventually by 1846 both Old and New Testaments were available in Literary Mongolian or 'high language Buriat'. Here was the first complete Mongolian Bible.

The Old Testament was never circulated in Buriatia as a complete volume, but only as individual books. The New Testament however, completed and reprinted in London, has been called 'a masterpiece for its time' which was used for about a hundred years. It subsequently underwent another two major revisions. (This constant revision process is needed for all translations.) Being in the literary form of the language meant it was not familiar reading for the common people, even if read to them. But it was the right choice for that time. The LMS missionaries were aware of its limitations so gave time, too, to preaching, teaching and setting up schools. By 1853, over two thousand New Testaments had been distributed.

The Bible in vernacular

Still wanting to see something in the vernacular, the British and Foreign Bible Society started work on a revised New Testament in 1877 using the proper Mongolian font. The New Testament's most recent revision was released as late as 1953, by a group from The Evangelical Alliance Mission, working with Mongols. It has been used consistently in Inner Mongolia, and can still be bought from the Hong Kong Bible Society today.

What happened to the Buriatia missionaries?

Edward Stallybrass moved to England and settled in East London where he was married for the third time, to Sarah Bass. Together they ran an academy for young girls until Sarah died in 1855. Edward married his fourth wife, Mary Oughton in 1861. He also outlived Mary who died in 1874. He died aged ninety in 1884.

William Swan resigned from the LMS in 1841, following the closure of the Buriatia mission, and went to teach at the

Glasgow Theological Academy. He also worked for the BFBS and the LMS in Scotland, showing a continued interest in mission, and helping with promotional work for a number of other mission agencies. William lived long enough to advise on the reopening of the LMS mission to Mongolia, but died in 1866 before James Gilmour left for Mongolia. Hannah Swan died in Edinburgh in 1890.

Robert Yuille, after his dismissal from the LMS in 1838, didn't leave Buriatia until 1846. How he supported himself is a mystery. He eventually returned to Glasgow, and died there in 1861. Whether he was reconciled to the LMS is not known, although his cantankerous personality would lead us to doubt this. John Abercrombie returned to the Scottish colony at Karass and lived there until at least the 1870s. He was described as 'a venerable old man, with fine regular features... coal-black sparkling eyes, and a long grey beard that would have done honour to a patriarch'.[6]

A huge personal cost was paid by the LMS missionaries in their desire to be faithful witnesses to Christ among the Buriat Mongols. The Yuilles' son, Robert junior, a very sickly child, died of fever in 1823. Susannah Stallybrass died in 1825 at just a few months old. The same week she died, both Elisabeth and Janet Yuille also died. Benjamin Stallybrass, the youngest of six Stallybrass children died in infancy. Of thirteen children of the mission, only eight survived to adulthood.

James Gilmour visited Selenginsk and Onage Dome in 1871, thirty years after the mission's closure. At Selenginsk he found the graves of four of the mission who died there: Martha Yuille (d.1827), two of her children and a young Stallybrass. At Onage Dome, he found two more graves, those of Edward Stallybrass's wives, Sarah and Charlotte. Monuments to these missionaries, erected by those in grief, have stood up to the ravages of 170 Siberian winters and are still there on the banks of the rivers in Buriatia. He lamented the premature closure of the mission station, finding only the odd tract or part of Scripture in one or two nomad *gers*.

The hope of Robert Pinkerton and John Paterson that the liberal policies of Alexander I could make Buriatia a springboard for the evangelisation of China proved too ambitious. The potential they saw in basing the work at Irkutsk was misinformed, and the probability of success highly exaggerated. Ultimately the mission was overwhelmed by the conservative autocracy of Nicholas I.

Yet the mission was not a total failure. Its achievements were respectable: a Bible translation, some contribution to Buriatian education, a handful of Christian believers. Among the people of Selenginsk, Khodon and Ona, a small legacy remains. Something of the missionaries' teaching or way of life must have stuck: the local Buriats still tend those lonely graves.[7]

I downloaded Hidehiro's disks onto my computer and searched quickly through the Old Testament files to the *Psalms*. Figuring I'd be able to read something simple, like Psalm 23, I enlarged the Cyrillic script, formatted it nicely and printed it. I wanted to see how my Mongol friends would read it.

I gave the printout to Magnai, a Mongolian colleague with whom I was working on some distance learning material. He was quite unaware that there was another Mongol Bible dating from last century. He read through it slowly.

'This is incredible,' he said. 'Where did you get it?'

I explained about the Buriatia mission and my meeting Hidehiro the day before. He gazed at the text and read it again, slowly.

'It's written in *deed khel*,' Magnai volunteered. 'The language is quite formal and there are several old words we don't use any more. It reads quite... ' he paused, lost for words. He was muttering the lines to himself: 'Jehova is my shepherd.... '

He turned to me. 'It reads majestically. It's got some wonderful expressions and phrases. I think it's probably more formal than your English King James Version.'

I was aware that the modern *Shin Geree* was a dynamic equivalent translation written for modern Mongolians. It was full of idioms and pithy, common speech.

'Can I have this?' Magnai asked, folding the printout and placing it in his pocket.

'Of course,' I replied. Scanning through the Windows File Manager, I showed him the list of files. 'There's plenty more where that came from.'

'I'll show it to some of my friends. I think it will bring a good balance to our appreciation of the Bible. If they like it, I'll just come back and copy the disks. OK?'

NOTES
1. C.H. Robinson in Charles R. Bawden, *Shamans, Lamas and Evangelicals: The English Missionaries in Siberia* (Routledge and Kegan Paul: London, 1985),p.xi.
2. *Nicholas I.* Micropaedia of Encyclopaedia Britannica, 15th edition, 1990.
3. C. Silvester Horne, *The Story of the LMS*, 2nd edition (London Missionary Society: London, 1895), p.144.
4. Frans August Larson, *Larson, Duke of Mongolia* (Little, Brown and Co.: Boston, 1930), p.264.
5. Marshall Broomhall, *The Bible in China* (1934), p.129.
6. Charles R. Bawden, *op.cit.*, p.352.
7. This was communicated to the author personally by Charles R. Bawden in August 1998.

<table>
<tr>
<td>Chapter
29</td>
<td><h1>James Gilmour,</h1>
<h2>Consecrated Pioneer to the Mongols</h2>
'I doubt if even St Paul endured more for Christ
than did James Gilmour.'
Anonymous colleague of James Gilmour</td>
</tr>
</table>

Beijing railway station is an awesome place. Initially I was intrigued by it. It hinted at the enthralling chaos of Old Delhi station through which I'd been countless times as a boy. Beneath the simmering mass of humanity which was jostling, shoving, sitting, sleeping, waiting, staring, running and searching was an order imposed by a wily group of men in green uniforms.

Obviously foreigners were expected to look after themselves as there was not a word of English anywhere (except a sign that said 'foreign trains'). All I could say in Chinese was 'hello', 'New Zealand' and 'thank you'. When these words were strung together, this very complex sentence usually got me out of most tight spots.

We'd decided to catch the train back to Ulaanbaatar after two weeks in Beijing for medical check-ups for our daughter Anjali who had developed some sort of respiratory problem. It was July, midsummer. We headed for the 'foreign trains' sign and dumped our luggage. It was 7am. I had half an hour to find our train.

At 7.25 I returned from a thorough exploratory circuit of the whole of the station. I had shown my tickets to about thirty people. No one knew anything.

'Can't find it,' I said to Karen who'd been guarding the luggage. 'I'll just check with this custodian again.'

That custodian had obviously grown suspicious of Karen's prolonged wait. When she saw the ticket, she burst into an agitated high-pitched diatribe, dragged Karen by the arm, and dived into the masses of people in the main hall. I grabbed the remaining seven pieces of luggage (unlike Old Delhi station, there were no porters anywhere) and tried to follow the sound of her animated babble.

It must have been something like 'make way for these stupid foreigners who are about to miss their train', punctuated by a string of expletives, for an opening formed in the crowd like Moses parting the Red Sea. Zillions of eyes were watching us.

She disappeared into an underpass (that I had missed in my search; obviously the Mongolian train was not regarded as 'foreign') and by now had broken into a quick trot. She shouted abuse at the guard when he tried to stop us and check our tickets. We emerged on a platform, she pointed at a train, yelled at us the last time and disappeared. We scrambled on, dumped the luggage and collapsed.

I rubbed my bruised and battered shoulders; my arms felt like jelly.

Karen glared at me, opened her mouth to say something, then thought better of it.

'No worries,' I joked, 'we're a full minute early.'

Passion and conviction

In 1871 the London Missionary Society kick-started the Mongol mission. This time, instead of approaching Mongolia from the north, the LMS capitalised on the opening door through China. The pioneer of this second phase of the LMS mission was James Gilmour.

James Gilmour is perhaps the most famous of all missionaries to Mongolia. He ranks with heavyweights like William Carey, Robert Morrison and David Livingstone. His eccentricities and his unswerving commitment to Christ made him a household name in the late 1800s: 'If you pray earnestly, you cannot but work earnestly, and then you will also give earnestly, and I do not think we can be too earnest in the matter for which Christ was so much in earnest that He laid down his own life.'[1]

Gilmour's sense of call to Mongolia had come from a blend of logic and common sense. 'Is the kingdom a harvest field? Then I thought it reasonable to seek work where the need was greatest and the workers fewest.' He chose Mongolia.

Born in Glasgow, Scotland in 1843, Gilmour was converted in the revival of 1859 as part of the Evangelical Awakening. He graduated with a MA from Glasgow University, then joined the LMS in 1870. He set out almost straightaway for Mongolia, arriving at the port of Tientsin in China on 18 May.

Gilmour spent no time familiarising himself with the niceties of urban Chinese life. News of the Tientsen massacre was enough for him to steer clear of large Chinese cities and head for the remoteness of the Mongol steppe. On 5 August, only nine weeks after arriving in the country, he headed north-west to the border town of Kalgan, then across the vast Gobi steppe lands to Urga (modern-day Ulaanbaatar), and on as far north as Kiachta on the Russian border. After visiting the old LMS mission site at Selenginsk, he continued north to Irkutsk. Now he could get to know Mongol culture and start learning the language. His embryonic strategy was simple: to equip himself to preach and write Christian tracts. This initial tour of the Mongol heartland lasted for fifteen months.

Gilmour had made good gains with his language during this first trip. In Kiachta, he tried to secure a language teacher, but the Russian and Mongol authorities suspected his motives, so he chose to spend three months living in a *ger* with a lama. This had been an unexpected blessing, allowing him rapid progress with the language and the culture.

Gilmour spent that winter in Beijing, but was soon off on another trip onto the Mongolian steppe. He travelled mainly in north-eastern Mongolia and here he found that instead of being mainly nomadic, the Mongols were sedentary and agricultural. These Mongols could speak Chinese, but Gilmour found no sense of call to them. His call was to the nomadic Mongols of the steppe. Wintering in Beijing and spending the summer on the steppe became his pattern.

During the winter of 1872 to 1873, Gilmour took up residence at the Great Yellow Temple in Beijing, now called Yong He Gong, situated on the northern side of the subway circle in Beijing. He had discovered that Mongol visitors to China would gather there, usually on religious pilgrimage or for trade purposes, so there was good opportunity to meet people, and to continue studying their language. By this time, Gilmour had realised he would benefit greatly from some sort of medical training. He had frequently been accosted for medical treatment and had tried to provide what he could. So that winter he spent some time with Dr Dudgeon (also of the LMS) acquiring rudimentary knowledge of treatments.

On his trips into the hinterland, Gilmour himself suffered a type of sickness: intense loneliness that bordered on depression. The immense horizons, scarcity of human contact and vast distances have to be experienced to be believed. Loneliness became a torment. He appealed for help from the LMS, hoping the directors would send out a co-worker, which they did. He could see great potential need for medical missionaries. Gilmour was expecting a male medical colleague, but God provided a woman. In 1874, he married Emily Pankard.

Gilmour's family life

One could call this marriage quasi-arranged. Gilmour had heard a lot about Emily from her sister, Mrs Ann Meech. The Meeches were missionaries based in Beijing. Gilmour had stayed with them in 1873, and they had often talked about Ann's sister whose photo stood on the mantelpiece. With Ann's permission, Gilmour entered into correspondence with Emily: his first letter contained the marriage proposal, and Emily's response was her acceptance! They met for the first time at the dock at Tientsin after Emily's long voyage from England and were married a week later on 13 December 1874.

Emily threw herself into the dual role of wife and colleague, acquiring the Mongolian language rapidly, and accompanying

Gilmour on further travels onto the steppe. But soon her health broke down, due to the combination of the rough lifestyle and the demands of Mongol nomadic life. The psychological pressures of living as itinerant missionaries in a completely foreign culture built up; lack of privacy was the greatest challenge. Mongols were very interested in them: 'at our meals, our devotions, our ablutions, there they were much amused and interested, of course!'[2] In 1882, after a year of poor health, Gilmour took Emily back to England for a furlough. This rest did her good, and she returned to Mongolia rejuvenated. However, the relief proved only temporary and she succumbed to tuberculosis in Beijing in 1885 and died. James and Emily had had two boys, William ('Willie') and James ('Jimmie'), in their eight years of marriage. Both were sent to England for their schooling, a decision that added to his own distress and loneliness. Their absence tormented him.

Gilmour's strategy

Gilmour's strategy was simple. He combined common-sense medical treatments with tract distribution and preaching. Clusters of Mongol *gers* were dotted across the steppe, or at Naadam festivals. Mongols would come together for horse racing, wrestling and archery. Gilmour availed himself of the ever-open *ger* door and would quickly become engaged in spiritual discussion. The mere presence of this odd foreigner would draw the neighbours, and Gilmour had an audience for as long as he liked.

However, despite his commitment to the nomadic Mongols of the steppe, Gilmour later felt the Mongols would more easily be reached from a sedentary base, probably in China. He chose Kalgan, the border town on the main trading route between China and Mongolia.

His methods were novel for his day. Colleagues saw the evangelisation of the Chinese as the priority. They would build mission stations with high walls; small colonies of England surrounded by a mass of Asian heathen. Gilmour challenged this. His priority was the Mongols, and he would not be confined to any mission station nor naturally join in the social life of his fellow Britons. That he had so few converts seemed to prove his methods wrong.

Gilmour's passion carried him on. The reactivation of the LMS Mongol mission was not without its critics, mainly because of Gilmour's lack of conversions. His sense of call and his strong ethic of duty drove him. So after three major trips into Mongolia without any results, and with a frail wife, he still urged that the mission continue. He argued that the Mongols had just as much right to hear the gospel as any other race on earth. It was not so much results that were important, as a duty to 'preach the gospel to every creature'.[3] Therefore he would not abandon the mission. This steel-like willpower was certainly a strong trait in his character. One of his colleagues in Beijing wrote: 'I doubt if even St Paul endured more for Christ than did James Gilmour.'

Gilmour became convinced that personal one-to-one evangelism was the key to the heart of the Mongol, rather than public preaching. This conviction was part of the reason for shifting to a sedentary location. Nomads kept moving, and even though his name was widely known over the steppe, Gilmour could build only a few meaningful relationships. But in a border town, it would be different. Relationships could be maintained and evangelism could be personal. 'In the shape of converts I have seen no results. I have not, as far as I am aware, seen any one who even wanted to be a Christian; but healing their diseases I have had opportunity to tell many of Jesus the Great Physician.'[4] In 1884, thirteen years after arriving in Mongolia, Gilmour saw the first Mongol convert, a man by the name of Borjinto.

From 1870 to 1885, Gilmour devoted himself to the nomadic Mongols, believing the sedentary Mongols in Inner Mongolia should be reached by Chinese missionaries. By 1886, however, the American Board of Missions was well established in Kalgan, and setting up work among the sedentary Mongols in Eastern Mongolia. Three centres were established: Ta-cheng-tse, Ta-si-kow and Chaoyang. Gilmour may have moved to Chaoyang because of mission politics. His departure from Kalgan prompted American colleagues to invite the Moravians to Kalgan. The Moravians were unable to accept the invitation, but it did stimulate their mission to consider Mongolia, and indirectly caused them to establish a work in Ladakh, north India.

Gilmour's legacy

Gilmour had found the Mongol nomads slow to respond to the gospel. After the conversion of Borjinto, he saw only two more Mongol converts in Chihli province in north-east Mongolia, bringing the grand total to three. After relocating to the town of Chaoyang, Gilmour did manage to establish a solid work among the Chinese, and stuck ardently to his conviction: 'I am still of the opinion that our best way to reach the Mongols is from a Chinese base.' In a sedentary environment, his strategy remained essentially the same: heal the sick, preach the gospel and distribute literature. He himself wrote some tracts and catechisms. Those few Chinese converts whom he made were shaky in their commitment. One caused scandal, and another robbed him. One became a Christian because of the promise of work. Nevertheless, Gilmour did leave behind a small Chinese congregation in Chaoyang. Although this was in Mongol territory, he had dwindling contact with the Mongols in this second phase of his ministry.

Gilmour's most significant contribution to the evangelisation of Mongolia was not the number of converts or the size of the church he left behind. It was, perhaps, the publication of *Among the Mongols*. Written in 1883, this proved to be an instant best-seller in England. *The Spectator* wrote in its editorial: 'Robinson Crusoe has turned missionary; has lived years in Mongolia and written a book about it.'[5] It became one of those classic missionary stories that propelled another generation into the missions cause. The challenge of Mongol work appealed particularly to the Swedes, both those in Sweden, and those that had immigrated to the USA. Frans Larson, who later received the honorary Mongol title of 'Duke', felt called to Mongolia as a direct result of reading about Gilmour. Larson set up the mission station in Har Osso and he was followed by twenty-six other young Swedes to work in China and Mongolia, all around 1893. A direct result of Gilmour's legacy.

A further legacy of Gilmour was in medical work. Although untrained, he had offered much to the Mongol nomad in the way of simple hygiene and rudimentary preventative medicine. His clinic in Chaoyang was used by forty or fifty people a day. Mr Liu, a Chinese convert who could speak Mongolian, assisted him initially, until Liu was able to study medicine formally in Beijing. Gilmour promised a doctor and a hospital for the people of Chaoyang, and it was to this end that he kept pleading with the LMS to send doctors.

Gilmour gave a solid twenty years of service to Mongolia, his influence winning him the warm affection and respect of the people. One fellow worker writes, 'I doubt... if Christ ever received from human hands or human heart more loving, more devoted service.'[6] Gilmour had taken two verses of Scripture as promises that motivated him throughout his lonely efforts: 'Blessed are ye that sow beside all waters' (Isaiah 32:20); and: 'In the morning sow thy seed, and in the evening withhold not thine hand; for thou knowest not whether shall prosper, either this or that' (Ecclesiastes 11:6).

Gilmour did not live to see the development of the mission at Chaoyang. He died of typhus fever in 1891, aged forty-seven, and is buried in Tientsin.

The gentle sway and rhythm of the train lulled me into a distant gaze at the horizon.

'Look Dad, camels!'

I followed the direction of Anjali's pointing finger. A herd of two-humped bactrians were staring at us with their droopy eyes, their big floppy lips making fun of us. The last of their winter moult made them look patchy like the fluff from newly-laid carpet. A couple of calves tried to hide between their mother's legs.

A thunderstorm was gathering on the horizon. The dark, lightning-streaked clouds formed an imposing backdrop to the bright sun-drenched plain we were crossing. It felt good to be back in Mongolia, out of the teeming masses of China and the tightly-packed fields that jostled for space before succumbing to the arid Gobi chaparral.

'Do you want some aspirin?' Karen broke my thoughts.

My head was foggy from the night before. I had stayed up till 3am, gallantly fending off prying customs officers, trying to ensure the family had a good night's sleep. Chinese border guards had come onto the train and stamped us out of China. Then the train was shunted off to a long covered siding. Here we were shunted backwards and forwards so that all the couplings came loose, then each carriage was jacked up about two metres off the ground. I had watched all this from the open doorway at the end of the carriage. The wheels were then pushed out, carried off by an overhead crane, then new wheels were placed on the line, and pushed under the carriage again. Slowly, the carriage was let down. Apparently the gauge in Mongolia was different from the Chinese gauge. I looked at the track. There was about two centimetres in the difference. We had now been shunted right up to the Mongolian border and Mongolian border guards shone torches in our faces, stamped our passports and asked questions. All up, the whole routine took about six hours.

I swallowed some aspirin and my head slowly cleared. We were starting to climb ever so slightly up from the plain onto the rolling steppe that we had to cross on the way to Ulaanbaatar. We had been travelling for thirty hours and had another six to go. The grass was longer and greener, and small unchannelled rivulets snaked across the grassland, going nowhere in particular. Wild rhubarb, along with the hues of a hundred different types of wild flowers, shimmered in the breeze of the passing train. A shepherd called to his sheep in the distance. A dozen horses stomped and fretted at a water hole.

'This is probably the same route that was used for trading between Kalgan and Urga,' I said to Karen. 'I'm glad there's a railway now. It used to take over thirty days to make the journey by camel or ox-cart. I wonder if they had to change the wheels of the ox-carts at the border for the different-sized ruts?'

Occasional clusters of white *gers* speckled the green like dice randomly thrown across the carpet. Over the years, we did that train trip three times in all, and each time I was enthralled by the harsh beauty of the Gobi. Even in January, in deep winter, the trip had a certain magical charm to it, as long as the train heating stayed on.

Once we travelled with friends who were new to Mongolia. They had a daughter the same age as Anjali.

The two girls pressed their faces up to the window, and Anjali got all pedagogical.

'Look, Sala,' she said, 'those are *gers*.'

'Yeah' said Sala. Long pause. 'What are *gers*?'

'You know. Those white things,' Anjali explained. 'The Mongol tents. They're round and smooth...like Daddy's bald head!'

NOTES

1. *China's Millions*, North American edition, 1908, p.25.
2. C. Silvester Horne, *op.cit.*, p.379.
3. *Ibid.*
4. *Ibid.* p.378.
5. Marshall Broomhall, *op.cit.*, p.125.
6. *Ibid.*

Thomas Cochrane,
Medical Missionary to the Mongols and the Chinese

'Taifu hsinhao.' ('The Doctor's heart is good.')
Chinese patients of Thomas Cochrane

'Just one packet thanks,' I said to the young boy selling chewing gum. 'And I'll take the English newspaper.'

Since 1993, young Ulaanbaatar entrepreneurs had set themselves up at most bus-stops and thoroughfares, selling mainly single cigarettes, *undaa* (the local fizzy drink), chewing gum, chocolate, newspapers and the like.

I wandered away a distance and watched the crowd of about twenty waiting for the bus. Two were children, somewhere between eight and twelve years of age, and one was an old man with his legs bent in a singularly severe arch from hip to toe. You could bounce a basketball through them without them noticing.

'Rickets,' Karen said. Karen was a nurse and had seen plenty of rickets while practising in a small mission hospital in Chile. 'It's really bad in Mongolia.'

I unwrapped my gum and popped it into my mouth.

'What's with the gum?' Karen didn't approve.

'Trying to enculturate,' I responded feebly. Of the crowd waiting for the bus, over half were chewing gum. 'Look, everyone does it. It's a Mongol thing.'

We were returning from visiting Mongolian friends. My pocket was full of boiled sweets that I'd successfully intercepted between the hostess and my children. The Mongols love to give boiled sweets to children, mine especially. When we gave gifts to Mongol children we tried to give them stuff that wouldn't wreck their teeth, like books or crayons.

By the time the bus arrived, the little sugar in the gum had all been chewed out. I wondered if enculturation couldn't be achieved by some other means.

We squeezed forward to the front of the bus and Anjali took refuge on my lap from the crowd.

'Remember Namona!' she said moralistically. She was referring to a girl who had visited our place once to play. Namona was about six, had a bubbly personality and a very pretty face. Until she opened her mouth. Inside was a dark cavern of rotting pegs, more to be expected from an eighty-year-old tramp. I winced the first time she smiled. The dental bill would bankrupt most people. I was quick to give an object lesson to Anjali about 'moderation in all things', especially boiled sweets. 'Remember Namona!' had become a phrase in our family much like 'Remember the Alamo'; it spurred us on to consider the consequences of wrong choices.

I thought it best that my four-year-old daughter not outdo me in the morals I preached myself, so I folded my gum into the wrapper and put it in my pocket.

As the bus pulled away from the stop, I saw the two kids with rickets trying to run and jump up onto the bottom step of the door-well. They were a desperate sight with their odd waddle; their feet pointed at each other and their legs looked as if they'd snap under the pressure.

'It's so easy to prevent.' Karen was reading my thoughts. 'The diet lacks key vitamins, and they swaddle their babies so tightly that they never get any sunshine: the babies are inevitably jaundiced. That and the long winters means that vitamin D just never gets efficiently synthesised in their skin. And there are all sorts of superstitions attached to it. There's cultural stuff too. The Mongols think we're nuts when we let our babies wave their arms and legs around for exercise. They bind their newborns so tight they're immobilised for the first three months.'

I opened my English newspaper and read the headlines: 'Health Ministry quarantines plague area'. I read on with interest. Bubonic plague had broken out in one of the *aimags* (provinces). I remember when this happened in India once, and the internationl media made a song and dance about it. Here in Mongolia it was endemic, and broke out periodically.

You picked it up from contact with *tarwag*, the prairie-dog-like marmot that lived on the steppe. The Mongols loved to hunt them. Last summer, one of our church's evangelistic teams was delayed due to a quarantine slapped on an area they were passing through.

'Hope that meat you bought gets well cooked,' I said to Karen.

The Chaoyang mission

After Gilmour died, the LMS made several attempts to replace him at the Chaoyang mission. With Mongol-Chinese fighting in the area, an immediate replacement was impossible. Eventually a Dr Case came to Chaoyang. Liu returned from medical studies and assisted him. Others followed. Dr Roberts came in 1888, but left within a month due to a reappointment elsewhere. Dr Purves Smith followed that same year, but his wife's health broke down and he left a year later to continue work with the LMS in Shanghai. John Parker succeeded him. Parker was convinced that if he plodded on, then Gilmour's foundational work would bear fruit. He too appealed for more colleagues, especially doctors. However, his health broke down too, and he had to retire early. W.E. MacFarlane arrived in 1891, but had to resign after four years because of continual dysentery. He was replaced by Dr Thomas Cochrane in 1897.

When Cochrane arrived there was 'a handful of loyal Chinese Christians, an austere little building rated as a chapel, half a dozen Sunday-school children and the Mongol lease of a plot of land adjoining the small compound'. During Cochrane's time, the Rev. and Mrs James D. Liddell from Scotland (parents of the later famous Eric Liddell) took up work in Chaoyang, spending time mainly in evangelism and Bible teaching for the small Chinese congregation. But then they moved on to Siaochang, Beijing, and then Tientsin.

Chaoyang is only a short distance inside the 10,000 Li Wall,[1] or the Great Wall as we know it in English. The town itself is Chinese, but the hinterland was populated by Mongol tribes. It had all originally been Mongol territory, but Chinese immigrants had taken over. It was an economic and religious centre, having large markets and a famous lama temple, Wu-Tai. The Mongols would come into Chaoyang to trade their dairy products for grain, oats, and copper and brass utensils. During fair days and religious festivals, the Mongols would come on pilgrimage to Wu-Tai. Because of this constant movement of Mongols in and out of the town, it was an ideal site to use as a base for Mongol evangelism. This was Gilmour's original dream, and the LMS wanted to build on it.

In 1900 the Chaoyang LMS property was totally destroyed by the Boxers (see Chapter 40), and most of the congregation was scattered, heading into the hill country. The missionaries were encouraged to withdraw to Tientsin on the coast, and in attempting to re-establish the mission after the Boxer uprising, it was decided in 1901 to hand it over to the Irish Presbyterian Mission of Manchuria. These small groups of believers were under the direction of the Irish Presbyterian Mission for only ten years. LMS statistics for the district in 1907 stood at eighteen expat men, five expat women, forty-eight native preachers and up to 2000 church members. There were few, if any, Mongol Christians. The vast majority, if not all, of the local preachers and church members were Chinese. This small beginning was eventually handed on to the Brethren in 1912.

Thomas and Grace Cochrane

Thomas Cochrane was a 'hardy Scot' who described his commitment to God at the age of thirteen simply and forthrightly: 'I have vowed myself to be God's, with his help for ever.' Cochrane had first considered Sudan, but he became a prime candidate to fill Gilmour's shoes. During his LMS missionary interview he was told that Sudan was closed, so where would he like to go? He replied 'to the neediest place there is!' With this open offer, the LMS sent him to Mongolia to replace Gilmour who had died six years previously.

Thomas Cochrane qualified from Glasgow University Medical School in 1896 and arrived in Shanghai in 1897 with his bride of four months, Grace, heading for Chaoyang. John Parker had followed Gilmour, and Cochrane was able to work with Parker for some time before Parker left.

Cochrane came to Chaoyang with the ambitious resolve that 'all of Mongolia could be evangelised in one generation', reflecting the mission commitment of that era. He inherited Lien-yi as an assistant: John Parker had trained him up as an evangelist. Lien-yi and Liu would later go on clinical tours north of Chaoyang around the outlying stations that Gilmour had set up. This was an exceedingly dangerous enterprise as the hinterland was infested with bandits which they encountered on several occasions. However, in surrounding Mongol, Chinese, or mixed race villages, they were generally well received by the peasants. The LMS had struck upon a strategy — medicine — that was to gain much contact with both Mongol and Chinese alike. For all the medical skills that Gilmour didn't have, Cochrane did.

'The Doctor's heart is good'

Cochrane's medical skills were pushed to the limit. He had to deal with smallpox, rabies, bubonic plague, malaria, pneumonia, venereal diseases, cholera, typhus (Gilmour had died of typhus fever), diphtheria, tuberculosis (Emily Gilmour had died of tuberculosis) and a host of skin diseases (scabies was especially common) due to appalling personal hygiene. Added to this was the growing addiction to opium with all its social problems. Cochrane felt overwhelmed by the task:

> I stood at the door of our little Chinese bungalow, and romance, if there were any, merged into reality. I looked over the great plain shut in by encircling hills, and I became

aware of an enveloping depression, as it came home to me that I was the only medical man in thousands of square miles of bandit-ridden territory, and that it would be as much as my life was worth if I should happen to perform an unsuccessful operation.[2]

This was the pre-antibiotic era, and Cochrane did not have the drugs we have today. The challenge was not merely to tend the body, but to couple medicine to the preaching of the gospel such that both complemented each other, and a person received ministry in both body and soul.

This is where Lien-yi came in. While Cochrane and Liu did the medicine, Lien-yi spoke to patients of spiritual matters. Lien-yi was a master of story-telling, having a good wit and plenty of charisma. He adapted the Bible stories to the Chinese medium and spoke in Mongolian to the Mongols. The sedentary Mongols who were residents of Chaoyang were the poorest in the city. They had been relegated to the slums by the Chinese, and those right at the bottom of the pile were those Mongols who had intermarried; they were the 'half breeds'. A Mongolian-speaking evangelist was therefore indispensable. It brought hope to the Mongols and great joy to Cochrane. Lien-yi's rapport was so good that his audience would often beg him for more. This adaptation to use the gifts of local Christians seems obvious to us today. Lien-yi even advised that Cochrane discard his Western clothes for Chinese, which he did, and this helped to dispel lingering mistrust among the Chinese.

From Chaoyang to Beijing

Thomas and Grace Cochrane had to depart abruptly and unceremoniously from Chaoyang in 1900. They managed to get away only hours before the Boxers looted then destroyed the LMS station. They had spent a total of three years there, and three sons had been born to them: Edgar in 1897, and twins

Robert and Thomas in 1899. The local Christians hurriedly dispersed into the mountains.

After a furlough back in Scotland, the mission assigned Cochrane to Beijing where he reopened the LMS Mission Hospital. The mission had started medical and educational work in Beijing as early as 1839. The hospital had been founded by Dr Lockhart, the first LMS doctor to China in 1861. 'The Free Healing Hospital' as it was known had treated about 1.5 million patients in its first forty years before being razed by the Boxers. It was Cochrane's job to rebuild it and reopen it. Dr Li Hsiao Ch'uan, employee of the Free Healing Hospital, showed Cochrane around the ruins and left him to make his own conclusions.

Having worked alongside Liu in Chaoyang, Cochrane reckoned that his own skills would be multiplied hundreds of times over if he could establish a teaching hospital, and here was his opportunity to do so. He was not merely to rebuild a forty-year-old hospital; he knew that to gain the goodwill of the Chinese, especially after all the anti-foreign sentiment expressed in the Boxer uprising, he would have to get the Empress Dowager, Tzu-Hsi, on his side. Official patronage and sanction was paramount.

Tzu-Hsi had been the effective ruler of China for the previous forty years. It was in Cochrane's favour that she was interested in medical things and saw herself as knowledgeable in diagnosis and prescription. However, Cochrane was not going to compromise the Christian teaching at the hospital, so a delicate process had to be undertaken: how would he gain the Empress' patronage, and still maintain the LMS hospital as Christian? It was a strategic appointment at a crucial hour in China's history. After the Boxer uprising, Cochrane became convinced that Christian missionaries would not have access to China indefinitely and so it was imperative to build up a genuinely Chinese church as fast as possible; one that could grow without foreign assistance.

How the Peking Union Medical College began

Cochrane's big breakthrough was in containing a cholera plague in Beijing. He had gained the confidence of Prince Su, a Mongol prince in the imperial court whom he had literally bumped into in the street, and later met properly. With the Prince's approval, health management notices were posted up all over Beijing and the epidemic was contained and eradicated. This gained Cochrane a huge leap forward in the eyes of the imperial court. He was invited to attend to the health of hundreds of eunuchs in the court. This meant regular visits into the Imperial House, and ultimately led to the imperial patronage of his work that he so prayerfully had required.

In 1903, work started on rebuilding the LMS hospital. During this year, Cochrane saw over 20,000 outpatients, and cared for nearly 250 inpatients, in three sub-standard clinics on the outskirts of the city. He slowly gained the approval of the Empress-dowager and the Grand Eunuch, and established the Peking Union Medical College (PUMC) in 1906. In 1911, PUMC attracted the interest of the Rockefeller Foundation, transforming it into an advanced medical training and research centre.

Cochrane was keen that the hospital and medical college should be a 'union' institution. As the Protestant missionary societies restaffed their work after the peace treaty following the Boxer uprising, Cochrane was amazed that none worked together. There was too much sectarianism, and this proved confusing to the Chinese. He was keen that a common name should be adopted for the churches in China and that all foreign denominational names should be dropped, as they were meaningless to the Chinese anyway. His dream was to have a church union. Gradually, due to his enthusiasm, a union committee came into being.

Another passion of Cochrane's was the need to train the Chinese to do the medical work themselves. This education would have to be at the highest possible level and within a regime of rigorous academic study and clinical practice. Neither was it to be divorced from Christian evangelism:

> China wants our education, our secrets of applied science, but what if in giving up these secrets, we destroy the ethic which has influenced China for three thousand years and did not give it in its place... an ethic purer than that of Confucius? Give China the science without the Christianity, and woe betide us. We should have raised up a dragon of portentious size and strength, a competitor without scruple or conscience; and woe to the rest of mankind.[3]

The PUMC was founded jointly by five mission agencies.

Cochrane's legacy

Cochrane's legacy is profound. He was the only doctor in the Chaoyang district for three years, ministering to Chinese and Mongol. He rebuilt the hospital in Beijing after the Boxer uprising and it was this hospital that became the first ever training college in Western medicine for the Chinese. He was the first missionary to stand before the Dragon throne of China as he secured the patronage of the Empress Dowager and the Grand Eunuch.

Cochrane embodied the original aims of the LMS in that he was a unionist at heart. He abhorred sectarianism, but he was not unique in his unionist sympathies. The handful of converts in Buriatia had found their way into the Orthodox Church after the LMS mission was closed. In Kalgan, Gilmour's convert Borjinto was discipled by other missionaries. His book Among the Mongols propelled a whole raft of other denominations into the Mongol and Chinese mission field. In Chaoyang, the church was given to the Irish Presbyterians, then to the Brethren. Finally, in Beijing, this non-sectarian ethic, embodied in the constitution of the LMS, found full expression in the foundation of the PUMC. Gilmour's vision, that medicine must be part of evangelism to the Mongols (and the Chinese), along with the LMS commitment to a non-sectarian agenda in mission means that PUMC still stands today in Beijing as a testimony to the foresight and wisdom of these first missionaries.

––––––––––––––

Two bus-stops before ours, we started fretting. Getting off Ulaanbaatar buses is an art form, requiring the agility of a gazelle and the brawn of an elephant. Our stop was called 'Jukhov Museum', named after a Russian General. His four-metre bust, in true Communist fashion, graced the end of the access road to our housing estate.

'*Buukh uu?*' I asked the people who obstructed the door. 'Are you getting off?'

This question actually meant: 'I want to get off. I'd advise you to get out of my way so that you don't collect my sharp elbow as I vigorously barge through the 50 people between me and the door, before the driver slams the door in my face, or I get my pocket picked and my bag slashed in the squeeze. I'd advise you to start making way for me right now because I can see my bus-stop fast approaching and I am about to panic. If you don't move then I will start spitting like a camel and bucking like a horse. Should you have failed to make way for me by the time this bus stops, I will start yelling, "Plague, plague," at which time you have only yourselves to blame if the rest of the passengers assault you for your lack of grace extended to me and my family.'

The bus stopped. We popped out of the door like peas from a pod.

Karen sighed. 'Anjali's missing a shoe. It must have come off in the final shove.'

Just then, as the doors slammed behind us and the bus started pulling away, her shoe came spinning out of a window in a trajectory that nearly clipped me on the side of the head.

'*Ikh bayarlalaa*, thanks a lot!' I yelled at the anonymous ally who must have been one of the sea of faces staring at us as we tried to regain some dignity at the curb.

I loved this language. So much meaning could be packed into so few words.

NOTES
1. A Li is a unit of measurement: approximately one third of a mile.
2. Margaret Aitchison, *The Doctor and the Dragon* (Pickering and Inglis: London, 1983), p.18.
3. *Ibid.*, p.109.

Part **7**

Catholic Mission Since 1783

Chapter 31

Evariste Régis Huc and Père (Joseph) Gabet,
Lazarists reintroduce Catholicism into Mongolia

'I will go and see if my old mother is still there; if she is alive, I will make her enter into the Holy Church. As for my two brothers, who knows whether they will have enough sense not to believe any longer in the transmigrations of Buddha.'
Samdachiemba, valet to Huc and Gabet

The trip from Hong Kong to Macau is exhilarating. Although less than an hour away, and only on the other side of the Pearl River delta, it is an international journey.

Tim and I checked out of Hong Kong and bordered our jet-foil. Jetfoils, Jetcats and hi-speed hover-ferries plied the delta regularly. The Hong Kongese travelled to Macau frequently because of the attraction of the casinos on this tiny colony.

'This is like an aeroplane,' I remarked to Tim as the pilot opened up the throttle and we lifted up onto the foils. There was a faint smell of aviation fuel and a high-pitched whistle from the turbines.

Tim was a Fijian and colleague of mine working in Mongolia. Our families were holidaying together in Hong Kong and Tim and I had decided to spend a day in Macau exploring because we were both interested in its Christian history.

'Feels like South America,' I said to Tim as we walked along the Avenida da Amizade from the ferry terminal into town. Portuguese language and culture surrounded us. 'I think the Portuguese is close enough to Spanish. Karen grew up in Chile; she'd be able to read all this I guess. I wonder if the Chinese here speak Portugese?'

A pedicab driver accosted us in broken English as we walked past the Casino Lisboa but we said we preferred to walk. Tim checked the map. 'There's a Catholic church on just about every street corner,' he remarked. 'Apparently the ruins of St Paul's Cathedral is the grandest.'

After breakfast in a hole-in-the-wall cafe, we found St Paul's. Only the facade is standing now, after the main part of the building burned to the ground in 1835. The facade has become the tourist symbol for the colony. We gazed up at this massive face of classic Catholic Iberian architecture with niches for statues of various saints. In the centre was the Virgin Mary. Behind us a bus belched out its tour group of Japanese who chattered away and took lots of pictures.

A cornerstone had the date 1602 carved into it. Tim checked the tour-guide. 'It says here that to the cathedral's right was the training college for the Jesuits. All those Jesuits who entered China in the seventeenth century must have been trained here,' he remarked.

The Catholic mission so far

We return now to Catholic mission to the Mongols. There is no record of Franciscan endeavour past 1368 when the last Mongol Yuan emperor, Toghon Tumer, fled to the Mongol hinterland in the face of the rising Ming. The Ming dynasty (1368–1644) practically sealed China from the outside world. In the seventeenth and eighteenth centuries Mongolia was brought under the suzerainty of the Manchus, or the Qing dynasty (1644–1911). However, the story of Catholic mission to the Mongols does not stop with the demise of the Yuan dynasty.

The Jesuits

If the Franciscans embodied the first Catholic contact with the Mongols, the second wave of Catholic mission to China was undertaken by the Society of Jesus, better known as the Jesuits. Pope Paul 3 (r.1534–1549) approved the founding of this order in 1540. This was not so much to counteract the Reformation, but in response to the self-reformation that Ignatius Loyola (?1495–1556) had started, and that had taken root among his followers. Ignatians merely wanted to imitate Christ, and at first had no intention of forming an order. Nevertheless the Pope commissioned Ignatius to draw up a constitution and then commandeered him and his followers on mission service to foreign lands. The aim of the order soon became the spreading and strengthening of the Catholic faith everywhere. The challenge of Islam in Spain was its initial focus. Jesuits soon sent missionaries to India, Japan, Canada, Central and South America, and China.

Francis Xavier was the first Jesuit who attempted to go to China. He died in 1552 trying to get to Macau and Canton. In the same year, the Italian Matteo Ricci was born, and Ricci arrived at the Portuguese territory of Macau in 1583, meeting the Jesuit fathers who had managed to establish a base there. It was Ricci who then penetrated north to Beijing in 1595, opening a way for further Jesuit mission into the heartland of China. At its height, the Jesuits had four colleges, one seminary and forty stations in China. In 1773, when the Jesuit order was suppressed by the papacy and the Chinese mission had to close, there were fifty-four Jesuit fathers in China. The first Jesuits in China had been mainly Portuguese, but from 1687, the mission in Beijing was staffed mainly by French Jesuits.

Unlike the Franciscans, the Jesuit fathers had no distinct mission to the Mongols. However, there is some evidence that they had contact with Mongols. Jesuit fathers accompanied Emperor Kang-Xi (1662–1723) on his campaigns in Mongolia and assisted him in mapping Mongolia.

First attempts via literature

There is reason to believe that works of two Jesuit fathers from this time, Ricci and Alenio, had been translated into Mongolian.[1] The Jesuits were involved in a number of different endeavours, including advising the imperial house on mathematics and astronomy. More interest was shown in Ricci's theological works, because Ricci wrote in a Chinese genre. His works *The Twenty-Five Words*, *The Paradoxes*, and *The True Doctrine of God* attracted a lot of attention.

The True Doctrine of God (*T'ien-chu-she-i*) was a catechism dealing with fundamental Christian beliefs, including the unity of God, creation, doctrine of the soul, and reward or punishment in the future life. It appealed to both reason and Scripture. It refuted the Chinese worship of idols and belief in the transmigration of souls. Ricci included arguments and proofs from ancient Chinese books, which gave it great acclaim. It was a masterful work of apologetics. It went through four printings and 'led countless numbers to Christianity, and aroused esteem for our religion in those readers whom it did not convert'.[2]

In a similar vein, Giulio Alenio (1582–1644) published many works in Chinese on a variety of topics. Alenio arrived in Macau in 1610 and distinguished himself in mathematics and theology, travelling throughout Jiangsu and Fujian provinces. His more famous works were *The True Origin of all Things* and *The Life of God, the Saviour, from the Four Gospels*. Both of these outlined Catholic doctrine and argued against the perceived errors in Chinese religion.

We do not know exactly which of Ricci's or Alenio's works were translated into Mongolian, but given the esteem that their literature acquired, it could have been any or all of those mentioned. Baptisms were reported from Henan province, Manchuria and Mongolia during the reign of Qian Long, who ascended the throne in 1736. These baptisms must have been due to the Jesuit influence in these areas. How many Mongols (as distinct from Chinese) were baptised has not been recorded.

The Lazarists take over from the Jesuits

When the Jesuits were suppressed by the Pope in 1773, China was assigned to the Lazarists (or The Congregation of the Mission). The Lazarists had a centre in Beijing, but abandoned this in 1834, moving to Hsi-wan-tzu, in Chih-li province. This shift was mainly due to persecution by the emperor. Lazarist fathers had been resident in Hsi-wan-tzu from 1829 and the place had become a refuge for persecuted Catholic Chinese generally. Many Christians had fled and gone over the Great Wall to Mongolia where they leased land from the Mongolian princes who permitted them to cultivate vegetable plots.

Such an arrangement at first appears very altruistic, but issues of land use were to plague the Catholic mission at Hsi-wan-tzu. Nevertheless, this station gave the Lazarists much greater access to Mongols. It was situated 'at the gates of Mongolia', about fifty kilometres north-east of Kalgan, and it became the centre for their work among the Mongols, and later for that of the Congregatio Immaculati Cordis Mariae ('The Congregation of the Immaculate Heart of Mary' or CICM).

By 1842, the Lazarist mission had become strong enough for Pope Gregory XVI to designate the 'Apostolic Vicariate of Mongolia'. Monsigneur Joseph Martial Mouly, previous Bishop of Beijing, but resident in and Superior of the Lazarist Mission in Hsi-wan-tzu from 1836, was assigned as Vicar Apostolic of this new church province of Mongolia.

It is reasonable to assume that at this time the Lazarists viewed the Mongols as quite distinct from the Chinese. The very first mission station of the French Lazarists was in the hunting park of the Manchu emperors in Jehol province of Eastern Mongolia, and staffed by two Lazarists by the name of Huc and Gabet. That this was later shifted from Beijing west into Mongol territory, rather than south is also significant. When the Apostolic Vicariate of Mongolia was formed, Monsigneur Mouly commissioned Huc and Gabet to tour the Vicariate to establish its borders and determine the potential for work among the Mongols. The record of their journey is well known among the travel writings of central Asia.[3]

Huc and Gabet team up together

Evariste Régis Huc shifted to Hsi-wan-tzu in 1841, and then in May 1843 to Har-us ('Black Water'), another Lazarist mission station in Mongol territory, 80 kilometres north-west of Kalgan and 225 kilometres from Hsi-wan-tzu. Here he concentrated on the study of Manchu and Mongol languages under the direction of Père Gabet.

Père Gabet (sometimes called Joseph) was five years older than Huc and had much more experience in Mongol matters and better Mongolian language. Before Gabet moved to Har-us, two Buddhist lamas were converted in Jehol province in 1837 through his witness. One was twenty-five years of age and was baptised 'Paul'. The other was Garudi (1820–1893) who was converted at the age of twenty and baptised 'Peter'. Peter later went to Macau and was ordained in 1854 becoming the first Mongol Catholic priest. He became known as the Lazarist Peter Fong.[4] Gabet also made a journey to Urga and tried to get up to Kiachta on the Mongol/Russian frontier in the summer of 1839, with these two converted lamas.[5]

Gabet improved his language greatly on this journey into heartland Mongol territory. In a letter to Pope Pius IX, colleague Planchet praises Gabet's linguistic skills. After Paul's conversion in 1837, Gabet drew up 'a small collection of prayers in the Mongol tongue' and 'a small elementary Catechism of Catholic doctrine'. In his own words: 'we wrote in Mongol a complete statement of Catholic doctrine drawn from the Council of Trent and set out in the form of question and answer; then an historic treatise on the Christian religion with a refutation of the superstitions of Buddhism; and, finally a tract for teaching purposes on the existence of God.'[6] Later, in 1842, Gabet wrote a Manchu grammar and then 'a tract on the connections between this language and the Mongol tongue'.

Huc and Gabet — men of mixed reputation

It was a natural choice then for Mouly to assign Huc and Gabet the task of surveying the new vicariate. Huc understood that they had been appointed by Mouly to 'ascertain the nature and extent of the diocese'. Mouly writes in March 1845:

[we sent] two European missionaries... to the northern part of Mongolia. They set out on September 10th, 1844. They were M.M. Gabet and Huc, both fairly well acquainted with the Manchu and Mongol languages, and knowing enough Tibetan to enable them to carry on their ministry usefully among the nomadic Mongols and to attempt to found a mission in their midst. A subsequent letter of Mouly dated 8 February 1846 records: 'We have had no news of... Gabet and Huc, who left almost two years ago to evangelise the nomadic Mongols of the north.' One of Gabet and Huc's own letters reveals that they were clearly instructed to go to the north-west into Outer Mongolia, that is, the country of the Mongol Khalka tribe, towards Urga. None of the territory was known in detail although some knowledge had been acquired from the Jesuits' maps.

For some reason, Huc and Gabet turned south-west rather than north and stayed in the Tibetan centre of Khumbum for eight months, then went down to Lhasa, Tibet. This could have been due to a misunderstanding between the two and Mouly, or a deliberate decision against his wishes. What Mouly's brief actually was is confusing. There may well have been a directive to go down to Lhasa, but this is not explicit.[7]

Huc and Gabet certainly did go north to begin with, but not as far as Urga or Kiachta. In 1844, disguised as Mongol lamas, they visited Catholic congregations in the north and west, and then turned south towards Tibet. They took with them a Mongol called Samdachiemba.

Samdachiemba was a Buddhist lama from south-west Ordos

who had been converted, instructed and then baptised 'John-Baptist' under Gabet's ministry. His testimony was clear: 'I belong to Holy Church, and know that these things [divination] are wicked and prohibited.' On revisiting his home district after eighteen years, Huc records him as saying: 'I will go and see if my old mother is still there; if she is alive, I will make her enter into the Holy Church. As for my two brothers, who knows whether they will have enough sense not to believe any longer in the transmigrations of Buddha.' Samdachiemba acted as camelier, cook and valet for Huc and Gabet. His Christian commitment continued to be genuine even after leaving their service. In 1888 he was employed by CIM missionaries Mr and Mrs Cecil Polhill-Turner in Sining, some thirty kilometres from Khumbum, to teach them Tibetan and Mongolian.

Huc and Gabet's sojourn at Khumbum allowed time to write various tracts and enter into debate with Buddhist lamas. Here Huc composed a summary of the Christian religion which he distributed freely among the lamas. In Lhasa he did likewise and noted that some aspects of Buddhist ritual seemed similar to Catholicism, leading him to speculate that the lamas had adopted various teachings and practices from previous Catholic missionaries to Tibet.

Huc and Gabet were successful in their navigation of the new vicariate, but have received considerable criticism. They were deported from Lhasa in 1846, and Huc returned to France, allegedly due to bad health. This may have been so, but there is reason to suggest that they had conducted themselves beneath their priestly vows, and both finished their priestly careers ignominiously in Europe. The problem was their behaviour, rather than their doctrine.

The quality of their writing has also been questioned. Pelliot notes that although Huc had good powers of observation and memory, he also had a vivid imagination and he 'cannot be trusted in details'. Another critic refers to the 'plagiarisms of Father Everiste Huc'. Some doubt he ever went to Tibet, on the grounds of his imaginative accounts of the journey. The journey very likely did happen, but it would be unwise to classify their observations as 'scientific'. Huc seems to have had little 'geographical sense', and is plainly inaccurate in geographical data. We note that, regarding Chinese history, 'no Orientalist would ever dream of looking to the works of Huc for authoritative information'.[8]

The Catholic Vicariate of Mongolia grows

Within the newly-formed Catholic Apostolic Vicariate of Mongolia, the Lazarists enjoyed some success among the Mongols. The mission station at Har-us became something of a small Christian realm. Huc refers to it as 'the little Christendom of the Valley of Black Waters', but does not say whether this 'Christendom' was comprised of Mongol or Chinese Christians. We know that Chinese Christians fled Beijing and found refuge here, but we don't know if any Mongol Christians were there as well. The Lazarists eventually opened stations in eastern Mongolia, and for more than a century were the only Christians working among the Ordos Mongols within the bend of the Yellow River.

Until the Apostolic Vicariate of Mongolia was formed, Catholic administration of Mongolia had been under the Catholic Diocese of Beijing from 1690 to 1838. Up to the time that Huc and Gabet toured the new vicariate, no Catholic fathers had been based in Mongolia proper. After 1783 the new Mongolian Vicariate was administered by the Lazarists. As the Lazarists had inherited the work from the Jesuits, in 1864 they gave it to another Catholic order, the CICM. It was handed over in sections, first eastern Mongolia, then central. And finally western Mongolia in 1866.

'Let's check out this fort,' I suggested after we'd long soaked in the atmosphere of St Paul's. The Monte Fort overlooks St Paul's and is on the highest place in Macau. It was built by the Jesuits and came into its own when the Dutch tried to capture Macau in 1622. A well launched cannon ball landed exactly in the middle of the Dutch ship carrying the magazine of armaments and blew the lot to smithereens.

We explored around the fort, then found our way through the rabbit warren of hilly streets, past small Catholic grottoes and big corner churches, and emerged in a typical Iberian plaza. In the corner there was a high white-washed wall, broken by a small unimpressive gateway over which a small plaque announced 'Protestant Church and Old Cemetery (East India Company, 1814)'.

'A glen of Protestantism in a jungle of Catholicism,' I muttered to Tim as we stepped through the gate, relieved to enter a tranquil courtyard away from the clutter of Macau traffic, tourists and Catholic symbolism. 'I guess this will be full of sailors, merchants and petty bureaucrats who succumbed to cholera, typhoid, malaria and gunshot wounds from pirates.'

A small, white Anglican chaplaincy church greeted us and we looked at the notices on the board by the door. 'Morrison Chapel' the board read.

'Morrison. Didn't he have something to do with translating the Chinese Bible?' I asked Tim.

The cemetery behind the chapel had two levels and we enjoyed an hour or so wandering around. It was remarkably well kept, a tribute to the loving care of the late Sir Lindsay Ride, Vice-Chancellor of the University of Hong Kong.

'Nineteen children,' I announced to Tim.

'That's ten percent of the graves,' he replied. 'I counted them. Mainly British, but a few Americans and Europeans. There's a grave I think you'll be interested in over in the corner there. It has a huge memorial stone in Chinese next to it.'

I stood looking at the grave, trying to fathom the significance of this moment. Here we were standing in a small plot of land wrested by the East India Company from the Catholic masters of Macau, surrounded at every turn by the culture of the Jesuits. The Jesuits who had penetrated as far north as

Beijing and who had paved the way for a fuller Catholic mission to the Mongols later in the century.

'He worked for the East India Company as a translator, but look,' said Tim, pointing to the text on the gravestone, 'the London Missionary Society sent him to China originally. Wasn't that the same society that translated the Mongolian Bible in 1840 in northern Mongolia?' It was more of a statement than a question.

I knelt down and read the inscription carefully:

Sacred to the memory of
Robert Morrison, DD
the first Protestant missionary to China
where after a service of twenty-seven years cheerfully spent in
extending the kingdom of the blessed Redeemer, during
which period he compiled and published
a Dictionary of the Chinese Language
and for several years laboured alone on a Chinese version of
The Holy Scriptures
which he was spared to see completed and widely circulated
among those for whom it was destined.

NOTES

1. Pelliot's introduction to R.E. Huc and Gabet, W. Hazlitt, trans., *Travels in Tartary, Tibet and China: During the Years 1844–1846* (1928), p.xxxii, footnote 1 reads: 'Gabet was not aware that old translations of the works of Ricci and Alenio into Mongol and Manchu existed.'

2. J. Brucker, 'Ricci, Matteo' in CG Herbermann, et al, eds, *The Catholic Encyclopedia* (The Universal Knowledge Foundation Inc.: New York, 1912), vol. 13, p.36.

3. R.E. Huc and Gabet, *op.cit.*, 2nd reprint edition (The Open Court Publishing Co.: Chicago, 1900), and R.E. Huc, *Christianity in China, Tartary and Tibet* (Longman, Brown, Green, Longmans, and Roberts: London, 1857).

4. This name implies he was Chinese. However, Pelliot, in writing about these conversions, implies that both were in fact Mongols. Pelliot in his introduction to RE Huc and Gabet, op.cit., (1928), p. vi, doesn't explicitly say these are Mongols, although implies it from the context. J. Van Hecken affirms both as Mongols: J. Van Hecken, 'Mongolia' in *New Catholic Encyclopedia* (The Catholic University of America, 1967), p.1058.

5. Pelliot's introduction to R.E. Huc and Gabet (1928), p.xxxi. J Van Hecken, *op.cit.*, (1967), p.1058, says that Gabet 'visited outer Mongolia in 1838 with two converted lamas'.

6. Pelliot's introduction to R.E. Huc and Gabet (1928), p.xxxii.

7. However, Markham says they were 'appointed by their ecclesiastical superiors to make their way to the city of the Dalai Lama (ie Lhasa)' and Sir Thomas Holdich agrees: Mouly 'deputed Huc (with one companion Gabet) to visit Tibet'. See Pelliot's introduction to R.E. Huc and Gabet, *op.cit.* (1928), p.xviii.

8. *Ibid.*, p.xvi.

Chapter 32

Théophile Verbist, Antoine Mostaert and the CICM Fathers,
the Catholic Commitment to the Mongols

'[Verlinden] is convinced that the solid knowledge of the language is an important means to promote the conversion of the Mongols.'

Daniël Verhelst

'*Egch-ee!*' I called the sales assistant over. 'Can I look at that fridge there?'

She said nothing, undid the rope and let me into the display area. There was an assortment of old washing machines, beds, tables, chairs, and one fridge in the far corner. I plugged it in and listened to the motor. It sounded all right. I looked at the price tag: 48,000 *tugruks*. I did a quick calculation in my head: US$200.

'It's too expensive,' I said to the lady. Again she said nothing. The service in post-Communist Mongolia needed some revving up, I thought. I turned around and leaned on the front desk. The idea was to make a nuisance of myself, and then she'd drop the price just to get rid of me.

'I've got a fridge if you want to buy one,' someone whispered in my left ear. I just about jumped out of my skin. The last time someone did that to me was in Kathmandu, and it was hashish, not fridges, he was selling.

'Sure,' I said. 'Where is it?'

'In my *ger*,' he replied.

It was 1992, and all I'd heard about life in the *ger* suburbs around Ulaanbaatar was bad: poor roads, bad sanitation, muggings, the odd rape. Although half of the city lived in the *ger* suburbs, not too many foreigners had ventured into them at that stage.

But I was always in for an adventure, so I jumped into his Lada and we bounced off up the hill through dusty alleyways and broken wooden fences to a *hasha* that had a huge green door with the traditional Mongolian intermeshing plaited design on it. There was only one cottage in the *hasha*. The Mongols tend to take their *gers* down in the summer if they can live in a cottage.

'This is it,' he announced as we entered the cottage.

'*Sain bain uu*,' I greeted the woman who must have been his wife, or sister, or aunt or grandmother. I wondered if she really wanted to let her fridge go.

The fridge was perfect. The motor purred nicely, it was the right size and was in good condition overall. I really wanted it. After a hearty cup of *su-tai tsai* we started to talk about the price.

'$200,' he announced. I wasn't closed to the idea of buying it in foreign currency. People wanting to get ahead had to get foreign exchange so they could go to Russia or China for trading. Inflation was running at about 300% per annum as well.

I had $80 in my pocket. I also knew it wasn't worth $200.

I proceeded to point out all the faults of the fridge and that I didn't really need it and that I was doing him a big favour by offering to take it off his hands.

'$50,' I offered.

After another five cups of tea, three nips of vodka, and some help with one of the children's English lessons, we settled on $80, 5,000 *tugruks*, and delivery to my place — about $100 worth all up.

'We'll lie it down and put it up on the roof,' he said.

So we did. It was too big for the roof rack. We tied it on with twine. At every pot-hole and bump we drove over, I expected the fridge to come crashing down onto the road. I could just imagine him suddenly braking, and the fridge launching itself forward with the momentum and sliding off down the street, collecting the jaywalkers on the way.

It wasn't a problem as the Lada's brakes didn't work, and so we never stopped suddenly.

I had to let the fridge stand for two days for the freon to settle.

Five years later, I was visiting a colleague's apartment, and there was our old fridge, still going strong.

The CICM enters Mongolia

The CICM was founded in the 1860s in Scheutveld on the outskirts of Brussels by Théophile Verbist. In August 1864, the decision was made for the mission, or the Scheutveld fathers, to take over the work of the Lazarists in Mongolia. They won this territory against a bid by another Catholic order, the Foreign Missions of Milan, who were also interested in China. A transition time was assured so that the Lazarists would not leave until the Scheutveld fathers were well established.

The Lazarists wanted out of Mongolia because they said they didn't have enough missionaries to service it. Monsigneur Emmanuel Verrolles, then Vicar Apostolic of neighbouring Manchuria, wrote to Cardinal A. Barnabò in Rome criticising the change:

> The missionary work is very difficult due to the climate, the vast distances and the bandits for the last five to seven years. Mongolia is a facsimile of the mission in Manchuria. A missionary society that knows what is going on in China can never accept isolating itself in this underdeveloped region [of Mongolia]... The Lazarists who are in charge of this mission really cannot just drop Mongolia under the pretext that they have a shortage of missionaries.

The CICM's entry into Mongolia was not altogether smooth. There was first the 'issue of the passports'. Belgians couldn't enter China because they had no representative in Peking, and therefore had to go through the French embassy with French passports. This entailed political manoeuvring and diplomacy with the French ambassador in Peking, but it eventually worked. That the CICM fathers were taking over from the Lazarists, who were also French, probably compounded the problem. Verbist wanted fourteen workers in the first sailing for China, but had to start with only four, who accompanied him to China in 1865.

On arrival, they wanted to have a full year just learning the language, but the Lazarists did not agree or co-operate. Writing on 20 April 1866 Verbist comments:

> unfortunately, I have not been able to carry out my plans. Arriving in Mongolia, I had hoped that the Lazarists would agree to let us devote a full year to the study of the Chinese language. A full year is certainly needed in order to have a reasonably good commmand of it. We could then take over the administration of the [Mongolian] Vicariate.[1]

A further set-back to the CICM mission was the death of Verbist after only three years. By 1868 he and one other had died of typhus. Nevertheless, his original companions continued with the founding of the mission. Further controversy with the Lazarists ensued. The overlap period ended up being only six months instead of a year. It became clear that the Lazarists really only wanted to be relieved of the eastern part of their Mongolian territory initially, but the CICM was expecting to take over the whole Mongolian portfolio. Relationships between the orders remained cool.

Back in Belgium, Jaak Bax took over the administration of Mongolia. Growth was rapid. He reorganised the training college and between 1865 and 1887 the CICM sent seventy-four missionary fathers to Mongolia.

The territory in which the CICM worked was well defined and originally it was straightforward to continue the work of the Lazarists. Little effort had to be spent in setting up new initiatives. The CICM took over the Lazarist centres which were ethnic Chinese communities, but in Mongolian territory. Hsi-wan-tze, previously a Lazarist centre, became the CICM head-quarters. It had 1000 inhabitants and a further 2000 people within a six-kilometre radius. All except three families were Catholic.

Although this work was among the Chinese, the CICM did not neglect the Mongols. Their initial commission was to Mongolia: bordered on the south by the Great Wall, the east by the Manchurian border, the west by Gansu province, and the north by the Gobi desert. Several CICM fathers had a particular interest in the Mongols and made witness to them their life ministry.

Father Antoine Mostaert ordains the first Mongol priest

After establishing themselves at Hsi-wan-tze, the CICM fathers founded what was to become another 'flourishing Mongolian Christian community' in Boro-balghasu. Boro-balghasu is south-west of Ho-hot (the modern provincial capital of Inner Mongolia) in the Ordos region, within the great loop of the Yellow River. Catholic work here was more successful than in Hsi-wan-tze due mainly to the foundation laid by Father Antoine Mostaert.

Mostaert arrived as parish priest in November 1906. Until 1925 he committed himself to the study of the Mongolian language and culture, collecting a vast array of specimens of folk literature and manuscripts of rare Mongolian works of history, epics, prayers, rituals and folklore. He also wrote what has become a famous dictionary on the Ordos-Mongol dialect. He was one of the founders of the Catholic University in Peking, and he is credited as being instrumental in forming Mongolian studies into a modern science.

But he was committed to more than scientific endeavours. The Catholic community grew to 800 by 1920, double the size it was when Mostaert arrived in 1906. It was in Boro-balghasu that he ordained the first local Mongol into the priesthood.

Munkhjargal (Ma Yuan-Mu in Chinese) was ordained in 1937, and took the Christian name Joannes-Baptiste (or John-Baptist). Munkhjargal's ordination was the first of three in the following decade. In 1947 two Mongols from Boro-balghasu were ordained for work in Ninghsia, and one of these went on to study agronomy at the Catholic University in Beijing.

CICM fathers produce scholarly resources

Mostaert's legacy in Boro-balghasu resulted in church growth and in Mongol leadership for that church. In 1934, Father Gasper Schotte founded a training college there and it was from this college that Munkhjargal and the two other priests graduated. It catered for twenty-seven students who were exposed to a general education, including Christian teaching. Students were mainly Chinese. Schotte was later appointed Vicar Apostolic of Ninghsia, and he continued to promote missionary work among the Mongols.

Schotte had also set up a printing house in 1835 in Boro-balghasu, which was used to print catechisms, tracts and language learning aids. One such endeavour was the production of an 11,000-word Mongolian-French/French-Mongolian dictionary of the spoken Mongolian language for the use of the young missionaries to Mongolia. The original is in the archives of the Vatican, and there are no other known extant copies (although possibly fifty had been printed). They may have been destroyed in a fire which tore through Boro-balghasu in 1900 during the Boxer uprising.

Further scholarly work was done by other CICM fathers. Henri Serruys contributed to the study of the Mongolian language and the history of Chinese Mongolian relations. Likewise, Joseph van Hecken brought much to modern understanding of Inner Mongolia through his publication of many works including research of CICM history in Inner Mongolia.

Persecution of the Catholics

Boro-bolghasu was totally destroyed during the Boxer uprising of 1900 along with all the churches in South Ordos. Most Christians fled to a centre called Baga-gur ('Small bridge' or Hsiao-ch'iao-pan in Chinese), which successfully fended off the Boxers throughout August and September that year.

For a further four years, the Catholic congregation in Baga-gur was plagued with conspiracy against it. In 1903 a plot came to light which was begun by three Chinese who had tried to recruit local Mongol support. The aim was to destroy the church at Baga-gur. Keng So, one of the Chinese conspirators, had told a certain Tyun Fu-shih-erh: 'my elder brother is bringing six salaried soldiers from the south to join the Mongol soldiers who are now ready, and they say that they will take the Church of Little-Bridge.' A letter dated January 1904, written by Arbin-bayar, the Mongol prince ruling Ordos, to the CICM father Edmund Vereenooghe confirms this:

> Chinese and Mongols conspired and decided to kill to the last man... all priests and Christians; they prepared flags, vests with distinctive markings, arrows of command and letters with seals affixed, swords and (other) implements ... [They have] plans to do away with all of us without reason and to lay hands on all our possessions.[2]

The plot was motivated by old-fashioned lust for power and the desire to loot. There was probably resentment too over land issues. However, the conspirators could not gain the full support of the neighbouring Mongol banners due to their own inter-sectarian strife, and so the plot fizzled out and was exposed.

The CICM mission in the Ordos region continued to be subject to political unrest well past the Boxer crises. In the 1930s, the Chinese Nationalist Government noticed the impending Communist revolution in Inner and eastern Mongolia. In the

Otog Banner of the Ordos League Communist agitators under the leadership of two Mongolian Communists, Oldshe Dalai and Amer, set up a people's army aimed at opposing the princes of the Otogh Banner and also the European Catholic missionaries in the Boro-balghasu area. Tussles between nationalists and Communists in 1946 resulted in the town and mission centre being looted, 'hundreds' murdered and all the mission buildings except the orphanage burned down.

This, however, was not the end of CICM mission work among the Mongols. Boro-balghasu had certainly been the centre of the first modern Catholic work among the Mongols, but gradually the entire population of the area eventually became Chinese.

CICM's priorities

The CICM had several priorities in their mission in Mongolia. Language learning was deemed essential. Verbist insisted on at least a full year of language learning in Chinese before any religious vocation was started. After that it was a case of learning on the job. All new missionaries continued to spend time on language study daily; to learn the language thoroughly was seen as crucial.

Mention has already been made of a CICM college. There were actually at least two 'colleges' and a number of schools. The Lazarists had started a college at Hsi-wan-tzu by 1859, and the CICM built a small college in Boro-balghasu in 1934. The Hsi-wan-tzu college maintained its student numbers at around twenty-seven from 1859 till 1865. Students were mainly Chinese, but Mongols had access too. Munkhjargal, the first Mongol priest, graduated from the Boro-balghasu college in 1859. (This was his home town.) Classes for enquirers and for candidates before baptism were taught separately. Periodic retreats were also held for the strengthening of Christians.

A further priority of the CICM Fathers was to gather the Catholic converts into Christian communities and villages. The

Catholics would tend to baptise whole families, rather than individuals. Because of this the Catholic presence in Hsi-wan-tzu was very visible: there was a twenty-five-hectare farm, three orphanages, some schools and a pharmacy, plus leased land supported by the money earned from the farm. 'In Mongolia... thanks in part to the policy pursued by the Vicar Apostolic of the Scheutveld fathers, there were numbers of Christian settlements... around which catechumens were colonised.'[3] We have already explored some of the issues regarding the acquisitions of land. Mongols understandably resented the encroachment of Chinese settlers on their pastures.

Medical work was also important. In 1923–1924, the CICM started a hospital in Hohot (then called Kuei-hua-ch'eng). This hospital was located on ten hectares near the railway station, and had one hundred beds. As with the seminary, there is little mention of Mongols having access to this hospital, but plenty of mention of Chinese involvement. We can assume Mongols had access to the hospital due to their proximity.

Because of the vast distances between places in Mongolia, the CICM fathers took to travelling as a method of witness. They embarked on preaching tours and the priests toured the villages to hear confessions and administer the sacrament. Catholic fathers in Inner Mongolia tried to visit each Christian community three times a year, and aimed to stay for between four days and three weeks in each place.

The CICM spreads out to other Mongol areas

Although the original work of the CICM was mainly among the Chinese, the Mongols were specifically targeted from 1872 when a decision was made to expand, and to work among the Mongols of the plain of Chahar. The CICM fathers first built a church at Hsi-ying-tzu to which Father W. Meyer was appointed as priest in 1874. Later CICM fathers to Chahar made a priority of learning the Mongol language, and a small medical ministry developed.

By 1878 work commenced in Gansu province and in 1884 in Xinjiang, the most westerly province of China. Whether the CICM saw itself as in continuity with the previous Franciscan mission there is not known. Five centuries separated the two endeavours. The district was populated with Mongols, Chinese, Kazak and Russians. CICM work in the Ili area began in 1884 at Kuldja, and by 1906 there were six missionary fathers working in two other stations: at Ch'ing-shui-ho-tzu, and Sui-ting (also known as Huo-ch'eng), along the Ili River.

By 1920, the work had five mission stations (adding Sui-lai and Ti-hua), with a total of 300 Catholic Christians. Joannes-Baptiste Steeneman was the longest-serving member of this mission, succumbing to typhus in 1918 after thirty-five years. We do not know the ethnic make-up of the converts, but because it was in Mongol territory and because the Franciscans had also had a centre there, we could hazard a guess that some Mongols had converted to Christianity. George Hunter, CICM missionary in Urumqi from 1908 to 1946 refers to Mongols who showed an interest in the gospel during his travels in the hinterland, so it is not unreasonable to assume some converted to Christianity through the work of the Catholic mission. The Ili mission was abolished in 1922 by Pope Pius 11, presumably because of the growing border tensions between Russia and China and the rise of Communism.

'We need a fridge,' said Carol.

'It's not a problem,' I replied. 'I'm getting good at buying appliances.' Since my first expedition into the *ger* suburb, I'd bought another two fridges and a washing machine for other people. Carol and her husband were new to Mongolia and were setting up house.

'I understand the Catholic fathers have a fridge they want to sell,' chipped in Sue. 'I'll check with them.'

Sue introduced me to the Catholic fathers later in the week. I'd hired a truck and roped in some Mongol friends to get the fridge. I was intrigued about these fathers though, and couldn't help dawdling to ask some questions.

'We're both from the Philippines, and the third is from Belgium, but he's not in right now. We're CICM fathers. We've been here since 1992,' they replied.

'Do you meet for Sunday services anywhere? How many people come?' I asked naively.

'We meet here in this apartment for mass each Sunday. We've got about ten regulars — mainly embassy staff from the Eastern European embassies.'

'No Mongols?' I asked.

'Not yet. We're in no hurry. We're an embassy from the Vatican as well as missionaries. We'll be here for ever now.'

What an unusual attitude, I thought. He summed up my thoughts perfectly:

'You Protestants are tearing around planting churches and evangelising and teaching because you think the doors to Mongolia are going to close again soon. You never quite know if you're legitimate or not. On the other hand, we have religious visas. We're here by invitation of the President himself.'

I was intrigued and translated the conversation into Mongolian for my helpers.

'Thanks for this fridge.' I paid him and we heaved and grunted it down the steps to the waiting truck.

'Invited by the President himself,' I said again to my Mongol helpers as we tied the fridge on. 'I guess they'll be around for some time then.'

NOTES
1. D. Verhelst, and N. Pycke, *CICM Missionaries, Past and Present, 1862–1987* (Leuven University Press: Leuven, Belgium, 1995), pp.42–43.
2. H. Serruys, 'Mongol Texts Regarding an Anti-Christian Conspiracy in 1903', *Mongolian Studies*, IV, p.51.
3. Beckmen in K.S. Latourette, *A History of the Expansion of Christianity* (Eyre and Spottiswood: London, 1947), p.281.

Chapter 33

Joseph Van Hecken,
The Legacy of the CICM and its
Arrival in Ulaanbaatar

*'The CICM missionaries in Ulaanbaatar] want to be
increasingly known for what they are, Catholic
missionaries. They envisage activities that bring
them in close contact with the local population,
and that are seen as a service to the society at
large.'*

Paul Van Parijs, Vicar General of the CICM

'The only Catholic service I've been to is a requiem mass,' I said
to Jasper. I almost had to jog to keep up. Jasper was a long-
legged Dane who always walked quickly. Jasper and his wife
Charlotte and I were heading to the thirteenth microdistrict of
Ulaanbaatar for the opening of the new Catholic centre. It was
April 1996.

'Just relax. It will be like any other church service. There will
be a few officials I think. Embassy people. Vatican hierarchy
from Taiwan and Hong Kong.'

The new Catholic centre was easy to find. It was the only
building in the thirteenth micro that looked new. And it was
finished too. Its red-brick façade stood out against the dirty
white prefabricated canyons of the surrounding apartment
buildings. A variety of cranes and piles of building paraphernalia were enclosed behind a number of *hashas* that we passed,
testimony to grand visions but broken budgets. There was obviously money in the Catholic building.

A plaque on the wall read 'Apostolic Nuncio's Residence:
Catholic Church Mission'.

'*Sain bain uu*,' I said to the Mongolian usher at the door.

'Good morning,' he replied in perfect English. Obviously the
English language programme the Catholic Church offered had
some good students. 'Go on up to the second floor, please.'

As I sat among the hundred or so guests, I couldn't help

noticing how foreign everything looked. All the light fittings were imported, as were the curtains and furniture. The building itself was quite innovative: folding side doors led to extra small rooms. There was a kitchenette on this floor, and five apartments for the fathers on the south side of the building, I was told. The room we were in did not look like a chapel. It was a multi-functional building. I smelt paint and fresh upholstery.

'I was impressed with the service,' I said to Jasper and Charlotte as we enjoyed the generous spread of food laid out for the guests afterwards. 'It emphasised thanks to God for his faithfulness and asked God to continue to bless the work of the mission in the future.'

'Yes, it didn't have too much Catholic ritual, I thought,' Charlotte said. 'We've been coming to the Catholic congregation on and off now for a few months. There are about thirty regulars with a growing number of Mongols.'

Joseph Van Hecken records the story of the CICM

It is difficult to get a full picture of the CICM work in Inner Mongolia because any original materials are still in private collections or stored in Vatican archives. However, Father Joseph van Hecken published a large work between 1970 and 1976 about the mission's history of the territories in Inner Mongolia where the fathers had been active since 1872. The first series focuses on eastern Mongolia and was published privately in nine volumes in Flemish, but no English translation has been done yet. Julian Pas, Professor of Religious Studies of the University of Saskatchewan, found an edition of this in Japan in 1977 and has outlined the contents in a helpful journal article.[1] In a second series, Van Hecken records the CICM mission history of south-west Mongolia. Pas is in high praise of Van Hecken's account and laments that it is not available more widely. Pas does translate for us some key paragraphs, and they are included here. He records the clear goal of the CICM in

Ordos-Mongolia: 'The exclusive purpose of the foundation of a mission in Ordos had been the conversion of the Mongols with the exclusion of the Chinese.'

The CICM fathers had originally thought that the Mongols would be easier to convert to Christianity as they seemed more 'primitive' than the Chinese, and their religion was less organised. He continues:

However, the true situation made the missionaries [that is, the CICM fathers] very soon aware that the Mongols were not free to embrace any other religion but lamaism, and certainly not Christianity... They were often strongly attached to Buddhism through family ties, since most families counted a member among the lamas. Add to this their moral corruption and the satisfaction of their passions, which they would have to curtail in the Christian religion.... However, the greatest hindrance for an Ordos Mongol to convert to Christianity was his total dependence on the [Chinese] magistrates and [Mongol] nobility.

The socio-religious feudal system was stifling. A corrupt hierarchical government meant that any bureacrat could 'dispose of far-reaching powers. Punishments for crimes [consisted] of whipping with the black whip, or fines of money or cattle and of forced labour'. Within this feudal system, the Mongols were virtually slaves 'prepared to do or avoid whatever pleased the official'. When it came to religious conversion, 'officials did not allow their subjects to convert or to go over to the foreigners, for they believed that they would lose them for their slave services and financial contribution.... They were entitled to use any kind of violence to prevent such a defection and actually widely abused their authority.' Van Hecken explains that this abuse of power was due to the old Mongol system of dividing the population into nobility and serfs. The nobility were descendants of Chinggis Khan and:

each nobleman disposes of several families of serfs over whom they exercise the fullest right, whereas the serf has only duties. If a nobleman forbids his serf to convert to Christianity or to have contacts with Europeans, it becomes impossible for the [serf] to do so. His lord is entitled to impose on him all possible punishments no matter how unreasonable they are.

When the CICM fathers entered Ordos, they were hopeful that they would not meet much resistance from the Buddhist lamas because a Muslim rebellion had resulted in the massacre 'of thousands of Ordos lamas... and almost all temples in the Ordos region had been destroyed'. But Van Hecken tells us that this was not the case. As well as the feudal social structure, lamaism presented a seemingly insurmountable obstacle to conversion.

The few remaining lamas still exercised an all-powerful influence upon the minds of the superstitious Mongols: the lamas knew how to threaten them to instil into them a superstitious fear of divine punishments. They skilfully exploited the misfortune of some converted Christians by explaining [the misfortunes] as divine vengeance.

Several times the lamas themselves did not hesitate to use brutal force.... The threats of punishments for transgressing taboos by which the Mongols were strongly chained had a powerful influence on the hearts and will of the ordinary Mongol.

Van Hecken concludes that 'dependence on lamaism [was] the strongest obstacle for their conversion to Christianity'. He also bemoans the Mongols' 'moral corruption', accusing lamaism's celibacy rules of sapping their strength and bravery and causing them to sink into immorality. 'The lamas wandered through the desert and passed the nights here and there living with the women of their relatives who did not dare to oppose them.' Other vices were inherited from the Chinese: 'Chinese itinerant merchants had introduced into many families their own vices of smoking opium, gambling [and] concubinage.'

Van Hecken then relates that the CICM fathers, although still working in Ordos, turned their efforts to the Chinese: 'After all efforts of the missionaries to convert the Mongols had failed, they turned to the Chinese and thus the Ordos Mission has become a mission among and for the Chinese.'

The CICM mission work left only a flickering light among the Mongols of the Ordos: 'There was only one exception; the small Mongolian "appendix" at Boro-balghasu where the missionaries for many years have fought a strenuous battle against the four antagonistic elements.' Others had described this work at one time as a 'flourishing Mongolian Christian community'.

Pas summarises Van Hecken's history of the CICM mission in Inner Mongolia:

> The information contained here constitutes a particularly moving document of human adventure in the service of an ideal. [The whole story] is lively and fascinating. One feels admiration for the author who painstakingly collected the sources and reconstituted the history of an episode of Christian missionary activity which has perhaps left no more traces in the very land where the events took place.

The Mongol aspect of the CICM work died in Ordos. However, the CICM found further work among the Chinese fruitful. The Chinese residing in the Ordos were all people who had lost their means of existence in the interior. Thanks to the missionary action they had rediscovered a decent human life through becoming Christians.

Not all Mongol work was finished though. In a short table in the *World Christian Encyclopaedia*, Van Hecken records in the entry 'Mongolia' that there were thirty adults and fifty 'affiliated' Catholics. He believes there were 'scattered secret believers' during the Communist era. This edition of the encyclopaedia was published in 1982, so Van Hecken must be referring to either Mongolian Catholics in Inner Mongolia or in the Mongolian People's Republic itself. The implication is that it is the Mongolian People's Republic. There is no verification of this from other sources to date. On the other hand, from the evidence of Van Hecken's testimony itself as translated for us by Professor Pas, he must surely be referring to Inner Mongolia, and the centres of Hsi-wan-tze and Boro-balghasu where the most successful Mongol work was conducted. If, at the most, eighty Mongol Catholic affiliates survived the traumas of the Chinese Communist state through to the 1980s, then this is a respectable legacy.

The CICM arrives in Ulaanbaatar

The CICM soon focused on Urga, deep within the Mongol heartland. In February 1922, Pope Pius XI restructured the Central Mongolian Apostolic Vicariate and assigned Outer Mongolia *missio sui juris* to Bishop Jeroom Van Aertselaer. This meant that in theory Outer Mongolia would become an official church district. The aim was to establish a CICM mission station at Urga. Van Aertselaer carried the title 'administrator' of the Urga mission, but it was never staffed, due to the intrusion of Soviet Russian troops in 1921 and then the proclamation of the Mongolian People's Republic in 1924.

Urga (now Ulaanbaatar) remained a 'paper' vicariate; only since 1992 has it been staffed. Ironically the initiative came from the Mongolian government. In June 1990, the government contacted the Holy See to explore possibilities of establishing diplomatic relationships. Monsigneur Jean-Paul Gobel, representative of the Holy See in Hong Kong, visited Mongolia on a fact-finding tour the following year, and Father Jerome Heyndrickx later in the year. In January, 1992, a unanimous decision was made by the CICM to staff the mission in Ulaanbaatar, and in April official diplomatic relations between Mongolia and the Vatican were established. The first three fathers to staff the mission, Wens Padilla, Robert Goessens and

Gilbert Sales, arrived in Mongolia in July. Nearly a year later, in April 1993, the papal nuncio, Archbishop Giovanni Bulaitis, presented his credentials to Mongolian President Ochirbat. In May 1996, the CICM mission opened a mission centre in the thirteenth microdistrict of Ulaanbaatar from which its ministry continues.

Today this mission in Ulaanbaatar enjoys a status and privilege that no Protestant agency does, as the Catholic fathers fulfil a dual role. They are officially the Vatican's ambassadors (and therefore political diplomats) and also religious missionaries. Father Paul Van Parijs, Vicar General of the CICM, admits that the Mongolian government sees the relationship 'on the diplomatic level. The Vatican for them is one window on a wider world beyond Russia and China…. The local officials certainly think very much in terms of social projects and development help.'[2]

The local fathers want to be more than just ambassadors of the Vatican. Van Parijs outlines a threefold strategy for Mongolia as 'presence, dialogue and evangelisation'. The fathers 'want to be increasingly known for what they are, Catholic missionaries. They envision… activities that bring them in close contact with the local population and that are seen as a service to the society at large.'

With respect to 'dialogue', the CICM fathers want to

approach the local religious tradition [that is Shamanism and Buddhism] with due respect and openness…. Our confrères hope gradually to build up good contacts with Gandan monastery, the major Buddhist centre in the capital. The contemplative Buddhist tradition, with its monasteries as centres for prayer and meditation, might provide a model for a Christian centre of prayer and recollection. It would be a model which Mongolian people could easily understand.

Alongside this they recognise the important role of proclamation. (Van Parijs implies the Protestant missionaries are doing this well enough.) Presenting the gospel in a culturally appropriate way is of major importance for the CICM fathers. In evangelism, 'as soon as the language skills are acquired, our confrères will face the task of developing a presentation of the faith in an inculturated way'.

We walked back from the new Catholic centre in the late afternoon.

'I've got to stop and buy a Pepsi for the kids,' I said. 'I get one every Sunday. It's a weekly routine we have. It helps as a time marker, especially during the long winter months.'

We stopped at a *tuz*, one of the numerous small food kiosks that line any well-frequented route in Ulaanbaatar. Everything from soft drinks, biscuits, chewing gum, bags of apples, toiletries, tinned fruit, bread, plastic toys and jam competed for space in the *tuz* window. The shop assistant was in there somewhere.

A warm wind licked around the buildings. It was nice to have some longer days and a stronger sun.

'That building cost a million dollars,' said Jasper.

'What? This *tuz*?' I joked.

I doubted very much if my home church in New Zealand could come up with a million dollars for a comparable building as a gift for the Mongolian church I attended. 'One of the advantages of the Catholic Church is that there is only one of them. The CICM is it here in Ulaanbaatar.'

'Plus there's accountability,' Charlotte chipped in. 'Accountability brings stability. I bet they don't ever have any visa problems. The government knows who they are, why they're here and what they're doing. It must be nice to be able to do Christian ministry on a religious visa.'

I agreed, being well familiar with the major headaches of getting and keeping Mongolian visas, especially in the hectic years of 1992 and 1993.

'They're obviously here for the long haul. They've got English lessons going, plus a developing social programme including ministry to street kids. They have a good number at mass each week now too.'

I paid the lady for the Pepsi and shoved it into my bag.

'Yes. It's really the third wave of Catholic mission to the Mongols,' I suggested. 'First the Franciscans, then the Lazarists, and now the CICM. It's been a long-haul effort. Seven centuries. Us so-called Protestants expect everything instantly. Including church growth. Fast and instant — it pervades our Anglo-Saxon cultures.'

'Three Snickers, please,' Charlotte asked the saleslady.

'Why do you call these kiosks *tuz*? I thought they were called *mukhlag*' Jasper said, unwrapping his Snickers bar.

'*Mukhlag* is the generic word for kiosk. *Tuz* is an acrynom. T.U.Z.' I replied. I often made use of the hundreds of *tuz* around the city. They were great for quickly grabbing a bite to eat on the way to language school or even church on Sundays.

'So what's it stand for?' Jasper was curious.

'Fast-service-spot,' I replied. 'Perhaps a metaphor for our Protestant churches?'

NOTES
1. J.F. Pas, 'Missionary Efforts in Inner Mongolia: A Review Article', *Zeitschrift für Missionwissenschaft und Religionswissenschaft* 69 (January 1985), pp.63–70.
2. P. Van Parijs, 'CICM in Mongolia', *Missionhurst CICM* (October – November 1993), pp. 11–13.

Part **8**

Evangelistic Strategies in the Twentieth Century

Frans August Larson,
Mongol Duke and 'Tentmaker'

'I crossed and re-crossed Mongolia in every direction, distributing Bibles for the [British and Foreign] Bible Society. Men, women and children listened attentively when I read to them from my Bible, and they bought many thousands of copies to read themselves or keep until a traveller passed who could read.'

Frans Larson

'Have you seen this newspaper article?' Buya asked me. We were walking along the footpath, making our way home after a Wednesday evening worship time at church.

I looked up from the footpath where I had been carefully negotiating all the lopsided pavement stones, so as not to trip.

'You're going to have to explain it,' I said. 'My Mongolian isn't that good.'

Buya had flown in from Korea the day before. He'd been in Seoul for about four months visiting a large Korean church, where he'd been sent with a few other potential church leaders by a Korean pastor in Ulaanbaatar. This had made me very nervous as I could just imagine the team returning with all sorts of false hopes and expectations about what could be done with the Mongolian church. I'd therefore kept in touch with Buya during this time, by post.

I looked over the article he handed to me.

'There's my name!' I said incredulously. Sure enough my name appeared about three times in the article, along with Buya's. I recognised some Christian terminology as well. 'What newspaper is this anyway?'

We came to an intersection and waited for a break in the traffic so as to cross the road. This was an unnecessary habit I had acquired from home. Buya merely strode out on to the road. I gingerly stepped over an open service hole, held my breath and followed. Why does every city planned by Communist planners have a 'Peace Avenue', I thought. Cars, trolley-buses, RVs and jaywalkers all jostled for territory on the road. It was anything but peaceful.

Buya must have had an invisible, protective force field around him, for he just kept on talking, oblivious of the surrounding mayhem. 'It's a tabloid newspaper that is highly speculative and publishes mainly crime and detective stories.'

We landed on the other side. I felt nauseous from the fumes. I checked to see if I still had all my body parts.

Buya continued: 'This journalist has published a letter that I wrote to you from Korea. I sent you three letters. Did you get this one?'

I looked at the article again and tried to get the gist of it. 'I don't recognise it. I only got two letters from you.'

Buya was getting agitated and unconsciously started walking faster. 'I have no idea how this journalist got this. He quotes my letter word for word and speculates about all the Christian terminology in it. He thinks that we are part of a subversive plot, and because he doesn't know the Christian meanings of these words, he thinks these are coded instructions.'

'You're joking, right?' I said nervously.

'Not at all. This is a serious breach of privacy. I'm going to hunt down the journalist through the newspaper's office and demand a written published apology. I'm going to get a lawyer on to it. You'd better take it seriously too.'

'Why's that?' I asked, not liking the last bit of advice.

'He speculates that you're a spy.'

The opportunistic Swede

Frans Larson was an opportunist. He arrived in Mongolia from his home country of Sweden in 1893, and throughout his thirty years there he lived life to the full, giving himself enthusiastically to whatever job was at hand. He was equally at home in a Mongol's *ger* drinking *su-tai tsai* (tea with milk) and eating boiled mutton as sitting for long hours at a desk translating Scripture tracts in a tent on the isolated steppes of Mongolia.

Larson first settled in Paotow on the Chinese/Mongol border. Frustrated with this, he wanted to get into Mongolia proper but found it difficult acquiring residence. Nevertheless he started learning the Mongolian language in Paotow with a tutor. But there was nothing written of any help, and he made slow progress. His real desire was to go out and live with the Mongol people on the steppe, for although he had good contacts with Mongols in Paotow, they tended to be travelling through on business or pilgrimage elsewhere.

Things changed when the feudal Khan of the province of Ordos (which Paotow borders) allowed Larson to visit the wedding festivities of his son. The Khan invited him to stay on in the royal residence and assigned him a language teacher. Larson lived with the Khan for three months, enjoying rides into the countryside and quickly acquiring the Mongolian language.

Larson made many friendships with young Mongol *noyons* of Ordos due to common interests in hunting and sports. Over the years he also developed good links with government ministers and top lamas and their families. He knew the prince of Hanta well, and his son, and also Prince Lob-Tsen Yen-Tsen, who had first trained as a lama, but in later life took a government job. Prince Tsereng Dorch, minister of foreign affairs, and the prince of Sunit were both friends of Larson. These relationships were genuine and close. Larson wrote: 'I have attended more weddings in Mongolia than I can count.' His rapport with the Mongols was so good that he was eventually created a duke by the Living Buddha in Urga, with full rights equal to those of a Mongol prince's son.

Larson had originally come to Mongolia with the Scandinavian Alliance Mission and worked with them until 1900. However, the Boxer uprising that year made conventional missionary work impossible and Larson fled north to

Urga to get out of the turmoil. Unable to draw missionary salary, he worked with the Mongol Ore Mining Company from 1900 to 1902 to support himself. In 1903 this company folded and so Larson joined two Swedish engineers who were surveying for a railway from Verkhne-Udinsk (Russia) over the Gobi to the border of China. He also spent some time as a merchant, building up a respectable trading business in horses (a total of 200,000), wool and furs. This sense of belonging, rapport and at-home-ness on the Mongol steppe led him later to take a two-year posting in republican China as Mongol advisor to the Chinese president.

Larson as BFBS agent

After his stint with the mining company and the surveying team, Larson joined the British and Foreign Bible Society in 1902 as its agent for Mongolia. His work meant that he was able to travel extensively throughout Mongolia still, this time selling Bibles and Scripture tracts. The Bible that Larson distributed was the Literary Version of Stallybrass and Swan. In 1902, from Kalgan, he travelled 3,200 kilometres east and north-east. Between 1904 and 1905 he undertook a total of six long journeys, visiting as far west as Uliastai (in modern Mongolia's mid-west) as well as Urga.

Larson changed his residences frequently, visiting Urga nearly every year. As a base, he set up his *ger* in a place called Tavan-uul ('the five hills'), about 140 kilometres from Kalgan on the Urga road. He preferred Tavan-uul to the confinements of Kalgan, yet was close enough for the supplies which Kalgan offered. In all, Larson lived in four different places, all of them near to the Mongols: Paotow, Kalgan, Tavan-uul and Urga.

He had met Mary Rodgers, an American in Kalgan during an earlier summer. They were married two years later and had two daughters, Mary and Katherine. She continued to work among the Chinese in Kalgan, while Larson worked among the Mongols. From their summer base in Tavan-uul, Larson worked on translation projects and, together with Mary produced a Mongol-Swedish-English dictionary. They used Schmidt's German-Russian-Mongolian dictionary as their model, and were in effect translating it into English and Swedish.

Larson became dissatisfied with the LMS Literary Version of the Bible, mainly because of the literary form of the Buriat dialect, and because the Mongols whom he was with each day were of the Khalka tribe. Others in Kalgan also thought it time to do some revision. Anton Almblad, also of the Scandinavian Alliance Mission, suspected that the Literary Version did not communicate well so hired a local Mongol, Gendun by name, to work on a revision with him.

Together they started by reworking the Literary Version of *Genesis*, based in Tavan-uul in the summer of 1911. They also had a go at the New Testament but it is probable that they revised only the four Gospels and *Acts* at this stage. In the autumn of the same year, Almblad and Larson crossed the Gobi to go to Urga to get their revision checked by scholars there.

Here a curious sequence of events unfolds. On arriving in Urga, Larson found that the Living Buddha was very friendly to him, and interested in his work. A high Mongolian govern-ment official was asked to appraise the new Bible revision. The Living Buddha (or Bogd Khan, that is 'Holy/Divine King') assigned this work to Ponsok Searim, secretary to the Mongolian Department under Beijing, where 'every verse in the four Gospels and in *Acts* was subjected to a rigorous criti-cism'.[1] Larson and Almblad had certainly found themselves a powerful and influential man to check their work. Perhaps too powerful. Like the closure of the Selenginsk mission, the trans-lation got caught up in the gusts of changing political winds.

Urga and the rest of Outer Mongolia were under Manchu-Chinese domination at the time, and administered from Beijing until 1911. That same year Urga rebelled against Beijing and threw out the Manchu governor and Chinese garrison. This paved the way for the Bogd Khan to become the religio-political leader, and Ponsok Searim was promoted to the position of commissioner of customs. There ended any hopes, so it seemed, of a thorough translation check by a native speaker.

But with great courage, and perhaps pulling the high-level strings which Larson was able to do, he and Almblad appealed to the minister of foreign affairs, Prince Hanta Dorch, who surprisingly released Ponsok Searim from his government duties to work with them until the checking was complete. Considering the traditional hostility of lamaism towards Christianity, this was indeed a great concession. The revised and checked version of the Gospels and *Acts* was then printed individually in Yokohama and released by the BFBS in Shanghai in 1913, two years after the revision had been started. At this point Larson resigned and handed his work over to Almblad.

Larson was quite at home in Urga, spending part of each year there. After throwing out the Manchurian governor posted by Beijing, the Mongols enthroned the Bogd Khan in 1911. Because Larson was in Urga at the time, he witnessed this enthronement. Larson gave him the first motor car ever seen in Urga, a Ford. This relationship with the Bogd Khan had started back in 1894. The rapport he built up gained him the title of 'duke'; not only that, but the Mongols also wanted him to be on their delegation in the tri-partite Mongolian-Chinese-Russian negotiations at Khiakta on 6 June 1915. Larson wisely declined this as he knew the Russian and Chinese delegations would not accept him.

Larson's legacy

Larson was well aware of walking in Gilmour's footsteps. In the early 1900s, Kalgan was attracting a growing number of missionaries committed to the Mongols. However, Christian witness was often tedious and fruitless. Larson concludes: 'despite all the mission work which has been done on the [Mongolian] plateau, there are a very few Christian converts. The Mongols do not easily give up the way they have followed through the centuries.' It seems that Larson had found the same dynamic as

Gilmour. One can slave away for years witnessing to the Mongols, but because of the power of their lamas, and the all-pervasive influence of Buddhism, they are slow to convert to Christ.

This opposition didn't detract Larson, however. He was a 'people person' with tremendous rapport with the Mongols, preferring their company to the niceties of mission station life. On one journey he was camped near a Mongol priestess who would come to his *ger* almost every day and they would talk about the books of the Bible. Larson had the confidence of Mongol princes and Chinese governors. He was also willing to take secular jobs to keep himself, while endeavouring to do Christian work. Today, we'd call him a 'tent-maker', after the example of the apostle Paul who supported himself by his trade, making tents, while living among local people and teaching them the gospel.

Despite his priority for the Mongols, Larson also helped the missionary community as they fled during the Boxer uprising of 1900. During the uprising he escaped to Har-us ('Black Water') on the Mongolian plateau, where he had a summer home. There three missionary families joined him while they waited for other north China missionaries. The others never arrived so Larson, together with Mary and their two girls, led this band of seventeen adults and six children (both Swedes and Americans) across the plateau to Urga. The journey took thirty-six days and on arriving in Urga he heard that all the property of the mission in Kalgan had been destroyed, including the Swedish-Mongol-English dictionary over which he and Mary had worked so hard. The loss of the dictionary has been bemoaned by linguists to this day. After the Boxer upheaval, Larson and his family returned to Kalgan in 1901 to rebuild their home and continue their ministry.

Fellow missionaries perceived Larson as a replacement for Gilmour. On his first arrival in Kalgan, he had travelled in the environs of Kalgan for a full month, acquainting himself with the hinterland, then decided to open a mission station at Har-us, the home place of Borjinto, Gilmour's convert, 'so as to follow up Mr Gilmour's work'. That following summer he bought a *ger* and pitched it next to Borjinto's in Har-us.

Larson had that same unassailable restless pioneering spirit that characterised Gilmour. He was, however, less idiosyncratic, and managed to build a rapport with the Mongol nobility which Gilmour never could. He stayed committed to the nomads on the steppe, while Gilmour shifted his focus to the sedentary agricultural eastern Mongols of Inner Mongolia. Both Gilmour and Larson were committed to travel and language learning, but Larson had one further asset. He exploited every opportunity to remain on the steppe with the Mongols. He was not locked into any mission strategy, nor did he have to conform to the expectations of mission boards thousands of kilometres away. He was flexible, entrepreneurial and opportunistic. By the end of his years in Mongolia, Larson was able to comment: 'In many states I have known the father as monarch, and then his son as monarch, and now know the little boy who is growing up to rule.' Larson always had an open door to the hearts of the people: 'during thirty-five years, I have stayed with many Mongolian rulers.... If I am ever in need of a home, I am welcome there for as long as I wish to come and stay.'

I met Buya about three weeks later and he explained the sequel to the newspaper article.

'I tracked down the journalist in his home. Apparently I'd addressed the letter wrongly. I got the post-box numbers mixed up and it went to his instead of yours. He opened it, read it and saw it as good fodder for that article.'

'Still, he shouldn't have opened it if it was addressed to me,' I interjected. 'That's a breach of privacy.'

'Of course. The newspaper promised he'd write a full apology in the following edition,' Buya explained. 'I haven't seen it yet.'

We let the incident slide. Nobody else had mentioned the article. I was hoping that people wouldn't take it too seriously considering that tabloids are renowned for stretching the truth.

It's not every day one has the heady privilege of being slandered in the press. I knew that the government was wary of English teachers coming to Mongolia and using their teaching position as a platform for proselytising. The last thing I wanted was my teaching position at the polytech jeopardised by some rogue journalist.

'You'd better not be so involved in our church,' suggested Buya. 'The government may misinterpret your reason for being here.' Buya was still wary that the ashes of Communism may spark back to life again.

'I have a visa to teach English at the polytech. I am a trained teacher, fulfilling my professional calling. The polytech invited me to apply for the job.' I felt like I needed to justify myself. 'The polytech knows I'm a Christian. My head of department knows I'm a Christian. The passport visa section know I'm a Christian. I submitted copies of my Bachelor of Theology degree along with my teaching certificates when I applied for the job. Nobody's questioned my motives. I'm certainly no spy.'

Buya chuckled, then chipped in. 'I think it must be difficult for you having to do that teaching job so that you can work in the church.'

'I don't see it like that,' I responded. 'I have a responsibility first to my employer, the polytech. I have a vital Christian witness there. I arrive at class on time, I don't skip classes, I prepare my lessons well, I don't let the students cheat on their tests. I conform to all the normal routines that any Mongolian colleague has to. To do anything less than this would compromise my integrity and cheat God. I know I'm not allowed to use the Bible as a teaching text so I don't. It would be unethical of me to use my teaching position as a platform for preaching. I'm not allowed to do that in a school in New Zealand, so why should it be different in Mongolia? Incidentally, I get paid in *tugruks* too.'

Buya must still have been listening, although I'd just dumped all this justification on him. 'Aren't some of your students members of our church?' he asked.

'Sure,' I said. 'Teaching is a pastoral activity too. I'm more than willing to talk with students about what it means to be a Christian, both in class and out of class. I think there'd be something wrong with me if I didn't get any questions about being a Christian. They have to initiate the questions though, and if it looks like I may be tempted to compromise my position at the polytech, I talk with them out of class, or ask you or one of the other church leaders to pick up the relationship. Even the other teachers are quite curious about why I'm different.'

I knew Buya knew all this, but I felt I needed to tell someone in Mongolia that I was OK. He listened graciously, then changed the subject.

'We had a church leaders' meeting last night and have decided to have a large Christmas celebration on the twenty-fourth night. Will you be able to come?'.

Christmas was about three weeks away, and I knew that the polytech had a Christmas concert planned for that same night. All the English teachers had been instructed to prepare a song for the concert. 'Jingle Bells' had already wafted through the corridors periodically as classes started to prepare. I was determined I wasn't going to be associated with the hollowness of a Western Christmas and was starting to scout around for some appropriate music. I saw it as a good opportunity to invest some Christian content into the evening. I also knew that I would have to work on 24 and 25 December as neither of these were public holidays.

'I'd love to come,' I said to Buya. 'But I'm not going to be able to make it.'

Buya was disappointed. The previous year's Christmas celebration at church had been an outstanding success with many new people coming, and we had packed a hall that sat 600. I too was disappointed I couldn't make it.

'Why's that?' Buya asked.

I replied simply: 'I have to be at work.'

NOTE

1. Marshall Broomhall, *op.cit.*, p.131.

Chapter	# George Hunter and Percy Mather,
35	### Bringing Christ to the Mongols of Chinese Turkestan

> *The harvest's great, the reapers few,*
> *but ask what [God] would have you do,*
> *And to his sacred trust be true,*
> *regarding wild, wild Gobi.*
>
> *For his name's sake some hardship bear,*
> *to break his last command beware*
> *Go, preach the gospel everywhere,*
> *e'en in the wild, wild Gobi.*
>   George Hunter, eighth stanza of 'Wild, Wild Gobi'

'See if you can get us an invitation into those *gers*', I asked Dorj, our translator. We'd been in Mongolia for two weeks and this was our first trip to the countryside. Having enjoyed a nice mild early-September day by the river, I was very keen to have a look inside a *ger*. There was a cluster of them nearby.

'Oh, you don't need an invitation,' Dorj replied. 'If the door is open, then you are free to avail yourself of their hospitality. This is the unwritten rule of the steppe. If you are travelling, and you need accommodation, then you are free to just drop into any *ger*.'

So we did.

'Tie up the dogs!' Dorj hollered as we got out of our Russian Lada. This I discovered was the most common greeting on the steppe. And a very wise greeting too, considering the dogs looked something like a cross between a bear, a wolf and a crocodile.

One of the brutes growled at me as the host showed me through the door. 'Don't stand on the threshold,' Dorj hissed this last bit of advice as I was just about to. 'It's an insult. Like standing on the host's neck.'

The hosts seemed as interested in us as we were in them. In

hindsight, I think it was a Khazak *ger*, not a Mongol *ger* as the door was not facing south, and there were no Buddha idols or images in the *hoymon*. (The *hoymon* is the most sacred place of the *ger*: it is the area directly opposite the door; the furthest you can go into the *ger*, and there is usually an idol ledge with offerings on it.)

'*Deshe so.*' The host was beckoning me. 'Come and sit higher.'

I was milling around in the empty space immediately inside the door, not quite knowing what to do next, and was relieved to be told what to do. I followed his pointing hand and sat on a stool up close to the *hoymon*. He sat on the stool immediately in front of the *hoymon*, ordered his wife to make teá, and commenced to pass his snuff bottle around.

Dorj explained that we were new to Mongolia and didn't know all their customs. At this the host burst into laughter (his neighbours had joined us by then too). Everyone relaxed and our host proceeded to give us a long and involved lesson in Mongol etiquette.

Xinjiang: a strategic location

George Hunter, a Scotsman from Aberdeen, left his homeland for China in February 1889, and started work in Lanchow, the capital city of Gansu province, with the China Inland Mission (CIM). In 1906 Hunter shifted to Urumqi, then known as Tihwa in Xinjiang province (or 'Chinese Turkistan'). He was to spend the next twenty-five years there without a break.

In 1914, Percy Mather joined him. Together, Hunter and Mather had constant daily contact with all the people groups of central Asia, for Urumqi was a town where Turk, Chinese, Mongol and Russian interests all converged. Hunter and Mather were not the first Western missionaries to take up residence in Xinjiang province however. It was already perceived as a key strategic area for reaching the peoples of central Asia. The

CIM had previously located a Dr Landsdell and a Mr Parker in Urumqi as early as 1876. They had undertaken some translation and tract distribution, along with some medical work, and had penetrated as far west as Kuldja in the Ili River valley, on the Russian border.

Urumqi was near a branch of the Siberian railway, on the Russian side of the border. One could catch a steamer down the navigable Irtish River, and catch the train on the other side of the border. A Swedish couple, a Mr and Mrs Eneroth, had set up work in Chuguchak (north-west of Urumqi, also on the Russian border) in 1898, but this was short lived due to Mrs Eneroth's poor health. The Mongols of the area were located in Karashar (south-west of Urumqi) and the Torgut/Kalmuck Mongols north-west of Urumqi. Hunter estimated the Mongol population north-west of Urumqi at about 42,000.

George Hunter

George Hunter was 'a dour man with a character compounded of severity, sternness and obstinacy, but he was sterling to the core and showed occasional facets of faithful affection and even tender-heartedness... [he was] simple, unpretentious, unassuming'.[1] The lonely life of isolated Urumqi, well away from the pettiness of mission compound life in China, suited Hunter. He was a pioneer at heart, and could endure long periods of loneliness and a comfortless life. He was 'tall and well built, with dark grey whiskers' and had a 'passion for reaching primitive people in remote localities'.

Hunter quickly developed a pattern of evangelism. He became highly mobile; his strategy was to travel out from Urumqi, preaching and selling tracts and Bibles in the bazaars, and generally taking every opportunity afforded him to share the gospel with whoever would listen to it. It seems he had some success.

His first journey was west to Kuldja in the Ili River valley, which was where the Franciscans had been working. He chose to camp where Mongols camped and to rely on Mongol hospitality. His language was adequate to the task, finding on one occasion that he had to mediate between arguing Tungans and Mongols over the local horse tax.

His practice was to sell Gospels for goods in kind: milk, cheese, *argol* and the like. He would dialogue with Mongolian lamas en route, and make sure he had in his satchel both Mongolian and Tibetan Gospels and tracts for this purpose. They were his currency for trading, and sometimes used as gifts for hospitality received or favours done. Journeys were long. His total trip to Kuldja was seventy-five days, covering around 1600 kilometres on horseback.

Hunter undertook several short trips from Urumqi. He felt at home among the Mongol encampments and in the company of princes and living-Buddhas. On one occasion he went to Sin-si-hu ('new Western Lake') in 'Mongol country', recording in his diary that a Mongolian man brought a gift of two watermelons and wanted Mongolian books.

In 1920 he embarked with Mather on a more ambitious journey to Kobdo and Altai. This is not Gobi-Altai, the provincial capital of Altai *aimag* in western Mongolia. It is likely to have been the Altai or Shar Sum on the River Kran, a tributary to the Irtish River that flows west into Russia. Kobdo was that in modern western Mongolia. This trip is well documented as Hunter sent reports of it to *China's Millions*, the magazine of the China Inland Mission. The Chinese north-west frontier was then the centre of a power struggle between the Chinese and the Russians, and Hunter's trip through the area was the last of any foreigner.

Hunter's journals show that the local Khazaks and Mongols received them well. He went equipped with Scripture tracts 'in all the languages of central Asia', including Mongolian, and took with him his Kalmuck-Mongol helper, Nimgir. Nimgir had been given to Hunter and Mather on a previous trip by a Mongolian living-Buddha and his main duty while they were travelling was management of the horses and their protection from thieves.

Hunter's contacts with the Mongols on this journey are recorded in his diaries: on one occasion he camped among the Torgut Mongols; on another he met fifty Torgut Mongols carrying telegraph poles and gave them Gospels and tracts. On another occasion he camped near the Hobuk River and traded with the Mongols there, distributing tracts. On that journey he met a Mongol and asked whether he wanted to buy a book. The Mongol's reply was that he already had one, reaching into his *del* and producing a well-worn Kalmuck Gospel. This presumably was the Gospel of Matthew translated by the Moravians. Apparently the Mongol had had it for four or five years having received it from another Mongol who bought it in Urumqi, presumably from Hunter or Mather. This man was already a few days' travel from home, and said that he carried it everywhere he went.

Preaching, book-selling, tract distribution and dialogue with lamas characterised Hunter's trips. Although Kalmuck Mongols dominated the local hinterland, he met Mongols from a variety of sub-tribes. On one occasion he met a Khalka lama doctor with whom he traded Gospels for butter and cheese. He met Ölöt Mongols, a sub tribe of the Kalmucks, and gave them Gospels. He gave tracts to the Urungu Mongols. Arriving in Kobdo he pitched his tent a couple of kilometres from the river above Kobdo, near some lamas' *gers*, and traded Gospels and needles and thread for milk and butter. Into this encampment several young lamas rode wanting books.

On the streets in Kobdo, Hunter sold Gospels in Chinese, Mongolian, Kalmuck, Khazak, Sart and Russian. This provoked a response from the local Mongolian customs official who demanded to examine all that they were carrying. This inspection turned out for the good: he himself bought books in Mongolian, Kalmuck and Tibetan. In fact, Hunter and Mather sold out of Mongolian and Tibetan Gospels in the Kobdo bazaar.

Hunter was reasonably successful in his distribution of Mongolian Christian literature. On the whole of the Altai journey, he and Mather had distributed Gospels and tracts to the people in a language they could understand. He left books in strategic places, like the telegraph office and the government salt station. His diary is punctuated with entries like 'sold books and preached' or 'I distributed a number of books and preached on the street' or 'on July 4th, I sold a number of Chinese, Tibetan and Mongolian Gospels and also sold or gave away quite a number of books the days following'. On one occasion he was greeted by a Mongol he had met several years previously. He gave him a warm introduction to the people of the neighbourhood who poured out to see him; this presented an excellent opening to preach and distribute further tracts and Gospels.

Hunter's linguistic strategy was different from that of his colleagues in Kalgan. Rather than trying to learn Mongolian fluently, he attempted to learn an adequate amount of all the local languages such that he could converse simply about the gospel with whoever he met. The surrounding languages and dialects of Urumqi were far more numerous than Kalgan, and so this seemed to Hunter to be a necessity. He learned the languages from the people on the street and the nomads on the steppe. He was a self-taught, need-to-know linguist. Mildred Cable and Francesca French, his biographers, record that he could 'make himself understood' in Mongolian and eight or so other languages of the area.

Percy Mather

Hunter's sidekick, Percy Mather, was more focused. He was absolutely convinced of his call to serve with Hunter: 'great is the need [in darkest Turkestan]; I feel I must be where the need is greatest and the work hardest. Not only is it my desire... but I feel absolutely certain that God has called me, and that I am in line with His will.'[2] After arriving in Urumqi and taking up residence with Hunter, Mather immediately warmed to the Mongols in particular.

Learning the Mongol language proved a challenge, due to the lack of textbooks, reading materials and of a teacher. Mather hit upon an idea. He was in constant contact with Mongolian carters and caravans but had no access to Mongolian Scriptures, or literature, so decided to learn the language himself, using Chinese as a medium, which, presumably, he already knew. However, no one in Urumqi knew Chinese and Mongolian, except a recently convicted criminal. The governor would not let the prisoner out, so Mather asked to be locked into the cell with the prisoner every day. This was certainly an effective way of learning the language, much to the humour of the town. Mather stuck at it through the burning sun, derision and disgrace. Emil Fischbacher, who visited Urumqi much later, observed that Mather 'speaks Chinese fluently, and also Kalmuck Mongol'. Fischbacher comments that Mather can preach in these languages, 'and is in fact specially interested in work among the Mongols'. His Mongolian language must have been quite good as he produced a Mongolian-English dictionary, and a Mongolian grammar book before he died in Mongolia in 1933. Mather also knew Turkish and Russian.[3]

Apart from his linguistic prowess, Mather was also a musician and an amateur doctor. He played the fiddle and mouth organ, which would inevitably attract a crowd. Hunter would then preach and Mather administer some rudimentary medicine. During one furlough, Mather spent several months studying at the Manchester Royal Eye hospital to get some skills to minister to the Mongols with their eye diseases. After returning from England, news spread that he had equipped himself with proper ophthalmic equipment. He writes of one Sunday: 'I had to attend to eighty patients after I had taken Sunday service; so many people come to us for medicine. A Mongol has just been in with trachoma and ulcers on the eye. [He paid with] 3 lbs of lump sugar, a 2 lb box of biscuits... 70 large tomatoes, 10 lbs potatoes, 6 huge water melons, 20 cayenne pods and 4 large cabbages.'[4]

The duo

Hunter and Mather formed a good partnership. Hunter was a generalist and Mather a specialist. Hunter was the austere senior missionary, Mather the younger innovator. Together they criss-crossed Xinjiang with their helper, Nimgir: Hunter witnessing to the central Asians in general, and Mather to the Mongols. Nimgir was their adjutant, translator, manager, dresser and administrator as well as their protector and horse-minder.

Together they distributed thousands of Scriptures throughout a huge area. 'During the twenty weeks I was away, I travelled some two thousand miles and sold Scriptures in eight languages… [including] twenty-four Mongol Gospels… besides a quantity of tracts in Chinese, Tibetan, Turki and Mongolian. These were sold mostly in Kobdo, Altai, Zaisan and Chuguchak.'[5] When Mather first arrived in Urumqi, he had brought with him 5,000 Gospels to restock Hunter's supply. On another occasion we know that Hunter was ecstatic at the arrival of a caravan of camels with eight boxes of tracts and Gospels in various languages, including Mongolian. It had taken two years to come from Shanghai. The caravan had been diverted to Urga due to troubles in the Gobi provinces and the caravan had not been able to get through.

They also worked together on translation projects: dictionaries, *Pilgrim's Progress*, parts of Scripture 'in practically all the languages native to the province', including Mongolian.

Hunter records that he baptised two people in 1908, but then there is no mention of any more. He feared new converts would backslide, disgracing the name of Christ, and so he did not keep any baptismal records. He believed himself called not to baptise but to preach the gospel. Evangelism was his passion, but then when new converts came to the point of professing their faith publicly, Hunter stalled. This can be explained by a combination of his cautious personality, his passion for the renown of Christ and his knowledge of the temptations of Urumqi's city life. Mather brought a balance to this difficult quirk in Hunter. They argued passionately about church affairs: Mather's more level approach led to some responsibility being delegated to local leaders. This was imperative as Hunter and Mather were often away for long periods, and weekly teaching had to continue.

Mildred Cable and Francesca French wrote biographies of Hunter and Mather separately. They leave us in no doubt that Hunter was a man of passionate convictions, committed to the evangelisation of Chinese Turkestan's many and varied peoples. But it is Mather who is clearly portrayed as the missionary specifically to the Mongols. They comment that

> among the Mongols he became as a Mongol.... He was interested in all their affairs... and the erection of a tent, the management of a restive horse, the building of a camp fire were things which he delighted to learn.... In return for their kindness, he used his simple medical skill to relieve their ailments.... To the Mongol, Percy Mather always showed himself the friendly man, helpful, capable, approachable, eminently understandable and obviously without guile. At the mention of his name, the Mongols raise both thumbs in the highest expression of praise they know.[6]

On visiting his grave in Urumqi they comment that 'Percy Mather brought Christ to the Mongols'.[7]

After my first lengthy lesson on Mongol etiquette, I became a lot more comfortable in a Mongol *ger* and had many chances to enjoy Mongol hospitality. I came to enjoy *su-tai tsai*, their 'with-milk tea', mutton soup, and *aral*, one of their many dairy products.

Ulaanbaatar, Mongolia's capital. Churches have been strategically planted throughout the city.

The Catholic centre in Ulaanbaatar which doubles as an embassy and a church.

Communism's legacy is still
visible in modern Ulaanbaatar.

Gandan temple complex dominates the western sector of Ulaanbaatar today.

Tibetan Buddhism has experienced a renaissance in the 1990s, with many temples being rebuilt throughout the country.

Erdenzuu, south west of Ulaanbaatar. This Tibetan Buddhist temple now dominates the site of the ancient Mongol capital Karakorum.

The façade of St Paul's Macau. Macau was the centre of Jesuit missionary enterprise in Eastern Asia.

Mongolian Christians meet for worship and leadership training today.

MONGOLIA TODAY

THE MONGOL EMPIRE IN THE 13TH CENTURY

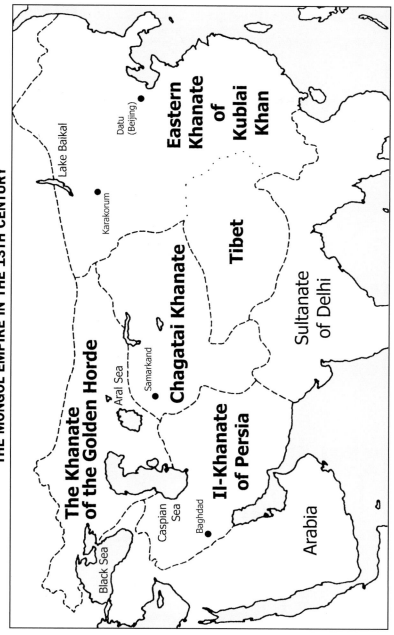

The Khanate of the Golden Horde

Chagatai Khanate

Eastern Khanate of Kublai Khan

Il-Khanate of Persia

Tibet

Sultanate of Delhi

Arabia

Lake Baikal

Karakorum

Datu (Beijing)

Aral Sea

Samarkand

Caspian Sea

Baghdad

Black Sea

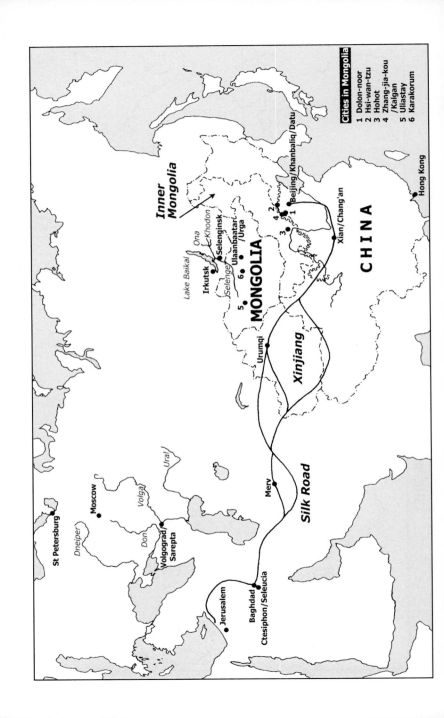

Cities in Mongolia

1 Dolon-noor
2 Hsi-wan-tzu
3 Hohot
4 Zhang-jia-kou
   /Kalgan
5 Uliastay
6 Karakorum

I'd noticed that in Ulaanbaatar, the Mongols' apartments would often have the same spatial arrangements as a *ger*. The man's bed would be against the left-hand wall as you entered the room, and the woman's on the right. Chairs would be against the wall, and there would be an area at the opposite end of the room where the idol was. In an atheistic-Communist home, the *hoymon* would have pictures of the generations before: uncle who died in the war, grandfather in front of his *ger* in the countryside and the like. The Mongols also like to hang their large ornate carpets on the wall. I guess this was to give them the cosy feeling of the *ger*. With a currency that was inflating at 300% annually, I suspected that the carpets were also investments for the future. Mongols visiting our home always walked around our carpet on the floor, or took their shoes off before walking on it.

'*Gidis?*' I was on my own now. No translator to excuse me. I'd been plotting my avoidance of *gidis* for several months. I had managed to squirm out of situations where *gidis* was likely to be offered to me. And *gidis*, I'd been told, was the delicacy of delicacies in Mongolian cuisine. To me it looked like tripe, liver, kidneys, heart, lung and intestines. Which is what *gidis* is. We call it offal in New Zealand.

The hostess had shoved a plate of cold *gidis* under our noses and left the room. Karen turned white. I didn't mind hot, sauted kidney or liver. Still better if in a curry. But cold? I could just about see the botulism on it. There was no dog I could feed it to. I was trapped.

So I did the only thing I could. I ate it.

'It's OK. I feel fine,' I lied to Karen who had pushed hers onto my plate.

When we left an hour later I felt a bit woosy.

When we got off the bus, I felt nauseous.

When we got to our apartment I threw up. Seven times.

I apologised to my language teacher at the end of the week for missing a couple of classes that week, and explained what had happened.

'She should never have served you the *gidis* cold. That was quite rude of her to do that,' my language teacher sympathised. '*Gidis* should always be served well cooked, hot and fresh.' I was relieved. I figured anything was edible if it was freshly cooked and hadn't been sitting around in an overheated apartment collecting every species of bacteria on it.

'You must come and have some real *gidis* at my place,' my language teacher continued. My stomach went into a spasm. 'And you must try the specialty from my native *aimag*.'

'Specialty?' I looked at her suspiciously.

'Yes, hot camel's milk.'

NOTES
1. Mildred Cable and Francesca French, *George Hunter: Apostle of Turkestan* (CIM: London, 1948), pp.38,54.
2. Mildred Cable and Francesca French, *The Making of a Pioneer: Percy Mather of Central Asia* (Hodder and Stoughton: London, 1935), p.88.
3. Marshall Broomhall, *To What Purpose?* (CIM/The Religious Tract Society: London, 1934), p.71.
4. Mildred Cable and Francesca French, *The Making of a Pioneer*, p.233.
5. Quoted from Hunter's diary in Marshall Broomhall, *op.cit.*, p.144.
6. Mildred Cable and Francesca French, *The Making of a Pioneer*, pp.154–155.
7. W.J. Platt, *Three Women: Mildred Cable, Francesca French, Evangeline French: the Authorised Biography* (Hodder and Stoughton: London, 1964), p.178.

Chapter 36

Cecil and Eleanor Polhill-Turner,
A Strategic Inn for Mongol Pilgrims

'The Lord make us to be inextinguishable firebrands, so that no matter how cold the reception of our message may be, the fire may burn on and on.'

Cecil Polhill-Turner

I am in Beijing again, and my curiosity to explore has been stirred. I've been through Beijing numerous times while flying to and from Mongolia. This time I am on my way to Mongolia to be a consultant on a variety of educational projects. There are still so many unexplored corners in this city.

I know I have to leave a full day to get my Mongolian visa. I've worked out a routine: flag a *miandi*, one of the small yellow Daihatsu vans, around 7am and point out where the Friendship Store is on the map of my Lonely Planet guidebook (now well soiled after many such trips). The taxi driver then snakes his way through the now teeming assortment of early morning commuter traffic. Old Chinese ladies do their morning shadow boxing exercises on the pavement. The driver delivers me, not to the store, but to the cafe next door. By 8am, after pastries and coffee, I head off on foot into the Jianguomenwai Embassy Compound. One block in, one block over and opposite the Ethiopian embassy: here I find the back gate to the Mongolian embassy.

This morning, I'm the only one there. I'm prepared for a long wait and come armed with *Freedom in Exile*, the autobiography of the Dalai Lama. I like to think I'm at least on acquaintance level with the embassy staff as I've been there so many times before. I recognise the woman behind the counter and try to impress her with my Mongolian language. She looks long and hard at the number of previous Mongolian visas already in my passport. I have to show my official invitation. Everything's in order. The boss arrives an hour late to verify it. (Once a colleague waited a full day to get his visa because the embassy staff were all out at the airport trying to fly a cadaver back to Mongolia.) I offer translation assistance to some confused tourists, then I'm out of there by 10am. Quickest I've ever been through. Now it's off to get my air tickets confirmed. I'm finished by 10.30. I now have the rest of the day to go exploring.

I'm tempted to go to the Ancient Observatory which stands at the corner of the outer limits of Kublai's old city, but is now bordered by two of Beijing's busiest arterial roads and straddles Jianguomen subway station. It is an impressive site, looking like a small castle with spheres, astrolabes and other stellar apparatus probing the Beijing smog. It had been built by Jesuits during the Ming dynasty in an attempt to keep the confidence of the Ming emperors while the Jesuit fathers taught the Christian faith among the Chinese intelligentsia. It was a noble effort at enculturation, but resulted in very little fruit for the kingdom of God.

I've been through the observatory before so when I get to the door, I check my Lonely Planet guide again to see what else might be worth visiting. I am on my own, so it is time to get adventurous. I notice that the Beijing lama temple is only five subway stops away. I head underground at the adjacent subway door. I stare up at the huge Chinese characters and painstakingly match them against the English map in my guidebook. I don't want to get out at the wrong station. It takes me about ten minutes and I miss three trains. I successfully emerge from the subterranean gloom at Yonghegong station. I decide the city council must build all its subway stations under significant historical sites. The lama temple wall is shared with the subway station.

Having grown up with Tibetan friends in India and become familiar with things Tibetan, I know what to expect at the lama temple. I suspect that this is the temple where the Panchen lama of Tibet had been resident. The Panchen Lama is second only to the Dalai Lama, but during the turmoil of the 1950s and 60s, tended to be more pro-Chinese than Tibetan. I look forward to finding some solace from the frantic city outside, wandering the neatly laid out gardens and exploring the gradation of buildings leading into the inner sanctuary. The guidebook says 'this beautiful Tibetan temple features lovely gardens, stunning frescoes and tapestries and incredible carpentry'. This is indeed true and I am not disappointed. It is then I notice the short sentence: 'the temple is in active use again'. And it certainly is. On entering the outer courtyard I am immediately hit with the powerful aroma of incense. Other foreign tourists meander around. Local Tibetan and Chinese have come to revere the gods.

I stand for a long time outside each building in each courtyard watching these devotees. They prostrate themselves in front of the idols that sit with their demonic expressions gazing down with lifeless eyes. The idols' facial contortions are the substance of nightmares. The worshippers walk around them, murmuring their *mantras* and waving their incense sticks.

I think of James Gilmour. He once sat here. He came to this temple to learn the Mongol language and witness to the pilgrims and lamas. He'd lived here for a whole winter one year.

Location: a key concept

Historically, the Mongols have been fairly inaccessible. The Mongolian heartland is distant from the sea, and only in this century has a main railway line been put in. The sparse population and the enormous distances between centres, coupled with severe winters and short summers has meant that few have penetrated into Mongolian heartland with the gospel. Along with this, the Mongolian tribes (or 'banners') are well spread out across central Asia, and also have a number of dialects, making language acquisition difficult.

How then could missionaries take the gospel to the Mongols? Most missionaries of the nineteenth and twentieth centuries have been primarily focused on the Chinese, but a handful had a specific burden for the Mongols. How could this handful of enthusiasts sustain an ongoing mission to the Mongols, if the Mongols were so difficult to get to?

The simplest strategy was to locate oneself strategically. It made sense to set up a mission station away from the Chinese among the Mongol tribes. Several missions did this across Inner Mongolia and Xinjiang. Nomadic Mongols were then accessible in the immediate vicinity of the station. Alternatively, missionaries would place themselves on a route which Mongols frequently travelled for trading or for religious pilgrimage. Then when Mongols passed through town, they could talk with them or give them Bibles.

Religious centres

It was good to be at or near religious centres, as opportunities for witness arose to those who were visiting the temples or monasteries. Mongols would go on very long pilgrimages to religious places in China and even to Tibet itself. The routes were well known and the inns did a brisk trade in food, accommodation and animal care. In 1889, a Frenchman, Gabriel Bonvalot, made his way to Tibet using the track of a recently returned caravan travelling from Lhasa to Mongolia. In 1892, Rockhill (Secretary of the US Legation in Beijing) took a journey to Tibet passing through Koko-Nor and met Mongols returning to Mongolia having been to Tibet on pilgrimage.

Mongol pilgrims could be found at any number of religious sites: Wu-t'ai-shan ('The Five Peaks') is a sacred Buddhist retreat centre in Shansi province where Mongol pilgrims would worship. At Kang Lung lamasery, three days' journey from Kanchow, Mildred Cable mentions meeting a Mongol prince on his way to the lamasery. At the lamasery at Mai-mai Chen, Inner Mongolia, Reginald Sturt, a Brethren missionary, spent two days distributing Scriptures and explaining them to 'the three living Buddhas and the abbots': seven of the twelve abbots accepted the literature. Sturt also regularly visited Ta Pan Shang, a 'mongol centre' in eastern Mongolia where he set up a Gospel tent and Bible stall for the fair at the temple. Although the Chinese authorities were co-operative, Sturt recognised the desperate need to have a Mongol or Mongol-speaking person based there. Jehol city too was of great significance with large religious sites.

The lama temple in Beijing also attracted numerous Mongol pilgrims. Gilmour spent time there learning the Mongol language and witnessing to the pilgrims. Percy Knight, from the China Inland Mission, wrote in 1907 of a visit he had made to the temple. He found boy lamas in training who were 'motley, vicious, unwashed', indeed all the lamas had a 'vacant, ignorant or sensual expression'. Knight was moved by the potential of evil among these boys condemned to celibacy. All their prayers were in a 'Mongol tongue' (probably actually Tibetan). The priests were in ignorance as to the meaning of their worship according to Knight and there was an entire absence of joy and intelligence. Knight wondered at the hold this type of worship would have on their hearts and longed for the day 'when the idols shall be utterly abolished and these false systems with their enslaving power will be swept away by him who is the Way, the truth and the life'.

Dolon-noor, or 'Seven Lakes' (modern Duolun in Inner Mongolia, and Lama-miao in Chinese) was also a key strategic site for evangelism. Large bronze and brass foundries were located there and it was the place where most of Mongolia's idols and religious trinkets were cast. A large lamasery was nearby. Robert Stephens, the first Brethren missionary in Mongolia (from 1897) found it strategic for preaching and selling Tibetan Gospels. There was a huge number of resident lamas, and many nomads and visiting lamas would arrive, coming to purchase Buddhas for their own lamaseries. Reginald Sturt frequented the border towns and Dolon-noor in particular. These missionaries believed that the border towns were key places to preach because of the constant movement of Mongols through them. The Ching administration of China had established lama hostels in Beijing, and at Jehol, Wu-t'ai-shan and Dolon-uur as part of their policy to decentralise lamaism and so bring it under their control.

The Polhill-Turners in Xining and Kumbum

Cecil Polhill-Turner and his wife Eleanor began pioneering work in Xining from 1888 shortly after they were married there. Xining was the capital of Qinghai province and the governor of Koko-nuur district lived there. Located on the Tibetan borderlands, it was an important administrative and military centre. The CIM had opened a station there three years previously 'in the hope of reaching Tibetans and Mongols' for Christ.[1] The residents of the town were 'Chinese, Aboriginals, Mohammedans, Tibetans and Mongols', although resident Mongols were comparatively few. The CIM station was the only Christian presence in the city, and comprised a boys' school and a small dispensary which had a constant flow of Muslim, Chinese, Tibetan and Mongol patients through it.

Kumbum lamasery, one of the most important and biggest Tibetan-Buddhist sites outside of Lhasa, was located about thirty-two kilometres from Xining. It was called the 'Lamasery of the Ten Thousand Images' and had been the residence of the reincarnation of Tsongkapa, the great reformer of Tibetan Buddhism. The Polhill-Turners were committed to evangelism among the Tibetans in the first instance and so took a special interest in the activities of Kumbum and the pilgrims who frequented it. First though, they managed to arrange to study Tibetan language from the old Catholic Mongol called Samdachiemba, who had accompanied the two French Lazarists Gabet and Huc on their travels.

During festival time at Kumbum, the Polhill-Turners distributed tracts and engaged the lamas and pilgrims in religious discussion. Quite a few of these lamas were Mongols. At times like this, the number of Mongols could swell by thousands. The

Polhill-Turners found this evangelistic work difficult, not knowing the Mongols' language. They resorted to distribution of tracts and Gospels in Mongolian and Kalmuck.

During the following year they did a reconnaissance of the vicinity of Xining into the 'border' areas (ie of China with Mongolia and Tibet). For Cecil, it was a delight to be back in the saddle again. He was one of the famous 'Cambridge Seven', a group of rising stars from Cambridge University in England who turned their back on lucrative and high-status positions to go to China with the CIM. After graduating from Cambridge in 1879, he had joined the Bedfordshire Yeomanry, then was 2nd Lieutenant in the Dragoon Guards (The Queen's Bays), rising to the rank of Lieutenant by 1884. The adventurous, if somewhat romantic life of the army, accompanied by his love of horses, put him in good stead for long journeys across the Qinghai steppe. Cecil and Eleanor found that news of their teaching spread ahead of them, and they were inundated by questions from many Mongols.

Their first love was the Tibetans, and initially they stayed in Xining for only two years. They relocated south to Sungpan in western Szechwan province, and also spent some time ministering to Tibetans on the Tibetan-Indian border. They returned to China again, but were withdrawn to the coast during the Boxer uprising of 1900. Cecil must have been injured in the uprising, for he was invalided home to England and doctors forbade his permanent return to China. Undaunted by this, he made a further seven trips to China, although never took up residence there again.

In 1923 he and Eleanor hit upon a strategy for evangelism which was both novel and successful. They purchased a property and started the Tibetan Gospel Inn back in Xining. The aim of the inn was to offer hospitality to pilgrims coming to Kumbum. To do this it not only had to accommodate the people, but also their camels and horses. It was mainly aimed at Tibetans (there were two Tibetan evangelists associated with the inn) and by 1929 'a number' of Tibetans had already professed Christ as their Lord.

However, Cecil and Eleanor didn't limit their ministry only to Tibetans. The inn was open to the five main people groups of the area. The flag on the opening day represented these groups by five different colours: red for China, yellow for Manchuria, blue for Mongolia, white for Muslims, and black for Tibetans. The Mongols were definitely part of the original vision for this outreach. The 'holy classics' (that is the Bible in some form) were printed and distributed from the hostel in all five languages: Chinese, Arabic, Tibetan, Kalmuck and Mongol (presumably the Khalka dialect). The inn provided free accommodation, and guests cooked their own food in the communal kitchen. And it had a preaching hall which could seat about fifty people.

Some opposition to the gospel arose at Xining, fired by a Mongol lama who handed out tracts warning of 'dire consequences of listening to heterodoxy'. However, Mongol pilgrims did use the inn. On one occasion a Mongol prince arrived with a caravan of more than a hundred camels. He had to send most of them to another inn as the Gospel Inn had room for only thirty.

The Polhill-Turners had an unusual ally at Kumbum. Cecil had given a Tibetan lama called Mina Fuyeh copies of the Gospels. This lama treasured John's Gospel and committed most of it to memory. He could quote it accurately and argue intelligently from it about the incidents in Christ's life. He 'believed thoroughly in Jesus' but couldn't see the need to renounce Buddhism. He expounded the gospel and Christian doctrine 'with all the famous lamas and pilgrims from the far interior, even from Lhasa, as also from Mongolia... teaching them to pronounce for the first time the name of Yesu Mashika'.[2] He was the means of unconsciously spreading the gospel among a wide and diverse number of lamas and pilgrims.

There are other stories of Mongols converted through similar ministries in key locations. For example, a Mongol called

Yappel travelled from Mongolia to a monastery in Lhasa on pilgrimage with his parents and stayed in Tibet until his parents died. With no further responsibility and no one to support him, he trekked south down to Darjeeling in India. This town, set in the foothills of the Himalayas close to Tibet, acted as a natural conduit for refugees, traders and pilgrims. Several Christian ministries were based here, including the Tibet Mission Band, committed to work among the Tibetan-Buddhist peoples of central Asia. Yappel heard the gospel and was converted in Darjeeling.

It was a wise strategy to locate Christian work on the main pilgrim routes. It gave easy and open access to the Mongols. The idea of giving accommodation to pilgrims was new and meant that there was time to spend with pilgrims. However, there were natural spiritual dangers associated with being in or near a lamasery. Missionaries have many stories of the evil they witnessed at the lamaseries and the spiritual bondage the lamas were under. Entering the lamasery and debating face to face with the lamas may not be the best strategy, but one-to-one fellowship with weary travellers, ministering to their physical and spiritual needs, was a strategy that had some effect in Xining.

I sit there watching the people at the temple for a long time. I'm a voyeur, an outsider looking into something intimate. I start to get a headache. I need to move away from the incense. Maybe I had too many pastries for breakfast. I wander through the medical school, but find it disappointing. Same with the astronomical building. A few interesting maps and charts, but nothing intellectually satisfying. More idols, more *tankas* hanging on the wall, and a young novice guarding each hall, all the time muttering his *mantras* and counting his beads. I move down to the main hall where there is a huge Buddha staring down at me. He looks serene and harmless enough. For some reason he appears in the *Guinness Book of Records*. There are butter lamps burning at his feet, and offerings of fruit in dishes.

My head is splitting. I feel heavy and tired. I have to sit down. I watch the orange-robed lamas sitting in the sun on the opposite side of the courtyard. I try praying for them. James Gilmour must have prayed for the lamas in this temple too.

My praying becomes confused. I feel dizzy. My arms and legs feel heavy. The demons look down on me from the temple's roofs. They are laughing at me. The *mantras* of the lamas are stuck in my mind. The walls are closing in on me.

A gust of cold spring wind brings me back to my senses. I pick up my bag and head for the gate. As I run through the last gate, away from that oppressive place, the heaviness lifts and my headache disappears. The lesson is timely. I ponder as I sit on the shuttle bus back to the hotel. In seeking to be a good Christian witness to the Buddhist, I had persuaded myself that a short inconsequential visit to a local temple would equip me better as I would know more of my Buddhist neighbour's culture. True enough, but dangerous too. I had started to dance with the devil, and the devil obliged.

NOTES

1. Marshall Broomhall, 'The Province of Kansu', in Marshall Broomhall, ed., *The Chinese Empire: A General and Missionary Survey* (Morgan and Scott/China Inland Mission: London, 1907), p.195.
2. Dr Susie Rijnhart, quoted in F.D. Learner, *Rusty Hinges: A Story of Closed Doors Beginning to Open in North-east Tibet* (The China Inland Mission: London, 1934), p.63.

John T. Gulick,
The Strategic Role of the City of Kalgan

'Behold, I have set before you a door.'
Revelation 3:8

'Zhang-jia-kou,' I announced, trying to get my tongue around the Chinese consonants. The train slowed to a stop and I opened the window. A slight hint of coal dust wafted in. Chinese military music blared over the loud speakers. Huge large-character hoardings dominated the main station. A clock said 10.50 am. There was still a morning nip in the air.

'It amazes me how they can run this train exactly on time.' We had travelled from Ulaanbaatar and this was our third stop over the Chinese border, which we had reached at 1.51 precisely. We were heading for Beijing. The full journey would take thirty-six hours.

We'd woken that morning to a miracle. The vast trackless expanse of the Gobi desert had been transformed into the rich green of densely-packed Chinese cultivated plots. Small confined red-brick courtyards were home to piles of horded family utensils from farm equipment to bicycles and old beds. Everything was a dull grey from grime, smog and coal dust. We were looking into the lives of unknown people — spectators in time as we clattered past, peering out from our encapsulated vantage point. And all the roofs were tiled.

The station was sterile. No bustling activity of vendors. No one got on. No one got off. A few guards in ill-fitting green uniforms mingled around. Past the station building I could see the concrete apartment buildings and the tangle of overhead street wiring, and hear the general hubbub of a modern Chinese city. Mountains dominated the skyline. We seemed to be in some sort of amphitheatre.

'This is the old town of Kalgan, isn't it?' said Karen, peering out of the window.

'Yes. "The Gate" between Mongolia and China. This is a significant mountain pass. We should go through the great wall after we leave here.'

Kalgan

Kalgan was a flourishing business centre about 225 kilometres north-west of Beijing. The name means 'the door', and it was the door or gate between China and Mongolia, straddling the mountain pass through which the Great Wall is also built. The Chinese word for the Mongolian regions is *kow-wai* meaning 'beyond the gate'. The modern Chinese name for the town is Zhang-jia-kou (spelt variously) meaning 'mouth or entry into the court of Lord Zhang'.

Kalgan was the capital of Chahar province of Inner Mongolia at the turn of the century. Traditionally it was one of the chief towns on the northern branch of the ancient Silk Road, and the main transfer point of Chinese tea on its way overland to Europe. It was also the start of the main caravan route from China to Siberia, via Urga, and a major junction town for trade going west to Turkestan. Mongol camel pullers were the only ones capable of shipping freight across the Gobi desert.

The significance of Kalgan can be seen from its trade figures. In 1906, for example, the tea trade between China and Siberia, all processed through Kalgan, employed about 100,000 people, using 1.2 million camels and 300,000 ox carts. 408,000 kgs of tea went to Urga alone. Trade to eastern Mongolia through Kalgan comprised 25,000 horses, 10,000 horned cattle, 250,000 sheep and hides. Trade with western Mongolia totalled 70,000 horses, 30,000 horned cattle and between a half and two million sheep.[1] Mongols came here regularly to trade with Chinese merchants: the Mongols would sell livestock, wool, hides, salt, soda and timber, and buy manufactured goods from the Chinese: tea, silks, cloth, saddles, boots, needles and thread.

The ethnic make-up of the city was diverse. In 1871 it had a population of 17,000 of Chinese and Mongol mix, as well as about 10,000 Russian merchants. One missionary writing in 1871 observes that:

> the streets are wide, and lined with some of the best shops I have seen in China. The roofs of the houses are all made of mud, on which may be seen crops of grass, which give a very curious appearance to the town. The streets were crowded with long caravans of camels, bound for Kiachta [on the Russian-Mongol border], laden with brick tea; oxen, and carts drawn by men, laden with the produce from Russia, coming the other way: Mongols, camel-drivers, hurrying here and there, mounted on ponies or camels, keeping the stragglers together, dressed in various coloured clothes, and looking most picturesque. The sight presented to us was so different to anything we had ever seen before — it was like the realisation of one of the scenes in the Arabian Nights tales... If bustle and animation are a sign of prosperity, Kalgan must be ranked foremost in that category, and I believe it is the most prosperous town in China for its size.[2]

During the early 1900s Kalgan attracted a large expat missionary Community and during the Boxer and Communist uprisings, a large Mongolian and Chinese refugee Community. During the rise of Communism in the late 1940s, many Mongolian refugees congregated here, mainly Buriats from their pastures in the north. Officially, they were to be rehabilitated on pastureland along the northern bank of the Yellow River. Several Buriat Communities grew in and around Kalgan. By 1948 about 200 Buriats were still living in the town, and others in a small hamlet called Jang Bei about 65 kilometres north. More wealthy Buriats had emigrated down to Beijing.

Kalgan eventually fell to the communists, and all missionaries retreated to the coast, then left China for other fields.

The influence of the Gulicks

Because of the constant flow of Mongols through Kalgan, mission agencies saw it as a strategic site for Christian work. Many used the town as a base for evangelism on the steppe. Because of its higher altitude, cooler climate and picturesque surrounds, missionaries also came for rest and recreation. It was for reasons of health that John Gulick and his wife arrived there in 1865. They became so impressed with its potential as a site in which to base Mongol work that they recommended to their mission, the American Board of Commissioners for Foreign Missions (ABCFM), that it set up ministry there. This mission had been in China since 1830.

John Gulick was son of Orramel Gulick (1830–1923), well-known American missionary first to Hawaii, then to Japan. He and his wife were now the first ABCFM missionaries to the Mongols, and John would tour the steppe every summer, preaching, praying and planning strategy for evangelisation. Their first contact with the Mongols had not been entirely voluntary. Not long after they arrived in Kalgan they were driven from their rented accommodation by a mob of Chinese and found refuge with friendly Mongols sixty-five kilometres to the north. Their first convert was their cook, but we don't know if he was Mongol or Chinese.

Reinforcements for the ABCFM mission in Kalgan soon arrived. Mark Williams and his wife moved there in 1867 for one year, and in 1868 the Reverend T.W. Thompson joined them. But tensions over priorities soon arose: to which people group should most time be given? Since the first ABCFM missionaries in Kalgan were China orientated (they'd either been working elsewhere in China or understood their calling first to the Chinese), priorities soon drifted from the Mongols. 'To the Chinese first, and also to the Mongols'[3] was the motto.

However, the Gulicks themselves kept the Mongol work alive. They went on furlough to America in 1872 and managed to recruit the Reverend and Mrs W.P. Sprague specifically for Mongol work. The Spragues arrived in Kalgan in 1874, but overlapped with the Gulicks for only two years, as ill-health forced the Gulicks to transfer to Japan. Thompson left the same year, again for health reasons. Over these years, there were more responses to the gospel in the countryside than in the township, perhaps because Kalgan's population was so transitory and follow-up was difficult. However, through the labours of the Gulicks and others, the ABCFM work became well established in Inner Mongolia.

Specifically Mongol statistics are lacking, but a rough picture can be painted from general data. In 1886 James Gilmour recognised that the ABCFM was so well established in Kalgan, he felt freer to move east and set up work among the settled Mongols in eastern Mongolia. In north China (Manchuria and Inner Mongolia), the ABCFM had ninety-six places of regular meeting, and ten organised churches with 2931 communicants and 5000 adherents.[4]

Other mission agencies set up in Kalgan

The Gulicks' pioneering vision for Kalgan was caught by other mission agencies. In 1892 Sprague and Roberts invited the Moravians to join in the Mongolian work in Kalgan after the departure of Gilmour, but the Moravians couldn't oblige at the time. (However, the invitation prompted the Moravians to consider Mongolia, and indirectly led to their work in the Himalayas.) Other agencies would respond, and both Protestant and Catholic groups set up in Kalgan as a deliberate strategy to evangelise the Mongols. Missionaries interpreted Kalgan ('the gate/door') with respect to Revelation 3:8 — 'Behold I have set before you an open door.' They saw the advantages as numerous: Mongolian language teachers could be easily hired, caravans for travel could be easily employed, and utilities like winter clothing were readily available. Hospitality was another crucial part of the ministry of all the agencies. The city's proximity to Beijing and the Mongolian hinterland together proved it to be a good staging post and rehabilitation centre after long journeys on to the steppe.

It was not surprising that several other mission agencies followed the ABCFM. The Methodist Mission, the British and Foreign Bible Society, the Russian Orthodox, the Norwegian Alliance, the Seventh Day Adventists, the CICM, and the Missionary Canonesses of St Augustine. All these agencies had left Kalgan by the time of the cultural revolution.

We pulled out of Zhang-jia-kou exactly ten minutes after we had arrived there.

'No sign whatsoever of any of its past missionary history,' I commented to Karen as we settled down again.

Karen was arranging a stack of instant noodle packets she'd bought at the station. Each packet was a sealed polystyrene bowl. 'We'll just get some boiled water and fill these bowls up for lunch.'

Our carriage had a small coal-fired copper water-heater at one end, and the guard would fill thermoses for passengers from it.

I gazed out of the window watching the hustle and bustle of Chinese urban life transform itself slowly into the rhythm of the Chinese countryside again. The train moved slowly, obviously pulling hard because of the gradient. The mountains drew in closer around us, and the cultivated plots succumbed to natural forest vegetation. The occasional walled hamlet could be seen among the dense vegetation as we alternated tunnel, bridge and valley, winding our way slowly along the tracks.

'There it is!' I announced. 'The Great Wall of China.'

It was nothing much the first time we saw it. We had actually gone through it — it was an odd assortment of old masonry hidden by dense vegetation. We were pulling into a remote mountain station, from which we merely left again three minutes later back in the direction we'd come. I guess they switched the points as we now crept downhill even more slowly but in another valley.

'There it is again,' Karen said, pointing to a ridge opposite us. Suddenly the wall was everywhere. Running along that ridge, snaking up the other side of the valley, winding its way along the mountains in the distance. It was a huge piece of masonry in various states of disrepair. Some sections were well preserved, others crumbling.

Three Mongols came over to look out of our window. We'd got to know them a little during the journey. They had insisted that we try their Chinese *Tsing Hao* beer the evening before — as a sort of farewell toast to Mongolia before crossing the border. We had declined it which had upset them, but then we ate their *tsagaan edee*, an assortment of 'white food' — cheeses, yoghurt and the like — which redeemed us somewhat.

'*Eeshee so*, sit down,' I beckoned.

'The Great Wall,' one murmered. He introduced himself as Bat, and seemed to be the more extrovert of the group. He'd entertained us with Long Songs of the steppe the night before. Now he became pensive and glassy-eyed. 'It's a symbol of the animosity between our two countries.'

The wall was a recognised boundary. When the Mongol Yuan dynasty ruled China, and when the Chinese Manchurians ruled Mongolia, both these eras are recognised as a breach in the wall. Both Chinese and Mongol armies had marched through the pass at Zhang-jia-kou at some stage.

'The wall was built to keep the Chinese out of Mongolia,' I said to Bat. He looked at me, realised I was joking, and burst into laughter.

'Well the wall isn't very strong then,' he chuckled, opening another bottle of *Tsing Hao* beer. 'Look. Best beer in Mongolia is Chinese!'

NOTES

1. Marshall Broomhall, ed., *The Chinese Empire*, p.352.
2. W.A. Whyte, *A Land Journey from Asia to Europe* (Sampson Low, Son and Marston: London, 1871), p.49.
3. James H. Roberts, 'Work for the Mongols near Kalgan', in Marshall Broomhall, ed., *The Chinese Empire*, p.360 .
4. D. MacGillivray, ed., *A Century of Protestant Mission in China: 1807–1907* (Christian Literature Society for China: Shanghai, 1907), p.296.

Chapter 38

Reginald Sturt,
Saturating Mongolia with Gospels and Tracts

'His every aim, energy and thought spent itself for the glory of God, and the salvation of the Mongol people.'

A.G. Crompton, Reginald Sturt's biographer

Reginald Sturt was born in 1881 in Brighton, England. Raised an Anglican, he made a personal commitment to Jesus Christ at the age of sixteen, and a commitment to mission work a year later. Reginald wanted to be a doctor, but his own health broke down and his life was threatened by TB. On medical advice, he emigrated to New Zealand for 'an outdoor life', initially settling in the province of Canterbury, in the South Island.

His acceptance for work in China was announced in the mission magazine *Echoes of Service*: 'For China: Mr Reginald Sturt, who has long desired to serve God in China is leaving for Mongolia, December 11th, 1906.' Sturt was affiliated to the Brethren and commended from both England and New Zealand. He was in China between 1907 and1942 and between 1947 and 1948. His first location was the province of Jehol in Inner Mongolia, but a passion for the nomadic Mongols on the steppe soon started to grow, possibly from his reading of mission books about others working among the Tibetans and Mongols. He was also inspired by reports of revival among the Presbyterian churches in Manchuria and wished the same for Mongolia.

The toll on Reginald's personal life in his ministry in Mongolia was high. He was plagued by poor health and was often quite sickly. He was married three times, first to Gertrude ('Truda') Twite in 1912. Gertrude had already been working in China between 1909 and 1912 before they met; she died in 1923. A year later Reginald married her sister Margaret, but she died in 1929. In 1931, he married Marjory McCabe. Marjory outlived him by two years, dying in 1950.

Here Reginald Sturt's son, John, reflects:

I was born in Beijing in 1929, but my mother died soon afterwards. I was fostered by another missionary family, who lived in Hada (Chifeng), in what was then known as Manchuria, and later Inner Mongolia. By the time I was three, my father, Reginald Sturt, had remarried, so I was united again with my family and we continued to live in Hada. Later I attended boarding school in Chefoo (Yentai), but would join my parents for the long school holidays once a year.

We lived in a typical local mud-brick house, ate local food and dressed in the same kind of clothes the people around us wore. In the winter I remember wearing a padded coat and trousers, thick felt boots, a fur-lined leather coat and hat to go outside in temperatures of 20-30 degrees below zero. One house we lived in was also very cold. The window framing was covered with paper, not glass. We slept on a brick bed, which was heated by a fire underneath it at one end, with the smoke and heat permeating through tunnels to a chimney the other end. Often, one end of the bed was too hot and the other not warm enough!

One holiday, I arrived home to find I had a new adopted Mongolian 'sister' about my own age, with long black hair done into a big plait down her back. She was shy and spoke little English at that stage, and I knew less Mongolian. She stayed in our family for about two years.

In the summer months my parents used to travel across the Mongol plains to visit lamaseries, and spend time with some of the nomadic Mongolian clans (or banners) especially when summer fairs were being held. They would preach, distribute portions of Scripture and treat people with illnesses. Dad was a fluent speaker of both Mongolian and Chinese, and he prepared a primer and grammar to help either English-speaking or Chinese people learn Mongolian.

Their mode of transport was often by ox cart, at a slow six kilometres an hour. When my father travelled alone he would go by horse-back, and covered many thousands of kilometres in the Gobi this way. One of his accomplishments was the making of an accurate map of the area, as none was available then. Later they purchased a car, which enabled them to cover greater distances with more comfort and reach greater numbers of people.

There were those who responded to the gospel message and a few small local churches were established. Two I know of were at Ta Pan Shang and Lin Hsi, as well as the mainly Chinese-speaking church at Hada. But their missionary activities were increasingly restricted after the Japanese took over Manchuria, renaming it Manchukuo. At one stage they were accused of being spies and put in a common prison for a month. Along with many other missionary families we were made prisoners of war in December 1941, after the Japanese entered World War II. We were some of the fortunate ones to be repatriated about nine months later. All contact was then lost with Mongolian and Chinese Christians in Inner Mongolia.

Literature saturation

Sturt used Jehol city as his base, and travelled with James Duthie, another New Zealand Brethren missionary, distributing literature, selling Scriptures and preaching in streets and market places throughout the vicinity of Jehol. Due to lack of personnel, no one could give sole attention to the Mongols, and they had to split their time between Chinese and Mongols: 'I do not intend attempting the Mongol language until I have a good hold of Chinese, say in another eighteen months or two years; although Duthie and I have great desires Mongolia-wards.'

In a personal letter to the author, Mary Sturt, Reginald's daughter writes: 'My father did a lot of itinerary work among the Mongols: visiting lamaseries and *ger* communities with the gospel and Bibles....' On one of his first journeys from Jehol, Sturt was struck by the fact that no one was targeting the Mongols to the north of Jehol and on the inner table land. His strategy was simple: ride out to the market-places on the market days in the villages nearby. Take lots of literature, and distribute it as widely as possible. His journeys often took him away for three or four days at a time, travelling sometimes up to 500 kilometres.

1925–1927 were 'remarkable years... of journeys through unexplored country with the Mongol and Tibetan Scriptures'. He went north of Hada to the Mongol border area and for three weeks travelled solely through Mongol territory. One journey was for over five months. Sturt met many Mongol princes and high lamas and always left gifts of books for their hospitality: copies of *Genesis*, the Gospels or *Acts*. Booklets from Scripture Gift Mission, and copies of a catechism that Gilmour had written found their way into many *gers* in the Mongolian hinterland.

This was no random wandering across the steppe. Sturt developed a systematic pattern: 'the whole of the Mongol-speaking territory, nominally controlled from Jehol, had been carefully and systematically traversed and "pioneeringly sown" with portions of the Word of God and much other gospel literature, all in Mongolian and Tibetan.'

Sturt had contact with many different tribal groups. He travelled among eleven Mongol banners and in three or four of these he plied his literature thoroughly. He visited fifty or so lamaseries in these banners alone. He also contacted the Aru-Khorchin banner, and the Abaga banner on the north-west of the Khingan Mountains all the time leaving Gospels and tracts among the nomads and lamas. Sturt also visited the Barin Banner, Keshikten Banner and Sunit Right Wing Banner. The prince of the Ujimchin Banner on the north-eastern slopes of the Khingan Range was also interested in his literature. On occasions Sturt stayed at the lamaseries for hospitality. He summarises: 'thus the printed word and a clear presentation of the gospel has been placed in the hands of the princes and officials of the tribes, the living Buddhas, and leading abbots of at least ninety lamaseries visited by us as guests, and in the innumerable homes of the people.'

Sturt targeted strategic towns, for example Wu-Dan-Cheng on the Mongol-Chinese frontier. It was an important trading centre. Here he sold books to both Mongols and Chinese. Similarly Hada in Jehol province, where Mongols would come to trade in grain and salt and use it as a transfer point to unload goods for the coast.

The Buriats living near Kalgan attracted the Sturts' special attention. They had been forced off their northern pasture lands due to Communist exploitation and had migrated down through Kalgan into Inner Mongolia. On one occasion he joined a truck convoy to give relief to Buriat refugees, taking food, clothing, money and implements to about one hundred families. Mrs Sturt recalls singing in the small encampment called Jang Bei north of Kalgan to the very poor Buriat Mongols there. They were all very friendly and receptive until one of their lamas came and 'the atmosphere changed; everyone jumped up and stood all the time, and he occupied the centre of everything, doing most of the talking'.

Sturt was an opportunist, capturing every moment either to preach, distribute Christian literature or engage someone in conversation about spiritual matters. He also gave medical assistance where he could, drawing on his limited knowledge. At a Barin banner festival on another occasion, he preached from dawn till sundown to the Mongols who would gather at his *ger* door. The Mongol prince accepted a Mandarin Bible and assured Sturt that he regularly read the Mongolian Bible which Sturt had given him five years previously.

Sturt distributed literally thousands of tracts, books and Scriptures in Mongolian, Chinese and Tibetan, giving them or selling them to a whole variety of people in squatters' huts, temples and palaces. One year he complained that he hadn't managed to move as much as the previous year ('barely 500 copies in Mongolian, Tibetan and Chinese'). Between 1929 and 1930, he took to using a 'Gospel Coach', a Dodge 6 van, for literature distribution to fairs and clusters of *gers*. He was received well by people, priests, a Mongol prince and Chinese officials. With the changing political allegiances in China, he was arrested in 1940 for being too close to a military zone.

Douglas Broughton, another New Zealander who arrived to help the Sturts in late 1939, tells of selling 5000 Scripture portions and thousands of tracts at the annual fair at Tai Ming where an estimated 30 000 people had gathered. Adopting a similar strategy to Sturt, and often working alongside him, Broughton too travelled around the countryside. It was Broughton who kept the Gospel Van going, both as driver and chief mechanic, through 'deep sand and thick mud, dry rocky valleys and rivers swollen with torrential floods, washed-out roads, boulder-filled and flooded creeks, steep ravines and dangerous passes'.

Stories, stories

Personal anecdotes abound of conversations and encounters. Sturt reflects on a personal encounter with a lama regarding merit when walking around the Tai-ping pagoda. At the lamasery at Mai-mai Chen, Sturt spent two days distributing Scripture and explaining it to the three living Buddhas and the abbots. Seven of the twelve abbots accepted the literature. On one occasion Sturt just missed meeting the Panchen Lama but left Mongol and Tibetan Scriptures with his retinue. Two living buddhas and officials received his books.

The story of Altantsetseg illustrates Sturt's commitment to the Mongols. Altantsetseg, a girl of about sixteen, was dying. She was an orphan and only child, looked after by a granny. Hygiene in the *ger* was poor. Sturt, with other missionaries, visited her throughout one summer. At each visit Sturt would tell Altantsetseg another story about Jesus. On one occasion he tried to describe heaven to her from *Revelation* 21 and 22.

Naturally she wanted to know if Jesus would make her better. On what turned out to be his last visit Sturt heard the lama performing his last rites in the next room. Despite this Altantsetseg still wanted to see Sturt.

Sturt was unable to follow up with Altantsetseg, being driven out of the village by the Japanese. However, a Chinese Christian stayed on in the village and was later called by the granny to come to Altantsetseg when she was finally dying.

'Well, Altan, how is it? Have you given your heart to Jesus?' he asked.

'Yes I have', she replied.

Six or seven Chinese 'and also several Mongols living in and around Ta Pan Shang' professed faith in Christ. A Mongol police-soldier at Tien Shan professed faith in Christ. He had heard Sturt preach and had bought Gospels from him two years previously. Stephen followed on from Sturt, and during a later trip he found literature which Sturt had circulated: it was 'everywhere in evidence, true seed of the word pregnant with harvest'.

Some criticism has been levelled at Sturt for failing to establish churches in the wake of such a highly mobile widespread literature ministry. Sturt believed that converts should be left to form indigenous churches from the start, rather than have foreign missions establish them and run them with foreign funds. For Sturt, 'evangelism was the church's chief business, to which everything else was secondary'.

Sturt acquired some stature among the missionary community. He led devotional times with Swedish missionaries in Kalgan, and many testified to the inspiration he was to them in his Bible teaching.

Sturt's Mongolian Grammar and Primer — a labour of love

Sturt's *magnum opus* was a Mongolian Grammar and Primer published in 1941. When it was completed, a Mr C. Baehr photographed it in Chefoo and sent two copies to the USA. One was lodged at the University of California, and the other ended up with Stuart Gunzel of whom suggested amendments were asked. Gunzel believed it needed some major changes, and helped Sturt revise it. Sturt had high acclaim for Gunzel's knowledge of the language: he had an 'expert knowledge of colloquial Mongolian'. After Sturt did revise it, an unnamed missionary wrote 'it seems that his [Sturt's] efforts to produce a Mongolian grammar in English have not produced any satisfactory results'. However, the missionary making the crictisms had no working knowledge of Mongolian! In a letter from Owen Lattimore to Sturt, Lattimore implies that Sturt's Grammar is in the Kharchin dialect of Mongolian.

Revision was carried out in Kalgan with the help of his daughter Eleanor who had become a missionary to the Mongols in her own right. Checking was done with a competent Mongol who knew some English and German and could also read Russian and Japanese.

Sturt freely acknowledged that the Grammar and Primer had its limitations and in its introduction he readily credits the sources that he draws on, namely Whymont and Soulie. Professor F. Simon of the School of Oriental Studies at the University of London was keen to have it published 'in spite of acknowledged defects'. Sturt reworked it in 1946 and submitted it for criticism to 'those fluent in the colloquial'. This revision had over 2500 alterations, but there was still a feeling that the end product was not complete: war and repatriation had eaten into time and resources. Disappointingly he had to leave the manuscript behind when the Japanese took over. Sturt's other regret was his inability to finish the Mongol books he'd been working on due to sickness and continual Communist harassment. He had hoped that other missionaries would be able to use them in the future and wanted Stuart Gunzel to finish them.

Sturt's legacy

Sturt died in Ninghsia in 1948. No one committed to Mongol evangelism followed him after his death: 'then the dark curtain rolled completely over Mongol lands'. Sturt had been motivated by the 'inward urge to do something about the evangelisation of Mongolia... it gripped his attention and desire'. He had saturated the land with Gospels and evangelistic tracts. He was not afraid to engage lamas, nobles and common nomads in conversation about Christ.

Sturt's travel in Mongolia has not been surpassed. His maps of the area were later used by explorers, scientists and ethnographers. They were so accurate and detailed that Owen Lattimore, impressed by how extensively Sturt had travelled, recommended he be admitted to the Royal Geographical Society.

Sturt's writings included his Mongolian Grammar and Primer, an English-Mongol/Mongol-English vocabulary which he hoped would grow into a dictionary, a re-issue of Gilmour's catechism (then out of print) and some language revision of the Bible (that is, the 1840 LMS edition).

H. Funnell, once home director of China Inland Mission in New Zealand, said of Sturt that he 'became one of the great pioneers of Mongolia'. Reginald Sturt's commitment to the Mongols was equalled only by James Gilmour. His life was given for 'the evangelisation of the Mongols, to which [end he was] bound as by a "singular vow" '.

Eleanor Sturt

Eleanor (or 'Tufty' to the family) was the daughter of Reginald and his first wife, Gertrude. Eleanor believed herself called to missionary work like her father in Mongolia and trained as a nurse at Auckland Hospital, New Zealand. She was sent out from the Brethren Assembly of Eden Hall, Auckland.

She went to China via India in 1945, first working in Gansu

Province, then on to Beijing for language study. Her initial goal was to learn the language then work in Inner Mongolia 'just over the border from Suchow' as a nurse. However, along with Reginald and Marjory Sturt (her stepmother), she settled in Kalgan in 1947 to work among the Mongols. Here she started a small school for refugee Mongol children, using the rooms of the Norwegian Alliance's disused hospital. She then moved to Pa-tse-balong, about 160 kilometres west, in 1948, where the Gunzels were also working. She visited Mongols in their villages, treating diseases and teaching Scriptures. Reginald and Marjory accompanied her in this ministry, then all went to Ninghsia at the end of that year.

After Reginald died, Eleanor and Marjory stayed on. Stuart Gunzel managed to find them a Mongolian language tutor, an educated Mongol who had been converted under Sturt's ministry. Eleanor, along with Marjory and Jessie D. Smith, then went to Zhongwei in 1949 where two Norwegian CIM women were also working. This trio worked with the women and children, reaching the Mongols in the area on camel-back.

John Sturt continues:

Over fifty years later, in August 1994, my wife Agnes and I had the privilege of spending a month in Ulaanbaatar. I found it a moving experience to be once again on Mongolian soil, even though about 1,500 miles west from where I had lived previously. I felt at home with the people and countryside, and enjoyed listening to the language which I had not heard for so long. I delighted once more in the splendour of the deep blue Mongolian sky, though now it was often criss-crossed with vapour trails left by jet planes.

Living in a multi-storey tenement building, heated in cold weather by hot water radiators was a very different way of life from the old days. We enjoyed staying one night in a *ger* outside the city, and having a ride on a Mongolian horse again. The autumn colours in the trees were magnificent at that time, and we were excited one morning to wake up to find the vast plains and hills covered in a beautiful blanket of snow.

It was special for me too [Agnes] to be in Mongolia, because I had heard so much about the country. My cousin Douglas Broughton had spent about three years working with Reginald Sturt in Inner Mongolia. I still had vivid memories from reading his book, *Mongolian Plains and Japanese Prison Camps*, and from listening to the interesting stories he told us. So in a way, we both had a sense of 'coming home'.

The Mongolian people we met in Ulaanbaatar were much the same as I [John] had remembered them to be from my childhood, though most were now wearing Western-style clothing. However, so many of those we passed in the streets seemed to have sad faces and empty eyes. What a contrast we found when we met up with Mongolian Christians, who expressed a joy in their new faith, and great friendliness in their smiles and greetings. We were truly amazed at what God is doing in Mongolia today. How my father would have rejoiced to see the growth of the church there now!

Chapter

39

Stuart and Margaret Gunzel,
Revisers of the Mongolian New Testament

'Cannot the Lord save the Mongols as well as others? I know he can, and I trust him for it.'
Stuart Gunzel

'I love Hong Kong,' I announced to Karen. We were on the Cheung Chau island ferry looking back at the wharf in Central. The narrow straight of Victoria Harbour between Hong Kong Island and Kowloon was churned up by a dozen ferries, several junks, the odd hovercraft and the Macau-Hong Kong jet-foils. A huge American nuclear-powered battle-cruiser dwarfed the dock buildings. Overhead three aeroplanes were lining up for that ever-precarious landing at Kai Tak International. The multi-storeyed apartment blocks and glass-towers stood as sentinels protecting the power and wealth invested in them. And always the background hum of the Asian mega-city.

'You can keep it,' Karen replied. 'I'm looking forward to two weeks of lazing on a beach at Cheung Chau.'

Beaches were few and far between in Hong Kong. And usually polluted with plastic bags, aluminium cans, general sludge and the algae that fed on it all.

But we had discovered Cheung Chau island, and we had come here every January, during the deepest part of winter in Mongolia, for our annual holidays.

Cheung Chau is a dumbbell-shaped island that you could walk around in one day; there are no cars on it. It has a fascinating Chinese market, and a well-sheltered harbour choked with fishing boats. It takes about an hour on the ferry from Hong Kong, and many companies, religious institutions and schools have holiday guest houses there. A core of Hong Kong commuters live there also. We had discovered a guest house for

Christian workers and enjoyed its wonderful hospitality three years in a row.

'Dad, can we have a root beer at the top of the hill?' To get from the ferry to the guest house meant climbing a few hills, and we had managed to bribe the kids with a root beer from a shop at the top of the first. It had become a family tradition. It was the only way we could get them up, short of carrying them.

'Sure,' I said. 'You've got a good memory. I haven't had a root beer since we were here last year.'

We all plonked ourselves on the stone bench outside the shop, cracked open our A&W root beers, and contemplated the path we'd just struggled up. There was a hint of bougainvillea on the cool sea breeze. A motorised trolley was slowly chugging its way up the hill with all our luggage.

'I'm glad we don't have to carry that stuff up to the guest house.' Karen summed up our thoughts nicely.

I looked out across the maze of TV aerials below us to the solid cliffs of the island opposite.

'Lantau Island — that's where the TEAM missionaries worked on the revision of the Mongolian Bible,' I mused aloud. 'I bet they didn't have root beer to keep them going!'

Early days

Stuart Gunzel, a Canadian, went to Inner Mongolia in early 1933 and lived in the home of a Mongolian prince, Sunnit Wang. Gunzel taught the prince's son English, and in exchange learned Mongolian. This life on the steppe proved excellent orientation for Gunzel, but he soon became distracted by a new lady missionary, Margaret Lier, who arrived in Beijing in 1935. They were married at the end of the year, and spent the rest of their lives in ministry to the Mongol people.

Stuart and Margaret were with the Scandinavian Alliance Mission, based in Chicago, which recruited from Scandinavian immigrants in the area. It later changed its name to The

Evangelical Alliance Mission (TEAM). The Gunzels wanted to start a work at Pailingmiao, then capital of Inner Mongolia, which Stuart had visited in 1934, but he was told by the Mongol prince that he would not be allowed to preach the gospel there. The local Mongols had responded to the gospel message with laughter and accusations of madness, but were grateful for some medical treatment given to them. So the Gunzels worked in Patsebolong, Suiyeun province (160 kilometres west of Kalgan) until 1946.

Stuart Gunzel proved an able Mongolian language scholar. He was closely involved in the 1952 revision of the LMS' literary Mongolian New Testament, such that some call it 'Gunzel's revision'. He also produced a Mongol-English dictionary and assisted Reginald Sturt with his grammar book.

First fruit

In November 1936 occupying Japanese forces shut down all mission work and expelled the missionaries from Patsebolong. The Gunzels moved to Chao Ho, but the Mongols suspected them of spying, and after six months, Chao Ho fell to the Japanese. However, the Mongols eventually spoke favourably of the missionaries in the face of the Japanese occupation, enabling the Gunzels to stay where they were until 1940. However, they continued to be on the receiving end of animosity, and found things difficult as they pressed on with no Mongol co-workers.

Gunzel would often head off onto the steppe, witnessing to the nomads with a train of eight camels behind him, loaded with tracts and Bible portions. He would wander between encampments and summer fairs, giving out tracts, selling Scriptures, ministering to the sick, and always praying. These were difficult years. By the time they left Chao Ho, they knew of no born again, baptised Christian.

They did learn later that one Mongol had been driven out of the district because of his faith in Christ, and that two people had expressed a desire for baptism, one a former lama and the other a Mongol-speaking Chinese.

The Gunzels left China in 1940 to return in 1947, this time joined by Edvard and Jenny Torjesen and Angeline Bernklau, new TEAM recruits. However, all TEAM missionaries were evacuated in 1948. The Gunzels headed off into Qinghai province to survey strategic opportunities there. Gunzel's proficiency in Mongolian gave many openings to minister along the way and in scattered villages.

The 1952 Bible revision

The political scene was changing quickly in the early twentieth century in both Mongolia and China. Gunboat diplomacy of the colonial powers had opened up treaty ports around China's coast, and the Boxers had rebelled and killed many Chinese Christians and Christian missionaries in 1900. Missionaries who had taken up residence as far inland as Urga were expelled by 1924. The Manchu dynasty was crumbling, and republicans and Communists were jostling for power, resulting in civil war. This, combined with the invasion of Manchuria by Japan, threw China and Mongolia into turmoil for decades.

Translation work did not stop with the rise of the republic in China. Photographic reprints of the LMS' Literary New Testament were being produced in Shanghai from the press of the British and Foreign Bible Society as late as 1948.

After the Second World War, the Literary Version of the New Testament was revised by TEAM missionaries, the Swedish Mongol Mission, and three Mongol linguists. Work on this began in Kalgan, under the leadership of Stuart Gunzel, but the base shifted to Momingan, Lanchow, then Hong Kong, with the ever-widening threat of Communism.

The Scandinavian Alliance Mission (SAM) had had several missionaries working among the Mongols before this major project was undertaken. Almblad, who had worked on the previous revision of the Literary New Testament with Larson, had been a member of the SAM, as had David Stenberg before him, who had done work on the Khalka New Testament. Stenberg, along with four other SAM missionaries, met an untimely death at the hands of the Boxers in 1900. The SAM involvement in Mongolia had been costly and without much result.

Gunzel's passion for Mongolia was evident from his early days in Sunnit Wang's camp. He wrote from Mongolia to the editor of the mission magazine:

> there is not any revival in Mongolia. We are not able to give any report of people seeking their Lord and Master. Cannot the Lord save Mongols as well as others? I know that He can, and I trust Him for it. Last evening I walked the floor of my room with tears in my eyes as I thought of the blood of our dear fellow missionaries that has been poured out.... Does the blood of our brothers have to call out these thirty-three years and then see the work go backward instead of forward?[1]

The decision to revise the Mongolian Bible was made in 1935. The Literary Version of the New Testament had been translated by Stallybrass and Swan a century earlier. Whether the translation team also worked from the Larson/Almblad revision or the Pozdneev revision, or had on hand only one received version, we do not know. However, Anders Marthinson explicitly links the original Literary Version and the final new edition of Gunzel and team.[2] Margaret Gunzel, Stuart's widow, insists it was a revision, not a new translation.[3]

Joel Ericksson and Miss Gerda Ollén, both of the Swedish Mongol Mission, were also prime movers behind the project. A final committee of three Mongols and four foreign missionaries worked on the project. Exactly who was involved and at what times is difficult to ascertain, but Gunzel, Ollén, Torjesen, Ericksson and Marthinson are all foreign names associated with the work, and Matthai, Genden and Erinchindorj are Mongols who were involved.

The Swedish Mongol Mission had worked in Mongolia for a total of fifty-three years (1897–1950). The missionaries viewed their expulsion from China as an opportunity rather than a setback. TEAM eventually took up work in Taiwan and Japan.

After Edvard and Jenny Torjesen had been expelled from China in 1948, they went to Lantau Island off Hong Kong and founded the 'Institute of Mongolian Studies', where the revision team was based. (Lantau Island is where the new Hong Kong airport is located.) This revision was printed in 1952 and released in its final form in spring 1953, titled *Shin Testament* or commonly called the '1952 Revision'. It is in *mongol bichig*, the vertical script. Because of the Communist hold on China by this time, the only way to distribute this new edition was to courier it personally to believers, or mail it. This was done for over ten years through a Christian contact in north China.[4] It can be purchased today from the Hong Kong Bible Society, and some Christians in Mongolia have acquired copies of it.

Taking the gospel to Mongols in other countries

Thousands of Mongol refugees left China and ended up scattered around the world. Many settled in Taiwan, travelling via Hong Kong. The TEAM missionaries (the Gunzels, Edvard and Jenny Torjesen and Evangeline Bernklau) realised that the Communist government would close the doors to mission work, so moved their base to Taiwan with the refugees where they planted a small but significant Mongol church. Some who came were Christians, others were drawn out of curiosity at hearing a Canadian speak Mongolian. The TEAM missionaries also started English classes among the refugees, and through these, a good number became Christians.

In Taiwan, Mongol refugees represented their people in the government. The Torjesens found a fruitful ministry among the Mongols in these roles, and write about three who professed Christ openly. These were a representative to the National Assembly of China, the seventeen-year-old son of the secretary general of the Mongolian National Assembly, and the seventeen-year-old daughter of a representative to the National government.

Erinchindorji was one of three Mongol linguists working with the TEAM missionaries in Hong Kong on the 1952 revision. His widow, Mrs Fu, later lived in Taiwan. Their daughter Hannah married Joseph Chiang the pastor of the TEAM-related Chinese church in Taipei. They are lasting Mongol fruit from these years.

The Gunzels wrote numerous articles for *Horizons*, TEAM's magazine, between 1932 and 1954. In his last visit to Asia in 1966, Gunzel was instrumental in arranging for Mongol gospel radio programmes to go out on a regular basis from Korea. Stuart died in 1995, aged ninety, with a sense of a job faithfully done. In a personal letter to the author, Margaret Gunzel writes, 'We are so happy for what the Lord is doing among the Mongols [today], the people we have worked with and prayed for for many years.'[5]

Our two-week holiday at Cheung Chau was over. We'd swum, played on the beach, eaten ice cream and sugar cane, eaten out, watched videos, pottered around in rock pools, shopped and explored Hong Kong. We were all a bit subdued on the ferry back to Central. We knew that the Air China flight that afternoon would deliver us to Beijing where it was 0° celsius, and then the next day to Ulaanbaatar where it was likely to be about -20° celsius.

'How was your time at the United Bible Society office and the OMF library?' Karen broke the drone of the throbbing engines.

'Good, thanks. I met a couple of guys at UBS who have been consultants to the Mongolian Bible translation and they filled in some gaps as to the history of the Mongolian Bible. They didn't realise that the 1952 *Shin Testament* revision committee had worked on it over there on Lantau Island. The OMF library in Mongkok has lots of back-copies of their *China's Millions* magazine that have some references to the early missionaries' work in Inner Mongolia.'

A Macau-Hong Kong jetfoil went screaming past our sedate ferry. A nauseous waft of fuel from its jet engines enveloped us, and then it was gone. We rocked on the wake.

'I'd quite like to explore Lantau some time to find where they worked. I doubt that there'd be a sign on the gate though, but somebody might know,' I said.

Karen flicked open her Lonely Planet guide. 'It says here that Lantau is home to a huge Buddha on one of its peaks. It's also one of the biggest outlying islands, so you'd have real difficulty finding any trace of the TEAM missionaries' house. Lantau's also where they're building the new airport. I guess it must be on the other side.'

The engines died and we angled and drifted into the dock. About two hundred people all stood up together and moved to the side where we'd disembark. The ferry leaned alarmingly.

'Dad, look!' The voice came from down by my knees somewhere. It was my four-year-old daughter Anjali. I looked in the direction she was pointing.

'Look Dad, men in the water!'

I looked furtively to see who had fallen overboard, then remembered the maritime lesson I'd given her two weeks ago.

'Buoys, Anjali, buoys.'

NOTES
1. Vernon Mortenson, *God Made it Grow: Historical Sketches of TEAM's Church Planting Work* (William Carey Library: Pasadena, Ca., 1994), p.164.
2. Anders W. Marthinson, 'The Revision of the Mongolian New Testament', *The Bible Translator*, vol.5, no. 2. (April 1954), p.74.
3. Personal letter to the author from Margaret Gunzel, dated 2 June 1994.
4. Stuart Gunzel and Donald E. Hoke, 'The Mongolian People's Republic', in D.E. Hoke, ed., *The Church in Asia* (Chicago: Moody Press, 1975) p.447.
5. Personal correspondence with the author dated 2 June 1994.

Chapter 40

The Boxers,
A Short and Brutal Setback

'pao, kua, mieh yang' ('Protect the country, destroy the foreigner.')

Boxer slogan

'Did you say there were two hundred Spanish speakers here in Ulaanbaatar?' Karen was incredulous. 'Why do Mongols need to speak Spanish?'

Karen had grown up in Chile and was bi-lingual in Spanish and English. She hadn't spoken English until she was twelve, and even today expresses herself in Spanish phrases when she can't find the right English expression.

'It's the Cuban connection,' Chicken answered. 'There are three Cuban teachers at the university.' Chicken was a girl of about eighteen whom we had met at church. Her name wasn't really Chicken. It sounded like the Mongolian word for chicken, and Anjali, then three, had latched on to this. So she was always 'Chicken' to us. We were sitting in our flat drinking tea, enjoying the last bit of warmth from the autumn sun that came beaming in through the window. Pigeons cooed on the balcony.

'I'm learning Spanish at the university. There are twenty in my class. I want to be a tour guide in Spain when I finish my degree. I was told you speak Spanish, Karen. Can I come to have conversation practice once a week?' Mongol dreams and aspirations never ceased to amaze me. We agreed to the weekly Spanish practice, but tried to show Chicken that realistically, being a tour guide in Spain was next to impossible.

Karen replied: 'You can come every Thursday for lunch. We'll read the Spanish Bible together, and then we'll talk about it.'

This seemed like an excellent idea to everyone. Chicken was a new Christian, having made a profession of faith only two weeks before. This way she got her Spanish practice, and Karen was able to disciple her a bit.

We'd come to Mongolia, all keen to learn the local language, enculturate and identify with the people. So why not do it in Spanish? I pinched myself to make sure I hadn't nodded off in the warm sunshine and missed something somewhere.

The doorbell rang that Thursday and there was Chicken. She burst through the door, red eyed and crying. I opened my mouth to ask her....

'I've been kicked out of home. My mother says I have to leave. My uncle is a lama and he says that having a Christian in the house is bringing bad luck to everyone. I tried explaining to him that Christians are good people and that Jesus...' Karen gave her a tissue and sat her down. 'My brothers and sisters have ostracised me for the last two weeks. My youngest brother is sick and the lama says it's my fault and that if I'm a real Mongol I would never be a Christian but a Buddhist. None of my other family will take me in. I have an aunt living on the other side of town, but my uncle has already warned her about me and she won't open the door to me.'

Karen looked at me and I looked at Karen. This was the first instance I'd found of someone being persecuted in Mongolia for being a Christian.

'You can stay here until we sort this out,' Karen said.

The fearful Boxer rebellion

The causes of the Boxer uprising of 1900 are numerous. There was growing resentment among the Chinese about the foreign armies seizing port cities and territories; resentment at the interference of missionaries in lawsuits; resentment that mission agencies were acquiring property; resentment at individual foreigners, mainly Christians who were culturally insensitive and whose teaching was deemed to be divisive and offensive. Foreigners misunderstood Chinese customs and the

Chinese misunderstood the foreigners. There was discontent by those made redundant after employment in the railways, steamboats and telegraph. Rumours were prolific about foreign customs; it was alleged that at every bend in the railway a Chinese child was buried; photo prints were rumoured to be made from grinding up the eyeballs of Chinese children. This, with an underlying conservatism among the official and educated classes, mixed with the general riff raff of listless youth, meant that a cauldron of discontent was brewing for some years prior to 1900. The spark came by way of an official decree on 24 June 1900 by the Empress Dowager to 'kill all foreigners in the empire' and this led to a sudden outburst of violence and killing across northern China.[1]

The Westerners gave the name 'Boxers' to the para-military groups that roamed the Chinese countryside, from their name *I Ho Ch'uan* or 'Righteous Harmony Fists' and because of the gymnastic exercises they did. The Boxers adopted the mottoes *'pao kua, mieh yang'* ('protect the country, destroy the foreigner'), *'li kua, mieh yang'* ('establish the country, destroy the foreigner'), and *'pao ch'ing, mieh yang'* ('protect the Ching dynasty, destroy the foreigner'). Placards around Beijing during 1900 read: 'Within three months all foreigners will be killed or driven away from China' and 'During forty years the Empire has become full of foreigners', and 'they [the foreigners] have divided the land'.

The uprising was swift, brutal, devastating, but nevertheless short lived. It was essentially against foreigners, not against Christians *per se*, but thousands of Christians died in those few weeks. On the coast, ambassadors and merchants were slaughtered, and in the hinterland the Christians bore the brunt of the uprising. It was essentially a Chinese uprising, but it extended into Mongol territory and Mongol bandits got involved, if for no other reason than to capitalise on the general anarchy, and loot and pillage for their own ends. The Boxers did not distinguish between missionaries to the Mongols or to the Chinese, and all foreigners became subject to their wrath. Any atrocities perpetrated by Mongols against the missionaries were more to do with random looting and banditry, rather than systematic killing due to ideological convictions.

Escape through Urga

A small band of Mongolian missionaries managed to escape the uprising. Five members of the ABCFM from Kalgan joined three Swedish families at Har-us for refuge. The magistrate however was unfriendly and expelled them, warning that the Boxers would imminently arrive. The only option was to cross the Gobi and seek refuge in Urga. The British Consul at Shanghai had been planning a cross-Gobi journey, but was unable to get away, and so made available his twenty camels, six camel carts and nineteen horses. The band swelled to twenty-two with more Swedes from Kalgan. One of the Swedish women had been 'almost clubbed to death' and one of the men 'presented a frightful spectacle, covered with blood and dust'.[2] They set out on 30 July, still with the constant risk of running into bandits or Boxers until they reached Siberia proper, accompanied by all the dangers of crossing a desert in summer. Frans Larson gave able leadership and provided food with his rifle. 'For eight days there was nothing to be seen but sand.... The heat was intense.... We all suffered greatly.... Day marching was impossible.... We ineffectually tried to snatch some sleep in the daytime, drawing up our caravan in horse-shoe formation, and keeping the necessary lookout. We were completely isolated.'[3]

They reached Urga on day thirty-eight to a warm welcome by the Russian consul-general. However, he warned them that 10,000 local Mongols were gathering for a festival and there were 2,000 Mongol troops in the city. He himself expected the imminent arrival of 350 Cossack troups for his own protection and could not guarantee the safety of this rag-tag collection of missionaries. The band headed north to Kiachta on the border (meeting the Cossacks going south on the second day), and finally made it back to St Petersburg, Russia on 18 September.

Another attempt at escape

News of this escape inspired another band of missionaries in Guihuacheng (modern Hohot, capital of Inner Mongolia) to escape across the Gobi as well. Two former CMA missionaries, Mr and Mrs Helleberg, accompanied by a new recruit, Emil Wahlstedt, covered over 300 kilometres before being murdered. Another seventeen CMA adults and twelve children delayed their escape 'until one member's confinement was over'. When they did get away they were constantly harassed and even robbed of their clothing, such that they took refuge with four Catholic fathers. On 22 August the Boxers arrived and 'the whole place was burned and the missionaries perished'. C.L. Lundberg and Emil Olsson, the leader of the band, escaped, but were soon caught and beheaded.

All up, the CMA lost twenty-one of its thirty-eight missionaries in Inner Mongolia, and fourteen children of missionaries were killed. Other Protestant agencies in Inner Mongolia suffered as well. In the final count, several dozen missionaries and thousands of Christians, mainly Chinese, were killed in Mongolia, and more died of privation. Around 225 missionaries were killed in China altogether, along with up to 30,000 Chinese Christians, mainly Catholics. The deaths of three Mongol Christians is documented.[4]

Slaughter of Catholics

In Inner Mongolia, the Catholics had heavy losses, but their attackers were Mongols, rather than Chinese. There was a conspiracy uncovered in their centre at Borobalgasu to exterminate the foreigners and the local church. This mission station was totally destroyed in 1900, along with all the churches of south Ordos (except Hsiao-ch'iao-pan). The killings had begun in June, and lasted through the summer. The worst of the uprising was in Shansi province, spreading northwards into Inner Mongolia and west into Ordos. The CICM had 40,000 Chinese

Christians and over a hundred missionary priests in Inner Mongolia, plus a number of schools. The Franciscan order Sister of Mary had orphanages and these two orders paid a huge price. In another place two European priests were executed and their heads were exposed publicly. Three Catholic fathers, Jozef Dobbe, Désiré Abbeloss and André Zijlmans paid the ultimate price in their own church when it was burned to the ground on 22 August. At one stage, 4,000 Catholics were besieged.

Fr Alois Goossens, missionary in eastern Mongolia for twenty-one years, tells of the martyrdom of Father Joseph Seger on 24 July 1900 at the hands of the Boxers:

> A couple of days later came news of the imperial decision that all Christians must renounce their faith and all Europeans must return to their country.... On 21 July, Father Segers was loaded onto a cart... and delivered into the hands of the Mandarin.... The Mandarin cursed him once more for being a European devil... meantime others were digging a grave on the bank of the river.... When they came to the grave they tore the clothes from Father Segers; he tried to speak but one man beat him, another split his forehead with a sabre blow and the others threw him, still alive, into the grave, which they filled immediately with sand. After some time they dug up the corpse and threw it into the river.[5]

Bishop Hamer, Vicar Apostolic in the Ordos banner, put up a valiant resistance. A Mongol *noyon* had warned Hamer of the impending uprising and of the massacres of Europeans in Beijing, but Hamer refused to leave his post, preferring to stay on with his flock. The Boxers arrived, cut his fingers and toes off then dragged him around from town to town. They then tied him to a tree and tortured him for six hours. He was finally put to the torch but his body didn't burn well and so they beheaded him.

Bandits followed the Boxers, and mission stations along the wall took months before fully recovering. Catholic missionaries in T'ie-ko-tan-kou in Hou-pa who sheltered Protestant mission-aries from the Boxers were robbed of everything.[6] Houses owned by the Catholics in Kalgan were burned down in the Boxer uprising, before the Mandarin of Kalgan intervened on behalf of the Christians.

The recovery after the Boxer rebellion

In spite of the sudden burst of violence and the heavy loss of life, the mission stations made a quick recovery, most of them up and running and restaffed within two to five years. By 1911 Chihli province had the largest number of Christians of all the provinces that had been attacked by the Boxers. The number was 360,460, mainly Chinese but with some Mongols. The CICM reports that between 1905 and 1912 in south-western Mongolia, the number of Christians more that doubled.

Friedstrom returned to the SAMM work and soon records that there were 'about fifty persons attending our meetings'.[7] After 1900 the mission went on to open up work among the Mongols west of Pao-tow. One can only guess at how news of the Boxer deaths had shocked churches whose members had died cruelly, but it did not stop candidates applying to missions working in the area. In 1904 Mr and Mrs A. Magnuson arrived, followed by Mr and Mrs A. Almblad in 1905, both couples for work in Mongolia, based initially in Kalgan. The Magnusons were to serve for fifteen years, basing themselves in the SAMM mission station of Patsebolong. By 1916, the SAMM had built its numbers up to a total of fifty-seven members in China as a whole, including the Mongolian borderlands.

Mr and Mrs A. Godfrey Lindholm arrived in Mongolia in 1929 for language study at Kalgan and were assigned a lan-guage teacher called Daktoho. They went to Patsebolong to inspect an agricultural project, but within a day's journey of the town both were kidnapped and held for ransom. Daktoho, who had accompanied them, negotiated a ransom and on payment they went free. Despite this experience, Lindholm adopted the strategy of itinerant evangelism, based from Kalgan. Later they moved to Patsebolong but as the work there was more among the Chinese, they determined to move back into Mongol territory. However, with the threat of the Japanese, they had to hand over the work to seven Chinese Christians and go on furlough. The Japanese took control of SAMM mission stations in 1936 and ordered all mission work to stop and the missionaries to go home. The Lindholms were able to return in 1940 to relieve the Gunzels for furlough.

Through all the trials of the early 1900s, the Mongolian aspect of the SAMM was not submerged under the Chinese work, and evangelistic trips into Outer Mongolia continued until World War II. The SAMM changed its name to TEAM, but by 1950, due to the rise of Communism, there were no more TEAM missionaries left in Mongolia; several had followed the refugee Mongols to Hong Kong and Taiwan.

Chicken stayed with us for two weeks and merely camped in our lounge, as was the Mongol custom. She learned a lot of Spanish, and we learned a lot of Mongolian.

I'd struggled with the idea of a Mongol Christian being persecuted for her faith. There had been ostracism, some slander in the press, building administrators who reneged on church rental agreements, but no front-on individual persecution. I thought the wider extended family structure of the Mongols would provide accommodation for just about any member who had fallen out with anyone else. But not so with Chicken. She really had been kicked out, and no one would take her in.

We had to broach the topic of her return some time.

'I've talked to the church leaders,' I told her one night, 'and they would like to go and talk with your mother. They said they wanted to explain what Christian faith was all about, who Jesus is, and let your family meet some genuine Mongol believers. Hopefully by doing this, they will be seen to be normal people and not some *mangus* from hell.' I wanted the church leaders to own the problem and resolve it in a Mongolian way. Besides, I certainly did not have enough of the language even to think about effecting a reconciliation.

We prayed about it, and a delegation of three were chosen and sent. They successfully negotiated peace with the family and Chicken returned. They did such a good job, that the following *Tsagaan Sar* festival in February, Chicken's family invited us for the feast.

'My mother is quite open about Christian things now,' Chicken informed us enthusiastically. 'I think the young people the church sent convinced her that we're quite normal people. My uncle is still antagonistic, but my mother told him to stay out of it. I gave him a Bible to read.'

I was amazed at the turn around and prayed a silent prayer of thanks.

In spite of the assurances that all was well at home now, I was still nervous about going to see the family at *Tsagaan Sar*.

'When we come to your home for *Tsagaan Sar*,' I asked Chicken one day, 'will I have to speak Spanish?'

NOTES
1. For a dramatic account of one missionary family's escape from the Boxers, see A.E. Glover, *A Thousand Miles of Miracle* (OMF/Christian Focus Publications), 2000 centenary edition, complete with letters home from the author.
2. A.J. Broomhall, *It Is Not Death to Die*, book 7, p.335
3. *Ibid.*
4. K.S. Latourette, *op.cit.*, p.517.
5. A. Goossens cicm, 'Letter from Inner Mongolia — 1900', *Missionhurst CICM* (October – November, 1993), p.15.
6. D. Verhelst and N. Pycke, *CICM Missionaries, Past and Present, 1862–1987* (Leuven University Press: Leuven, Belgium, 1995), p.89.
7. D. MacGillivray, ed., *op.cit.*, p.507.

Chapter

41

Greta Nillson and
Dr Gerda Ollén,
The Scandinavian Mission in Urga

'So the "girl doctor" came. She had walked the long way to the tent of the Mongol woman, even though she was pale and looked tired. The lady...liked watching nurse Greta caring for the sick one. When nurse Greta burned out [from work] and had to leave Urga, the lady stood at the square in the early morning, shaking from sobs and tears.'

From *Stäppens Folk*

I first learned about the Swedish mission to the Mongols when I met Elon Svanell, the director of the Evangelical East Asia Mission (EEAM) in Ulaanbaatar in 1993. He'd come to Mongolia to deliver, among other things, a letter to the Ulaanbaatar city mayor, to plead his case for getting back some property his mission had owned until 1924.

'I don't like your chances,' I told Elon.

'I reckon I've found the building,' he said. 'It's been reno-vated somewhat, but it's definitely the right one. You can tell because it has a touch of Scandinavian style to the architecture.'

I was intrigued by this. 'Where exactly is it?' I asked.

'It's in the eastern part of the city. The Russians had their consulate in the eastern sector of Urga too.'

Elon didn't have the time to take me to it, but about six months previously I'd bought a map of old Urga from a vendor on the street. I found the Russian consulate, but no record of the Swedish clinic.

Now it's March 1997 and I'm teaching a seven-lecture course to forty students at the small Bible school in Ulaanbaatar. We're in the nineteenth century and exploring various evangelistic strategies that missionaries used in Inner Mongolia. We learn of James Gilmour, George Hunter, Mildred Cable, Reginald Sturt,

Edward Stallybrass and Francesca French. Then we get on to taking a brief look at the Swedish mission to Urga. I show the students a photograph of the old medical clinic. I'd found this picture in a photocopy of a Swedish missions magazine that Elon had left me. It was in the Siberian style of architecture, one storey, with heavy shutters on the window. It had a fenced *hasha* with a bold gate that had a notice and a medical cross on it.

'This building is somewhere in eastern Ulaanbaatar,' I told the students. 'The Swedish missionaries used it for a clinic and a small school until the red Russians expelled them in 1924. There's a box of chocolates for anyone who can find it.'

How the Urga mission started

The first significant Christian work in Urga was started by two Norwegian brothers by the name of Naestegard in 1896. It is unclear what mission society they belonged to, and only a snapshot of Ola Naestegard is available to us in English. Another Scandinavian, Gustav John Ramstedt met Ola Naestegard in Urga some time around 1900.[1]

Naestegard had been living in Urga for nine years by the time Ramstedt met him. Ramstedt tells us that Naestegard would preach on the streets and in the squares, and at least one of these occasions was witnessed by Ramstedt. Ramstedt wasn't impressed and records that his 'attempts to preach... often ended abruptly and sometimes quite ignominiously'. Naestegard had 'meagre results', and Ramstedt puts this down to the fact that Urga was home to 20,000 Buddhist priests who often tripped him up in public debate. Ramstedt records an incident where Naestegard was not sure of his arguments, and even less sure of the gospel (according to Ramstedt's description of the event) and ends in a tangle with the priests. In Ramstedt's words:

For instance, once he was explaining... that men are saved and go to heaven solely by believing in Christ, when one of his listeners inquired in a loud voice, 'But what has happened then to all those who died before you came here? Are they all lost?' Naestegard answered without thinking, 'Yes, certainly.' Another Mongol, also a priest, then cried, 'But this is too cruel a god. After all, it wasn't their fault that you came here so late.' The next time Naestegard was on his guard and conceded that those who had heard nothing about Christ could be saved if they led a pious and honest life and were generous to the poor. This concession then inspired a priest, who had earlier listened to Naestegard's sermonising, to say aloud, 'But why did you come here then, since thus we don't need you and your religion here with us?'[2]

We're not able to verify Ramstedt's account of Naestegard's preaching. At face value, it seems that his theology endorsed a 'good works' doctrine. He must have found the public street preaching and debating taxing and in his latter days he preferred distributing Scriptures, being the Urga agent for the British and Foreign Bible Society. Mongols were keen to have them, often apparently using the pages for rolling cigarettes and starting their *argol* fires. Some ended up on the scrap heap on the hills to the west of Urga, among the decaying urban detritus and rotting bodies of the unburied dead.

The Swedish Mongol Mission

In September 1897, a missions conference was held in Bollnäs, Sweden. This had been instigated by Fredrik Fransson, world-renowned evangelist and eventual founder of fourteen mission societies. At this conference a young couple, Georg and Eva Eneroth, declared themselves willing to serve as missionaries in Mongolia. Fransson secured financial backing and in May 1898 the Eneroths started their long trip to Mongolia, via Omsk and Semiplatinsk, to start their work in Chuguchak in western

Mongolia.[3] Chuguchak is the modern Tacheng/Qoqek in the far north-western corner of modern Xinjiang province of China. This was Torgut Mongol territory, and was chosen because of the proximity of the Siberian railway line.

The Eneroths arrived in Chuguchak in September. But Eva fell severely ill and they were forced to return to Sweden in December, less than four months later. Georg Eneroth reflected: 'It truly felt hard to leave a country and a people where, as it seems, the doors stand wide open and the paths are prepared for the messengers of peace.'[4]

This initial setback did not deter those in Sweden who were convinced that a mission to the Mongols was in God's reckoning. In September 1899, the Central Committee of the Swedish Mongol Mission (SMM) was constituted under the chairmanship of Prince Oscar Bernadotte. Karl and Lotten Helleberg and Emil Wahlstedt were accepted as missionaries. They arrived in Shanghai in November 1899 and started work at Hallon-us ('Hot Waters'), 100 kilometres north of Kalgan. But the times were tumultuous and all three were martyred by the Boxers in the following year.

Again, this did not deter the home board. Other missionaries were sent and a considerable work was built up on the Mongolian-Chinese border. After starting in *Hallon-us*, the mission extended the work to Gulchagan, Hattin-Sum and Doyen. In 1919, SMM missionaries 'reopened' a medical clinic in Urga. The mention of a 'reopening' of a clinic must refer to the previous presence of the Naestegard brothers in Urga, but no record has been found of their actually conducting a clinic.

By 1929 the mission had eleven missionaries working in Inner Mongolia and one hospital and one dispensary with two doctors and two nurses. By 1947, fifty years after establishing work, the mission still had these three well-functioning stations and about one hundred converts.

The Urga clinic

Greta Nillson and Dr Gerda Ollén were the prime movers behind the Urga clinic. They visited Urga in 1919 for a reconnaissance, and were moved by the poverty and deprivation of the people. These two women believed it was time to start a medical work. Together they rented a building for a clinic, but Gerda returned to Inner Mongolia, coming back to Urga three years later.

The rumour about the arrival of a 'foreign medical man' spread throughout Urga. However, this 'man' was a woman. The citizens of Urga found it difficult to accept a single female doctor in their city, and Greta was addressed as 'girl doctor'. Prejudices were soon overcome and in the first four months of operating, between January and April 1920, Greta was swamped with 3,000 visitors to the clinic. Gertrud Falck arrived in the autumn of 1920 to help. By January 1922 they were processing between forty and fifty patients at the clinic daily, as well as doing house calls. (Gerda Ollén returned that year, with Signe Folke and Dagny Hansen.) The medical workload alone, apart from the harassment of local lamas and the growing threat from Soviet soldiers took its toll on Greta. Her health collapsed. On the way back to Sweden she died and was buried in Rangoon, Myanmar on 15 April 1924.

Most people in Urga would not come to the medical clinic unless the lamas deemed it auspicious. Urga was a powerful centre of lamaism and the people went to consult the lamas for every event in their lives. They had to ask the family lama who, by drawing lots, made the decision for or against a visit to the clinic. They often found it 'a good omen' to ask 'the girl doctor' for advice. In most cases it was the poor people who came, as the lamas had nothing to gain from keeping the poor in their own care. Greta Nillson left her mark on the city. One story tells of a typical encounter:

She had walked the long way to the tent of the Mongol woman, even though she was pale and looked very tired. The lady saw that her hands were so soft and tender when she touched her poor sick child. She liked watching nurse Greta caring for the sick one. It was like a warm sunbeam, melting the ice and reaching deep inside... When nurse Greta burned out [from work] and had to leave Urga, the lady stood at the square in the early morning, shaking from sobs and tears.[5]

Despite the departure of Greta, the work continued to grow. The clinic was moved into larger rented buildings in late 1920 and over the door it had written 'Medical personnel here sent by the Christian Church in Sweden to receive the sick and the suffering to bring loving help'. In the waiting room there was always a missionary to make friends with patients and their families and to spread Christian literature.

Signe Folke and Dagny Hansen had come up from Hallon-us, and took up residence in the former clinic which the mission had purchased. Signe was a teacher and together with a Mongol called Enkh-bileg (also from Hallon-us) set up a small school in a shed next to the clinic. This school attracted some young people and some soldiers. Scriptures were always available and some interest was shown in them. Like the tracts that Ola Naestegard distributed, however, Bibles would often be torn up to use as wicks for fires, or for cigarette papers.

The growing mission also purchased land in the spring of 1923 on the north-west hills of Urga to start a farmlet. Magnus Björklund ran this with Magnus Johansson-Havermark, who had previously been working at the mission's four stations in southern Mongolia.

The legacy of the Urga mission

Between 1921 and 1924 Urga was thrown into turmoil first by the White Russians and then the Red Russians. A foreign presence in the city naturally drew the attention of the Russian authorities who initially forbade the farmlet. The sequence of events is recorded in the SMM magazine:

At present all our... optimistic plans and hopes for missionary work in Urga are dashed to the ground. At first the mission was forbidden to cultivate the fields of the farm outside Urga. The missionaries found out that they were 'shadowed', and that all their activities were closely checked. Suddenly one day many soldiers arrived at the new plot where missionary Johansson lived. An extensive house visitation took place. Books and printed material were confiscated as well as purchase-deeds [for] the old clinic-yard, the new plots as well as the farm. The expeditionary body carried on to the clinic. The missionaries received upon request no explanation for these house-visitations. Missionary Johansson waited several times upon the authorities but all this [was] without success.

Because of the rapport that Greta had built up in the city due to the medical service, she and the mission enjoyed the Mongols' trust. The result was that 'the Bolshevik masters found [it] difficult to present solid reasons for expelling the missionaries'. Nevertheless, expulsion was inevitable. Some attempt was made to go through official channels to overturn the Russians' decision. The Council of Sweden and the Swedish Foreign Service offered immediate protection to the missionaries and tried to secure their property. Promises of assistance from the Mongolian envoy in Moscow came to nothing.

The end result was a notice to leave the country due to 'unauthorised activities', the missionaries having 'preached the Scriptures without consent from the authorities'. Missionary Johansson considers this statement as untrue, because long and extensive interrogations took place before their arrival in Urga at the time they applied for a visa. The missionaries had then fully accounted for their planned assignment.[6]

The written banishment came on 27 May 1924 and all the SMM missionaries were compelled to leave Urga. The extent of the medical work, by numbers alone, must have left its mark on the city. And the volume of Scriptures distributed must have been significant. But on departure, the missionaries report merely 'some inquirers', but no open converts.

There was no church established in Urga. 'Even the smallest attempt to go over to Christianity...would have been quenched by violence or cunning.' The good rapport with the Mongols was overtaken by the 'violence, lies and anti-religious attitudes'[7] prevailing in Urga as well as at all other places under Bolshevik rule.

And so we come to this recent attempt to regain the properties of the SMM, now renamed the Evangelical East Asia Mission (EEAM). The clinic building was identified in 1992 by the director of the mission who wrote to the Ulaanbaatar City Council in February that year:

> Our organisation bought a piece of land and a building and also a farm outside the city. There were a few nurses who... opened a medical clinic. They also had some classes to teach people to read and many soldiers came to the clinic to get something to read. In 1924 the building was confiscated (sic) by the red army, and those Swedes had to leave the country. While I was in Ulaanbaatar, I happened to see that building.... Now our organisation would like to continue the work which was started in 1919 on the educational field.... We would appreciate [it] if you could find out the possibilities of getting that building back or giving another piece of land or building instead of that one in Ulaanbaatar. The sum we paid in 1924 was today a value of Swedish Crowns 190,750 (in US$ 33,194).[8]

There were several old Siberian-style buildings in eastern Ulaanbaatar which were possible candidates for the old mission clinic. One was directly in front of our apartment building. It was of log-cabin construction with small windows and heavy-looking window frames. Large shutters and clay packed between the logs gave it a very solid look. Nothing about the building was plumb. Nevertheless, no north wind was going to blow it over.

We'd observed the function of the building changing numerous times. It was first a state ration shop, then a private *delguur*, selling a whole range of food and knick-knacks — we'd often taken the kids there to buy the Mongolian soft drink, *undaa*. Later a private company took it over and truckloads of goods, presumably from China or Russia, were off-loaded and warehoused there periodically. But it didn't really match up with the picture I had from Elon.

'Did anyone find the Swedish clinic?' I ask a week later in class, plonking a box of chocolates on the front desk to remind them of the stakes involved in their detective work.

'*Bagsh-aa*,' a student near the back gets my attention by waving a newspaper clipping around. 'I found this in the newspaper recently. It's about Frans Larson, a Swedish missionary who worked on the Mongolian railway from 1900 to 1902. Also, I was talking to a Russian who lives in my building and he says the old Russian Orthodox Church is still standing. He says he would take me and show me if I liked.'

I have one more question for the class. 'If we found this building, do you think the City Council would give it back to the EEAM?'

Everyone says no, and the box of chocolates remains unclaimed.

I pass them out and we eat them anyway. The packet says 'Made in Sweden'.

NOTES

1. When Ramstedt was in Urga is not clear, and there are conflicting dates in the two resources to hand. Hoke (1975) says the Naestegard brothers started work in Urga in 1896, but then adds that they 'fled the Boxer uprising and never returned'. The Boxer uprising was in 1900, which would mean that they were only in Urga for four years. However, there is little evidence to suggest that the Boxer uprising extended as far north as Urga. Ramstedt mentions 'when we got acquainted with Naestegard the missionary, he had already been in Urga nine years' (Ramstedt, p.41). This would mean that Ramstedt was visiting in 1905, but then this does not square with Hoke's comment about the Boxer uprising.

2. G.J. Ramstedt, J.R. Krueger, trans. *Seven Journeys Eastward 1898–1912* (The Mongolia Society, USA, 1978), pp.41–42.

3. Spelt Tjugutjak in Swedish.

4. 'Bland Stäppens Folk: År ur Svenska Mongolmissionens historia', *Evangelisk Östasien missionen*, nr 6, (Juni/juli 1987), Årg 6, 29.

5. *Ibid.*, 33.

6. *Ljusglimtar från Mongoliet,* (1924), pp.74–75.

7. *Ljusglimtar från Mongoliet,* (1937), quoted in 'Bland Stäppens Folk', 33.

8. A photocopy of the letter was given to me by Elon Svanell in 1993. The original letter was dated 14 February 1992.

The Missionaries of the Swedish Mongol Mission,
The Birth of a Mongol Church in Inner Mongolia

'Our Mongol evangelists have come back from their summer evangelisation. Never before have the doors been open like this. How wonderful to welcome them when they arrived, filled with joy that God had shown himself to them.'
Elsa Skallsjö, 1933

It was 7.40am and -32° celsius in mid January. Five-year-old Anjali stomped her feet and flapped her mittens together in an attempt to keep warm. She was so toggled up against the cold that all you could see were two eyes, and these had a faint white dusting of frost around them already.

'Here comes Monica now,' she announced, peering through the pitch blackness. Monica was shuffling over the ice from her apartment building. She was a teacher at the Ulaanbaatar International School which Anjali was attending, and I'd wanted to catch her before getting on the school bus. The smell of coal dust wafted up the valley from the power station and made me cough.

'Hi!' Monica said. 'Here's the translation you asked me to do. I hope it's OK.' She shoved a bundle of papers into my hand and I stuffed them into my inside coat pocket. I felt like a KGB agent making a rapid clandestine contact by the half-light of an over-head street lamp. Her breath froze on her scarf as she spoke.

The school bus pulled in and the twelve or so waiting kids piled on. 'The magazine is the 1987 hundredth jubilee edition of the EEAM. I was deeply moved to find that my fellow Swedish countrymen had played such a significant role here in the evangelisation of the Mongols. Gotta go. We can talk later,' she said, and the bus door closed.

I waved goodbye to Anjali through the window which was rapidly fogging up with the sudden influx of body heat, and walked briskly back to the apartment. A large cow had managed to break down the rather flimsy door to the rubbish enclosure at the end of our lane and was lazily redistributing its contents along the footpath as she looked for morsels from the day before. Three stray dogs approvingly joined her.

Once inside my apartment, I stripped off my hat, mittens, and down jacket and warmed up by the radiator.

'I made a batch of scones,' Karen said. 'There was no bread in the shops yesterday.'

'Sounds great. I had to meet Monica to pick up that translation.' I flicked through the papers she'd given me. 'This is terrific. It looks like this is going to fill in a whole lot of gaps. The original is in Swedish. These are all short biographical sketches with heaps of quotes from the missionaries themselves. I could probably just use it as it is.'

After the Urga mission was forced to close down in 1924 due to the influx of red Russians, the Swedish Mongol Mission concentrated its efforts south in Inner Mongolia. Over a twenty-four-year period it established four stations which became the base camps for a wide-ranging mission across Inner Mongolia. Halun-us, Goltjaggan, Doyen and Hatin-sum are the names of these 'steady points'.

Halun-us

Along with the medical work in Urga, the SMM set up medical work in Halun-us ('Hot-Waters') from 1920 and it developed quickly, under the leadership of Dr Joel Eriksson. Syphilis, endemic on the steppe, was treated effectively, and Eriksson even did surgery: amputations, tumours, gunshot wounds, and some eye surgery, gaining the 'foreign medicine man' an excellent reputation.

The mission also started literature work. The first Christian Mongol, Gendun, translated tracts from Chinese to Mongolian, including *The Pilgrim's Progress*, and a songbook. Two Mongolian Christians, Enkh-bileg and Dash-jav, travelled extensively during the summer months on an ox cart distributing tracts and Bibles. Enkh-bileg had been the evangelist and teacher at the Urga clinic.

Soon there were baptisms and a church began. In 1920, five Mongols were baptised, including Dash-jav. In June 1923 seven more men were baptised.

After being expelled from Urga in 1924, Magnus Björklund came south to work at Halun-us, where he tried to develop veterinary work:

> The Mongol is totally dependent on his animals... and among them disease ravages. To bring help to the Mongols, Magnus Björklund travelled to the University of Nanking to learn rudimentary veterinarian skills. However when he tried to persuade the Mongols to let him treat their animals, he was met with disbelief. Eventually resistance died down and consultations dribbled in from the villages on the steppe.

New recruits joined the mission between 1924 and 1927, including Sven Skallsjö, Elsa Berg and Vivian Almqvist. The Mongol church continued to grow with six more baptisms in 1925 and five in 1926. Both medical work and Bible distribution continued. In 1926 the number of patients treated at Halun-us reached 4,670, about half of them Mongols. The same year, over 7,000 Bible portions and even more tracts were handed out. Gerda Ollén, now no longer able to continue work in Urga, translated some booklets, and in the winter of 1926–1927 a Bible study course was held at Halun-us.

The Christian Mongols met hard resistance from their countrymen. 'Tåchtå[1] was baptised, a man who later backslid and caused the missionaries great grief, and also the mother of

Gallinder, who at this time was mightily touched by God. The communion on the evening of the baptism was an unforgettable experience and Garma afterwards said: ' My heart is overflowing of joy. I didn't know there was something like this. O, that our Mongols knew of this joy.' But after some happy years with Jesus and his friends the dark forces of the old hedonism sucked her into worship of the so-called living-gods [ie living Buddhas]. After this, darkness filled her soul.

Around this time a Chinese provincial administrative change in the area occurred. The result was that the Chinese actively colonised the area and the Mongols were forced to move north. The SMM therefore thought it necessary to move, and so they closed the station in 1927. The work was moved to Hatin-sum ('Temple on/of the Rock/Cliff'), where a small lama temple was purchased to use as a mission site.

In 1922 the mission received a plea for medical assistance: 'A deputation of Mongols arrived at Halun-us from the province of Goltjaggan. These Mongols asked us to open up a mission station in their province also, because, as they said, we want to have a physician.' Magnus Johansson-Havermark and Magnus Björklund went on a reconnaissance to Goltjaggan province together with the evangelist Gendun and decided to build a new mission station there. Gendun and another evangelist called Nantji were, together with a young Christian Mongolian family, prepared to start the work there. The place was situated ninety kilometres east of Halun-us. There were good pastures and water. Soon Magnus Johansson-Havermark arrived and built a simple house with four rooms and a kitchen in the autumn of that year. The mission now had its second centre in Mongolia.

Goltjaggan[2] — a battleground against dark forces

In the autumn of 1923 Hulda Wiklund and Elsa Berg arrived in Goltjaggan. A year later Signe Folke and Magnus Johansson-Havermark arrived (and were married in December 1924). Signe was in charge of a school in Goltjaggan from 1923. However, their reception by the Mongols was indifferent:

The Mongols met the missionaries with benevolence, but it seemed difficult to reach their hearts with the message from God. A great deal of the Mongols here belonged to a tribe that had moved to this district from the so-called Bargott[3] country, where they for hundreds of years had refused to abandon the black Shamanistic belief for the yellow religion, that is, the lamaism.... Among these people the missionaries received a new and deeper insight in the darkness and superstition that holds the Mongolian people.

Within two years of work at Goltjaggan, there was a spiritual breakthrough. Goltjaggan became the meeting-place for the first Christian-Mongols' convention in the summer of 1925. They arrived by horse or in ox carts from east and west, and for the first time they experienced a widened fellowship in a festive atmosphere. The missionaries learned that the Christian Mongols had woken up to a responsibility for missions among their own people. They even took a collection for the support of an evangelist during the summer.

In the autumn of 1925, the medical ministry got a further boost with the arrival of Gerda Ollén's brother, Dr Teodor Ollén and his wife Maja. The next spring, Dr and Mrs Ollén and Joel Eriksson moved to Kalgan, where the head of the nationalist army had asked for medical help from the Swedish mission. While there Mrs Ollén caught a serious cold and died in May.

Back in Goltjaggan, the church continued to grow:

eventually the Goltjaggan station spread out and with its many houses here and there and clusters of Mongol tents it formed a little village. Quite a few Mongols gathered for the Sunday services and at grand occasions the visitors could be up to 150.... Twenty visits could be made in one morning [with the car] and also a great deal of treatments could be made.

A touching moment was the ordination of four teachers and evangelists: Bantji from Halun-us, Gendun and Enkh-bileg from Goltjaggan and also Dash-jav from Doyen. It was the first ordination that took place here.... The four knelt down on the floor before the congregation and through the laying on of hands received the mission of the congregation to be messengers of the gospel among their people.

With blessing often comes testing, and this was especially so in the years 1930–1934. Sven Skallsjö's time in Goltjaggan turned out to be short. He died of typhoid fever in February 1930. Dr Ollén died of typhoid a week later:

The Lord called his servant home. There was his new wife, and four little children, alone. It came down to me and some of the Mongols to dig a grave on the hill. It was no easy task. It was winter and the ground frost was several metres down. We had no choice but to light fires, and in that way defrost the ground. A couple of seeds had fallen into the ground of Mongolia.

This setback was short-lived, however, and a time of revival was at hand. On New Year's Eve 1933 a new chapel was opened in Goltjaggan. As one member later recalled with passion:

Finally the 18th February 1933 arrived, one of the greatest days in my life. That was the day when our converted Mongols were to receive the baptism. Nurse Dagny and Elsa Skallsjö came up to Goltjaggan to be present. It was a great day for nurse Dagny, who had fought for this place for years, as well as for Elsa Skallsjö, who had to bury her beloved husband here in Goltjaggan a few years ago. Twenty-six Mongols were to be baptised! Something had really happened in Mongolia.

More SMM missionaries came from Sweden. Anders Marthinson (who later helped revise the New Testament) had arrived in 1930 and his fiancee Svea Eliasson the following spring. Elsa Bengtsson arrived in 1933 and dedicated herself to the school and the orphans in Goltjaggan. In the autumn of 1934, Folke Persson arrived, who together with Paul-Georg Svensson was to lead the work in Goltjaggan.

However, the station came under attack in October 1933. Bandits kidnapped Gendun, Enkh-bileg, Sittjing Batto, and other Mongols with them. The emotion of this is captured in the following account:

Then soldiers from Kalgan arrived and drove away the bandits. Under a shower of bullets the bandits tried to break through but were pursued by the soldiers. During this the horse of Gendun tired out and refused to walk. Gendun turned towards the soldiers who prepared to shoot him. Then he was brought to the chief in command who was very friendly towards him. He rested a few days with the soldiers and then started the walk home. Our dear Enkh-bileg is dead, apparently killed by the Chinese soldiers. A Chinese followed us up at the hills, where they had brought him and here the headless, naked body of our dear Enkh-bileg was lying, bloody and cold. The 29th November the funeral took place. It was one of the most touching moments I have experienced. There has never been a time when it has been so difficult to be a missionary as it is now.

This was the beginning of much suffering to follow between the years 1935 and 1937. The winter of 1935–1936 turned out to be very difficult, with deep snow covering the pastures and much of the livestock freezing to death, threatening the Mongols' livelihood. Added to this was the political unrest, with the encroachment of the Japanese. Joel Eriksson writes in September 1937:

It hasn't been too easy for our people in Goltjaggan. Almost all the time the [Mongol soldiers] stay there. They have eaten from the stores... and fired their arms. One day when we arrived we ran into a couple of those unpleasant fellows. That day alone they had fired some fifty shots. They aimed at doves and were very careless in their shooting. Our missionaries had asked them to stop, but it didn't help. They say they are out to find deserters, but these soldiers themselves are not better than the bandits. On the way back from Goltjaggan we found a man they had shot. A horrifying perspective is developing — a taunting race war here at the border.

In 1940, Gendun, the mission's first Mongol convert, died. He had excelled himself as an evangelist and teacher, and also as handyman at the station. However, in spite of the loss of Gendun and the gathering clouds of war, the mission work, especially the medical ministry, continued until the Japanese shut it down in February 1943. For twenty-one years the Swedish missionaries had been working there, and the most dramatic happenings of the mission had taken place there. Goltjaggan, 'the Settlement of the Wild Spirits', had been a battleground where the kingdom of God had gained victory over dark forces in people's lives through frail human tools.

Doyen[4]

Another site chosen by the SMM after the Urga mission closed was Doyen mountain, seventy-five kilometres north-east of Goltjaggan, in Chahar province. The area was well inhabited by Mongols, and the ruling Mongol *noyon* were fairly obliging. In December 1924 Gerda Ollén, Dagny Hansen and Gertrud Falck arrived there with four Christian Mongols, establishing a tent station under some old elms.

The missionaries met with a reserved response from the neighbours. Some showed a hostile attitude. Not too many sick came to their small clinic either, except one old lady,

Altantsetseg, or 'golden-flower'. Two very cold winters were spent in tents here before permanent buildings could be put up in spring 1926. Magnus Havermark was 'building supervisor', and in October 1926 the Skallsjö family moved into a new home at Doyen.

Sven Skallsjö writes:

> We notice very well how the priests are counteracting what we do. Among the sick it's not as it is at other stations, where more well-off people are coming. Here all are paupers without exception. The priests probably don't consider the poor to have anything they could benefit from. I must admit that sometimes there's a fear coming over me that our friends of the mission and intercessors will grow weary, since they hear so little about success and victories from here.

Skallsjö later moved back to Goltjaggan in 1928, and Doyen had six years without a resident missionary. 'The daily care [of Doyen] was in the hands of [the Mongol Christian] Dash-jav, but twice a month the Skallsjös were to visit the station.' Ironically, when a Mongol was in charge, the first spiritual breakthrough occurred with the conversion of old 'Golden-flower'.

The reason for no resident missionary was the lack of medical personnel. Elsa Bengtsson and Dagny Hansen lived for a time in Doyen during two summers. Elsa writes: 'in none of the other places are there so many Mongols as here. But in order to be in Doyen one has to have medical training, because it is that which opens the homes, and it seems as if all people here are sick.'

Once while the missionaries were absent, a *gegen*, or living-Buddha visited. In a rage he broke the windows of the station and destroyed much of the missionaries' property. He demanded liquor and when none was to be had, he took their organ with him. However, later in 1938 the *gegen* fell sick and called for the missionaries. He got well again after this consultation and changed his attitude to the mission.

Joel Eriksson and Dash-jav started a revision of the Gospels in Mongolian in Kalgan, and shifted this work to Doyen in 1937. Later Gerda Ollén, after nine years back in Sweden, moved out again to Mongolia to rejoin this small translation team.

In October 1941, Ollén writes: 'God has worked in a special way in Doyen. Never before have we had such a stream of sick people as we've had this summer. Through this, the good news has been preached to many who never before have heard about Jesus Christ. There has also been a great willingness to listen and a peace during the meetings, which is not usual among the Mongols.' By 1944, the mission's annual report notes: 'There are only two baptised Christians in Doyen, Jattamba and his wife Ojen. Some seekers are also there though. Jattamba is a serious Christian, and we believe that he's trying to do everything he can to spread the gospel.'

The missionaries left Doyen after the dramatic but blessed summer of 1942. This epoch in the history of the Mongol mission was terminated after almost twenty years of uninterrupted battle between the light and the dark.

Hatin-sum

With the Chinese colonisation of the Halun-us area, Mongols started moving out, and a state of near anarchy developed with raiding bands of thieves and paramilitary groups. The missionaries were often visited, mainly because the bandits wanted help for their wounded. A patient invited the missionaries to move to his birthplace, where a desolated temple was situated, at Hatin-sum, 'the Cliff Temple'. After some trouble this temple was bought and then in the summer of 1927 a small missionary home was built, and the Joel Eriksson family, Vivian Almquist, some orphans and some Christian Mongols moved from Halun-us to Hatin-sum.

The station in Halun-us was torn down and the timber used to build the new buildings at Hatin-sum: a clinic, a small print shop, and accommodation for the Mongolian staff. News of the clinic soon got around and the demand became huge. From one temple area alone, some 100 kilometres north of Hatin-sum, a row of ox carts arrived with some twenty sick people who pitched their tents nearby and stayed for seven weeks.

A social work developed as well because of unseasonal climatic catastrophes. In 1929 the crops failed and the pastures dried out. The winter of 1936 was also catastrophic with heavy snowfalls in which most of the animals died. The mission came to the nomads' aid with medical assistance, the distribution of flour and oat flakes, and help in purchasing new livestock.

The church in Hatin-sum grew. In 1935 a chapel was built and dedicated on Christmas Eve with about 150 people present. The Japanese threat loomed large, but there was a good spirit. The meeting hall was filled regularly. Five Mongols were baptised and became members of the congregation. This sudden growth was in the face of much spiritual oppostion. Elsa Skallsjö writes in 1933:

They who deny the existence of a devil and a hell should come to Mongolia, where they'd see and experience his awful work. We hardly had the strength to ring the prayer bell. But we did, and a few showed up. During the whole first part of the meeting there was something dark and heavy that we couldn't get away from. But suddenly it was as if there was a transformation…. Our evangelists have come back from their summer evangelisation. Never before have the doors been open like this. How wonderful to welcome them when they arrived, filled with joy that God had shown himself to them.

Anders and Svea Marthinson managed Hatin-sum while the threat of the Japanese grew:

In 1937 when we came back to Mongolia after a period of rest in Sweden, the Japanese had invaded Inner Mongolia and their power reached out over an extended area. Back in Hatin-sum we had to deal with the usual work. I had the responsibility for the station and the print shop. Now and then trucks with Japanese soldiers stopped by outside the porch. Without showing the least consideration they barged into our dining area where we every time served tea and sandwiches.... After a couple of minutes they brought forth their notebooks and the questions showered over us: Where are you from? What are you doing? How many members are there in the congregation? Where do you get funds for the work? Where have you been before? Etc.

1941–1944 — the work closes

The isolation during the war created a lot of problems for the Mongol missionaries. Dagny Hansen writes in 1941:

During the past year we as Mongol missionaries have had the urge to pack our bags and leave; our work has seemed hopeless. This field has always been hard, but never as hard as it is now. As for me, I said to God: ' I'm not going to Mongolia again unless you do something new in me.' The new thing arrived with the Kalgan conference. The meetings didn't last the one week that was planned for, but seven weeks instead. We were fifteen different missions, representing ten nations, about eighty missionaries altogether. There was a unity and a love never dreamt of. Never before have I felt God that close, and never before have I heard God speak to his people as he did there.

There was renewal in Hatin-sum too:

In Hatin-sum we had a great celebration when ten Mongols were baptised. Among them was an elderly Mongol who has been working in the print shop for many years, and slowly but surely he's been convicted about the truth while he's been setting the Gospels. He used to be a priest and has been firmly tied to paganism and superstition. During the meetings last summer Dagny Hansen's Mongol girl, Sain-bileg, also made a commitment to the Lord.

Hatin-sum was the station where it was possible to stay on longest. But in March 1944 the Marthinsons, Vivian Almqvist and Gerda Ollén left and moved to Beijing, where most missionaries had been interned by the Japanese. They had left behind a small handful of faithful Mongolian believers. Hatin-sum was the youngest of the stations, but it brought with it the tradition from Halun-us — a total period of thirty-eight years. A lot had happened at these stations: medical work, itinerant evangelism, veterinary assistance, translation, tract and Bible distribution, and education. More importantly, not only was seed sown across the steppe, but some actually germinated.

From Alopen, to the Great Khans, to the Fransiscans: no unique Mongol church had ever been established. A small Kalmuck Moravian congregation had been planted in Sarepta, but now, here on the steppe of Mongolia, a genuine uniquely Mongolian church was finally born. This is a testimony to the hard work and prayerful persistence of the Swedish missionaries, and the fortitude and faith in God of the first Mongol converts.

'I'm fascinated by this Swedish thing,' I told Karen after breakfast. 'They've done some amazing work.' I'd found some stuff on other Swedish missions and had spread it out on the table. We rummaged through it together.

'Here's a Swedish Baptist Mission that entered China in 1892. This mentions a Reverend John Swordson and wife who worked in Mongolia. Here's something on a guy called Arne Nordmark. He was with the Swedish Free Mission and was able to stay on after the War. Looks like he was more west; in Xining and Gansu. Plenty of Mongols over there though.'

'More coffee?' Karen interrupted my thoughts. We'd managed to buy about fifty packets of Brazilian freeze-dried coffee for about fifty cents each at a Russian shop the week before. We'd learned you had to buy things when you saw them in the shops. Stock flow was a major problem in the market. It was about four years out of date, but nonetheless excellent. It should last us for about three years.

Karen paused and shuffled through some papers. 'Here's a Swedish Holiness Mission. North Shansi province, plus Kalgan it looks like. I wonder how many people they had?'

'No idea,' I replied. 'We really need to have a contact in Sweden to be able to hunt down some more of this stuff.'

'Well we have eight Swedish colleagues working with us now here. Someone must know something,' Karen suggested, filling up my mug with another coffee.

'Any milk?'

'Only Moloko.'

I selected one of twenty tins of Russian condensed milk we'd hoarded. It was only eleven years past the best-before date.

I broached the possibility with Magnus Kopman that night when he and his wife Sarah came to our place for dinner, of being a Swedish history-contact person. They were on a one-year contract, teaching English to Mongolian doctors in an Alcohol Abuse Reduction project.

'Sure,' Magnus said enthusiastically. 'I'm quite interested in the Swedish missionaries to Mongolia myself. I'll see what I can do when we get back to Sweden.'

That was the beginning of a very fruitful correspondence where Magnus spent a lot of time making contacts and rummaging through second-hand book shops hunting down accounts of Swedish missionaries.

One day in 1997 an email arrived from Magnus:

I've made contact with Paul Ericksson, the son of Dr Joel Ericksson. Paul was born in 1922 and he lived his first six years in Mongolia, at the Swedish Mongol Mission's stations in Golchaggan (sic) and Doyen. Then he went home to

Sweden to go to school. He went back to Mongolia in 1947 and stayed there for three years, and he finally had to escape from the Communists to Hong Kong in 1950. Later he moved to Japan with his wife, where he worked for a long time as a missionary. Paul showed Sara and me two-and-a-half hours of film from the 1930s and 1940s, mainly made by his father Joel. It was very interesting to see Joel, Anders Marthinson, Gerda Ollén and many other legendary Swedish Mongol-missionaries in action!

NOTES
1. This is the Swedish spelling. I haven't seen the name written in English at all.
2. This is the Swedish spelling. I suspect it is Gol-tsagaan, meaning 'white river', an illusion to its winter appearance, but the Swedish text translates as the 'settlement of the wild spirits'.
3. The area of this group is unclear. Perhaps if translated differently (the Mongol language has a 'g' that is often silent), this may well be the Buriat.
4. The Swedish spelling is Dojjen.

Chapter

43

Three Women of the Gobi,
Gossiping the Gospel

'Of course, I know about these three women. They are unmarried, they travel everywhere teaching their religion and doing good.'

A Mongolian living Buddha

Karen Kemp writes:

I kicked the dusty stones in frustrated despair as I walked home from our Ulaanbaatar language school. The battered, bruised and desperate girl I had met on that crowded bus had left me feeling powerless, inadequate and deeply grieved. The pain, anguish, desperation, helplessness and vulnerability of this child's face haunted me. She had tried to hide the bruises; she had been doubled over in pain.

Her so-called care-giver was wearing the uniform of the local State Hospital. The bus had stopped, she'd wrenched the child's arm, dragged her through the compact of people and tumbled her down the stairs onto the street. Hauling her to her feet on the pavement, she then dragged the now dazed, limp child, half walking, half carrying her until she disappeared from view.

No beds left in the hospital. (If she'd ever made it to hospital.) State taking her home. (If she had a home.) I felt the anger and the tears well up inside. I wanted to shout, to stop the bus, to create a scene, to demand justice.

My journal was full of anguished entries; periodically I had dissolved into pools of tears as I wrote. I felt profoundly inadequate to begin to address what I knew to be just the tip of the iceberg. Alcoholism. Unemployment. Extreme inflation. Pathetic wages. So much for the new-found liberties of democracy and the market economy.

As a young wife and mother struggling with already heavy demands, what could I possibly do to alleviate the suffering of one girl-child, let alone the thousands around me? I am a nurse. I work in a large Christian organisation. I can design a project. I can find sponsors. I can do a strategic plan! But these ideas never got further than my journal. I was simply overwhelmed.

The wall of spears

The Gobi desert has been described as a 'wall of spears'.[1] Situated in a large sweeping band from north-west China to south of the steppe of Mongolia proper, it stretches west into Xinjiang province of China. In southern Mongolia, it is not so much sandy desert as grainy chaparral: Mongolian nomads can graze camels commercially on the succulent perennials of the Gobi.

But when the spring winds come, the Gobi is truly a wall of spears. Sand, gravel and hail all mix in a cauldron of vicious velocity, relentlessly hurling itself at any traveller who is unfortunate enough to be caught in the open. The wall of spears strips paint off buildings, blinds unprotected eyes, fills up wells, and reduces grand civilisations to oblivion, leaving ghosts to howl in the shifting sands of marching dunes.

And to this wall of spears came Evangeline French, her sister Francesca, and Mildred Cable.

Three women

Evangeline French grew up in the cosmopolitan city of Geneva, Switzerland, and her younger sister Francesca was born in Bruges, Belgium. Their father was a small landowner with estates in North Africa. They shifted later to Portsmouth, England, where Victorian society seemed rather a let-down after the stimulating cultural and artistic crossroads of Geneva. Eva, a somewhat restless and 'stormy petrel' was challenged by hearing of the plight of women and children in China. The ideals of the Salvation Army appealed to her adventurous spirit;

working among the poor of society struck a chord with her strong sense of social justice. But it wasn't until 1890 that she made a commitment to Christ. The key to her conversion was her younger sister, who quietly said to her one night, 'Eva, there is no need [to take the world's misery] upon yourself. It was done long ago, on the cross.'

Francesca was a 'placid lamb' as a child, and of the two, the quieter and more level-headed. Eva sailed first for service in China, as Francesca stayed home caring for their mother. When their mother died, Francesca trained in midwifery. Both sisters, Eva the tempestuous and Francesca the meek, loved working with women and children.

During her first furlough in England, Eva teamed up with Mildred Cable, nine years her junior, who sailed back with her to China. Mildred was from Surrey and known for her lively sparkle and humour. She was a qualified chemist, and self-taught in anatomy, surgery and midwifery. She worshipped at Westminster Chapel, then under the pastoral oversight of the famous preacher Campbell Morgan who said of Mildred: 'I have never recommended anyone for missionary work with more heartiness or stronger conviction.'

On returning to England on furlough, Eva and Mildred invited Francesca to join them. This she did, and since then they have been known as the 'Cable and French trio' or simply 'the Trio'. In their own words: 'our objective was to take the knowlege of God to people who were given up to idol-worship, and no one ever went to the Gobi on more important business.'[2]

Initial work in Hwochow, Shansi province

The initial work of the Trio was in Hwochow, in a China Inland Mission station comprised of missionaries' houses, clinic, church and school. Their work here was mainly among women and children, dealing with the social curses of foot-binding, opium smoking, poor literacy and the aftermath of the Boxer uprising. Mildred put her medical training to good effect. But among the rhythms of mission compound life, their greatest love was meeting people.

'Gossiping the gospel' was really what mattered. They were never more at home than chatting to patients, schoolchildren, and their mothers. They loved to visit Chinese homes. And they loved to talk with the students from far away who had made the effort to come to Hwochow, including Mongols.

During their years there, the Trio conformed to accepted mission thinking. Gilmour's policy still held, that the best way of reaching the Mongols was from a Chinese base. The Trio took this one step further, insisting that it was the Chinese church's responsibility to evangelise the Mongols. In 1909, Mildred said to an audience in England while on deputation: 'The purpose of our Bible school and teacher training [in Hwochow] is that China must be evangelised by her own people.' At the time Chinese were flooding into Mongolian pastureland and taking it over for cultivation. This move was indirectly supported by mission stations, and so Christian mission became associated with Chinese colonisation. Mildred admitted that the Chinese had not had a good record of evangelism among the Mongols because of colonisation, but she felt the Chinese Christians would have to work this out themselves. It seems the Trio were at the same time innovative in training locals to do the evangelisation, and products of their own colonial heritage. Ultimately, they became uncomfortable with station life and cast their eyes towards Mongolia: they defined Mongolia as lying 'immediately north of the great wall of China and Chinese Turkistan'.[3]

'Gossiping the gospel'

Life in Hwochow had afforded the Trio a panorama of passing traders and pilgrims of all the minorities of China: Buddhists, Muslims, Turks, Tibetans, Mongols, Manchus and even Russians. By 1920 they felt that the church in Hwochow was strong enough to survive without them, and started pondering the needs of the peoples passing through. Although the wrench from Hwochow would be painful, their hearts became set on central Asia. In June 1923 they set off for the wall of spears, aiming to visit every city of the Gansu province situated beyond the great wall. This took them decisively into Mongol territory.

The Trio have written numerous books of their journeys in the Gobi, still readily accessible in secondhand bookshops and church libraries. W.J. Platt's *Three Women: The Authorised Biography* (Hodder and Stoughton: London, 1964) provides a comprehensive description of their travels if the reader wants to explore their wider ministry.

Mildred described their strategy as 'gossiping the gospel'. There was no strategic planning, projected budgets, professional consultations, prayer walking, short-term visits, contracts with aid agencies, united mission co-operation, or quarterly visits from the home director. They did nothing more than wander around the Gobi, gossiping the gospel:

Many of us commenced our evangelistic work in China by going from village to village, visiting the women and living with them. No days or hours are more precious to us than those, as we saw God's grace and love take possession of their hearts.... In unevangelised villages, we rent a room, and two [of our Chinese] Bible-women live there two or three weeks.... All our people should be trained to know that it is their business to pass on the Good News.[4]

In all, they travelled the old Silk Road between Suchow and Urumqi four times, and the total western sector of Gansu province six times. They were, by any reckoning, outstanding travellers of the twentieth century.

Many opportunities presented themselves for the Trio to evangelise Mongols. Suchow, thirty-five kilometres within the western boundary of the great wall, had a suburb that was used by Mongolian camel drivers for stalling their beasts. The women saw Suchow as strategic and opened a small Bible school there.

Kanchow, the city of which Marco Polo had once been governor was also a key place: Mongol pilgrims had to pass through Kanchow to reach Kang Lung lamasery, a famous pilgrim destination, three days' journey away. Here they had opportunity to meet a Mongol *noyon*, a thirty-six-year-old Kalmuck Mongol chieftan from the Altai mountains, on his way to the lamasery. Dr Kao, a Christian doctor resident in the town, had once rescued this prince who had lost his route to Kang Lung lamasery. He had approached the caravan and discerning that the prince's nine-year-old son was ill, invited him to the mission hospital. With prayer from the Chinese Christians and his own medical skills, and some rest in the Christian compound, the prince left with a cured son. In gratitude for the boy's healing, the prince declared himself a 'sworn friend' of Dr Kao, and because of this invited the Trio to visit his banner, two months' journey away in the Altai mountains.

It seems the story of the prince's son spread among the Mongols of high rank, as Kao later met a living Buddha who knew of him through the first prince's testimony. The lama said, 'I have heard so much about you and about the religion you hold, that I want to come and see you and have a talk.'[5] This lama then spent 'many hours' talking about Christ with Dr Kao: 'I desire in this life to be your friend, and for the next that we should enter heaven as brethren,' said the lama concluding his conversations. The lama took Scriptures and there was also interest from his entourage.

On another occasion the living Buddha of Altai sent a messenger to the mission compound at Kanchow commandeering cart and horses for a spiritual pilgrimage. The Christians granted his request. When he returned the equipment later, he 'listened with great interest to stories of the life of Christ, and bowed reverentially at each mention of his name'. He was now reading the Scriptures daily, and had given Dr Kao a passport to safeguard him through the whole territory of which he was spiritual chief.

Kao, not only proficient in medicine, was also an evangelist. The Christians of Kanchow, under the Trio's direction, set up a gospel tent for four days, a huge marquee which held three hundred people. There Kao preached with simple, apt illustrations, relating Christian truth to local life. The tent was crowded to capacity with Turks, Tibetans, Chinese and Mongols.

This constant exposure to Mongols prompted the women to travel north-east of Suchow into Mongol territory proper, to Kinta and up the Edzingol River valley. The main tribal grouping of this area was the Torgut, a sub-tribe of the Kalmucks who had gone to Russia in the early seventeenth century, but returned when the politics of China had allowed it (see Chapter 23). The Torgut Mongols had been evangelised by the Moravians in Russia, and perhaps some of them came back to China as Christians. They never regained their original grazing grounds, and had been relegated to the Edzingol by the Chinese emperor.

In Edzingol, the Trio stayed in nomad tents, spending time with whoever would receive them. They talked at length with the Torgut *noyon* Wang-Ye. However, the prince was in two minds about Christianity in light of the new doctrine of Communism. He had read the Christian books they had given him, and held them in high regard. But they gained his audience on the same day he received a Communist ambassador, and the prince was undecided.

Gossiping with the Scriptures

Like Reginald Sturt and other missionaries travelling the Mongolian steppe, the Trio gave out vast quantities of Christian literature. Mildred Cable records her joy at receiving in the mail Tibetan Gospels of *Mark*, Chinese New Testaments, Arabic Gospels of *Matthew*, the Russian Bible and Mongolian

Gospels of *John*. This must have been the 1840 Mongolian John's Gospel, translated by Stallybrass and Swan.

They had a passion for the written word and saw a high priority on Scripture distribution. During their entire missionary career in central Asia, they kept a close relationship with the British and Foreign Bible Society. There was a constant demand for Mongolian Scriptures. The total number of Scriptures (in whole or in part) distributed by BFBS in central Asian languages by 1929 was 3,591,809.[6]

Topsy

The Trio had a special place in their hearts for the children of central Asia. Contact with children often led to invitations to their homes. While in Suchow, sing-songs would attract the children, especially the orphans and street kids. Thus they came upon a Mongol deaf-mute girl, whom they initially called 'Little Lonely'.

'Little Lonely' was the offspring of a one-night stand of a Mongol pilgrim and a Tibetan peasant woman at a festival in China. The baby had not been wanted and therefore was sold to a foster mother. This was not an uncommon practice; children were often bought and sold, especially unwanted girls. These girls were often no more than slaves in their new households, doomed to a life of servitude and sexual abuse. Little Lonely's adoptive mother worked her as a house servant, looking after her reasonably well, until it became obvious she was both deaf and mute. Now a liablility, the foster mother turned her out into the streets of Suchow to join the other beggars. The Trio learned of her plight when she knocked on their door one morning, hoping for food. This grew into a daily routine of coming to their home for hot soup and bread.

Hearing her story from neighbours, they decided that they would buy Little Lonely themselves. Thus on Christmas Eve 1928, she joined their household for seventeen shillings and sixpence and from that day on they became her 'three mamas'.

The formal written adoption was transacted by the local Mandarin. She was now their own daughter: a true Mongol, fearless and proud, and completely at home with a horse. Once given care and attention, she developed a hugely pleasant and extroverted personality.

The Trio renamed her 'Ai-Lien', meaning Love-bond, but she became known as 'Topsy' as she couldn't lip-read the two sounds Ai-Lien. When applying later for a British passport, she became 'Eileen' (anglicising the Ai-Lien) and took Mildred Cable's Chinese surname of 'Gai', thus becoming Eileen Guy. Topsy outlived her 'three mamas' by nearly forty years, dying in south London in 1997.[7]

Realists

The Trio were powerful communicators, and sent regular letters home. On furlough they would fill large halls, and when Topsy arrived as an adopted daughter, she was soon welcomed into the hearts and prayers of a huge British Christian public. An account of a valedictory meeting in Kingsway Hall, London, just before they left for their last term of service in August 1935, appeared in *China's Millions*, and is worth quoting at length. It shattered any romantic notions of life in the East for these women and their endearing Mongolian child:

Miss Eva French centred her remarks around a question she had been frequently asked, namely, 'Are you not thrilled to be going back?' Picturing conditions of the Gobi, its stony floor, the filth of its inns, the hard bread and unappetising food, the uncertainties of life, the rumours, the brigands, etc, these things made poor thrills. But contacts with needy souls, the evidences that kind deeds did bear fruit, were thrills worth while. But the only true thrill was to be able to say, as the Master did, 'I delight to do thy will.'

People had asked if Topsy was thrilled to be going back to her native land, but Topsy's bitter experiences in the land of her birth were poor preparations for being thrilled at the prospect of return.

But there were a few things that Topsy wanted to say, and though she had been born deaf and was consequently dumb, she had been taught to know about five hundred words. At Miss French's invitation, Topsy then rose and said, 'Goodbye,' and, 'Forget-me-not,' waving her hand as she did so. Topsy will not be forgotten, and the memory of her will speak for her people.

Then Miss Cable immediately transported us to the realities of the Central Asian roads. She almost felt the desert grit. At home all was for speed, but the ancient roads, with their three miles per hour, were better suited for the great business of preaching the gospel. Christ had joined himself to two discouraged disciples on the road, and the talk had been about great things. The great question of the road was, 'Whence do you come, and whither are you going?' Think what you lose by your speed, she said. You can't talk of these great and everlasting subjects when speed is the passion.

[The reporter then added] What a traveller puts in his hand-luggage could not fail to be a revelation, and Bunyan was her choice.

With the Trio, Topsy was 'an aggressive missionary', showing anyone she could her picture gallery of Scripture scenes.[8] She wasn't the only orphan they adopted: Grace, too, a crippled Chinese girl joined the family. Why anyone would adopt a street waif, let alone a deaf, dumb or crippled street waif, was in itself a megaphone of love to the people of central Asia.

Legacy of 'the Trio'

The Trio took on the whole of the north-west China, from Kanchow, through the north-west corridor of Kansu province, along the trade routes to Urumqi, where George Hunter and Percy Mather were based. This was their parish. No town ever became home: they travelled everywhere by donkey cart. They were never in a hurry to get anywhere. They rented a room in this town, slept in a tent in that village, or under their cart on the way. The journey itself was as much their destination as they went where the need was, or where they sensed God had called them.

To gossip the gospel was their calling: to take every opportunity, in whatever language to whomever they met. Sometimes this would be by picture book, sometimes by tract, sometimes by debate, sometimes by medical healing, sometimes by the casting out of a demon. All the peoples of central Asia jostled for their attention, but the Mongols were high on their agenda. They went nowhere without Mongol Bibles to sell; they deliberately sought out Mongols for conversations, especially those on religious pilgrimage who were seeking the truth. Every individual counted. One by one. Whoever they spoke to had their full attention.

History eventually caught up with the Trio. Like the shifting sands of the wall of spears, Communism, republicanism, imperialism and the onward march of modernism swept through southern Gobi. Yet there is an irony here. It is because of the ideological clashes of the early twentieth century which were played out on the desert of the Gobi that they enjoyed such freedom to travel around. Warlords came and went. Mandarins came and went. There was no central authority who ruled that they couldn't be there: their presence was due merely to the rapport they had built up among the people. Even the lamas respected them, and on occasions protected them. Three spinsters, with a deaf-mute Mongol orphan in tow confronted the wall of spears, speaking to more people about Jesus and distributing more parts of Scripture than I can imagine.

Eventually these three intrepid women were forced to return to England. With Topsy, they continued an active life promoting the work of the Bible Society, writing, and recruiting another generation of missionaries for China and Mongolia. Their missiological principles were simple and practical. They came to believe that co-operation between agencies was an imperative for the future. Missionaries must be of a simple nature to fit in with nomadic habits: it was no good retaining the imperialism of the mission compound mentality. A missionary had to be with the people, eating their food, sleeping in their tents, travelling as they do, dressing as they do. The Trio were holistic: friendship evangelism was the only mission paradigm they had; everything they did was evangelistic, educational and medical all bundled up together. They did not compartmentalise either deeds or time.

One criticism levelled at itinerant evangelists is that they have a weak ecclesiology: they manage to have large numbers of converts, but leave few churches. Not so the Trio. Where possible, for example in Suchow and Kanchow, they linked with the local Chinese church. In Urumqi likewise. Their understanding of church was where two or three were gathered in Jesus' name. They emphasised teaching new converts, indeed they often stayed on for weeks in a village discipling and teaching. The modern cell-church movement is neither new nor innovative: Mongol, Chinese and Turkish converts of the Gobi were meeting in cell-churches eighty years ago, under female leadership. The Trio writes, 'the hope of the future lies not with scattered converts, but in such small living groups'. The church, any church, whether English, Mongol or Chinese should be 'a self-supporting church, full of evangelistic fervour, sending forth its witnesses to the furthest limits'.[9]

Karen Kemp continues:

I am kneading dough in my kitchen, looking out from the top floor of our apartment building located on a gentle rise in the eastern sector of Ulaanbaatar. Soviet-style apartment blocks surround us. It is spring: wind, dust, rain and snow yesterday. All together, at the same time. The Gobi had come to pay us a visit. Clear today except for the wispy trail of an international jet, going some place else. Trees' swollen buds pregnant with the promise of green, poised to make the sudden appearance we've longed for all winter.

I gaze into the distance. A ribbon of steel betrays the trans-Siberian railway in the distance; a frozen river, white twists on open grey expanse of grassland. Then that startling, vivid, clear blue Mongolian sky. So vast and brilliant an expanse, Mongols of old worshipped it as god above all others. Drab buildings; brilliant sky. The contradictions embody this land and its people. The people of this magnificent vastness live in small round felt tents scattered across valley floors and mountain sides as if to shelter from the hugeness of the steppe and the desert.

Mongolian hospitality, as expansive and generous as the land, masks a deeply reserved and outwardly undemonstrative character, legacy of a culture where trust can be a stranger even in the closest relationships. Fermented mare's milk vodka, while being the sign of greatest honour when served to a guest, also gives expression to Mongolia's deepest pain: the scourge of rampant alcoholism, crime and child abuse. Prisoners, orphans and street kids. The prisons are neglected cesspits of the outcast: the victims of a corrupt bureaucracy which damns souls for minor offences. Street kids living under the city, hugging the hot water pipes for comfort while it is -35° celsius up on the street.

The 'truth' of Communism has been replaced by the 'truth' of material ambition and secularism. This is the Mongolia that Jesus Christ, full of grace and truth, has come into. Mongol believers throughout this vast land are finding in him a new understanding of themselves and their culture; bringing hope and meaning to a time of disillusionment and confusion. Making sense of the contradictions.

The vast blue sky is no longer intimidating, no longer to be feared and placated. The same one who chooses to come and dwell among us is a constant companion through the changing seasons of nomadic existence. The one who changes the victim of a system to a uniquely valued child. One at a time, one by one. Would I ever meet again that abused girl-child on the bus to tell her this?

These beflagged piles of stones on the high passes no more commanding ritual by the argument of antiquity ('to be a Mongol is to be a Tibetan-Buddhist'). An elderly, devout Tibetan-Buddhist grandma who, on her first reading of the New Testament in Mongolian, impresses on her granddaughter: 'This Jesus, these words: I recognise them as the truth. Study them and follow him!'

As I look out of my room with a view, I marvel at all God has done in such a short time in Mongolia. Spring is here, summer will come. I can't solve Mongolia's problems on my own. But one by one, as they come to my door, as I meet them on the street, the poor, the abused, the neglected; perhaps a kind word, a hot meal, an item of clothing, a smile, a hug. This summer our Mongol church will again send out teams to every province of Mongolia, preaching that Emmanuel, God who came to be with us, is alive and active in Mongolia.

My few minutes' reverie leaves me feeling humbled, privileged and deeply thankful that God has brought me here at such a time as this. More than that, as I turn back to kneading the bread on the table in front of me, the single-minded discipleship of my Mongol brothers and sisters stays with me: a challenge.

NOTES

1. This is the title of one of Cable and French's books: *Wall of Spears; The Gobi Desert* (Lutterworth: London, 1951).

2. *Ibid.*, p.12.

3. M. Cable, F. Houghton, R. Kilgour, A. McLeish, R.W. Sturt and O. Wyon, *The Challenge of Central Asia* (World Dominion Press: London, 1929) p.59.

4. W.J. Platt, *op.cit.*, p.93.

5. M. Cable and F. French, *Dispatches from North-West Kansu* (CIM: London, 1925), p.13.

6. M. Cable, F. Houghton, R. Kilgour, A. McLeish, R.W. Sturt and O. Wyon, *op.cit.*, pp.72–73.

7. Paul Broomhall, brother of CIM historian A.J. Broomhall, and for many years chairman of the UK Interserve Council, became Topsy's guardian after the Trio died. His daughter took over this responsibility when he died, so Topsy was treated as part of the Broomhall family for the rest of her life. Mildred Cable and Francesca French wrote *The Story of Topsy* (CIM) which was read by many generations of Western children.

8. E. French, M. Cable and F. French, *A Desert Journal: Letters from Central Asia* (Hodder and Stoughton: London, 1934), p.162.

9. M. Cable, F. Houghton, R. Kilgour, A. McLeish, R.W. Sturt and O. Wyon, *op.cit.*, p.76.

David Stenberg and N.J. Friedstrom,

Experiments with Agricultural Colonies

'[We] had a meeting with the missionaries and came to the conclusion that the best way to gather the Mongols is to purchase a piece of land and teach Mongols to cultivate same.'

David Stenberg[1]

'What was the final outcome of that fencing?' I asked Markus. We were bouncing along in our sixty-nine jeep with a trailer-load of turnips, on a wide plain in Gobi Altai province, south-west Mongolia. The turnips were the first harvest of 'Waterfalls', a large agricultural project in Gobi-Altai which Markus was co-ordinating. He was an agronomist from Switzerland. 'The fencing looked good when we went to the site yesterday. Did you go down to the Chinese border to buy it?'

'I delegated the job to one of the workers.' Markus had to shout over the noise of the engine. 'He went down to the Chinese border OK. I'd signed over 100,000 *tugruks* to him, but he didn't return with any fence posts.'

'Couldn't he get them?'

'Oh yeah. That wasn't the problem. The Chinese traders at the border are so wily, that they talked him into buying a satellite dish instead.'

'A satellite dish won't be much use for keeping camels out of the vegetable plot! And what will European donors say when they find how your worker spent their money? Or have you written a new cable television service into the agricultural project?' I thought the whole episode sounded ludicrous, but this was only the beginning.

'We'll never get the cash back. We actually bought the fence posts from up north in the end. They're not Chinese, but Mongolian.'

Just then the driver pulled up to an abrupt halt in a cloud of dust. He carefully surveyed each horizon. On our left was a range of mountains, and his eyes probed each valley that opened out onto the plain. 'They'll be in that valley there,' he said, pointing about ten o'clock from where we were. All the valleys looked identical. How a Mongol navigated across the steppe totally escaped me.

Introduction

There is one major problem in nomad evangelism: nomads keep moving. To overcome this, missionaries have three options.

1. They could move with the nomads. A missionary could set up a *ger*, attach himself to a Mongol *noyon* and move with his camp. Today we call this indigenisation. The missionary dresses like a Mongol, eats Mongol food, speaks and acts as a Mongol. In mission thinking last century, the closest the missionaries got to this strategy was travelling with them. They rode horses or camels, going from tent to tent, encampment to encampment, preaching, offering elementary medical assistance and distributing tracts and parts of Scripture. James Gilmour and Reginald Sturt adopted this method. The Cable and French trio excelled at it. In many ways, it was a 'pre-evangelism' strategy. It gave opportunity to challenge the worldview of the nomads. Some Mongols became Christians, but there was little fruit from this approach.

2. They could set up a 'station' out on the steppe. This was the preferred pattern. A good site was located, perhaps in a trading town or near a large monastery; buildings were erected including a house for the missionary, a school and a dispensary. If Mongols were to hear the gospel then they had to come into the station. Medicine and education drew them in. Mongols

contacted out on the steppe would then ride by the station for further literature or medicines, or stop by when going on pilgrimage or trade. The SMM stations of Hallon-us, Golltjagan, Hattin-sum and Doyen enjoyed some success with this model.

3. They could form an agricultural colony. Instead of trying to keep up with nomads, why not entice them to stay still in one place? Why not try to change their ways to becoming sedentary, and then the missionaries would have as much time with them as they needed. If the missionaries taught them some agriculture, then vegetables would supplement their meagre diet of boiled mutton. And if their diet improved, sickness would decrease. The children could be educated, and there would be easier access to medical assistance. The advantages seemed endless.

What happened to the first colony

From the spring of 1899 to the summer of 1900, N.J. Friedstrom and Carl Suber, both of the SAMM, toured from Kalgan up into the hinterland of Mongolia as far as Uliastay, to explore church planting possibilities. While they were away, David Stenberg stayed on at Wuyuan and set up an agricultural colony. When Friedstrom and Suber returned, they were warned that Stenberg (and others) had been murdered by the Boxers. Suber went ahead to check and was likewise murdered. The four had been betrayed by a corrupt Mongolian official. On instruction from a friendly Mongol *noyon*, another Mongol personally escorted Friedstrom to Outer Mongolia because of the ongoing Boxer threat. Friedstrom was the only survivor of SAMM in the Boxer revolution. He returned to develop the colony.

Stenberg had been the one with the vision for a colony. The SAMM eventually had two colonies, one at Wuyuan and the other at Patsebalong. Both were mainly agricultural. Originally 6,000 acres had been purchased, but because of the Boxer rebellion, much of this stood vacant for 1900, as the missionaries who had intended living there had been murdered. So instead of the Mongols resuming their grazing, Chinese colonisers moved in to cultivate it, and ended up pushing the Mongols to the steppe. The hope of attracting Mongols just did not happen. Stuart Gunzel visited in 1934 and found that the original 6,000 acres had been reduced to a mere 30 over the previous three decades and all the work was in the hands of Chinese Christians.

'The investment of prayer, effort, money, strength and even lives seemed all out of proportion to the harvest reaped. Seed was planted. Some germinated. There has been a harvest even though it seems small. The Lord's teaching about the rescue of even one lost lamb helps to put this field in perspective.'[1] This is a rather glowing assessment of the colonies considering that their emphasis quickly shifted to the Chinese. The aim of the SAMM missionaries had been to 'make disciples' and 'plant the church', but the church that was planted was Chinese, not Mongolian, although in Mongolian territory.

James Gilmour may not have disapproved of this method. After years of travelling on the steppe he concluded: 'I am still of the opinion that our best way to reach the Mongols is from a Chinese base.' And Gilmour would have taken the strategy further, insisting that the evangelisation of the Mongols should be done by Chinese evangelists. This however seems naive as the Chinese were taking over the Mongols' pasturelands. So why should Mongols listen to the Chinese, when there was such resentment and longstanding antipathy? The Cable and French trio admitted that the Chinese did not have a good record of evangelism among the Mongols because of colonisation, but they too concluded that this was a problem Chinese Christians could work out for themselves. But with the underlying racial antagonism, they never did.

Catholic colonies

The Catholic method of evangelism was colonisation, and they established themselves by leasing land from the Mongols and building Christian villages on it. These were all Chinese villages encroaching on Mongol pastures.

The Catholics considered the steppe as vacant land and bought up vast tracks of it, especially in Mongolia, selling it on or leasing it to Chinese settlers. Sometimes the settlers were Christians. Those who weren't were required to accept Catholic instruction before land allocation took place. Either way a Christian community would form. In essence, the Catholics were buying their conversions. Here a huge injustice to the Mongols is obvious. For a pastoral nomadic people to have their land bought from under them in the name of religion, then to have it sold on to the Chinese, who were the Mongols' overlords, made the Catholic fathers appear evil middle men. The Mongols had no further recourse to that land as their beloved grasslands became vegetable plots. Mongol vengeance during the mayhem of 1900 was not surprising.

The emigration of Chinese into Mongol lands was very rapid. A paper to the Royal Geographical Society in 1903 noted that there were 'Swarms of Chinese spread beyond the Great Wall, ousting the Mongols. By 1899 the Chinese settlers had reached a mile or so beyond Chagan-balgas; [now they are] ploughing virgin soil near Dabasum-nor, ten miles farther north.'[2]

We can be harshly critical in hindsight. The Chinese Christians themselves were being persecuted by the Manchu emperor Chia-ch'ing, and the Lazarists wanted to move a lot of their converts over the wall to find 'peace and liberty in the deserts of Tartary'. Some Mongols were sympathetic to this and only too happy to lease or sell their land. The Christians were being persecuted by an overlord whom the Mongols hated too. It was from this initial 'good-faith' agreement that further exploitation occurred.

The Manchu government was aggressively relocating Chinese onto Mongolian pastureland. For example, in 1908 the whole of the banner of Bagharin was confiscated and turned over to Chinese settlers. And some Chinese colonisation was actually promoted by the Mongols. The prince of the

Mongolian banner of Üüshin (later to be the president of the Ordos league) promised the Chinese Manchu military governor I Ku that he would open his whole region to colonisation. He had enormous debts and needed the revenue. The Mongols of Üüshin protested. I Ku, however, fell into disgrace in 1908 and dragged down the prince with him. The banners themselves had no united policy on land leasing. Some became nervous about turning grassland into arable land as they then attracted a Chinese land tax. Sometimes tempers flared. The prince of the Mongolian banner of Alashan demanded his land of San-tao-ho back from the church which was leasing it from him.

The legacy of Catholic colonial policy

Land issues were a direct precursor for the mayhem at Hsi-wan-tzu during the Boxer uprising of 1900. The Manchu court put pressure on the Mongol *noyon* to raise revenue to help the Ching court pay indemnities to the Western powers. Traditional Mongol pasturelands of Ulanchab, Yeke-juu and Alashan were confiscated by the Manchu government and signed over to the Catholic mission as part payments for previous losses during the Boxer rebellion. This meant the Mongols now lost both pasturelands and revenue. In the Teng-ko region of Alashan this Catholic occupation of land caused great hostility with the Mongols, who naturally resisted conversion to the church. Although the Catholics were in the Ordos region for more than a hundred years, there were just a handful of Mongol converts. Those who did convert abandoned nomadic life and settled near the mission stations.

In 1887 there were forty-nine CICM fathers in three Mongol vicariates, or church administrative areas, as well as Kansu and Ili. By 1888 there were 10,545 Catholics in the Central Mongolian vicariate and about 1,0000 catechumens, but according to Verhelst, these were all Chinese. By 1,900, before the Boxer uprising, the CICM had over a hundred missionaries and claimed 40,000 Christians. Numbers declined due to the

Boxer uprising, but there was then tremendous growth in south-west Mongolia between 1905 and 1912. By the end of 1912 the total of Catholics in all three Mongolian vicariates reached about 80,000. By 1913 the number of CICM fathers had grown to 169 throughout Inner Mongolia, Gansu and Xinjiang: all territories with large Mongol populations. Desmet records that 'in Eastern Mongolia there were 48 priests, 15 residences, 66 schools and a number of catechists'.[3]

Did the colonies succeed?

No. The SAMM's two colonies succumbed to pressure from Chinese immigrants, but some land was held for ongoing cultivation. No significant ongoing Christian witness to Mongols emerged out of it though, and no Mongol church was established because of it. The numbers of professing Christians associated with the colonies is astounding. However, these were all Chinese Catholics, and many of them bought by the promise of land and work. The deep antipathy of Mongol and Chinese meant the Catholic colonies worked against the establishment of a unique Mongolian church. It is not surprising that both Protestant and Catholic colonial policies failed.

'So where are we going then?' I asked Markus.

'We're going to find the guy who bought the satellite dish. Someone at Waterfalls said that his father's summer pasture is up this valley. So we'll go and see what sort of compensation we can get.'

I was intrigued. Markus obviously had enough language to negotiate these things, and I was curious to see a summer campsite.

The valley started to narrow. We unhooked the trailer half way up and threw the sixty-nine into four-wheel drive. Soon all we were driving on was a dry riverbed, hemmed in by towering harsh peaks on either side. And then, as if by some foreordained command, the ravine opened like a stage curtain and a perfect amphitheatre of green grass appeared before us. A group of four white *gers* sat neatly nestled together in the distance. There must have been a spring there. The distant baaing of sheep and goats was answered by a shepherd's call.

'*Sain batsgan-uu.*' We all greeted each other as we alighted from the jeep.

'We've got the right camp-site,' whispered Gertrud, Markus' wife, as we were offered *su-tai tsai* and *aral*. 'This is the guy's father and grandmother. He himself is not here. Which isn't surprising if he'd heard we were coming. We'd better make ourselves scarce when Markus has to do the negotiating.'

'I can't see any satellite dish,' I joked.

Soon enough we got a signal from Markus, and Gertrud and I, with baby Katrin in the back-pack, headed off up the meadows above the camp site. Markus went to 'look at the flowers' with the father, a euphemism for brokering a business deal. They moved out of ear-shot. I guessed we'd hear the result when they were done. I couldn't possibly conceive how this nomad family would be able to find 100,000 *tugruks* in cash.

The view from the top of the meadow was spectacular. We could see over the ridge to the vast plain below, with the shimmering emerald green of Waterfalls in the far distance. A cool breeze twisted around the peaks. A shepherd boy gazed at us from a distance, leaning on his crook and balancing on one foot. We were aliens from a distant universe.

'Well there it is,' announced Gertrud, turning to look back down the valley at the encampment. 'There's the satellite dish.'

Sure enough, well hidden behind the third *ger*, and about half the size of it, was the project's very own dish, sitting there in all its glory, pointing up into the heavens.

'Can't be helped really. I wanted to watch the Atlanta Olympics too.' I assumed the best, not quite seeing the relevance of Superstar Wrestling or MTV beamed in from Hong Kong. I still couldn't get past the surreal aspects of this adventure.

We said our farewells, and trundled off down the valley to pick up the trailer-load of turnips. The driver found a short-cut and connected back on the plain with the main route.

'So how did it go?' I couldn't contain my curiosity any longer.

'Oh fine.' Markus seemed rather casual about it. 'He's going to give us sixty ewes, two rams, ten goats, three steers, a gelding and thirty kilograms of potatoes.'

I was impressed. 'How are you going to get those down to Waterfalls?' I imagined one of those huge articulated stock trucks from New Zealand trying to make its way up that valley.

'We'll have to herd them to Waterfalls. But that's not our real worry. It's the principle behind it. I would be surprised if it took less than two years for him to come up with goods.'

And it took exactly two years to collect. In the end, Markus got all the promised livestock (and the potatoes), the project got its fences, and to this day, that satellite dish sits out on the Mongol steppe beaming in Star TV from Hong Kong to that nomad family's *ger*.

NOTES
1. V. Mortenson, *God Made it Grow: Historical Sketches of TEAM's Church Planting Work* (William Carey Library: Pasadena, Ca., 1994), p.111.
2. C.W. Campbell in a paper to the Royal Geographical Society in 1903, in M. Broomhall, ed., *The Chinese Empire*, p.347.
3. Desmet etc in K.S. Latourette, *A History of the Expansion of Christianity*, vol. 6 (Eyre and Spottiswood: London, 1947), p.288.

Part **9**

Present and Future

God's Word for a Nation,

A New Testament Translation in Modern Mongolian

'To make available the Bible in a form which is true to the original. And acceptable to the broadest range of readership.'

Aim of the Mongolian Bible Society

'I like the name,' David said. 'MCTEE. Do we get to eat McDonald's burgers at McTee?'

There were five of us in a steering committee and we had just inaugurated the Mongolian Centre for Theological Education by Extension or MCTEE. It was August 1995.

I tried to ignore his joke, although he insisted on calling the centre 'McTee' from then on.

'I think we should start by translating *Abundant Life*. It was developed in Spanish, but is used around the world now in translation. It will be an excellent foundation discipleship course,' I said.

The need for McTee had arisen because the Mongolian church was growing so quickly that good leadership training material had to be produced which everyone could use. The TEE model fitted perfectly with the situation in Mongolia. Students used a workbook at home, then met together in groups with a trained TEE tutor each week to discuss the personal life applications. Karen and I had seen this concept used very effectively in Chile, India and New Zealand.

'Getting the right terminology is going to be a real headache,' I said. '*Shin Geree* is the New Testament that the church is using now, but we'll have a new translation within a year. I understand it's using another set of vocabulary. Any suggestions Magnai?'

Magnai was about twenty-two years old, and shaping up to be the anchor-man of the project. 'We'll have to work with what we've got. *Shin Geree* is excellent for pre-evangelism and basic discipleship because it has quite a bit of explanation in the biblical text,' he said.

Less than a year later, we field-tested *Abundant Life* and trained the first graduates to be tutors. Suddenly everything in McTee snowballed.

'Do you have another course we can go on to?' asked one student.

'We need to have these courses out in the countryside,' said another.

'You'll need to make some changes to this course. Some of the grammar isn't right,' said a third.

Over the next year there was a flurry of proof-reading, retranslating, printing, graphics design, employing more people, field-testing, curriculum development and tutor-training.

'Are we still going with *Shin Geree*?' I asked. By now we had five working in the McTee office and the steering committee had increased in size.

'I think we should closely monitor what religious words the Mongolian church is actually using,' Charles said. Charles was director of another educational project in Ulaanbaatar. 'I think we should write a disclaimer in the front of our workbooks. We'd do the church a grave disservice if we alienated a section of it due to our insensitivity.'

The Mongolian Bible: a potted history

The first Bible in Mongolian was the New Testament and *Psalms* translated by the Franciscan father John of Montecorvino in the first decade of the 1300s. After this, nothing else was attempted until Schmidt's Kalmuck *Matthew*, published in 1815. A full Bible translation was completed by the LMS missionaries in Buriatia, the Old Testament finished in 1840 and the New in 1846. This is generally referred to as the Literary Version, and because the language was a high form,

TEAM missionaries tried to put it into more common parlance with their 1952 New Testament revision. A shift in the dialect occurred with this revision, from Buriat to Khalka, the most widespread dialect today.

Another Khalka Bible translation had been attempted in 1872 by two missionaries based in China. They were Dr Joseph Edkins and Bishop Joseph Schereschewsky. Together with a local lama they worked on a rough Khalka draft of *Matthew* based on a combination of the Literary Version, the Mandarin text and the Manchu. David Stenberg of the Scandinavian Alliance Mission then continued with the other three Gospels and *Acts*, until he died at the hands of the Boxers in 1900.

After this faltering start, there is no record of further work for another seventy-two years. A second translation project in the Khalka dialect was initiated by the United Bible Societies. This is a completely new translation done in the Cyrillic script for a modern society.

United Bible Societies (UBS) publish a modern translation

An Englishman by the name of John Gibbens started work on a Khalka dialect New Testament in Ulaanbaatar in 1972, when he first went to the Mongolian People's Republic to study language and history. It was completed seventeen years later in 1989. Thirteen days after the first free elections in Mongolia, in July 1990, the first 5,000 copies were being printed in Hong Kong, ready for immediate shipment. The translation had involved over thirty Mongols, five Bible translation consultants from Wycliffe Bible Translators and a consultant from the United Bible Societies.

A key person in this translation was a Mongolian university student who later became Gibbens' wife, Altaa. He met Altaa while studying at the university. She wanted to learn English, and Gibbens wanted to have someone to check his first manuscripts. Altaa was studying Thermal Engineering at the university in Ulaanbaatar, but 'her first love was languages'. She was persuaded by Gibbens to read the Russian Bible he gave her, after which she agreed to help with the Mongolian translation. She commented while reviewing the apostle Paul's letters that she wondered why letters of such good advice should be prohibited in Communist Mongolia.

In 1980 Gibbens was asked to leave Mongolia, as the Communist authorities claimed his visa had run out. Returning in 1987, he married Altaa. They returned to England, where Gibbens continued to work on the translation 'in consultation with speakers of Mongolian', based at the University of Leeds. Gibbens says that his part was to create first drafts and then to ensure the people helping did the necessary editing, checking and so on.[1] Of Altaa's role Gibbens declares: 'she turned it from a missionary translation into one that will be clearly understood by mother-tongue speakers.' Finally, the Mongols had a New Testament in their own idiomatic tongue, and co-translated by a Mongolian Christian.

From 1987 United Bible Societies was involved with the project and published the Gibbens' translation with the title *Shin Geree*. Its release was one of those divine appointments in history. Mongolia threw off Communism in 1990 and a modern colloquial translation of the Bible was waiting in warehouses in Hong Kong for an opportune time to be exported. *Shin Geree* is the New Testament from which the church of modern Mongolia has sprouted.

'High Literary' or 'Low Vernacular'; where do you pitch a translation?

During its history, the Mongolian Bible has been the subject of heated debate from time to time. Debate centres on fundamental translation principles: the target audience, the style they need, and the choice of vocabulary.

The Literary Version was the first to come under close scrutiny. Van Hecken, CICM father in Inner Mongolia, describes its language as 'far from perfect and full of mistakes'. The fact that the Literary Version was revised twice suggests that the missionaries did recognise its shortcomings and were attempting to rectify them. Van Hecken (writing prior to the 1952 revision) nevertheless concedes that it was 'useful'.

All the Protestant mission efforts in Inner Mongolia would have used the Literary Version of the New Testament. Mongolian churches were started using this translation. Granted, they were small and fragile. Later revisions were precisely to get the Literary Version into the more colloquial Khalka dialect.

Lowering a high literary form of a language into the colloquial is risky. The 1952 revision aimed to transform the original into 'as simple language as possible'. But this was not as easy as it sounds. There was cultural resistance to translating holy writings into the vernacular. Holy Scriptures should be in holy language.

It would be wrong to assume that a literary, or high form of a language, is less valid than the street-spoken vernacular. Marku Tsering, a researcher into the Tibetan language, notes that 'one of the dangers [of translation]... is that the [foreign] missionaries often see the "high" literary language as elitist and "bad" and the vernacular as popular and "good" and so miss the cultural advantages of an astute use of both.'[2] Stallybrass and Swan made a right choice in translating into the high literary form because it was the nobles and lamas who were literate, rather than the common people. It also gave the translation the status of holy writing, and hence worth reading and listening to.

The three Mongols who worked on the 1952 Revision project, namely Ganden, Matthai and Erinchindorji, all had a good knowledge of the vernacular Khalka. This was coupled with their use of the English Revised Standard Version and the Greek text. The final revision was checked against other English translations as well as Swedish, Japanese, Chinese and Tibetan ones. It has been transcribed from *mongol bichig* into the Cyrillic script and, although not formally published, is still available privately. A small number of Christian Mongols in Ulaanbaatar today use it regularly for worship.

Between 1990 and 1996, the most common New Testament in Mongolia was UBS' *Shin Geree*, translated mainly by the Gibbenses, with some portions translated by others. This is a completely new translation with no connections to the 1952 Revision. *Shin Geree* was done in an idiomatic style specifically for modern Khalka-Mongol speakers.

Criticism of UBS' *Shin Geree*

Although Gibbens has had some formal linguistics training, his work has been heavily criticised at times, mainly by colleagues in Ulaanbaatar. The issues are fundamental. Critics believe *Shin Geree* is 'a paraphrase' and has 'too much explanation within the text' and 'is not close to the original'. The ensuing debate reflects a clash of two translation models. On the one hand, a conservative model dictates that a translation should be literal, closely following the Greek and Hebrew original texts. Literal accuracy is the main parameter. These translations are called 'formal correspondence' translations. (A word-for-word translation would be an extreme example of this type of approach.) On the other hand, a 'dynamic equivalent' model looks for the meaning in each word or phrase, and then seeks to express that meaning in language that is understood by the readers. It is a meaning-for-meaning approach. Faithfulness to meaning coupled with overall comprehension is the main parameter.

UBS' *Shin Geree* is not technically a paraphrase. A paraphrase is a rephrasing of a text in the same language, as a student would be asked to rewrite a story at school. *Shin Geree* is a dynamic-equivalent translation, according to standard definitions used by UBS and Wycliffe Bible Translators. It is anchored in the Greek text, and has been checked by professional UBS consultants. Gibbens does concede that there is explanation in the text, but then all dynamic-equivalent translations do this.

This is needed, he says, for a first-generation church, because the reader has no background knowledge or cultural parameters with which to understand the text: 'throughout, semantic content has been the guiding principle of the work'. The Mongolian Bible Society (MBS), of which Altaa Gibbens until recently has been the Executive Director, is responsible for the distribution of *Shin Geree*. MBS has a clearly stated aim: to 'make available the Bible in a form which is true to the original, and acceptable to the broadest range of readership'.

Shin Geree was published at a unique time in history. There were no Christian Mongols in 1990 with adequate biblical knowledge able to review the translation thoroughly, like there are today. For Mongols working on the Bible, it was the first Bible they had ever seen. No readers would have access to commentaries or Bible dictionaries for many years to come, and therefore 'the aim was to give as much information as possible, and in a way which the totally uninformed would find comprehensible and easy to read'.[3] Today it is possible to test readership response, and the MBS has produced evaluation forms for this purpose. With over 40,000 *Shin Geree* sold since 1990, the potential readership response is enormous.

Can God be 'God'?

The debate centres on key vocabulary. Critics of UBS' *Shin Geree* believe that generic Mongolian words should be used, believing these to best preserve the literal meaning of the original Greek text. Central to this criticism is the word for 'God'. *Shin Geree* uses a phrase meaning 'Lord of the Universe', but critics argue that the word *burhan* should be used, believing it to be the generic word for 'deity'.

Gibbens argues that *burhan*, which is commonly used to refer specifically to Buddha, carries far too much Buddhist meaning in it. Is this actually the case? What does *burhan* mean? Is it in fact a generic word, and more importantly, how is it actually used today? Is it a word that can be used in a Bible translation and sanctified over time?

In the Buddhist literature of the Mongols, *burhan* means 'Buddha'.[4] Schmidt, translating into Kalmuck and Buriat Mongol, knew that *burhan* meant 'Buddha', as he gives only this meaning in a dictionary he published in 1835. Schiefner, in later revising the Literary Version, understood *burhan* to be a corruption of the Sanskrit word brahman. Others have dissected the word and suggested that the first syllable *bur-* derives from the ancient Chinese word *fut* (a sinicised use of the Sanskrit *brahman*), and the second syllable *-(k)han* comes from the Turko-Mongol word for king.

These suggested root words aren't really convincing. There is no substantial evidence in any ancient literature that the word *burhan* is a transcription or loan word from anywhere else. *Burhan* is an indigenous word deeply rooted in Mongolian and other neighbouring Altaic languages.

First, the element *-(k)han* is not the same as the word for king. *Khan*, the word for king, has a long vowel, whereas *-han* in *burhan* has a short vowel. Secondly, it is common knowledge that Siddharta Gautama, later to become the Buddha, never was a king. Therefore why assign him the title? Thirdly, the word *burhan* is used in a Shamanistic (rather than Buddhist) context among neighbouring peoples.

Likewise among the Buriat and Khalka Mongols, *burhan* is a Shamanistic word that is older than the introduction of Buddhism. For the Buriats, *Burhan* is the god of Lake Baikal itself.[5] In sum, *burhan* is a generic word of the Mongols meaning 'deity', or in its Shamanistic use 'image' or 'idol', and had this fixed meaning before Buddhism arrived. It was natural then that the word transferred its meaning to the Buddha as Buddhism merged with Shamanism and in some places replaced it. This adaptation of the word is natural as the sound of *burhan* and Buddha are similar.

Today in Mongolia, *burhan* certainly means 'The Buddha' or 'a buddha' as an idol. However, it has a generic sense that is not confined to meaning just 'Buddha'. When a Mongol talks about the deities in other religions that are clearly not buddhistic, he uses the word *burhan*. When a Mongol asks a foreigner 'do you believe in God?' then he uses *burhan* in the question. If the foreigner is a Christian, and replies, 'I believe in "The Lord of the Universe" ', then the Mongol understands this to mean that the foreigner's *burhan's* personal name is 'The Lord of the Universe'.[6]

Stallybrass and Swan knew that *burhan* meant Buddha when translating the Literary Version, but decided to take the risk of possible confusion. When James Gilmour reminisced about the Selenginsk mission station, he admitted that some Mongols had confused Christianity with just another dimension of their own religion.

Gibbens believes this risk is too high. In a culture now throwing off the shackles of Communism and undergoing a revival of Buddhism, Christianity cannot afford to be mistaken for another form of Buddhism. Granted, *burhan* does mean 'god' or 'deity' in a generic sense (and hence also means 'idol'), but in common use, it means 'The Buddha', and if an alternate can be found, then it should be used. Gibbens believes that the Mongolian phrase 'Lord of the Universe' is the most appropriate. He claims this is indeed a genuine Mongolian phrase, and not a contrived one, having found it in Nyamsuren's 1968 Mongolian-English dictionary. When Gibbens started using this phrase for 'God', one Mongolian said on television: 'The term used is insulting to Mongolians, because it describes a Lord of the Universe who is higher than all the other *burhans* down here; he makes all the *burhans* we worship at this level nothing; he is too high, and the term should not be used.'[7] On that basis, Gibbens used 'The Lord of the Universe' as his word for 'God'.

What about Inner Mongolia?

Critics also claimed that UBS' *Shin Geree* was out of synchrony with *Shin Testament* (the 1952 revision of the Literary Version) which uses *burhan*, and the result would be confusion in Inner Mongolia or among Mongols who have access to *Shin Testament*. Gibbens, in reply, argues that the confusion would be greater in Mongolia proper if in fact there were no immediate distinction between *burhan* in its Buddhist sense and 'God' as the revealed 'Lord of the Universe'. And, although *Shin Testament* has found its way to Mongolia, it is not used widely anyway.

The possibility of confusion in Inner Mongolia is not a valid criticism. The language in Inner Mongolia has dialectical differences and the number of Christians is different. Where the church in Mongolia is now in excess of 6,000,[8] the Mongolian church in Inner Mongolia would number a mere hundred or so.[9] Because of these two major differences, the need to be the same in both places is not so urgent.

Shin Testament has been used in Inner Mongolia since 1953, but in spite of this, the Inner Mongolian church has used the Chinese Bible more than *Shin Testament*. Even so, the Inner Mongolian church has tended to use the Chinese *shen* for God (possibly a Nestorian word originally) rather than *shang di* (the Chinese Protestant word), or the Mongolian *burhan*. Whether *burhan* or 'The Lord of the Universe' is used in the state of Mongolia then is irrelevant to the church in Inner Mongolia.

Nevertheless, Chinese Christians in Inner Mongolia have decided to do a translation of the Bible into the Inner Mongolian dialect, beginning this in 1995. The reason is to try to Mongolise a church that has become somewhat Chinese in appearance. This is part of the Chinese church's endeavour to reach the local Mongols with the gospel.[10] There are many manuscript copies of Mongolian books of the Bible and stories of the Bible that have been hand-copied from the Chinese Bible, but apart from *Shin Testament* — which is not by and large readily accessible to Inner Mongolians — there is nothing in the vernacular for a Mongolian Christian in Inner Mongolia.

This new translation in Inner Mongolia is going to use yet a third word for 'God', namely *tenger*. *Tenger* means 'heavens' or simply 'sky', but in ancient writings (and to a lesser degree even today) has a divine quality to it. Hence Chinggis Khan worshipped *munkh tenger* or 'eternal heaven'. It can be rightly argued that *tenger* has Shamanistic roots, but nevertheless it also has roots back into the fifth century when two Persian monks used it when they translated *Matthew*, *Acts* and *Psalms* into Han, a related language.

Because of cultural and racial persecution from the Chinese communists, the Inner Mongolians closed in on themselves more than those in the Mongolian People's Republic who adopted Soviet culture more readily. Buddhism acted as a social cohesive. As a result *burhan* maintained a stronger Buddhist meaning in Inner Mongolia and is now deemed inappropriate, and *tenger* is the more generic term.

Exploring a holistic Christian vocabulary

In addition to the lack of consensus on the word for 'God', other Mongolian biblical vocabulary is also unfixed. There are further significant differences between *Shin Geree* and *Shin Testament*. Stallybrass and Swan used a number of foreign words and phrases when they were unable to find a Mongolian equivalent. It was because of these that Van Hecken criticises the Literary Version. An example is the use of *baptislacho* for baptism. The Mongols at the mission stations in Buriatia would have known the meaning, but the further away people were from good teaching, the less likely they were to understand foreign words.

Ericksson and Ollen, in the 1952 Revision (that is *Shin Testament*) introduced the idea of 'holy washing' which is close to the term that Gibbens uses, 'wash with water'. Marthinson, one of the linguists on the project, claims that the local people understood this idea better than an introduced word, as the idea of water washing in a religious sense implied entrance into a new sphere of life.[11] Although at times the phrase is a little clumsy to use, the phrase 'wash with water' is widely accepted in the church today in Mongolia.

Another example is the word 'love'. Initially Stallybrass and Swan used the word *jeniklel*, but like 'baptism', people outside the immediate influence of the mission stations did not understand its unique Christian sense as *agape* love, since it carried the sense of filial and erotic love as well. In folklore, the word *jeniklel* was usually used in a base way. The choice of a right word for 'love' among the 1952 Revision team caused much soul-searching and debate. They did eventually agree and changed it to *khayar* which *Shin Geree* also uses. Although *khayar* does not carry with it the unique sense of the Greek word *agape*, it does have the sense of compassion and mercy, which makes it a lot more useable.

At times the debate in Mongolia has reached an impasse. Critics of *Shin Geree* set up a new translation committee in 1994 to work independently on a more literal version, using *burhan* and associated generic terminology. This committee is made up of local and expat. Christians working in Ulaanbaatar. It is called the Mongolian Bible Translation Committee (MBTC), and it published its New Testament in 1996 with the name *Bibil: Shin Geree*. This has been well checked by local Mongol Christians for readability and has had some external moderation. A Japanese academic has independently translated a few books of the New Testament which are now available, and the Witness Lee sect has published a dual column Mongolian-English Cyrillic transcription of the 1952 Revision, called *Shin Gerees*.[12] One or two individual churches have undertaken their own translations of single New Testament books as well. These are all in local Khalka Mongol. Between 1990 and 1996, UBS' *Shin Geree* was the only New Testament available in modern Mongolian. Since 1996 the MBTC version has gained a wide readership. Both these translations are now used in today's Mongolian church.

Individuals or committees?

Gibbens' name has been associated strongly with the UBS translation of *Shin Geree*, and most of the original work was either done by him personally or influenced by him. In this he has not breached any historical precedents. The vernacular versions of Europe were all the work of individuals originally. In China the first translators were all working separately, namely Marshman, Morrison and Gutzlaff. Even in the Mongol language, the original work was dominated by Schmidt, and Stallybrass and Swan worked separately, then compared their translations. At no time has a formal united Mongol translation committee been formed which represents the full spectrum of Christian expression.

Even though translations are often the work of individuals, there comes a time when a review by a committee is needed. This is certainly UBS' policy for all their projects, as it is with Wycliffe Bible Translators. A review committee is usually made up of representatives of the receptor language church, with no expat. missionaries on it. The final draft is either done by or checked solely by native language speakers. There is then rigorous field testing among the common people. UBS has conceded that *Shin Geree* has never had a wide formal review by the Mongolian church, because when it was published in 1990 there were only a handful of Christians. A UBS consultant reflected in 1993: 'We gave *Shin Geree* as good a check as we could, recognising the procedural gaps, and published it. In ten or so years, we will revise in better accord with our principles.'[13]

Any committee translation or review usually builds on a foundation laid by an individual. For example, the Authorised Version (AV or KJV) built on the work of Tyndale. Indeed, there were many versions of the English Bible done between the first translation of Wycliffe, published in 1384, and the AV of 1611. Several revisions of the AV appeared in 1616, 1629, 1638 and later. In the end, approximately 80% of the AV reflected the original work of Tyndale.

Likewise in Mongolia, the MBTC should not ignore either *Shin Geree* or the 1952 *Shin Testament*. The English versions show that translations built on the work of individuals do eventually become acceptable to most people if correct procedures are in place.

Gibbens has promised a revision of the New Testament when the Old Testament is published. Several Old Testament books have already been published individually by UBS in the dynamic-equivalent mode of *Shin Geree*.[14] Now the Old Testament is available, the extra textual additions in *Shin Geree* can be deleted, or shifted to footnotes. Good expository teaching by well-trained Mongol pastors will anchor the New Testament text in the Old Testament.

What is obvious to the casual observer is that the church in Mongolia is growing rapidly, from only a handful of believers in 1990, to a total church attendance on Sundays of over 6,000 nationwide by the end of 1999. This expansion has mostly been on the back of *Shin Geree*. Terminology disputes have not slowed the growth of the church. Granted, all translations have a shelf life and need periodic revision, and Gibbens has promised this for *Shin Geree*. Vocabulary is sanctified over time, and takes on new meaning. Vocabulary issues will best be resolved within a united committee made up solely of Mongol Christians representing the widest possible range of the Mongolian church.

I left Mongolia in August 1996, satisfied that the McTEE was in good hands, and with a working agreement that I was to act now as a consultant to it from offshore, returning three times during 1997. I left Magnai swamped with a fast growing student body.

My first return visit was in March 1997. I had three weeks in which to do a million tasks.

'The new MBTC New Testament has been published. Apparently 10,000 copies sold within the first few months,' Magnai greeted me at the airport.

Work had started already, and we hadn't even left the airport terminal.

'I guess it's a matter of waiting to see what shakes down in the church. I suspect it's the missionaries that get all worked up over biblical terminology. You're a Mongol. What do you think?' I challenged him. 'What translation will the church be using in ten years time?'

'Most churches are using the new MBTC version of the New Testament. One church is still officially using *Shin Geree*. If you look around in church on Sunday, most people are using the new translation. Ten years' time? I don't know. We'll have to wait and see.'

Magnai was typically non-committal. I'd noticed this with other Mongolian colleagues with whom I'd discussed it.

The three weeks were a whirlwind of long hours and late nights. MCTEE had published *Abundant Life* in its sixth and final format. One hundred and thirty-two students had completed the course, and half those went on to train as tutors so they could teach it in their churches and in the countryside. *The Life of Christ*, a six work-book leadership training compendium, was nearly finished.

I called the five office staff together for our final meeting. 'What do you think the priorities should be for the next three months until I return?'

Magnai spoke for everyone. 'We've been discussing this already. We think that we need to do another edition of *Abundant Life*. It's working well with *Shin Geree* terminology, but we think the pendulum is swinging. It's not an either/or situation, but a both/and. We should have two editions, each using the different set of vocabulary, and then review it after say five years.'

I was impressed with their mature solution, but felt overwhelmed with the amount of work ahead. 'It won't be a matter of simply using the find and replace function in the computer. You'll have to retranslate some parts and reformat.'

We tied off the other loose ends and enjoyed together a plate of *buudz*, those ubiquitous little steamed dumplings. Since my early days in Mongolia, I'd become a master of their consumption.

'I thought it would be good to have a camp in the summer when you come back. We could get all the church leaders together and promote the TEE courses. Plus we can ask them about where the terminology issue is at,' said Magnai.

I commended Magnai for his planning and diplomacy. So much of what happened in Mongolia was done by relationships. When the social context was right, then a lot of business could be transacted. I'd learned that 'event' was more important than 'time'.

'And by the way,' I said to Bolormaa, one of the translators, as we said farewell, 'I can actually watch what you're doing here in the office. I can see you from New Zealand, through the computer screen.'

She looked at me in a strange way.

I had left a message on her computer's screen-saver that would show up if the computer was left un-used for more than five minutes.

It said: 'Bolormaa, Hugh's watching you. Get back to work!'

I think she actually may have believed me.

NOTES

1. Personal correspondence of John Gibbens to the author, November 1997.
2. Personal correspondence from Tsering to the author, November 1996.
3. Mongolian Bible Society brochure, 1995.
4. This discussion of the etymology of the word *burhan* is based mainly on the paper of Berthold Laufer, 'Burkhan', *Journal of the American Oriental Society*, 36:4 (1917), pp.390–395.
5. Don Belt, 'The World's Great Lake', *National Geographic*, vol. 181, no.6 (June, 1992) p.23. 'Burhanism' is the name of the modern-day local Shamanism in Buriatia.
6. This is the gist of several conversations that I have had with Mongols. However, a Mongol on the street would not generally ask, 'Do you believe in God?' They would usually ask, 'What religion are you?' A Christian foreigner would probably then reply something like, 'I believe in Jesus', or, 'I am of the Christ-religion.'
7. 'Communists Help Translate the Name for God', *Church Scene* (September 1993).
8. Estimates of the number of Christians in Mongolia today vary tremendously; anything between 2,000 and 10,000. This author did a fairly accurate count with a colleague in the middle of 1994 and came up with the number 3,000. Assuming some growth (which is clearly observable), 6,000 seems a good number to work with for a head count by the end

of 1998. Some estimates put the number in the range of 12,000. What can be easily verified now is that there is a Christian presence in every province, whether it be a Christian family, a cell group or a fully-fledged church.

9. This statistic was relayed to the author personally by a Mongolian-speaking expatriate colleague living and working in Hohot, the provincial capital of China's Inner Mongolia Autonomous Region.

10. One China-watcher has questioned this motivation. If the Chinese church is a TSPM church (the official state church), then 'reaching out to Mongols' may be to bring them into the TSPM church, and thereby control them.

11. Anders W. Marthinson, *op.cit.*, p.76.

12. This in effect makes the text of the 1952 Revision accessible to us in English, and provides an English glimpse into the original text of Stallybrass and Swan. However, it is doubtful if the Mongolian and the English texts in the dual columns are adequate reflections of each others' meaning, as the English text at points reflects Witness Lee theology, eg the use of the word 'mingling'. The transcription was made by a Witness Lee missionary by the name of Kim.

13. Personal interview with a UBS translation consultant, Hong Kong, January 1995.

14. *Job*, *Genesis*, *Esther*, *Ecclesiastes*, *Ruth* and *Proverbs* are all available.

<table>
<tr>
<td>

Chapter

46

</td>
<td>

God's Time for a Nation,
Roots, Shoots and Fruits

'Winter, Spring, Summer, Autumn — four seasons
Companions of the mountains, water, sun and
moon.
Each man taking leave of the old and welcoming
the new-born
Through thousand years without a moment's rest.'

From 'Winter' by D Natsagdorj

</td>
</tr>
</table>

'Are you wintering well?' my friend would ask. The Mongolian seasonal greeting was a grammatical curiosity for an English speaker. In the other seasons the greeting would literally translate, 'Are you Summer-ing well? ' or, 'Are you Spring-ing well? ' or, 'Are you Autumn-ing well?'

'Yes, I'm wintering well,' I would reply. Truth proved to be a bit bendable with my responses. January each year was just the most awful time of winter, and we generally tried to avoid it by going to Hong Kong for a break. The temperature was mainly below -30° celsius, the sun didn't rise before nine o'clock and it set around four o'clock in the afternoon. Urban pollution and heavy traffic had blanketed and compacted the snow to a universal dull grey. Leaking pipes had spread sheets of ice across footpaths and thoroughfares. My breath used to freeze on my eyelashes.

Spring was even worse. The Gobi desert came to greet us more often than not by way of short sharp dust storms injecting fine yellow abrasive sand into eyes, ears, nose and mouth; snow, sleet, hail and sand could bombard you for a painful ten minutes, pinning you to any refuge you were sheltering in, leaving you with a mouthful of grit to grind. Then the storm would pass and the sun would come out as quickly as the storm had come and gone.

The seasons dominate life in Mongolia: the nomadic lifestyle is dependent on their rhythms. The extreme continental climate dictates long cold winters, and short very hot summers. A herd of livestock can be wiped out in one spring gale; poor snowfall means poor spring melt and hence poor summer pasture growth. Good summer rains can yield abundant autumn harvests.

Seasons of the soul

Mongolia is a country that looks to both the past and the future. Since the glory days of empire in the thirteenth century, it has borne the weight of Ming overlords, Manchurian exploitation, feudal poverty and Buddhist theocracy. During the twentieth century, it has emerged from seven decades of Soviet-style Communism until in 1990, when democratic elections created a new environment that brought social and political change. With these changes, the Christian church in Mongolia has sprouted from nothing to a body of thousands of national believers.

Why, after such a long period of spiritual drought, has the church burst into life with such powerful exuberance? Why has it grown so rapidly when in other parts of Buddhist central Asia it has remained unknown or struggled to exist? And what lessons does it offer for today? The answers to these questions, as with so much else in Mongolia, lies in the history and character of this remarkable people. By the end of the twentieth century, the Mongolian worldview had been shaped by four major influences: the veneration of Chinggis Khan, the religions of Shamanism and Tibetan Buddhism, and the secular philosophy of Communism.

The veneration of Chinggis Khan

In the early 1990s public pictures and statues of Lenin were replaced by memorials to Chinggis Khan. Slogans commending the glories of the Communist regime were replaced with the quotes and deeds of Chinggis. Young men and women wore lapel badges with the Great Khan's picture. School textbooks were rewritten; the Soviet (and Western) image of Chinggis as the 'marauding barbarian' was replaced with a vision of Chinggis as 'noble statesman'.

The modern Mongol sees himself in the light of Chinggis Khan. Chinggis is esteemed as a great political figure: the founder of the Mongol nation and the father of its people; the conqueror who established the greatest land empire the world has ever known. Chinggis' military prowess is the object of great pride. When democratic changes opened the door to new paths in 1990, there was much rhetoric about following in the footsteps of Chinggis: 'We were great once, and so we can be great again.'

The glorification of Chinggis Khan during the early 1990s produced a quasi-cult. He is venerated at shrines and held up as a model statesman. Sons, vodka, furs and travel agencies are named after him. His spirit, militant even yet, inspires Mongol youth to assert their Mongolian identity in the face of new forces jostling for priority. During the last decade of the twentieth century Chinggis was reinvented, reinterpreted and revenerated.

The formative dynamics of Shamanism and Tibetan Buddhism

Though Shamanism and Tibetan Buddhism play a huge role in shaping the Mongol worldview, their influence is not exclusive: the Mongol *yasa* enshrines religious tolerance in the national psyche, which finds practical expression in a pragmatic political policy. The khans did not embrace or neglect any one particular religion out of conviction. Religious tolerance simply made it easier to govern the conquered. Such tolerance was conditional, however, on absolute obedience to the khan, to whom politics and religion were distinctly separate.

The legacy of the *yasa* has influenced Mongolian religious

policy and worldview into the twentieth century. The post-Communist constitution of 1992, as interpreted in the Law of the Relationship of Church and State (November 1993) endorses three official state religions: Shamanism, Tibetan Buddhism and Islam, and ensures freedom of religious expression for Mongolia's citizens. The apparent tolerance implied by this law is perhaps better thought of as 'indifference'. As in the *yasa* of Chinggis, one's religion is seen to be inconsequential to the welfare of the state, so long as the state's citizens are obedient to the law. The law endorses three religions practised by the majority of Mongols; the law's intent was descriptive rather than prescriptive.

If Shamanism is the core belief system in the Mongol worldview by the end of the twentieth century, it has been overlaid in significant ways by the Buddhism which Mongols imported from Tibet. Outwardly, Tibetan Buddhism might seem to be the dominant partner. Tourists walking the streets of Ulaanbaatar today cannot help noticing Gandan monastery and its temple on the hill in the western sector of the city. In the provinces they might visit reopened monasteries and watch novices being trained; this all encouraged by periodic visits of the fourteenth Dalai Lama. On the surface, it seems that Tibetan Buddhism has been the main filter through which Mongols interpret their world.

Inwardly, however, Mongols still view Tibetan Buddhism as a foreign religion. Some are adamant that Buddhism was an import and have been quick to point out Tibetan words in the language as foreign words. For formal rites of passage many go to a Tibetan Buddhist temple, but the normal daily rhythms of life might well be dominated by Shamanistic practices. The local Buddhist lama may be consulted about the most auspicious day for a wedding, but the first ladle full of tea is flicked with the fourth finger to the four points of the compass as an offering to *tenger*, the ancient sky-god whom Chinggis worshiped.

A veneer of Communism

To add to this religious mixture, Soviet Communism has also influenced the Mongol worldview, although not pervasively. Atheistic Communism heavily suppressed all religion with purges in the 1930s, and the 700 odd Tibetan Buddhist monasteries in Mongolia were either levelled or turned into museums. Monks were killed or secularised while the nomads were organised into production units. The state took over everything and owned everything.

Communism as a worldview has now given way to a pragmatic atheism among the Mongols. It has bred a class of civil servants who in today's Mongolia are neither Shamanist nor Tibetan Buddhist. They were disillusioned that the Communist state to which they had given their lives, and which had such high ideals, collapsed overnight in 1990. The new generation of young people know nothing of either ancient Shamanism or Tibetan Buddhism. The result is a religious void in society. Older Mongols still interpret their world through the 'blue spectacles' of the ancient sky-god-based Shamanism, while a remnant of priests do so through the 'yellow spectacles' of Tibetan Buddhism (the Buddhist sect in Mongolia is the Yellow sect).

Changing economic fortunes from 1990 have brought new challenges to the Mongols: new television programmes, easier access to the Internet, new religions and cults arriving at the borders, and the ever-tempting lure of materialism. With an emerging worldview dominated by market reform and profit-driven consumerism, the almighty dollar has become a key frame of reference for the new entrepreneurial Mongols who have been importing all sorts of goods from China, Russia, and more recently from Japan and Korea. The early 1990s witnessed huge social upheaval, accentuated by the collapse of the state welfare system. Domestic violence, unemployment and underemployment, medical and nutritional mismanagement, and a poor work ethic have all contributed to social needs that are

overwhelming. Inflation, privatisation and market reforms
have left thousands poorer, indebted, abused and marginalised.

Birth of the Modern Mongolian church

Between 1990 and 1993, Mongolia experienced immense
changes. Democratic elections overthrew the Communist
Mongolian People's Revolutionary Party (MPRP), and the country went through two heady years of democratic reform. The
constitution was rewritten, there was talk of the country
becoming an Asian economic tiger, the Soviets began leaving,
and Mongolia threw its doors open to the outside world. A
check came with the re-election of a restructured MPRP in 1992,
but democratic and open-market reforms had come to stay.

These changes were not as sudden as they seemed. During
the mid-to-late 1980s reform had been in the air. Some
Christians had visited the Mongolian People's Republic on
tourist visas, praying for the day when it would open. Internal
restlessness grew and news of the changes in Soviet Europe
trickled back. A youthful groundswell, inspired by the rock
band *Honk* ('The Bell') picked up momentum, and it is only by
the grace of God and the constraint and wisdom of the nation's
leaders that Ulaanbaatar did not have a Tiananmen Square-like
incident in 1990.[1]

In these first three years, two tools were available for evangelisation: the United Bible Societies New Testament (*Shin
Geree*), and a film about the life of Jesus produced by Campus
Crusade for Christ, simply called *Jesus*. Both were used extensively throughout Mongolia. Groups of Mongolian Christians
would go to a provincial centre, show the *Jesus* film either out-
doors or in the local cinema, preach, sell *Shin Geree* (or *Luke's
Gospel*) and give an appeal for conversion. Such endeavours
would often bring a housegroup together and so a church
would be planted. Video editions of *Jesus* soon became available and continued to be used in homes and smaller venues.
The effect of the dual use of the *Jesus* film and the New

Testament *Shin Geree* cannot be underestimated: they were both distributed widely and they have been instrumental in hundreds of Mongolians coming to know Christ personally.

Shin Geree and the *Jesus* film spoke directly to a new generation of Mongolian youth who witnessed the collapse of Communism and for whom the Tibetan Buddhism of their parents and the Shamanism of their grandparents were unattractive, powerless and irrelevant. The first five years of Mongolian church growth was among the fourteen to twenty-five-year-old age group, and largely among girls. Nevertheless, by the mid 1990s this disparity had started to even out, with more young men and older people in the churches, often helped by specialist homegroups.

From a missions strategy perspective, Mongolia was a clean slate in 1990; a test-tube of opportunities. The country had no recent history of missions, no Western colonial history, no established church, no recognisable Christians, and no Bible. It was a grand opportunity to get evangelistic strategies right. It was also a tempting venue for experiments. It is significant that the two key evangelistic tools in the early days were interdenominational UBS' New Testament and the *Jesus* film. The expatriate Christians of the 1990s and the Mongolian Christians were all keen to evangelise Mongolia as quickly and effectively as possible. It was no surprise that the period from 1990 to 1993 saw a heady flurry of activity.

State tolerance or persecution?

In December 1993, when local papers published the text of the new 'Law on the Relationship of Church and State', expatriate Christians reacted quickly, claiming that it discriminated against Christianity on the grounds that it named Tibetan Buddhism, Shamanism and Islam (the third a concession to the Khazak minority) as Mongolia's official state religions. It declared Tibetan Buddhism the predominant religion which would receive state patronage. The implication was that to be a genuine Mongol, one was naturally a Buddhist.

This law was inevitable. Naming Tibetan Buddhism as the state religion was merely describing what already was, and conceding two other official religions reflected the indifference embedded in the ancient *yasa*. That Christian numbers had been growing so quickly between 1991 and 1993 was certainly a factor in its formulation. The timing of the law implied this, although nowhere was it stated explicitly.

The foreign media and the embassies showed immediate and intense concern over the new law. United Nations resolutions on freedom of religion were discussed, and eventually a small consortium of democrats and Christians took the government to the constitutional court, on the grounds that parts of the law were unconstitutional. The constitutional court sent the law back to parliament, ordering three clauses to be rescinded. In this revised version, the law allowed public preaching and witness, but still all *sums* (religious entities: churches, temples, mosques) had to be registered. No *sum* was allowed to meet in state-owned halls, and the state would control the number of clergy in any religion. The most immediate problem for Christian churches was that there were no alternative meeting places as private ownership laws had not yet been introduced, and consequently there were no alternative venues other than state or city-owned halls in which to meet.

Article 4.2 of the law put a high place on the unity of the Mongol people, their historical and cultural traditions and civilisation. Legislators saw post-1990 Christianity as a threat to this and that is partly why Tibetan Buddhism was reaffirmed as the official Mongolian religion. The challenge to the Christian church was to present Christ to the Mongolian people in Mongolian ways. Eventually, Christians settled down to wait and see what the outcome would be. Singapore and Hong Kong had similar laws regulating church-state relationships, and Christian churches there seemed to do fine.

Lessons learned in the first decade: 1990–1999

Among all the Tibetan Buddhist people groups in central Asia, the response of the Mongols to the gospel has been a pleasant reprieve in a hard-fought spiritual battle. In some ways, the people of Mongolia are different from other Tibetan Buddhist peoples; an underlying Shamanism, recent Communism, the legacy of Chinggis, political independence. In other ways, they are very similar. How can we account for the seemingly sudden success of Christianity? Are there lessons from Mongolia which apply to other parts of Tibetan-Buddhist central Asia?

As we think about these questions, first place must be given to the sovereignty of God in the birth of the church in Mongolia. It was God's time for Mongolia and Christians could only stand back, watch God at work, and rejoice. It was in fact a rebirth, considering that Christianity had a significant influence during the imperial era. Nevertheless, there were at least four factors vital to the church's rapid growth. These were:

- an accessible, easily readable translation of the New Testament;
- co-operation among Christians, and between Christians and the government;
- a focus on church planting;
- an emphasis on leadership training.

The New Testament: an update

In God's timing, there was a colloquial Khalka-Mongol version of the New Testament available as soon as Mongolia opened in 1990. Moreover, almost everyone in Mongolia was literate and could read it. Here was something new to Mongolia, well presented and well distributed: curiosity drew many to read it. The New Testament had a context; it was usually coupled with the *Jesus* film and good preaching. Any terminology questions were explained or discussed in the context of a worshipping Christian community.

Precedents from other countries, especially China, would suggest that the terminology debate might never be resolved, and that Christians will settle down to accept a number of different terms. However, with such a small population, and with a homogenous ethnic make-up of mainly Khalka Mongols, one hopes that resolution of the problem should be possible. In the providence of God, disputes over terminology do not slow the growth of the church.

UBS intervened decisively in Mongolia in 1999, believing the Mongolian Bible Society had been unable to demonstrate that it serves the interests of the whole church. Up to then it had been 'patient and understanding' in its dealings with the society. UBS has now 'terminated the current arrangements for the translation of the Mongolian Bible', and disbanded the Advisory Committee of the Mongolian Bible Society. Subsequently it has invited all the Christian churches and organisations in Mongolia to reform the committee so that it is broad-based and representative. UBS wants to recommence the translation work (major sections of the Old Testament need doing, as well as a revision of the New Testament) under a newly-formed translation committee, conforming more closely to international guidelines. At the right time, under the supervision of the new Advisory Committee, the Mongolian Bible Society 'will reopen according to UBS guidelines'.[2]

The Mongolian Bible Translation Committee which published its New Testament in 1996 (using the more generic set of vocabulary), has said that it will publish a full Bible under external moderation by the end of 2000.

A stronger witness through co-operation

With a clean missiological slate before them, it was tempting for expatriate Christians to act independently in Mongolia. Some did so, but most realised the benefits of working together. There was an encouraging amount of grass-roots co-operation, vision sharing, and praying together. Formal and informal partnerships gave rise to various aid and development projects, an international church and an international school, the Bible Training Centre, and the Mongolian Centre for Theological Education by Extension. Joint planning also resulted in an annual ministry consultation, city-wide evangelistic campaigns, a combined 'March for Jesus' through the streets of Ulaanbaatar, music-writing workshops, combined worship services, joint Easter and Christmas celebrations, and united legal efforts in response to the 1993 Law on the Relationship of Church and State. A single project in the countryside might feature an evangelistic team from one of the Ulaanbaatar churches, donated woollen clothing from a Christian aid agency, and a resident foreign teacher from yet another international Christian agency.

There was co-operation with the government, too. Christian agencies provided English teachers, vets, teacher trainers, agriculturists, doctors, aid-workers, financial consultants and environmental specialists either under direct contract to government departments or in partnership with inter-agency government projects. Christians promoted the spiritual welfare of the nation, but also witnessed to the love of Christ by providing vital services for the physical welfare of Mongolia. In this way Christians gained credibility with the government.

Joint work by Protestant, Catholic and Orthodox Christians was a frontier of partnership that was still being explored at the end of the 1990s. Exactly what form it would eventually take was not clear. Mongols have had exposure to Orthodox Christianity due to the large numbers of Russians who lived in the country during the Communist era. The Catholic order of CICM gained a presence in Mongolia due to an invitation by past-president Ochirbat for the Vatican to establish a papal embassy in the country. In the late 1990s the CICM had its own building, a viable congregation and was involved in much charity work in Ulaanbaatar. The Russian Orthodox Church returned to Ulaanbaatar as well, celebrating its first communion service on 16 March 1997 having been absent since 1931.

Church planting: a key strategy

Church planting was the major emphasis of the expatriate Christians who entered Mongolia in the 1990s. With a population of only 2.5 million, some saw the possibility of winning the whole nation for Christ, and many Mongol Christians believed this was attainable. Even though foreign Christians made a genuine effort to learn the language, it was the Mongols themselves who kept the momentum for the evangelisation of their own people. And who better to do it? Some churches set about praying for housegroups in particular stair-wells, then buildings. They went on systematically to evangelise housing estates, suburbs and whole towns.

In the summers, teams of Mongol Christians went out from Ulaanbaatar and travelled to the provinces to preach, distribute literature and show the *Jesus* film. The teams would often establish a housegroup, then stay on to teach the new believers for a number of weeks.

After a few months, emerging leaders would be brought to the capital for further training, or Mongolian Bible teachers would be sent to care for the new housegroup. Emerging daughter churches were encouraged to attend a winter and/or summer camp of the mother church in or near Ulaanbaatar for a week. Leaders were identified and given further training. The church I was involved with planted nineteen daughter churches before its own sixth anniversary: in November 1998, our first daughter church planted a 'grand-daughter' church.

Expatriate Christians wisely taught the great commission right from day one of preaching the gospel. The Mongolian church grew up familiar with its responsibility to reach out to its own country, and to the nations of the world. Mongolian evangelistic teams had gone to Buriatia (in Russia) and Hohot (in Chinese Inner Mongolia) by 1996. Within Mongolia itself, Mongols began to evangelise the Khazaks, the Chinese and the residual Russian population.

The key to the future: leadership training

With Mongols quite capable of evangelising their own country, expatriate Christians found themselves quickly (and rightly) working behind the scenes in a supporting role. Granted, 1990–1993 saw expatriates doing the evangelising, the organising and the church planting. But by 1995 the church was taking on a Mongolian face and fewer foreigners were to be seen 'up front'. The Law of the Relationship of Church and State demanded a lower profile for foreign Christians. Expatriate Christians found their place in teaching and training the emerging Mongolian pastors, evangelists and church planters. The 1990s saw a steady retreat of expatriate Christians to this second row.

Leadership training is now a high priority for mission in Mongolia, and this takes place on several levels. Churches train their own people: Sunday school teachers, home group leaders and the like. Alongside this, the Bible Training Centre, an interchurch and inter-agency Bible college, now offers high quality, in-country leadership training. The Mongolian Centre for Theological Education by Extension, started in 1995, provides distance learning courses to pastors who can't come into Ulaanbaatar for training. A number of Mongol leaders have won scholarships to seminaries and Bible colleges in America, Singapore, Australia and Europe.

Others have been called to produce resources for the church. A number of translation and research projects have been started to equip pastors with books in Mongolian so that there would be no need for them to learn other Asian or even European languages to use Bible references or to read Christian literature.

Witness among university and polytechnic students has potential for providing future church leaders. Several Ulaanbaatar churches have made it a priority to have student homegroups from as early as 1992, but recently the International Fellowship of Evangelical Students (IFES) has commenced student work in the Mongolian State University in Ulaanbaatar. IFES puts an emphasis on students being witnesses to students, and university Christian groups being led by students themselves; this means that a vital form of trans-denominational and non-sectarian leadership may well emerge.

The Mongolian church at the close of the century

At the beginning of the twenty-first century, Mongolian Christians face three long-term challenges. The first of these is to understand the Mongol Christian church's place in history, right back to the planting of the Nestorian Church. Christianity in effect pre-dates Tibetan Buddhism among the Mongols, and it can be argued historically that Christianity, especially Asian (as opposed to Western) Christianity has a legitimate place in Mongolia today. Christian Mongols also need to think clearly about their own culture, and experiment with ways of expressing Christian truth and worship in Mongolian ways.

A second challenge is the need to play a strategic role in nation building. In the late 1990s Mongolia began 'opening the books' on seventy years of Communism. Atrocities, missing persons, purges and mismanagement were starting to be addressed. There is now a great opportunity for Mongolian Christians to preach, demonstrate and lead the nation in acts of reconciliation, which would bring honour to Christ and his church. With the precedent for toleration set down by Chinggis in the *yasa*, the Mongolian church has every right to be in the forefront of political and social change.

The third challenge is that of Tibetan Buddhism. Social changes of the 1990s have led to a renaissance of Tibetan Buddhism in Mongolia as in other parts of the Tibetan Buddhist world, due to the renewed freedom to express again the religion of pre-Communist Mongolia. Idols have been rebuilt, novices recruited, lamas have begun writing in the newspapers, and once again are dictating the rhythms of family and national life. The Mongolian church is now aware of and seeking to address the great spiritual struggle ahead of it. It is a church reborn on solid historical precedents in a time when the nation has been at a critical turning point. In God's timing, and in his grace, Mongolia's modern Christian church will continue to bear a solid witness to Christ in the nation and graciously continue to live out the power and truth of the gospel.

I looked up at the huge statue of the Mongolian poet Natsagdorj, near the entrance to the children's park in downtown Ulaanbaatar. In his brief life, brought to a close by an untimely death in his early thirties, Natsagdorj contributed a wealth of wonderful poetry to Mongolian culture.

I pondered a poem we'd studied in class that day, simply called 'Winter', and thought of the metaphor of the seasons. Christian witness had gone through a full cycle of over a thousand years. Spring, summer, autumn. The last seventy years of Communism had been a severe winter. Now it was spring again: new shoots are pushing up through the desert and the steppe. Roots are pushing down to the water. Fruit is appearing. There are now Christians in every province of Mongolia. Mongolia is being reclaimed for Christ, steppe by step.

'Each...taking leave of the old, and welcoming the new-born, through thousand years, without a moment's rest.'

NOTES
1. In June 1989, thousands of Chinese youth gathered in Beijing's Tiananmen Square to demonstrate in favor of political reform. The Chinese army suppressed the demonstrators on 4 June 1989; this was the so-called Tiananmen Square Incident. A similar demonstration by Mongolians occurred in 1990 in Ulaanbaatar's Sukhbaatar Square. The demonstrations were allowed to continue and were not suppressed by the army.
2. Personal correspondence to the author from a UBS consultant to Mongolia, August 1999.

Appendix 1

Christian missions working among
the Mongols up to 1990

American Board of Commissioners for Foreign Missions (ABCFM)

Entered China 1830. Also known as 'The American Board of Mission' or simply 'The American Board'. Kalgan, on the China-Mongol border, was the third mission station, staffed by John T. Gulick and his wife from 1865. By 1906, in spite of a setback due to the Boxer uprising of 1900, the ABCFM had 9,573 communicants and 17,242 adherents. Although mainly Chinese, some were Mongols. In 1886 James Gilmour felt the ABCFM was so well established in Kalgan with work among the Mongols of the steppe that he was freer to set up work among the settled Mongols in Eastern Mongolia.

Brethren

Alternatively called 'Open Brethren', 'Plymouth Brethren' or 'Unconnected Workers'. Began in 1897 (or possibly 1887) in Pakou, 400 Li north of the Great Wall on the steppe by Mr Stephens. Brethren work is the oldest in Inner Mongolia. The Brethren in Jehol worked among the Djosotu and Djouda Mongol banners. In 1929, the Brethren had five stations and thirty-two missionaries in Inner Mongolia. Japanese missionaries took over the work of the Brethren from 1930s. Work in Jehol originally started by the London Missionary Society (Gilmour and others) was then transferred to the Irish Presbyterian Mission and, in 1912, to Brethren Assemblies.

British and Foreign Bible Society (BFBS)

Founded in 1804 to 'encourage the wider circulation of the Holy Scriptures without note or comment'. Came to China in 1843, and had a sub-agency at Kalgan. Huge numbers of Mongol Scriptures were distributed by the BFBS from Kalgan; for example, 10,600 Gospels between 1902 and 1906. In 1928, colporteurs distributed 176,000 books from Kalgan, 'mostly portions in Mongolian'. Mongolian Scriptures were in demand as far west as Xinjiang. By 1929 the total number of Scriptures and portions distributed by BFBS in all central Asian languages was 3,951,809. Frans Larson worked for BFBS from Kalgan for about ten years (1903–1913) then Anton Almblad took over from him in 1913.

China Inland Mission (CIM)
In 1865 Hudson Taylor started to pray for 'twenty-four skilful, willing workers' so he could assign two to each of the eleven provinces of China, with two for Mongolia. Lanchow station (capital of Gansu province, Xining and Ninghsia were opened in 1885 'in the hope of reaching Tibetans and Mongols as well as Chinese'. Annie Taylor, Cecil Polhill and the Torjesens of Hequ were all CIM missionaries to the Mongols.

China Mennonite Mission Society
With headquarters in Kansas, USA, in 1922 it had forty-two missionaries in seven stations and thirty-two outstations in China. Some of these were in Honan and three missionaries were in Inner Mongolia.

Christian and Missionary Alliance (CMA)
Founded by A.B. Simpson (1845–1919). In 1896 three large parties of Swedes from the USA arrived (total 'about sixty'). Their field was 'entirely beyond the Great Wall of China and comprised the northern part of Shansi and the eastern plain of Mongolia', using Kalgan as base for work done 'as far as to Urga'. CMA had sixteen mission stations strategically placed along the Great Wall to reach the Mongols of the steppe. Frans Larson was a CMA missionary. Major setbacks during the Boxer uprising of 1900. Twenty-one adults and twelve children were martyred; ten adults and six children escaped north over the Gobi desert, and after two months reached the trans-Siberian railway, which took them back to Europe. After the Boxer uprising the CMA work was taken over by the Scandinavian Alliance Mission.

Christian Workers' Mission (CWM)
An indigenous Chinese mission. In July 1954 at a meeting in Tientsin, they reported on Chinese evangelists who were working among the Mongols of Inner Mongolia. These Chinese evangelists travelled widely on the steppe, and saw several conversions among the Mongol nomads. In 1955 evangelistic meetings run by Chinese evangelists

were held in Hohot, the provincial capital, where a 'small-scale revival' broke out among the Mongols.

Congregatio Immaculati Cordis Mariae (CICM)
The Congregation of the Immaculate Heart of Mary. Also known as the Scheut Fathers. A Catholic Belgian order. Founded some time between 1860 and 1863 at Scheutveld on the outskirts of Brussels by Théophile Verbist who arrived in China in 1865. Verbist and four others went to China to take over the work of the Lazarists. It incorporated the ministry of the three Catholic vicariates of Mongolia. Between 1865 and 1887, CICM sent seventy-four Catholic fathers to work among the Chinese and Mongols on the Mongol steppe, centred at Hsi-wan-tzu. By 1913 there were 169 Scheut Fathers in China, including Inner Mongolia, Gansu and Xinjiang. Boro Balghasu, Hohot and Ulan Börügh are all Mongol centres where CICM work occurred. Main focus of Mongol work remained in the Ordos region. The CICM mission, along with Mongol Christians (including ordained priests), suffered heavy losses during the Boxer uprising of 1900. The Boro Balghasu mission station was totally destroyed in 1900, along with all the churches of south Ordos. Urga established as an ecclesiastical area in 1922, but not staffed until 1990. The Catholic Centre in Ulaanbaatar opened in May 1996.

Congregation of the Daughters of Mary and Joseph (CDMJ)
A Dutch Catholic order. 'The vicariate apostolic of Eastern Mongolia received its first European sisters, members of CDMJ' in 1923.

Council for World Mission
Current name for the London Missionary Society.

Danish Lutheran Mission
Commenced work in China in 1896, with work in Manchuria among the Mongols.

Dominicans
Catholic order formed in 1216, also called the Order of Brothers Preachers. These were itinerant preachers, with no monasteries. Some Dominicans were involved in the European mission to the Mongols

during the thirteenth century, including a Nicholas, who accompanied John of Montecorvino to Yuan China.

Evangelical East Asia Mission (EEAM).
Current name for the Swedish Mongol Mission.

Finnish Missionary Society (Finska Missions — Salskapet)
Founded in 1859, and from 1898 decided to work in Manchuria and Mongolia. Circumstances prevented this dream coming true due to the Russian usurpation of Manchuria, so work was initiated in China from 1901.

Franciscans
Catholic order founded by St Francis in 1209, also called the Order of Brothers Minor (or Lesser). Had no monasteries, and were itinerant preachers. The Franciscans were instrumental in carrying the correspondence between the Pope and the Khans during the thirteenth century. John of Montecorvino, long-time resident in Da-tu, was an Italian Franciscan. Rome created three vicariates at the end of thirteenth and early fourteenth centuries for the Franciscans to work in, but these mainly remained paper vicariates: Northern Tartary (includes eastern Turkistan), Eastern Tartary and Cathay established in 1320 (still under Mongol rule). The greatest Franciscan impact was felt in the Crimea and then with the conversion of Tokhtai Khan of the Golden Horde in Russia (r. 1291–1312).

Franciscan Sisters of Mary
Six sisters arrived in 1898 for Hsi-wan-tzu to look after the Holy Childhood day school and boarding-school girls. Hsi-wan-tzu was a large Catholic centre in Mongol territory.

Irish Presbyterian Mission of Manchuria (IPMM)
The LMS Mongol mission was handed over to the IPMM in 1901. This was after years of little fruit through Gilmour and the Buriatia mission. In 1906, IPMM formed the Manchurian Missionary Society with its aim 'to send Chinese missionaries to the unoccupied parts of the province (ie Manchuria), to Mongolia and to other peoples lying on the frontier'. Some success among the Mongols of Jehol was achieved,

although the Brethren assembly missionaries were invited to take over the work of the IPMM in 1912.

Lazarists
A Catholic order, also known as the Congregation of the Mission. Assigned to China by the papacy in 1783, after the Jesuits were suppressed in 1773. In 1844 the Pope assigns an 'Apostolic Vicariate of Mongolia', established to care for the Christians driven into Mongolia from Beijing by the persecutions of the emperor Kia-king. Abandoned their Beijing centre for Hsi-wan-tzu in 1834. Huc and Gabet were both Lazarists commissioned to explore the extent of the vicariate. Lazarists eventually had stations in Eastern Mongolia, Tumat and among the Ordos Mongols. For more than a hundred years, they were the only Christians working among the Ordos Mongols, involved in religious activities as well as research and publication on scientific and cultural aspects. Father Mostaert is credited as instrumental in forming Mongolian studies into a modern science. In 1864 the Lazarists give the vicariate to the CICM.

London Missionary Society (LMS)
Founded in September 1795, with an expressed aim of being interdenominational. First Protestant mission society to enter China, from 1807. Mission to the Mongols began in 1817 among the Buriat Mongols. Stallybrass, Swan, Yuille, Gilmour and Cochrane are all LMS missionaries to the Mongols, the last focusing on the sedentary Mongols of Chihli. Currently called the Council for World Mission.

Moravians (United Brethren)
First Protestant work among the Mongols was done by the German Moravians with the Kalmuck Mongols, based at Sarepta, on the Volga River, Russia, during the eighteenth century. From 1853 a mission to the Mongols was attempted, initially aiming to penetrate Mongolia from the north (Buriatia) but eventually settling among the Tibetans on the Indian border in the south. Pagel, Hyde and Jaeschcke are Moravian missionaries associated with the Tibetan church in Ladakh. In 1892 Sprague and Roberts of the ABCFM invited the Moravians to join in the Mongolian work in Kalgan due to the departure of Gilmour, but this didn't eventuate.

Nestorians

A Christian sect within the umbrella of Eastern Orthodoxy. Nestorianism is traditionally shunned by conventional church historians as a heresy condemned at the Council of Ephesus in the fifth century. Renowned as traders and travellers, being the first Christians to China in the seventh century. Since the discovery of the Hsian fu stone, gravestones and parchments throughout central Asia, opinion has become much more conciliatory to the Nestorians, with the general weight of opinion acknowledging their significant integration of the gospel into the central Asian *milieu*.

Norwegian Alliance

Probably the Norwegian Lutheran Mission and the Norwegian Missionary Society working together. The Norwegian Alliance Mission had a hospital at Kalgan during the late nineteenth century.

Pentecostal Mission

By 1907 a number of men and women in China were simply known as 'Pentecostal missionaries' working in Mongolia, Chihli and elsewhere. Pentecostal mission work was centred at Chang-peh, Inner Mongolia. The Assemblies of God were in Inner Mongolia from 1905, working in Chahar. The Canadian Pentecostal Mission also worked in Inner Mongolia in the first half of the twentieth century.

Russian Bible Society (RBS)

Founded with the sanction of Tsar Alexander during the Napoleonic wars. It was responsible for the Mongolian translation of the Bible, in liaison with the LMS missionaries in Buriatia.

Russian Orthodox Mission to China

The first Mongol-Russian school opened at the Voznesensky monastery in 1725 near Irkutsk; lasted fifteen years. 'This was the first school in Eastern Siberia where translators in Mongolian were trained, as well as Christian missionaries for the Mongolian and Buriat population'. Had its main centre in north-east Beijing near the Buddhist temple Yong-he-gong between 1901 and 1914, initially producing literature. By the end of 1914, the mission had thirty-two centres in Chihli, Hupeh, Honan, Kiangsu and Mongolia with 500 pupils in its schools.

Scandinavian Alliance Mission in Mongolia (SAMM)

Now known as The Evangelical Alliance Mission, or TEAM. Initially based in Chicago, among Scandinavian immigrants (sometimes called the Scandinavian Mission of Chicago). David Stenberg of SAMM entered Mongolia in 1895; joined by Carl Suber in 1896, and in 1897 by Hilda and Clara Anderson, Hannah Lund and N.J. Friedstrom. Experimented with farm colonies among the Mongols of Ordos. Personnel also based in Kalgan. Suffered a huge toll during the Boxer uprising of 1900. Gunzel and other TEAM missionaries were involved in the 1952 revision of the LMS' 1840 Mongol Bible translation. No TEAM missionaries left in Mongolia and China in 1950 due to the rise of Communism.

Seventh Day Adventists (SDA)

Entered China in 1888, and had a station in Kalgan with a printing press where Mongolian tracts and Scripture portions were printed.

Society of Jesus (Jesuits)

Mongolia and Tibet were brought under the suzerainty of Manchus in the seventeenth and eighteenth centuries, and it was Jesuit fathers who accompanied Emperor K'ang-hi on his campaigns in Mongolia, assisting him to map Mongolia. Jesuits Ricci and Aleni's Chinese works were possibly translated into Mongolian. Baptisms were reported in Mongolia during the reign of Ch'ien Lung (Qian Long), who came to ascendancy in 1736, probably due to Jesuit influence. The Jesuits were suppressed by the papacy in 1773, and were replaced in China by the Lazarists.

Soeurs Chanoinesses de S Augustin

A Catholic Belgian order, which in 1923 did some work in Western Mongolia.

Swedish Alliance Mission (SAM)

In 1900 a branch of the Scandinavian China Missionary Alliance (HQ in Chicago) was formed in Sweden taking the name of the Scandinavian Alliance Mission. In 1913 it changed its name to the Swedish Alliance Mission (Svenska Alliansmissionen). Worked in Shansi province north of the Great Wall and in Inner Mongolia (Sui yuan and Chahar districts), in association with the CIM. Most of the land was owned by Mongol princes to whom taxes were paid by SAM for mission centres.

Swedish Baptist Mission (Sallskapet Svenska Baptist Missionen)
Founded 1889, and entered China in 1892. In 1899, the Reverend and Mrs John H. Swordson joined the SBM after serving in Mongolia with the CMA.

Swedish Free Mission (SFM)
Arne Nordmark of the SFM devoted himself entirely to the Mongols from 1944, opening a station at Hwangyuan, near Sining. The SFM also had another outstation north of Hwangyuan on the Mongol steppe. Both stations were shut down by 1955.

Swedish Holiness Mission/Union (SHM)
The SHM possibly had some work among the Mongols near Kalgan in the early 1900s. Worked in Shansi province with some contact with Mongols.

Swedish Mongol Mission (SMM)
Known today as the Evangelical East Asia Mission (EEAM). First attempts to reach the Mongols were by the Eneroths in Chuguchak, Xinjiang, accessible by the Russian railway. Extensive and most successful Mongol work in four different centres in Inner Mongolia and also a dispensary in Urga until 1924. The SMM was the largest Protestant mission agency to work among the Mongols during the twentieth century. The work in Hallon-us started from 1899, then Hatin Sum, Golltjaggan and Doyen. Dr Erickson, located at Hatin Sum, and Dr Ollén at Golltjaggan did extensive medical work among the steppe Mongols. Responsible for the first genuine sustainable Mongol church. SMM missionaries Anders Marthinson and Gerda Ollén were involved in the 1952 Bible revision. By 1950 the SMM had left Mongolia and China and continued work with Mongols in Taiwan and Hong Kong, with some missionaries relocated to Japan.

The Evangelical Alliance Mission (TEAM)
See Scandinavian Alliance Mission (SAMM).

Tientsin and Shanghai Mission

The Reverend and Mrs J. Woodberry started work in Tientsin from 1895 among English-speaking Chinese mainly from the medical and naval colleges and Tientsin University. Evangelism was done solely by Chinese; evangelists and colporteurs were assigned to the eighteen provinces of China and also one to Mongolia.

Appendix 2

A Mongol Christian Timeline

Mongol history	Date	Christian history	Christian period
	650	635: Nestorianism	**Pre-empire:**
	700	arrives in central Asia	period of contact
	750		
	800		
	850		
	900		
	950		
	1000	1007–1020 Conversion	
	1050	of the Kerait to	
	1100	Nestorianism	
	1150		
1206: Temujin	1200		
ordained	1250	1245: Introduction of	**Empire:**
Chinggis Khan	1300	Catholicism with	period of
1335: Il-Khanate	1350	Carpini's mission	diplomacy
ends	1400	1368: Christianity	**Post-empire:**
1368: Mongol-Yuan	1450	disappears with the	period of neglect
dynasty ends	1500	fall of the Yuan	
	1550		
	1600		
	1650		
	1700		
	1750	1765: Moravian	**Pre-modern:**
	1800	mission among the	period of
	1850	Kalmucks	rediscovery
1911: Independence	1900		
from China	1950		
1924: MPR founded	2000	1991: Rebirth of	**Modern:**
1990: Elections in		modern Mongolian	period of
MPR		church	establishment

Appendix 3

Where's Where

Baghdad   Centre for Nestorianism during its height, between the eighth and thirteenth centuries. Residence of the Nestorian Catholicos. Capital of the Saracen Empire. Hulegu, first of the Il-Khans, sacked Baghdad in February 1258, but spared the Christians due to the advocacy of his Christian wife, Dokuz-hatan.

Boro Balghasu   Also Porobalgason. A village in the south Ordos region in the great loop of the Yellow River. Location of the first CICM mission station from 1874. Became a 'flourishing Mongolian Christian community'. Munkh-jargal, the first Catholic Mongolian priest was from Boro Balghasu. The Mongolist Father Antoine Mostaert of CICM was based here.

Buriatia   The homelands of the Buriat Mongols, north of the modern state of Mongolia, in southern Siberia. Ulan-ude is the modern capital. The LMS mission of 1817–1840 was located in Buriatia.

Chahar   District. Also spelt Chakhar. Inner Mongolia. The Swedish Alliance Mission worked in Chahar from 1913. The land was owned by Mongolian princes to whom mission societies paid taxes. Protestant mission work among the Mongols enjoyed some success in Chahar as the Mongol princes were not heavy handed and the Mongols were less migratory.

Ch'ang-an   Capital of the T'ang dynasty from AD 618. Modern Xi'an, Shansi province of China. Also Xian, X'ian, Chang-an, Hsian-fu. Chinese workmen discovered the Nestorian Stone in Ch'ang-an in 1625, which records the arrival of the Nestorians from AD 635. Biggest and most prosperous city in the world during the T'ang dynasty. Population 2 million with about 5,000 resident foreigners, including Nestorians, Manichaeans, Zoroastrians, Hindus and Jews. All were allowed to build their own religions buildings. Travellers through the city included Turks, Iranians, Arabs, Sogdians, Mongolians,

Armenians, Indians, Koreans, Malays and Japanese. SAMM had its headquarters in Xian from the late 1800s. In 1907 the city had a mixture of peoples in the northern sector of the city, including about 50,000 'tartars' (that is, Mongols).

Chaoyang   District and town. Modern Chaoyang, Liaoning province of China. Chaoyang means 'City facing the sun' or 'City of the Three Towers'. Site of the LMS station initiated by James Gilmour from 1886. The LMS station was handed over to the IPMM in 1902, who then handed it on to the Brethren in 1912, by which time the church in Chaoyang was solely Chinese.

Da-tu   Or Tatu, Da-du, Daidu, Taydo. The capital of Kublai Khan and subsequent Mongol Yuan emperors. Also Khanbaliq (the 'city of the king'). Located where the Forbidden City of Beijing is laid out.

Dolon-noor   Or Dolonnor, Tolon-nor. 'Seven Lakes'. District and town. Modern name is Duolun, Inner Mongolia. Also Lama-miao in Chinese, Nadan-Omo in Manchurian, Tsot-Dun in Tibetan. An ancient European map used by Huc names the town as 'Djo-naiman-soume' that is '180 Arrows'. A large Mongol trading town doing business with Kiachta in Russia. Location of bronze and brass foundries where most of the Buddhist idols throughout central Asia were cast. Robert Stephen and Reginald Sturt (both Brethren) distributed tracts to Tibetans and Mongols here.

Edessa   Centre for Eastern Christianity after Pentecost. Decian and Diocletian persecutions (third century) put pressure on Edessa, and the church centre moved east to Persia. Fell to Muslims in 1144, interpreted as the beginning of the end of the gains that the Crusades had made. After the fall of Edessa, Prester John rumours started circulating in Europe. Modern day Urfa in north-west Mesopotamia.

Edzin-gol   Also Etsin-Gol. Western Inner Mongolia. River valley in the south Gobi where the returning Torguts settled by permission of the Manchus. Modern Ejin Qi and surrounds. Cable and French trio visited here on evangelistic tours.

Gansu   Also Kansu. A province in north-west China. In the twelfth and thirteenth centuries, Gansu was a stronghold of Nestorianism. In 1878 the CICM commenced work in the province. The Cable-French trio spent much of their missionary career in this province. In the 1900s Gansu had a population made up of Chinese, Tibetans, Manchus, Mongols, Turks, aboriginal tribes and immigrants from all the other provinces.

Hada   Also Olaghan Hada, Ulaghan Hada, Ulaan-khad, Ulanhad. 'Red Rock/Peaks'. In Jehol district of Inner Mongolia. Also Chifeng. Trading centre for Mongols in grain and salt. Brethren missionaries (for example, Reginald Sturt) saw it as a strategic site from as early as 1899 in which to contact Mongols. The CICM founded a mission station in Hada under the leadership of T. Rutjes.

Hattin-sum   Also Hattin Sumu, Hat-um-sum, Hadain Sume. 'Temple on/of the Cliff'. In Chahar district of Inner Mongolia, two days north-west of Kalgan. Larson's original centre of work. Followed by SMM which started a Mongol church, school and medical work in the late 1800s.

Hohot   Modern Hoh-hot, provincial capital of Inner Mongolia. 'Blue City'. Also Kuku Hoto, Koko-Khotan, Xo Xot. Chinese: Tsingchau, Kui-hua-ch'eng, Guihuacheng, Hou-ho-hao-t'e, Hou-ho-shih. Nestorian centre and southern capital of the Nestorian Kerait before the rise of the Mongols. In this capacity was regarded as the capital of Prester John. Became a commercial and military centre during the reign of emperor Kang-hi. 10,000 resident Manchu soldiers. Famous for its trade in camels. Five great lamaseries, each with 2,000 lamas. Centre of the Catholic Ordos-Mongol church mission region. CICM had a hospital in the city as well as a large cathedral.

Hsi-wan-tzu   Also Siwantze, Xiwanzi, a village in Chihli district of Inner Mongolia. Sixty kilometres north-east of Kalgan. Centre for Catholic work among the Mongols. Headquarters of the Lazarists in Mongolia from 1829, then headquarters of the CICM from 1864. Catholic training school of twenty-seven or so students established here. Skirmishes between nationalists and Communists in 1946 resulted in the town and mission being looted, 'hundreds' murdered and all the mission buildings except an orphanage burned down. The town eventually became predominantly Chinese.

Jehol District and town. Summer capital of the Manchu court on the Mongol side of the Great Wall. Modern Chengde, Hebei province, north-east of Beijing. A large potala place and lamasery was located in Jehol, attracting Mongols and Tibetans on religious pilgrimage. The LMS was the first mission agency to locate in Jehol, followed by Irish Presbyterian then Brethren. Also a Catholic mission was located at Jehol.

Kalgan 'The Gate'. Also known in Chinese as Wanchuan, Chang-chia-kow, Chang-chia-k'ou, Changkiakow. Capital of Chahar district of Inner Mongolia. Modern Chinese city of Zhang-jia-kou, Hebei province of China. 'Mouth/entry into the court of Lord Chang'. Located at a narrow pass in the mountains north-west of Beijing, Kalgan was an important trading junction on the route from Beijing to Urga and also Ningsia and Turkestan. Many Western mission agencies that wanted to target the Mongols were based in Kalgan from 1865: the ABFMS, LMS, BFBS, Methodists, SDA and the Norwegian Alliance. Catholic orders of The Work of the Holy Childhood, CICM, Missionary Canonesses of St Augustine, Congregation of the Servants of the Sacred Heart. In 1952 the last missionaries were expelled from Kalgan.

Karakorum Chinese: Ho Lin. South-west of modern Ulaanbaatar, Mongolia. Ancient capital of the Uighurs in the second half of the eighth century. Later Karakorum was the northern capital of the Nestorian Kerait tribe. Was the seat of a Nestorian See as late as the thirteenth century. Originally a large encampment until Ogodei Khan built buildings at the site (possibly the site of a ruined Buddhist temple) and designated it the Mongol capital. Rubruk found twelve pagan temples of various nations, two mosques and one Nestorian church. Today the Buddhist temple of Erdenzuu has been built on the site, using the bricks and mortar of Ogedei's original buildings.

Khanbaliq See also Da-tu. Also Cambaluc. 'City of the King'. Turkish name for the Mongol capital at Da-tu (Beijing) that Marco Polo called it and by which it was subsequently known in Europe. As early as the seventh century, Khanbaliq became the seat of a Nestorian metropolitan with several bishoprics within it, all subject to the Patriarch of Baghdad. Birth place of Rabban Sauma.

Khodon Village and river. One of the three centres of the LMS mission in Buriatia. Home of Stallybrass, near Selinginsk, not far from modern Khorinsk. Site where the LMS printing press was located. A small group of Mongolian believers met together regularly on Sundays in Khodon during the era of the LMS mission (1820–1840).

Khumbum Also Kounboum, Khounboum. Chinese: T'a-erh-ssû (T'a-ri-si?). 'Lamasery of the 10,000 Images'. Thirty-two kilometres from Sining, Eastern Qinghai province of China. Centre for both Tibetan and Mongol pilgrimage. Residence of the reincarnation of the Tibetan teacher Tsongkapa. Protestant and Catholic mission in the area, including evangelism and tract distribution at the lamasery.

Lantau Island Hong Kong. Island where the 1952 Mongolian Bible revision team was based, renting five small vacation houses. Edvard Torjesen started the 'Institute for Mongolian Studies' here.

Ninghsia District in Eastern Gansu province of China. Modern Ningxia. Synonymous with the Ordos district. CIM missionaries arrive in 1885 with the aim of evangelising the Tibetans and Mongols of the district. Also a strong area for CICM work. In 1946 van Melckebeke is appointed Catholic bishop of the diocese of Ninghsia, and a year later ordained two Mongols from Boro Balghasu for ministry in Ninghsia. CICM experiment with agricultural co-operatives. All missionaries in the district were expelled by 1952 by the Communists. Reginald Sturt died here in 1948.

Olon-Sum 'Many Temples'. Archaeological site near Pailingmiao, Inner Mongolia. Walled enclosure of 914 by 548 metres with stone foundations. Discovered in 1929 by Houang Wen-pi of Sven Hedin's expedition in north-west China. In 1932 Owen Lattimore found stone pillars and tombstones with Nestorian crosses on them. Egami concludes in 1937 that it was the ancient capital of King George of the Ongut-Mongols. Later excavations in 1938 revealed the base of a Gothic chapel. The cornerstone has a Christian cross superimposed on a Buddhist lotus blossom (a Nestorian motif). In total, two churches were found, one Nestorian, the other Catholic. This was probably the church which Montecorvino reports to the Pope in 1305 that George had built in 1292. Probably Koshang, home town of Bar Sauma, and also King-tcheou of Chinese history.

Ordos Also Ortous. Synonymous with Ninghsia (Ningxia) district of Gansu province of China. Surrounded by the Yellow River on west, east and north, and the Great Wall in the south. Strong area of Nestorianism prior to the rise of the Mongols. The Hsia princes were overrun by Chinggis Khan in 1227. When the Ming rose to power, Ordos came under the sovereignty of the Khan of the Tchakar-Mongols who then submitted, with all seven Ordos banners, to the Manchus in 1635. Bronze artefacts with Nestorian crosses on them are still retrieved periodically in the Ordos desert.

Pailingmiao Modern Batukha'alagha, western Inner Mongolia. Olon Sum is thirty miles south-west of Pailingmiao. One time designated administrative capital of Inner Mongolia. Centre of Buddhism for the region and therefore a pilgrimage site for Mongols from all over the country. Gunzel wanted to start a work here. Visited in 1934, but was told the Mongol prince would not allow preaching. Response to gospel was laughter and accusations of madness. A small field conference in Patsebolong in 1935 recommended that Pailingmiao be made a proper mission station of the SAMM.

Paotow Modern Baotou, 200 kilometres north of Hequ, on the China/Mongolia border. Place where Frans Larson first settled. Scandinavian Mission of Chicago (Scandinavian Alliance Mission) started work among the Mongols west of Paotow after the Boxer uprising of 1900.

Patsebolong Also Patzupulung, Suihuen province, in the Ordos desert, just north of the Yellow River, 'fourteen days' journey' west of Kalgan. Gunzel of the Scandinavian Alliance Mission (now TEAM) located here for a time, working among Mongols. Sturt refers to the town as a 'former big Mongol settlement and mission centre where Mongols were found for hundreds of miles in every direction'. Sturt and Gunzel distributed Mongol Scriptures by camel-back around the

Mongol villages near Patsebolong. Where the SAMM set up an agricultural and industrial 'colony'. Stenberg was the first to recognise it as having agricultural colony potential and purchased it. Lindholm visited it in 1931 to assess it because the land had been carved up for sale by Chinese officials. The SAMM agricultural colony had originally been 6000 acres, but when Gunzel visited in 1934 he found that only thirty acres were left. Patsebolong had been gradually settled by the Chinese, pushing the Mongols further onto the steppe.

Rubruck   Also Rubrouck, Rubroek. Birthplace of William of Rubruck. Flemish town in northern France. William's journey was commemorated in July 1994 at Rubruck, at which time Rubruck became the sister town of Bulgan, Mongolia.

Sarepta   German colony on the Volga from which the Moravians worked among the Torgut/Kalmuck Mongols from 1765. Sarepta is now a part of the city of Volgograd. Approximately 65,000 families left the area to return to their original pasturelands in China in 1771.

Scheut   Town in Belgium, just outside Brussels, where the CICM order or Scheut Fathers originated. A novitiate is located here for training CICM missionaries for China and Mongolia. The Catholic fathers working in Ulaanbaatar during the 1990s were 'Scheut Fathers' of the CICM order.

Selenginsk   Small town on the banks of the Selenge river, Buriatia, where the LMS mission was for twenty odd years in the nineteenth century. The LMS station was located on the banks of the river opposite the town.

Seleucia-Ctesiphon   Original headquarters and residence of the Nestorian Catholicos (Patriarch) between 496/8 and 762. Transferred to Baghdad in 762. Ctesiphon was the political capital of the Persian empire while Seleucia, on the opposite bank of the Tigris River, was the banking and commercial centre of the empire.

Sining   Modern Xining, Qinghai (Tsinghai) province of China. Residence of the governor of Koko-nor. CIM station strategically opened here in 1885, to evangelise Tibetans and Mongols. Near

Kumbum temple complex (thirty-two kilometres away). Where Mr and Mrs Cecil Polhill-Turner worked and learned Tibetan. The station comprised a boys' school and a dispensary which had a constant flow of Moslem, Chinese, Tibetan and Mongol patients.

Taiwan   'Many thousands' of Mongols exited China with the rise of the Communists, many ending up in Taiwan via Hong Kong. Several foreign missionaries called to the Mongols went with them to Taiwan, including Gunzels, Torjesens and Bernklau. 'Quite a number' became Christians since settling in Taiwan and a Mongol church service was happening at one stage, as well as English classes among Mongol refugees.

Ta Pan Shang   A town in eastern Inner Mongolia which had a large Mongolian population, frequented by Reginald Sturt. Also local Christian resident Mr Hsu Shou En was active evangelising and practising medicine among the Mongols. Local population was bilingual, therefore strategic place for evangelism. Sturt used it as a base for further language training and preached extensively in and around the town. Sturt managed to give Bibles to the prince, leading lamas, the abbot and the living Buddha. Small group of Mongol children and at least two adults became Christians. Sturt wanted to use this town as a base for reaching the Barin Mongols.

Tartary   Medieval European term for generally ill-defined Mongol territory. Home of the Tartar people, ie Mongol descent. Among Protestant missionaries of the nineteenth and twentieth century, it usually meant anything over the Great Wall from Beijing.

Tavan-uul   Also Tabol 'Five hills'. Larson's summer residence, 136 kilometres north of Kalgan on the road to Urga. After 1901, in the employ of the BFBS, Larson used Tavan-uul as his base for Bible distribution itinerations into the Mongol hinterland.

Ulaanbaatar   Capital of modern Mongolia. Literally 'Red-hero'. The site was previously Urga, Ikh Huree and Da-Huree.

Urga   Name of the city where modern Ulaanbaatar is located. Also Da-huree and Ikh-huree. 30,000 resident lamas estimated when Larson visited Urga in 1900–1902. Political and religious centre of Mongolia. Also trading crossroads; most northern branch of the Silk Road, but more importantly the major staging post of Chinese-Russian trade. A 1911 uprising threw off the Manchu yoke and Urga enjoyed nine years of theocratic independence until in February 1920, the white Russian Baron Ungern-Sternberg attacked Urga (because the Chinese general Little Hsu had retaken it with 15,000 soldiers). The Russian Red army entered in July 1921 and the Communists, led by Sukhbaatar, set up the Mongolian People's Republic. Urga was named a Catholic vicariate and entrusted to J. van Aertselaer CICM by Pope Pius XI in 1922. However, this mission was unable to be staffed at the time.

Urumqi   Also Urumchi. Hung-miao-tze in Chinese ('Red Temple'). Also Ti-hua, Ti hua fu, Chichintalas. North-west Xinjiang province. Ancient Nestorian centre. Originally CIM missionaries George Parker and Dr Landsdell worked in Urumqi and environs from 1876, then George Hunter from 1906 and later Mather then Ridley. Urumqi church had 'Cassaks, Turkis, Mongols [mainly Torgut/Kalmucks], Chinese' in it, although the church service was mainly in Chinese. Major trading crossroads as well as centre of Russian-Chinese colonial power plays. Desiré Leesens founded the CICM Catholic work in Urumqi in 1907, but Frans Hoogers developed it by leasing land in or near the city.

Voznesensky   Monastery near Irkutsk where a Mongolian-Russian school was opened in 1725 that lasted fifteen years, used to train Russian Orthodox missionaries for the Mongolian and Buryat population.

Wu-t'ai-shan   Shansi province of China. 'The Five Peaks' is a sacred Buddhist retreat centre. Pilgrims from Mongolia and Tibet frequented the site. According to Gilmour: 'as Jerusalem to the Jews, as Mecca to the Mohammedans, so is Wu-t'ai-shan to the Mongols'. Sturt travelled through here and sold 'nearly a thousand' books to Mongols and Chinese.

Wuyuan   An agricultural-based colony established by Stenberg of the SAMM to attract Mongols in from the steppe to hear the gospel consistently and to disciple converts. Stenberg, Hanna Lund, Hilda and

Clara Anderson all moved to the area for the establishment of this colony. Corrupt Mongol official betrayed them to the Boxers and after spending twenty days and nights in the desert were killed by the Boxers in 1900.

Appendix 4

Bibliography

Athyal, Saphir, ed., *Church in Asia Today* (The Asia Laussane Committee for World Evangelisation: Singapore, 1996).

Bawden, Charles R. *Shamans, Lamas and Evangelicals: The English Missionaries in Siberia* (Routledge and Kegan Paul: London, 1985).

Bland Stäppens Folk: Är ur Svenska Mongolmissionens historia [Among the People of the Steppe: Years in the History of the Swedish Mongol Mission], *Evangelisk Östasien missionen* nr 6, (Juni/Juli 1987), Ärg 6, pp. 28–33. Unpublished English translation by Monica Ruderstum.

Cable, Mildred and French, Francesca, *George Hunter: Apostle of Turkestan* (CIM: London, 1948).

Cable, Mildred and French, Francesca, *The Making of a Pioneer: Percy Mather of Central Asia* (Hodder and Stoughton: London, 1935).

Cable, Mildred and French, Francesca, *Wall of Spears: The Gobi Desert* (The Lutterworth Press: London, 1951).

Cable, Mildred and French, Francesca, *The Gobi Desert* (Hodder and Stoughton: London, 1942, 1947; Virago Press, 1984).

Cable, M., Houghton, F., Kilgour, R., McLeish, A., Sturt, R.W., and Wyon O., *The Challenge of Central Asia* (World Dominion Press: London, 1929).

Canton, William, *A History of the British and Foreign Bible Society*, vols 1–5 (John Murray: London, 1910).

Compton, A.G. *Children of the Wilderness* (Wentforth Publishers: Auckland, 1953).

Dawson, Christopher, ed., *Mission to Asia: Narratives and Letters of the Franciscan Missionaries in Mongolia and China in the Thirteenth and Fourteenth Centuries.* Translated by a nun of Stanbrook Abbey. (Harper and Row: New York, 1966).

de Rachewiltz, Igor, *Prester John and Europe's discovery of East Asia* (Australian National University Press: Canberra, 1972).

de Rachewiltz, Igor, Hok-lam Chan, Hsiao Ch'i-ch'ing and Geier, Peter W., eds, *In the Service of the Khan: Eminent Personalities of the Early*

Mongol-Yuan Period (1200–1300) (Harrossowitz Verlag: Wiesbaden, 1993).

de Rachewiltz, Igor, *Papal Envoys to the Great Khans* (Faber and Faber: London, 1971).

Egami, Namio, Olon-sume et la decouverte de l'église catholique romaine de Jean de Montecorvino, in *Journal Asiatique*, 240 (1952), p. 56.

England, John C., *The Hidden History of Christianity in Asia: The Churches of the East before 1500* (ISPCK and CCA: Delhi and Hong Kong, 1996).

French, Francesca, *Thomas Cochrane: Pioneer and Missionary Statesman* (Hodder and Stoughton: London, 1956).

Gilmour, James, *Among the Mongols* (The Religious Tract Society: London, 1882).

Grousset, René, *The Empire of the Steppes: A History of Central Asia*, Walford, Naomi, trans., (Rutgers University Press: USA, 1970).

Gumilev, L.N., *Searches for an Imaginary Kingdom: The Legend of the Kingdom of Prester John*, Smith, REF, trans., (Cambridge University Press: London, 1970).

Heissig, Walther, *The Religions of Mongolia*, Samuel, G., trans., (Routledge and Kegan Paul: London, 1980).

Hoke, D.E., ed., *The Church in Asia* (Moody Press: Chicago, 1975).

Howorth, H.H., *History of the Mongols from the ninth to the nineteenth Century* (Burt Franklin: London, 1876).

Huc, Regis Evariste, *Christianity in China, Tartary and Tibet* (Longman, Brown, Green, Longmans and Roberts: London, 1857).

Hutton, J.E., *A History of Moravian Missions* (Moravian Publication Office: London, c 1922).

Jackson, Peter and David Morgan, eds., *The Mission of Friar William of Rubruck* (The Hakluyt Society: London, 1990).

Juvaini, 'Ala-ad-Din 'Ata-Malik, *The History of the World Conqueror*, Boyle, John Andrew, trans., (Manchester University Press: Manchester, 1958), 2nd ed., 1997.

Kahn, P., *The Secret History of the Mongols: The Origin of Chinghis Khan* (North Point Press: San Francisco, 1984).

Kara, G., 'Reading a New Mongolian Version of the New Testament', *Mongolian Studies*, vol XX (1997), pp. 39–63.

Kundan, Thespal, *The Moravian Church in India after 1985: The Himalayan Mission: Moravian Church Centenary, 1885–1985, Leh, Ladakh, India*, Bray, John, ed., (Publisher and date unclear).

Larson, Frans August, *Larson, Duke of Mongolia* (Little, Brown and Co.: Boston, 1930).

Laufer, Berthold 'Burkhan', *Journal of the American Oriental Society*, 36:4 (1917), pp. 390–395.

Lovett, R., ed., *James Gilmour of Mongolia: His Diaries, Letters and Reports* Fleming H Revell Co: New York and Chicago). (The Religious Tract Society: London, 1895).

Lovett, R., *The History of the London Missionary Society 1795–1895* (Oxford University Press: London, 1899).

Marthinson, A.W., 'The Revision of the Mongolian New Testament', *The Bible Translator*, 5:2 (April 1954), p. 74.

Moffett, Samuel Hugh, *A History of Christianity in Asia*, vol. 1: Beginnings to 1500 (Harper Collins: New York, 1992).

Morgan, D., 'The Great *Yasa* of Chingiz Khan', *Bulletin of the School of Oriental and African Studies*, 49 (1986), pp. 163–176.

Morgan, D., *The Mongols* (Peoples of Europe Series: Campbell, J, Cuncliffe, B, eds) (Basil Blackwell: Oxford, 1986).

Mortenson, Vernon, *God Made it Grow: Historical Sketches of TEAM's Church Planting Work* (William Carey Library, Pasadena, 1994).

Onon, U., trans., *The History and the Life of Chinggis Khan: The Secret History of the Mongols* (E J Brill: Leiden, 1990).

Pas, Julian F., 'Missionary Efforts in Inner Mongolia: a Review Article', *Zeitschrift für Missionswissenschaft und Religionswissenschaft*, vol. 69 (January 1985), pp. 63–70.

Peers, E. Allison, *Fool of Love: The Life of Ramon Lull* (SCM Press: London, 1946).

Platt, W.J., *Three Women: Mildred Cable, Francesca French, Evangeline French; The Authorised Biography* (Hodder and Stoughton: London, 1964).

Rossabi, M., *Khubilai Khan: His Life and Times* (University of California Press: Berkeley, Ca., 1988).

Saeki, P.Y., *The Nestorian Monument in China* (SPCK: London, 1916).

Serruys, Henry, 'Early Mongols and the Catholic Church' in *Neue Zeitschrift für Missionswissenschaft*, 19 (1963), pp. 161–69.

Stewart, John, *Nestorian Missionary Enterprise: The Story of a Church on Fire* (T and T Clark: Edinburgh, 1928).

Tsering, Marku, *Sharing Christ in the Tibetan Buddhist World*, 2nd ed., (Tibet Press: USA, 1993).

van Hecken, J., 'La Littérature Mongole Chrétienne', *Neue Zeitschrift für Missionswissenschaft* (1947). Unpublished English translation by Anne Windsor.

Verhelst, Daniël and Pycke, Nestor, *CICM Missionaries, Past and Present, 1862–1987* (Leuven University Press: Leuven, Belgium, 1995).

Yule, H., *The Book of Ser Marco Polo the Venetian Concerning the Marvels and the Kingdoms of the East*, 2 vols, Cordier, H, revised (John Murray: London, 1921).

English-speaking Interserve Offices

International Office:
PO Box 22140, 1588 Nicosia, Cyprus
Tel (357) 2 751844.
email: mail@link.com.cy
International website: www.interserve.org

Australia: PO Box 231 Bayswater, Victoria 3153, Australia
Tel (61) 3 9729 9611
email: info@aussend.org.au

Canada: 10 Huntingdon Boulevard, Scarborough, Ontario,
M1W 2S5, Canada
Tel (416) 499 7511
email: iscan@idirect.com

England and Wales: 325 Kennington Road, London SE11 4QH, UK
Tel (44) 20 7735 8227
email: enquiries@isewi.org

India: C-20 Community Centre, 1st Floor, Janakpuri, New Delhi
110058, India
Tel (91) 11 550 4334
email: isvindia@del2.vsnl.net.in

Ireland: 14 Glencregagh Court, Belfast BT6 0PA, UK
Tel (44) 28 9040 2211
email: 100517.3155@compuserve.com

Malaysia: Intercare Berhad, PO Box 13002, 50769 Kuala Lumpur
Malaysia
Tel (60) 3 794 8430
email: icare@tm.net.my

Netherlands: Krakelingweg 10, 3707 HV Zeist, Netherlands
Tel (31) 30 691 3741
email: isnet@compuserve.com

New Zealand: P O Box 10-244, Auckland 1030, New Zealand
Tel (64) 9 6300 981
email: hardplace@hardplace.org.nz

Scotland: 12 Elm Avenue, Lenzie, Glasgow, G66 4HJ, UK
Tel (44) 141 578 0207
email: info@isscot.prestel.co.uk

Singapore: Pasir Panjang Post Office, PO Box 117,
Singapore 911124
Tel (65) 281 1289
email: edwinlam@magix.com.sg

South Africa: P O Box 385, Plumstead 7801, Cape Town,
South Africa
Tel (27) 21 761 4234
email: issa@nis.za

USA: PO Box 418, Upper Darby, PA 19082-0418, USA
Tel (1) 610 352 0581
email: InterServeUSA@xc.org

English-speaking OMF centres

Australia: PO Box 849, Epping, NSW 2121
  Tel (02) 9868 4777. Freecall (outside Sydney)1800 227 154
  email: omf-Australia@omf.net   *www.omf.org*

Canada: 5759 Coopers Avenue, Mississauga ON, L4Z 1R9
  Toll free 1-888-657-8010. Fax (905) 568-9974
  email: omfcanada@omf.ca   *www.omf.ca*

Hong Kong: P O Box 70505, Kowloon Central Post Office,
  Hong Kong
  email: hk@omf.net   *www.omf.org*

Malaysia: 3A Jalan Nipah, off Jalan Ampang, 55000, Kuala Lumpur
  email: my@omf.net   *www.omf.org*

Netherlands: Eendrachtstraat 29a, 3784 KA, Terschuur,
  Netherlands

New Zealand: P O Box 10159, Auckland.   Tel 09-630 5778
  email: omfnz@omf.net   *www.omf.org*

Philippines: 900 Commonwealth Avenue, Diliman,
  1101 Quezon City
  email: ph-hc@omf.net   *www.omf.org*

Singapore: 2 Cluny Road, Singapore 259570
  email: sno@omf.net   *www.omf.org*

Southern Africa: P O Box 3080, Pinegowrie, 2123
  email: za@omf.net   *www.omf.org*

UK: Station Approach, Borough Green, Sevenoaks, Kent, TN15 8BG
  email: omf@omf.org.uk   *www.omf.org.uk*

USA: 10 West Dry Creek Circle, Littleton, CO 80120-4413
  Toll Free 1-800-422-5330   *www.us.omf.org*

OMF International Headquarters: 2 Cluny Road
Singapore 259570.